CABIN BOYS, MILKMAIDS, AND ROUGH SEAS

CABIN BOYS, MILKMAIDS, AND ROUGH SEAS

IDENTITY IN THE UNEXPURGATED REPERTOIRE OF STAN HUGILL

JESSICA M. FLOYD

University Press of Mississippi / Jackson

The University Press of Mississippi is the scholarly publishing agency of the Mississippi Institutions of Higher Learning: Alcorn State University, Delta State University, Jackson State University, Mississippi State University, Mississippi University for Women, Mississippi Valley State University, University of Mississippi, and University of Southern Mississippi.

www.upress.state.ms.us

The University Press of Mississippi is a member of the Association of University Presses.

Any discriminatory or derogatory language or hate speech regarding race, ethnicity, religion, sex, gender, class, national origin, age, or disability that has been retained or appears in elided form is in no way an endorsement of the use of such language outside a scholarly context.

Copyright © 2024 by Jessica M. Floyd
All rights reserved

∞

Library of Congress Cataloging-in-Publication Data

Names: Floyd, Jessica M., author.
Title: Cabin boys, milkmaids, and rough seas : identity in the unexpurgated repertoire of Stan Hugill / Jessica M. Floyd.
Description: Jackson : University Press of Mississippi, 2024. | Includes bibliographical references and index.
Identifiers: LCCN 2024022651 (print) | LCCN 2024022652 (ebook) | ISBN 9781496853127 (hardback) | ISBN 9781496853134 (trade paperback) | ISBN 9781496853141 (epub) | ISBN 9781496853158 (epub) | ISBN 9781496853165 (pdf) | ISBN 9781496853172 (pdf)
Subjects: LCSH: Erotic songs—History and criticism. | Sea songs—History and criticism. | Work songs—History and criticism. | Folk music—History and criticism. | Folk songs, English—History and criticism. | Hugill, Stan. | Sex in music. | Sex role in music.
Classification: LCC ML3780 .F56 2024 (print) | LCC ML3780 (ebook) | DDC 782.42162—dc23/eng/20240610
LC record available at https://lccn.loc.gov/2024022651
LC ebook record available at https://lccn.loc.gov/2024022652

British Library Cataloging-in-Publication Data available

To Gershon and Judith Legman, whose research, care, and generosity made all of this possible.

Contents

ix   PREFACE

xv   ACKNOWLEDGMENTS

3   CHAPTER 1. Chanteys: The Sailor's Work Song among His Brothers

53   CHAPTER 2. Hugill's Repertoire and Training an Interdisciplinary Lens on Expressions of Gender and Sexuality

90   CHAPTER 3. Words of Warning and the Ebb and Flow of Identity

130   CHAPTER 4. Heteronormative Economies and Shadow Admissions

171   CHAPTER 5. Looking Queerly and the Pleasures That Defy Category

205   CONCLUSION. "What Shall We Do with a Drunken Sailor" and His Comrades?

221   APPENDIX: Chantey Lyrics

240   NOTES

262   BIBLIOGRAPHY

273   INDEX

Preface

Since I can remember, I have been fascinated by the erotic world captured in literature. There has always been, I would say, a part of me clearly drawn to the obscure, the out of the way, and even the off-kilter. As a young student, my room was littered with books like *The 120 Days of Sodom*, *The Story of O*, and *Venus in Furs*, something that I think gave even my very liberal parents a slight pause. As an undergraduate, I worked primarily with the poetry and plays of John Wilmot, the Second Earl of Rochester, and later, in my master's-level work, expanded my interests to include other Restoration rakes of the period.

Because my chosen area of study was and is titillating, a bit scandalous, and great for cocktail conversation, one question always posed during a late Friday night or Sunday-dinner gathering at my parents' house focused on what bawdy or salacious poem or play I had discovered that week. In fact, on one particular night, the topic of discussion was my struggle with finding a topic for my master's degree capstone project. As there was never a taboo subject in my household, all were busy with drinking, laughing, and offering suggestions on what I might research to satisfy the requirements of my program. At one moment, my dad turned to me and asked, "What about chanteys?" I had never heard of chanteys. Without skipping a beat, my dad proceeded to sing, with a wry smile, glint in his eye, and the gusto of his baritone voice: "Who's that knocking at my door? / Who's that knocking at my door? / Open the door you filthy whore, says Barnacle Bill the Sailor." I was captivated and instantly struck by the connections I could see between bawdy Restoration poetry and the song that I had just enjoyed. My father explained that the song was "Barnacle Bill the Sailor," offering that he did not have a clear sense of where he first heard it, but that he had, perhaps, heard it sung in "some old movie" or as a kid watching *Popeye the Sailor*. I knew that I had to pursue the topic further and embarked on that charge the very next day. To me, there was a power and a vibration that this song brought with it: my father had, unknowingly, introduced me to something that I immediately knew was going to be larger than any project I had attempted or encountered before.

The scene at the dinner table is only a small window into how music permeated my life. I have always been surrounded by music. From the time that I was very young, I was immersed in different genres and was able to easily trace the sounds of different types of music, connecting different sounds and periods to each other based on what I learned from my father. My dad has a passion for music that is palpable. My family has often joked that he is a human jukebox, able to name any tune, describe and explain any genre, and call out a band or a singer having only heard a few lines of a song. Educated in music through a commitment and interest in the art, he can readily share the history of various songs and connect different musical genres to cultures, periods, and musical frameworks with a dexterity that most would expect from having formal training.

His passion does not end with only knowing music in this way. My father's workshop was attached to my childhood home, and I can recall hearing my dad's joyous, baritone voice booming over the sounds of wood saws, nail guns, and air compressors: cacophony interrupted by laughter and music. A cabinet maker by trade, my father has imbued his workstation with music and mirth to pass the time, entertain himself and his partner in the trade, Kenny, who passed away a short time ago, and participate in the music making that brings him happiness and sometimes nostalgia. Because of my father, I ultimately aligned music with work from a very young age.

Thus, when I began my early inquiries into chanteys, I almost took for granted the fact that the sailor sang songs while he was employed at work. When I began researching chanteys, I could easily imagine sailing men pulling on ropes together while shouting and singing over the din of the ocean and the weather, using songs in the same way that I watched my father use them: for a sense of connection (either to others or to the past), as an opportunity for entertainment and jollity, and as a means by which to ease the difficulty of a task, if only through the entertainment allotted by a song. I imagined the knowing amusement and the wry humor that must have been involved as music, wit, and toil seem to go hand in hand, at least in what I have encountered of working-class men and song.

My first brush with the chantey tradition—that night at my family's kitchen table—accessed and connected to an almost-spiritual knowledge that my work not only was going to take me through uncharted territory but also had the earmarks of becoming an important scholarly pursuit that would fundamentally impact research in the chantey tradition. That evening, excited by the prospect of investigating such a ribald song as "Barnacle Bill the Sailor," I embarked on a research path that ultimately led me directly to a manuscript that defied even my wildest expectations and rewarded my tenacious drive to find what so many told me might be impossible. As I went deeper into investigating the chantey genre, I began to register a growing refrain when I inquired about songs with lyrics like the ones produced by my father: they are few and far between, and there is only one possible repository yet to be located that would satisfy this pursuit. That repository was the unpublished manuscript compiled by famed chantey singer and collector Stan Hugill (1906–1992)—the self-proclaimed last chanteyman—before he died. Every mention of this manuscript, however, was followed by the admission that the texts were likely long gone, lost to time or hidden somewhere. I certainly would not have conceived, in those early days of inquiry, that I would be fashioning an analytical project to reproduce and critically investigate this highly sought manuscript of unexpurgated chanteys especially since even laying eyes on the manuscript felt like an impossible dream.

Gershon Legman's unpublished manuscript, which contains some of Hugill's unexpurgated versions of chanteys, was first suggested to me in a thread on Mudcat Café, a folksong and folk-ballad discussion board, which I encountered in my early inquiries in 2013.[1] I discovered the message board and discussion site through my first foray into tracking examples of unexpurgated chantey texts. My early models of the chantey tradition were Stan Hugill's *Shanties from the Seven Seas* and William Main Doerflinger's *Songs of the Sailor and Lumberman*. When I realized that these publications were fully expurgated throughout, I was forced to cast a wider net in an attempt to locate source material that ran closer to the tenor I encountered in the "Barnacle Bill" rendition supplied by my father. Clearly, dirty versions existed, otherwise people would not be repeating them.

In my early correspondences with folksong enthusiasts on Mudcat Café, I was told—and quickly gathered—that one of the few manuscripts of bawdy chantey material might be found in the then-missing Stan Hugill manuscript that Hugill prepared for Legman. Through my discussions with some of the contributors to the site, I was able to come into contact with John Patrick, the editor of the site the Jack Horntip Collection, which collects bawdy chanteys, sea songs, ballads, rugby songs, and the like, Jonathan Lighter, an amateur folksong collector, and Gibb Schreffler, a noted and respected critical voice in the field of chanteys. Throughout my conversations with these collectors, I was further apprised of the possible existence of a manuscript of unexpurgated chanteys that Stan Hugill transcribed and sent to Legman for eventual publication. In an email correspondence from Lighter, he maintained that "most of those [bawdy chanteys] come from Stan Hugill's now apparently lost (and irreplaceable) manuscript collection, which was once in the possession of Gershon Legman. Perhaps you can track it down? It very much would be worth doing, as it might be called the Holy Grail of chantey research."[2] The same sentiment was echoed by the curator of the James Madison Carpenter Collection, another unpublished collection of bawdy folklore materials at the Library of Congress. In an email communication, Dr. Robert Walser also called the manuscript "the Holy Grail of this topic."[3] The more that I heard about this missing manuscript and the secrets it contained, the more driven I was to attempt to locate it. It was—and still is—a literary researcher's dream.

Walser ultimately provided me with the contact information for Gershon Legman's widow, Judith, who now resides in Opio, France, indicating that if anyone knew the whereabouts of the manuscript, it would be her. I began an email correspondence with Judith Legman in the fall of 2014. The original manuscript now resides in the library at the Kinsey Institute at Indiana University along with other materials from Legman's years as a writer and researcher of erotic folklore and folksong. Judith held on to the manuscript of bawdy material, some items of which were collected chanteys, until around the time that I contacted her in October 2014. Serendipitously, in her first response to me, she indicated:

> But, your request is very timely. I have just sent off to the Libraries of the Kinsey Institute at Bloomington, Indiana, most of the manuscript that my husband had prepared when he was hoping to have a large compendium of uncensored folk songs published. BUT, I haven't yet mailed them the carbon copy, and if it would help you, I can make a photocopy of the carbon copy of the chapter on sea chanties and send it to you by postal mail.[4]

She very quickly promised to send me a scanned copy of the manuscript, which, for years, so many had searched for, and I could not believe my good fortune.

I was elated when the manuscript finally arrived at my home. Even the packaging carried a mysterious air: covered in stamps from France, betraying the miles of travel it took to arrive in my hands, weighty because of the pages the envelope contained. I could not contain my excitement as I opened the envelope. When I began perusing the materials, each section of the chapter meticulously ordered by paperclip, my excitement grew almost feverish. For a time, I too had thought that the manuscript was gone forever. Even

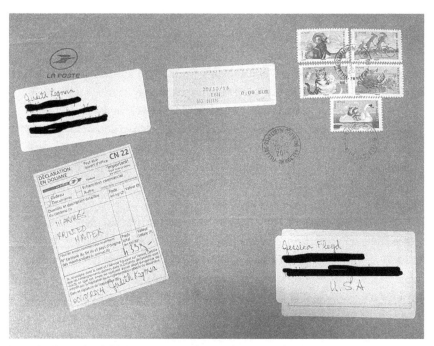

Image of mailer sent from Judith Legman containing the scanned manuscript of Gershon Legman's chapter "Sea Songs," October 20, 2014. Personal collection.

receiving the shipment from Judith felt like it was a long shot at best. As I flipped each carefully ordered page, I began to feel my fingers go numb a bit with the excitement spurred by what I was seeing. On several pages, interspersed between examples of other sea songs and chanteys, were entries that contained the name Stan Hugill and the title "Sailing Ship Shanties." The title was too close to Hugill's *Shanties from the Seven Seas* for me to refrain from making the obvious connection that I held in my hands the "unmasked" versions of Hugill's chanteys.

The manuscript eventually became the cornerstone of my research at the University of Maryland, Baltimore County, where I graduated with my PhD in December 2017. When I received the manuscript from Judith, it appeared to me that no one had been able to locate the manuscript because there was only one copy, lending a further air of mystery, intrigue, and rarity. Judith had held onto this sole copy, along with other pieces of Legman's work, until she was able to package the work and eventually send it to the Kinsey Institute. According to Judith, Legman amassed a huge collection of letters, materials for research and publication, and miscellaneous texts that she was attempting to sort, organize, and make decisions about whether to keep them for safekeeping in her home or to relinquish them to a storehouse. She indicated:

> I am seventy-four years old, and although I'm far from finished, it does seem time to delegate some things. I feel very fortunate to have found a home for the Legman Archive at the Kinsey Institute. Since you are connected with the academic world, maybe you know how difficult it is to find libraries willing to house and care for archival materials. This is all the more true when the person (me) doesn't have the means to endow the collection with some hefty sum for its care and feeding—or just care and housing.[5]

I retained the copy of the chapter "Sea Songs" that she sent to me just before she packaged the entire manuscript to be sent to the Kinsey Institute. As soon as I began my work with the manuscript, I registered a need to circulate this manuscript to a wider reading audience. Though, at this point, it was now safely housed at the Kinsey Institute, and I had held on to the copy of the chapter; I felt that it was necessary—indeed, I felt I was obligated—to share the manuscript with those who were so fascinated by the chantey tradition. Were this publication to have been abandoned or had I decided not to seek publication, Legman and Hugill's final and, arguably, most important work would likely remain in relative obscurity. *Cabin Boys, Milkmaids, and Rough Seas* is ultimately the product of combined and colliding passions. For me, this book is the capstone of a pursuit of rare chantey texts specifically and erotic texts more generally. It is a publication that was inspired by my encounter with "Barnacle Bill the Sailor," which opened this preface, and was fueled early on by the nascent passion of a fledgling scholar of erotic literature. When I finally received the manuscript of unexpurgated chanteys from Judith, my passion, too, collided with giant of erotic literature Gershon Legman, and through his passion, I also collided with sailor and chantey collector Stan Hugill. These intersections (passion, rarity, and uniqueness) imbue this book with a power and a sense of necessity. Unlike the time during which both Legman and Hugill wrote, we are now of a privileged epoch during which materials like erotic texts are able to be circulated and not solely under the cover of night. The same passion and dedication to authentic materials that run through *Cabin Boys, Milkmaids, and Rough Seas* is finally presented to the audience these men intended to reach all along, something that I will return to in the deeper discussion of the materials for this publication.

Acknowledgments

This project would not have been possible were it not for a number of incredibly generous friends, family, colleagues, and fellow researchers and chantey enthusiasts. I will be forever indebted to those I have met along the way who have aided me as I navigated this immense and complicated interdisciplinary project. First, I owe a debt of gratitude to Judith Legman. This project would not have been possible without your willingness to share your husband's collection with me and open your home to me nor without the countless emails we exchanged with each other along the way. You are always kind, encouraging, generous, and open, and I feel so fortunate that this project brought the two of us together. The work that Gershon accomplished over his career is an incredible contribution to the study of erotic folklore, and I feel privileged to have encountered one small part of his vast research.

In terms of colleagues and mentors, I am forever grateful to Laura Rosenthal and Amy Froide, who helped nurture this project from the very beginning. Indeed, Laura was present when the project was originally conceived when I was a master's student at the University of Maryland, College Park. Laura and Amy: you have both been a constant supportive force that I have turned to as I navigated this venture. I appreciate your time, thoughts, and care more than you know. I also want to thank Jonathan Allan and Steven Dashiell for their continued encouragement, support, and kind words as I traversed the sometimes very challenging moments of completing a project of this size. Your words, friendship, and encouragement mean more than I can capture here. Finally, I would like to extend my gratitude to Solimar Otero. You have been so generous with your time and have helped a new scholar without question nor need for introduction. Your kindness and willing spirit are what makes academia a more welcoming and inclusive place.

I would also like to extend a note of gratitude to James Engelhardt, who read multiple early drafts of this project and encouraged me to become "the captain of my ship" as I crafted the book. Your affability, insights, and belief in the project helped to make this all possible. A thank you, too, is in order for Susan Davis, who read the project and provided critical feedback that grounded the book more firmly in folklore studies. Your vast knowledge of Legman and of the field proved foundationally important to the final product. I would also like to thank all of the anonymous peer reviewers who read through drafts of the book and offered substantive feedback for consideration. Engaging in that process helped to generate deeper thinking around folklore, queer theory, and the position of an interdisciplinary project like this in so many different fields.

I am further indebted to several folks at the Library of Congress and also at Mudcat.org. Steven Winnick, Bob Walser, and Jennifer Cutting were integral to early inquiries into chanteys, as were Gibb Schreffler, Jonathan Lighter, and John Patrick. Longtime friends and acquaintances of Stan Hugill were also immensely important to me as I shaped a conception of the man who shared his songs with Legman, audiences, and the world: Chris Roche, John Townley, Lynne Noel, Janie Meneely, Keneeth Sweeney, Geoff Kaufman, and Jim Mageean. Thanks is due, also, to Edward Cray.

A number of chapters were also shared during presentations at the American Folklore Society, American Studies Association, the Northeast Modern Language Association, Popular Culture Association, and the Mid-Atlantic Popular Culture Association. Throughout these presentations, I had the opportunity to hone my argument and engage in critical feedback that undoubtedly positively impacted the final project. American Folklore Society was also where I had the good fortune to meet editors from the University Press of Mississippi. A special thank you to every person at UPM who played a role in the final product: I am immensely grateful to all that you have done to help me along the way. Thank you, too, to Peter Schmidt of Profs and Pints, who has given me the opportunity to share the history of chanteys, as well as my own approach to the genre, with a wider audience. Your platform has also informed how I view the chantey tradition. I would also like to thank the University of Maryland, Baltimore County's Dresher Center for the Humanities, whose funding and platform helped to support this project throughout its conception and completion. The Dresher Center funding provided me with the opportunity to meet with Judith Legman at her home, in Opio, France, and also supported the final revisions to the book.

Finally, I would like to thank my loving husband, my incredible family, and all of my friends. Cory, you have been there for every high and low, for nearly every presentation, and for the much-needed distractions I sorely needed in between. Thank you for being the one who consistently lifts me up, even when it has been difficult, and for always being the smiling and loving face in my corner. To my mom, dad, sisters, brother, and extended family: you have supported me from the very beginning, and I am forever grateful that you keep me laughing, humble, and dedicated. To all of my friends, near and far, thank you for loving me, cheering me on, and for believing in me. Behind every scholar, I hope, is the same loving and encouraging army of people who swoop in when the path becomes challenging, onerous, and, at times, alienating. Thank you.

CABIN BOYS, MILKMAIDS, AND ROUGH SEAS

CHAPTER 1

Chanteys
The Sailor's Work Song among His Brothers

Song is the rhythm of human existence. If we are open to it, we encounter musicality at every turn of our day. It is in the din of voices in an office, the hum of traffic and commerce in the streets, and even in the rise and fall of breath. The last item, the embodied musicality between body and breath, is perhaps the most important, the most overlooked, and the topic that is at the heart of this book.[1] The voice as it speaks or sings is connected to the organs that create and emit the sound, and what is produced through this intimate connection is nothing short of meaning making. It is sensual, it is visceral, and it is, perhaps, erotic. What, then, does this intimate connection among sound, body, and meaning making suggest about texts that are sung, coordinate movement, and contain within them the expression of intimate acts? *Cabin Boys, Milkmaids, and Rough Seas* is primarily concerned with answering this question as it pertains to chanteys, sailing work songs of the sea, and ones that are located specifically in the unexpurgated repertoire of a famed chantey singer and collector.

The chapters that follow seek to reembody a music that was intimately important to both the symbolic and actual lives of the men who sang them. In fact, more than any other type of music, the sailor's chantey provides an opportunity through which to consider music as a release valve for the confusing and complex facets of human existence. What this book will demonstrate is that sailors—and more generally, men—are complex and provocative artisans who shape narratives that expertly capture human quandaries and experiences, especially as they are lived in a constrained, homosocial space. While I went into my initial research into the field of chantey singing with the expectation that I would find blatant humorous and bawdy songs that suggested a desire for fellow men in a homosocial space, what I found, along with that, were sophisticated narratives that truly and fully represent what gender, sexuality, and life both at sea and on land actually mean. The songs present something of a kaleidoscope of identity: moving, changing, evolving, and almost undulating.

In the chanteys collected by erotic folksong collector Gershon Legman from the repertoire of Stan Hugill—men who will be further introduced below—readers immediately draw connections between other examples from homosocial song tradition, such as rugby ditties, freemason songs, and textile-workers tunes. They present as heteronormative on the surface, appearing to reify a staunch and categorical heteronormativity. What they prove, similarly to other homosocial traditions, is that such constructions are unstable, and what they ultimately articulate is a deep vulnerability and even liminality.

Who Am I, and How Do I Approach This Research?

It is worth laying out my own researcher identity, as well as the approach that I take in *Cabin Boys, Milkmaids, and Rough Seas*. I am in the sometimes-difficult position of viewing content using an interdisciplinary lens. I argue that such an approach is important for illuminating the complex realities inherent within cultural objects because they are not static things, despite their concrete quality in print spaces, and require interpretations that bring many lenses to bear on them. That said, I also recognize the unique challenge of writing an interdisciplinary project. It means, at times, that I might not meet the full expectations of one discipline or another and that parts of this project might feel as if there are readings, frameworks, or possibilities missing. What I encourage readers of all disciplines to imagine is that an interdisciplinary project like this, despite places where one might desire more, opens so many possibilities for deeper inquiry.

A folksong scholar might want to see a book that places the bawdy chantey against the backdrop of all number of all-male song traditions that evidences similar applications and narratives frames. A historian might want a book that explores the historical situatedness of the chantey as it arose within the confines of a specific social space during a very specific time. Gender and sexuality scholars might, similarly, want to have a book that plants the chantey texts within a specific time frame and read through configurations of gender and sexuality for a finite culture. Those books should be written and would add to the kaleidoscope of readings that I am beginning here. The chantey tradition is a complicated one for it is situated within and among all of these different fields and can be read through so many different lenses.

The choice of an interdisciplinary one is the best place at which to begin as it opens the trajectory for all of these other inquiries that would be inherently important to continued work in the field. Arguably, if I were to begin with looking at the chantey tradition only through the lens of a close literary reading, without the historical framework, readers would lose out on thinking through it as both literary artifact as well as historical register. If I were to read the chanteys from Hugill only as a part of a long tradition of men's work songs, the deeper analysis of what the songs are doing and saying would be subordinated to the project of creating connections among traditions. The work that I accomplish here requires that multiple lenses come together and highlight what I see as a deeply complex folksong tradition.

Chanteys are well poised for an interdisciplinary reading of them because they are cultural objects that are living and breathing entities. They contain characters and action that require a close literary reading, but they were also sung by men while they were at work at sea, which requires a level of historical, sociological, folkloric, and even organizational framing. The chanteys also capture unique renderings of sexuality and gender, which require theories of gender and sexuality in order to fully unpack the complex scenarios that are captured throughout the collected examples. As an interdisciplinary scholar, I see all of these lenses working together, overlapping with one another, and sometimes standing at odds with each other. Though complicated, they are all necessary in order to plumb the depths of a rich folk song tradition that has yet to be explored for what it represents about identity at sea. It is true that the circulation and instability of gender and sexuality is a theme that has been explored by many scholars to date; however, such focus has not been applied to the chanteys that the sailor used when he was at sea for sometimes months or years at a stretch.

Of course, my first instinct when confronted with content is to read from the literary tradition as I am trained as a close reader. Literary analysis is one that often engages multiple theories and disciplines that are then placed onto texts for interpretation. It is not uncommon to see a close literary reading that engages historical frameworks, theories from gender and sexuality, or even research in sociology and anthropology to illuminate what is communicated in text. In many ways, I approach my reading in a way similar to what Eve Kosofsky Sedgwick outlines as "reparative reading," taking pleasure in drawing out from the text what it is telling me and following the paths that open up to me while I am reading.[2] It is a process that provides pleasure for the scholar as she is bent to the task of reading, but it arguably also injects the text with its own power and voice. Indeed, the text leads me toward the interpretations and theories and even themes to explore as if words and phrases each open new worlds and associations at each turn. Charles L. Briggs notes that "my interpretations [of texts] rather emerged by bringing their words [informants] into dialogue with philosophy, history, folkloristics, anthropology, ethnic and racial studies, ethnomusicology, and other fields."[3] I am participating in a similar process of which I am going to the text first and bringing it into conversation with known fields that radiated out of those texts. Following this path of passion does not mean throwing out convention entirely, however.

Briggs says it best when he argues that "we might take a clue from Wittgenstein's epigraph and focus on maintaining a flexible, playful relationship to boundaries, jumping over them in such a way as to link and enrich the games being played on both sides."[4] I recognize, intimately, the discrete boundaries and expectations that attend the various disciplines that I am working with and within. They each contain their own set of rules and their own approach to research and writing, and, at times, they police those boundaries so as to ensure exactness and a degree of trustworthiness. In Briggs's argument, I see both a respect for and playfulness with these disciplinary boundaries and expectations. Research should be about fun and passion and knowledge and sharing ideas and doing so with the conventions that we have available to us. In the "jumping over," there is an understood *knowing* of those disciplinary boundaries and a conscious decision to jump over them, to "enrich the games" through knowledge of the rules and stretching them or refiguring them. I cannot help but think about Legman in Briggs's comment for he engaged in that same process of entertaining the disciplinary expectations while also infuriatingly transgressing those norms for his own dogmatic approach. Sarah Lash argues that Legman often chose a sometimes-haphazard or catchall organizational process on purpose, bucking the confines of scholarship and, in a way, becoming a sort of rebel scholar.[5]

It is worth noting that, as a female interdisciplinary scholar, I sit at the interstices in a similar fashion, at times, to the men who collected the manuscript and also to the working-class men who potentially used this content in their own workspaces. Because I do not land in any one place firmly, I am always at risk of being potentially suspicious, potentially associated with "scholars from other disciplines who 'dabbled with folklore,'" and therefore characterized as something of an "academic interloper."[6] I am, indeed, an interloper where these songs are concerned. As a female scholar, I have not ever sung chanteys while tasked with the grueling expectations of shipboard work. Coupled with my status as a female researcher is the reality that many early modern sailors likely would not have shared their songs with me nor felt it appropriate for me to engage with the songs as I do. Though I was raised in a working-class household, my position in the world is one that is far removed from that of the early modern sailor, and as such, it is important to highlight that I do not intend this project to "give voice" to a group through my status as a researcher. Researchers cannot become "voice boxes" for the subjects they are studying, even though the researcher is ultimately the one who will produce the scholarly work (and benefit from it). A researcher is tasked with the expectation that they will represent the data they find to the scholarly world, tempered with the caveat that the published perspectives are theirs alone. Likewise, in stating that one would be "giving voice" to a population is to usurp the power of the research subjects, intimating that the subjects cannot speak for themselves. I am intimately aware of the chasm between my position as a scholar and researcher and the working-class men who sang these songs as they battled the dangers of the sea.

The work of the interdisciplinary scholar is to dismantle thinking processes and frameworks that are insular or siloed, policed from within and without to ensure that all remains "solely to themselves." Interdisciplinary work seeks to demonstrate that all disciplines truly function together and converse among themselves, and interdisciplinarians attempt to eradicate the borders among them that are fiercely protected but largely arbitrary. This project will add to the reality that borders and boxes around identity provide ways through which we might understand the world, but they do not capture the reality of life and existence. In the same way, disciplinary boundaries help to structure the ways in which certain spheres view content and data, but that is not how data and content exists in the world.

A Note on Spelling and the Trouble with Chantey Scholarship

Before beginning to outline this critical study in earnest, I want to make a few distinctions in terms of chanteys. Specifically, I need to highlight my choice of the spelling "chantey" as opposed to other spellings the reader will encounter here and elsewhere (shantey, shanty, chanty, chantie, etc.). I also want to briefly provide discussion concerning the difference between chanteys and sea songs as these terms are often used interchangeably, even though they are quite different. In terms of the spelling that I have chosen for this publication, "chantey" closely resembles the actual act of singing the songs on sailing ships. According to the *Oxford English Dictionary*, the term is "said to be a corruption of French *chantez*, imperative of *chanter* to sing," with the definition being "a sailor's song, esp. one sung during heavy work."[7] Hugill, whose repertoire is the focus of this project, indicates, "Early shantying was, from what we know, little more than primitive chanting and wild aboriginal cries to encourage the seamen to keep time and work harder, and the fierce elemental yells on a rope known as 'sing-outs' were to be heard even in modern times aboard sailing vessels and occasionally aboard steamers while some sailing-ship shellbacks still remained to sail in them."[8] Though others have chosen to spell "chantey" using the many other options available, for me, no term comes closer to capturing the almost-ritualistic and community-building nature of the sailor's song in the same way that "chantey" does. Chanting produces an immediate, almost-spiritual connection between body, voice, and soul. The term comes close to apprehending the pervasiveness of the embodied quality of chanteys: it is in the voice, it is in the language, but it is also in the marriage between body and action. Additionally, the spelling with *ch* differentiates the songs under consideration from the catch-all term beginning with *sh* that is often used for songs that contain material about the sea and sailors but that are not always authentic chanteys in the strictest sense.[9] Some songs have been misidentified as chanteys/shanties when they are likely shore songs or fo'c'sle songs. The song "Barnacle Bill the Sailor" is often filed under the term "shanty" when it is actually a sea song and was created so as to be sung for an audience.[10] Scholar Graeme Milne also traces collections of the chantey genre and makes comments on the various issues inherent in the early collected examples. Distinctly, Milne captures the prevailing disagreements that attend the chantey genre and its early collection, meaning Milne points to some of the controversy around collectors and even collection processes. One of the primary issues he highlights is the struggle to claim authenticity and the often-slippery nature of categorizing materials under specific genre types.[11] Distinguishing a song as either a sea song or a chantey is inherently important to the study of the genre as the two types are distinctly different in application and therefore also as regards embodied meaning.

What distinguishing specific terms and spellings accomplishes is the identification of the content based on very specific applications, therefore allowing us to draw different conclusions depending on the classification.[12] Because chanteys are sung while the sailor is at work and the sea song or fo'c'sle song is sung in myriad other spaces and places, the position and use of the song has bearing on the ways in which scholars might read the text itself. One of the primary frustrations in working with the chantey tradition is authenticating chantey material and, thereby, claiming with certainty that a collection presents chantey material as it is sung at sea. The key reason that this identification is so difficult is the fact that early collectors often lumped all types of sea-related songs into collections and then circulated the material as chanteys to the wider reading public.[13] In presenting collected material in this way, early compilers of the chantey tradition merged sea songs with chanteys (or ballads and other songs about the sea), making it sometimes difficult to differentiate the two within publications currently in circulation. To outline the specific difference, "sea songs" are songs that are about the sea and sailors and are not interchangeable with the "chantey." "Chanteys," unlike sea songs, are songs that are *only* sung while men are employed in their shipboard work. The problem is that both genres (sea songs and chanteys) often focus on narrative material that is roughly similar, such as sailors or life at sea, ushering a conflation of the two genres, where one is mistaken for the other. Additionally, sailors sometimes borrowed sea songs and other shore songs and retrofitted them as chanteys. The grouping of these two genres is understandable though frustrating where research is concerned. In *Cabin Boys, Milkmaids, and Rough Seas*, I identify the manuscript material as containing examples of the chantey genre. There are some scholarly voices who will contend that the songs are, more likely, representations of the chantey genre as imagined by Stan Hugill, but I suggest that they are actual relics of the sea that run closest to how they were likely sung when they were originally conceived.

Hugill at least attempted to present true chantey relics to Legman in their correspondence. His defense of his knowledge of sailing work songs (especially the bawdy nature of them) and his presentation of learning those chanteys from early sailors convinced me that he had a working knowledge of the material he sent to Legman. In a more pointed defense of his knowledge of chanteys, Hugill showed Legman, in a letter dated September 2 (1962?), that he clearly knew the difference between a sea song and a chantey. He writes, "I agree with you [Legman] that every sailor song these days is a *shanty*—I have a hell of a job trying to explain the difference to the Philistines," which underscores the idea that Hugill understood the differences in the genre and sought to provide Legman with true examples of chanteys as he remembered them from his time at sea.[14]

Not all publications present this same, explicit defense and distinction.[15] Richard Bauman notes, "When an utterance is assimilated to a given genre, the process by which it is produced and interpreted is mediated through its intertextual relationship with prior texts," and in labeling Hugill's repertoire as examples of the chantey genre, I am making a conscious decision to treat those artifacts as a part of that genre, ultimately impacting the ways in which the songs are interpreted.[16] To view these songs as sea songs—and not chanteys— would change the lens to a degree. The interpretation of the songs as chanteys ties them to particular men in particular situations and to a longer tradition of a particular type of song. It should be noted, however, that Hugill did provide public and private productions of his repertoire, which opens his chantey examples to critique. This admission will be explored in greater detail; however, it is worth highlighting that Hugill did reproduce these songs out of the context of work that renders his publicly sung examples of the genre approximations.

What Are Chanteys?

Chanteys were considered an intimate part of the daily work of the early modern sailing ship. Though these songs appear humorous and entertaining to the modern reader, the sound of the singing and the lyrics of the songs were directly attached to some particular part of shipboard work, creating an intimate connection between what was sung and what was done. Prolific folklore, folksong, ballad, and chantey scholar and collector James Madison Carpenter captures the nature of the chantey best when he argues that "the chanteys were adapted, in movement, spirit and length, to the task in hand."[17] Chanteys were invented and deployed in order to coordinate the movements of men on ship as they completed the required tasks placed on them. To illustrate this embodied connection between voice and coordinated movement, Frederick Pease Harlow, in his *Chanteying aboard American Ships*, outlines, "Sailors were so accustomed to singing out when there was a pull to be made, that I have actually heard an old sailor give a 'Yo-ho-hip' when pulling on his sea boots."[18] It should be clear that the sailor viewed his voice as thoroughly linked to action: sound necessitated movement to the point where, at least in this instance, the connection was second nature. The relationship between and among song, voice, and work was intimately important, specifically to the sailor in the early modern sailing ship as compared to all other vocations in which song has been deployed at work or in homosocial spaces.[19]

Work song is an enduring genre and one that is at once finite and evolving. When dealing with chanteys, it is important to note that those songs are still sung today, though they are arguably approximations of the genre as it was sung during the days of tall ships. Because of their enduring quality, it is worth noting that movement from present to past tense, when discussing this genre, is predicated on the reality that chanteys were sung during a very specific time in history; however, they are also still sung and circulated today. I contend that the songs are most authentic as they have been attached to very specific working environments and conditions before the advent of the steamship; though, it is clear that these songs have been retrofitted to the work of and around sailing ships in our contemporary world.

The distinction for the early modern sailor, unlike others, was that his attachment to his work at sea might lapse into the intimate and even the erotic. Historian Greg Dening argues, "To a sailor, the text of his life was in knowing every degree of the relationship of his wooden world to the wind and sea and land outside it and the relationship of every place, role and action within it to himself. The pleasure of that text was as erotic for him as a composition could have been to Mozart, and just as self-identifying, and just as disturbing to others."[20] In Dening's own description of the sailor's life, it is impossible to miss the intimate and sexually charged quality of the sailing vocation and its specific relationship with *texts*. Within this description, the sailing man presents as a liminal figure, imbued and fueled primarily by his senses. Indeed, the excerpt from Dening takes the sailor directly to the realm of music, even identifying the sailor as akin to a composer, taking pleasure in the exchanges between the senses, the surroundings, and the composer himself. That relationship was embodied, personal, and deeply sensual. The sailor used certain types of chanteys for particular types of work. In fact, the chanteyman, a man on ship tasked with beginning the chantey and shaping its narrative, might be viewed as this composer described by Dening. The skilled chanteyman would deploy a song based on his understanding of the task at hand, the nature of the crew engaged, and the necessities of the moment: nothing less than a composer of sensation, emotion, and action. As the songs were deployed against the backdrop of a homosocial space and reignited with the erotic tension described by Dening, it is possible to consider the erotically charged circularity among song, homosocial space, and the men engaged in the process of sharing in specific cultural artifacts.

The chantey is a part of a homosocial work environment, and when I use the term "homosociality," I am considering the finite, all-male space of the sailing ship and the specific comradery and brotherhood that are endemic to that insular and sometimes-alienated space. The chantey, then, is an intimate object born of a very specific and privileged enclave and exists against the backdrop of the constrained, floating world of the sailing ship. The floating and near "total-institution" framework of the sailing ship, in fact, rendered this homosocial space almost doubly charged with the exclusive nature that courts other all-male spaces.[21]

The chantey itself is akin to other homosocial bonding mechanisms that function to facilitate bonds but also insulate the particular group who is sharing in the collective tradition and even work to articulate a distinctive identity. The homosocial environment is a single-sex space that often contains within it specialized rituals and artifacts that shape the space but also act on the bodies and identities of those participating in that restrictive context. Indeed, the cultural artifacts and rituals are a part of what distinguishes group members and also act as the objects that inculcate new members into the homosocial environment. Examples of homosocial enclaves and settings, other than the sailing ship, are fraternities, early modern freemason clubs, and all-male rugby groups, and vast scholarship exists that touches on not only how these spaces use cultural artifacts to differentiate group members from those outside and also initiate them but also how their objects and rituals often involve a degree of sexuality and sexual desire/expression. Sailing men, in fact, might be viewed as creating a "fraternity of the forecastle" through the ways in which they employ certain bonding, hazing, and rite of passage rituals to inculcate new sailing men into the sailing tradition. Marcus Rediker specifically ties chanteys to the bonding rituals of sailing men when he argues, "Such songs, in all their variety, were the very vessels of a collective consciousness at sea, the media through which tars expressed their common fears, hopes, needs, and social realities. The bonds that slowly and fitfully emerged from shipboard cooperation often found their way into song."[22]

Like the chantey, other bonding objects and rituals similarly function in the homosocial space to structure, demarcate, and initiate. In these homosocial enclaves, the homosocial and the homoerotic are distinctly dialectical. The work of Jane Ward, specifically, highlights the slippage between the homosocial and homoerotic in hazing rituals across homosocial enclaves and contends that "homosocial homosexuality is increasingly offered as a possibility for adult men who may have, in psychotherapist Joe Kort's words, a 'deep longing to experience the physical intimacy with other men that they are denied in a sexist and homophobic world.'"[23] Like erotic ritual in fraternities, Scott Fabius Kiesling and Michael Flood each investigate how particular erotic and sexually explicit language not only functions to create boundaries in the homosocial environment but also instructs members in new expectations of identity that align with shared values and approaches to the world both inside the fraternity and outside of it.[24]

The erotic capacity of the songs from Hugill should be viewed as not only wedding erotic content and even the erotic dimension of the sailing workspace but also arising as cultural artifacts imbued with the homosocial/homoerotic dialectic that Sedgwick recognized in *Between Men*.[25] Looking across different homosocial enclaves, it is possible to see, humming beneath the surface, the same homosocial/homoerotic slippage. This homosociality is key to understanding not only the function of chanteys but also the erotic undercurrents of this song tradition. Chanteys structure the bonds of the sailing ship, articulate and generate a specific sailing identity, and recycle narrative views of both the sailing and landbound world that complexly support a distinct homosociality that, unlike a place like the fraternity, is a matter of life and death, as well as appearing to dance around a desirability that is embedded in the frameworks of homosocial environments. Succinctly, the desire to be and the desire to be with are often in distinct relationship to one another.

Narrative of song is not static but rather evolves within the space it is sung. What I mean by "narrative" here and throughout is that song content contains something of a storyline: there is a beginning, a middle, and a sense of closure by the end for most of the materials contained in the manuscript. Barre Toelken's work is important for the ways in which I am thinking about and using the term "narrative" in the songs from Hugill. He writes that "most people refer to the narratives as 'ballads' and to the remainder as 'folksongs,'" going on to say that "the ballad develops an episode in which action takes place and is concluded, whereas the other folksongs focus on the articulation of feelings, ideas, fantasies, and attitudes without utilizing a narrative thread to achieve their ends."[26] Despite many of the songs being quite short and often nowhere near the narrative depth of something like a ballad, they do engage a beginning, middle, and end similarly to the structure Toelken mentions. The work of Peter Narvaez also supports my view of Hugill's repertoire.[27] Though some songs are clearly more lyrical in their construction, a vast number of the songs contains actual stories with characters who interact, clash, and resolve conflict in the ways that narrative tales also do.

Technically speaking, there are at least two types of chanteys that were employed in the work of the early modern sailing ship: capstan/windlass chanteys and hauling/halyard chanteys. Capstan and windlass chanteys were used for "heaving the anchor" and other "continuous process[es]," while "halyard or 'long drag' songs" were "intermittent."[28] The length and rhythm of the different types of songs each matched the particular processes for which they were employed and thereby structured and coordinated movement and collective effort. The rhythms of the song engaged the breath and the voice of the men, producing a physiological control, while the steady length and time of the song ordered and assimilated the shared task of working the ship by forcing the men to fall in line with one another and the rhythm of the work. Though, on the surface, the example of the sailor pulling on his boots or the sailor singing out as he pulls at the ropes might not seem erotic or sensual, the sailor was engaged in the same cyclical process that would, if done right, evoke a sense of pleasure or even, perhaps, release. The sailor, as he takes pleasure in singing out and pulling his boot strings, was registering, at least for a moment, the pleasure in the connection between voice and action. Percy Adams Hutchison observes, "The various tasks performed by sailors in working the ship are essentially rhythmic in their nature, which fact alone would be sufficient to impel many a man to accompany his work by rhythmic vocal utterances. The impulse to such vocal accompaniment may be regarded as the initial, or natural, *chantie-impulse*."[29] There is a distinct tie between body—both the corporeal parts and the spiritual—and the voice.

The complexities of chanteys truly lie within the nexus between the breath and the body: a continual and cyclical process. For sailing men, breath and body are directly tied to the process of work on the sailing ship, where the chantey serves as tying both breath and action together. The way through which to understand the connection between chanteys and their attachment to work is viewing them through the lens of Dorothy E. Smith's theory of texts regulating bodies, discussed in her "Texts and the Ontology of Organizations and Institutions." She theorizes how texts help to create, coordinate, and constrain spaces so that spaces become defined by their texts. Similarly, chanteys coordinate work, bodies, and identities within the ship, and songs are situated within work contexts in such a way that they might further articulate how texts coordinate the men and the environment of the ship. Smith argues, "The text itself, as a material presence (paper, electronic and so on) is produced, read, (watched, listened to) in particular local settings by particular people. People's activities in local settings are in this way connected into social relations organized by the text."[30]

The "text" of a chantey, in similar ways, orders not only the work of the ship, but also coordinates bodies to the particular task at hand, to particular positions and hierarchies in the work environment, and to a wider social community of the ship and the sailing world. An example of why such a theoretical underpinning is important can be understood through thinking about the narrative of "Sacramento," a song to be discussed in chapter 3:

> An' when I'm well an' free from pain,
> If I meet that whore, I'll fuck her again.
> Sing, me boys, oh, heave an' sing,
> Heave an' make her arse-ole spring.

The fragment is similar to the sexual nature of other songs from all-male bonding environments; however, the difference is that the narrative of the song, as it is applied to the work of the ship, would require the men to sing out the lines collectively as they are pulling or heaving at the work of the ship. The pulling and heaving, against the backdrop of the lyrics of the song, create a sexually charged shared experience for the men that is both controlling and regulating, as with other such texts outlined by Smith, but it is a controlled and organized text that is also erotically charged within a homosocial environment. The men are completing the work of the ship while they are also, consciously or unconsciously, simulating sex, ultimately a circular process that melds narrative with action—action that is virulently powerful. The sailors are regulated by the song; the singing and their bodies are tied to the task.

However, there is the added element that the narrative of the song includes specific characters that are a part of the ship, such as the heaving that occurs in "Sacramento." The sailors jointly "heave" themselves into the "arse-ole" of the woman, but they are also heaving at the capstan to work the ropes of the ship.[31] In this shared act, sailors essentially bond together through the brutalizing of a woman and also through the required tasks of the ship: all is accomplished through the wedding of breath, body, and voice. Indeed, it is possible to imagine that the frustrations of working the sailing ship in the early modern period were visited, collectively, on the body of the woman, and through her body, the sailors channeled further aggression to their collective work. In this way, the text, the bodies, and the work of the ship are organized, erotically charged, and also powerful. The breath, the voice, and the movements of the men's bodies are coordinated and arguably structured by the songs that are produced: the song engages the voice and the body—there is actual life within the lyrics that are deployed. The very nature of the chantey is evocative of the intimate connection between and among voice, body, and circulation.

When Were Chanteys Sung?

There is considerable disagreement concerning when chanteys were primarily sung. Essentially, arguments fall into two separate categories: an argument for dating chanteys at least back to the 1400s stretching into the 1880s and an argument that places chantey singing in a finite period between 1830 and 1860. I grapple with this question at length in "Engaging Imperfect Texts: The Ballad Tradition and the Investigation of Chanteys," in which I argue for an older dating of chanteys.[32] In 1928, Lucy E. Broadwood and A. H. Fox-Strangways

Plate I: image of sailing ship, with the parts listed, from Mystic Seaport Museum's 1856 edition of Richard Henry Dana Jr., *The Seaman's Friend: Containing a Treatise on Practical Seamanship, with Plates; A Dictionary of Sea Terms; Customs and Usages of the Merchant Service; Laws Relating to the Practical Duties of Master and Mariners* (Boston: Thomas Groom, 1851). Courtesy of Mystic Seaport Museum.

argued that chanteys can be traced back to as early as AD 200–400 or, with greater support, to 1480–1483. They note mention of singing "sea-songs" in *Daphnis and Chloe* and present various translations of the Greek that point to songs sung while rowers were toiling at their work. Broadwood provides a letter that was sent to her by Fox-Strangways that notes, "You have hit on a real *locus classicus* of the chantey man; he couldn't be better described."[33] Broadwood and Fox-Strangways go on to discuss the work of Felix Fabri, "a German monk of Ulm," who appears to provide descriptions of "occupational singing and music on board a Venetian galley."[34] These observations appear to note nascent chantey singing, but it is impossible to tell the exact content of the songs nor cull anything that would aid exact dating and comparison of these songs to chanteys beyond the use of song for work and the mention of call-and-response deployments. Importantly, however, Broadwood and Strangways note that "it would be impossible not to exchange songs, legends, dances and the rest whilst herding familiarity, for weeks and months on end, with fellow-creatures of the most diverse nations and degrees."[35] Broadwood

PLATE I.

THE SPARS AND RIGGING OF A SHIP.

INDEX OF REFERENCES.

1 Head.
2 Head-boards.
3 Stem.
4 Bows.
5 Forecastle.
6 Waist.
7 Quarter-deck.
8 Gangway.
9 Counter.
10 Stern.
11 Tafferel.
12 Fore chains.
13 Main chains.
14 Mizzen chains.
15 Bowsprit.
16 Jib-boom.
17 Flying jib-boom.
18 Spritsail yard.
19 Martingale.
20 Bowsprit cap.
21 Foremast.
22 Fore topmast.
23 Fore topgallant mast.
24 Fore royal mast.
25 Fore skysail mast.
26 Main mast.
27 Main topmast.
28 Main topgallant mast.
29 Main royal mast.
30 Main skysail mast.
31 Mizzen mast.
32 Mizzen topmast.
33 Mizzen topgallant mast.
34 Mizzen royal mast.
35 Mizzen skysail mast.
36 Fore spencer gaff.
37 Main spencer gaff.
38 Spanker gaff.
39 Spanker boom.
40 Fore top.
41 Foremast cap.
42 Fore topmast cross-trees
43 Main top.
44 Mainmast cap.
45 Main topmast cross-trees.
46 Mizzen top.
47 Mizzenmast cap.
48 Mizzen topmast cross-trees.
49 Fore yard.
50 Fore topsail yard.
51 Fore topgallant yard.
52 Fore royal yard.
53 Main yard.
54 Main topsail yard.
55 Main topgallant yard.
56 Main royal yard.
57 Cross-jack yard.
58 Mizzen topsail yard.
59 Mizzen topgallant yard.
60 Mizzen royal yard.
61 Fore truck.
62 Main truck.
63 Mizzen truck.
64 Fore stay.
65 Fore topmast stay.
66 Jib stay.
67 Fore topgallant stay.
70 Fore skysail stay.
71 Jib guys.
72 Flying-jib guys.
73 Fore lifts.
74 Fore braces.
75 Fore topsail lifts.
76 Fore topsail braces.
77 Fore topgallant lifts.
78 Fore topgallant braces.
79 Fore royal lifts.
80 Fore royal braces.
81 Fore rigging.
82 Fore topmast rigging.
83 Fore topgallant shrouds.
84 Fore topmast backstays.
85 Fore topgallant backstays.
86 Fore royal backstays.
87 Main stay.
88 Main topmast stay.
89 Main topgallant stay.
90 Main royal stay.
91 Main lifts.
68 Flying-jib stay.
69 Fore royal stay.
92 Main braces.
93 Main topsail lifts.
94 Main topsail braces.
95 Main topgallant lifts.
96 Main topgallant braces.
97 Main royal lifts.
98 Main royal braces.
99 Main rigging.
100 Main topmast rigging.
101 Main topgallant rigging.
102 Main topmast backstays.
103 Main topgallant backstays.
104 Main royal backstays.
105 Cross-jack lifts.
106 Cross-jack braces.
107 Mizzen topsail lifts.
108 Mizzen topsail braces.
109 Mizzen topgallant lifts.
110 Mizzen topgal't braces.
111 Mizzen royal lifts.
112 Mizzen royal braces.
113 Mizzen stay.
114 Mizzen topmast stay.
115 Mizzen topgallant stay.
116 Mizzen royal stay.
117 Mizzen skysail stay.
118 Mizzen rigging.
119 Mizzen topmast rigging.
120 Mizzen topgal. shrouds.
121 Mizzen topmast backstays.
122 Mizzen topgal'nt backstays.
123 Mizzen royal backstays.
124 Fore spencer vangs.
125 Main spencer vangs.
126 Spanker vangs.
127 Ensign halyards.
128 Spanker peak halyards.
129 Foot-rope to fore yard.
130 Foot-rope to main yard.
131 Foot-rope to cross-jack yard.

Plate I: "The Spars and Rigging of the Ship," from Mystic Seaport Museum's 1856 edition of Richard Henry Dana Jr., *The Seaman's Friend: Containing a Treatise on Practical Seamanship, with Plates; A Dictionary of Sea Terms; Customs and Usages of the Merchant Service; Laws Relating to the Practical Duties of Master and Mariners* (Boston: Thomas Groom, 1851). Courtesy of Mystic Seaport Museum.

Plate II: image of sailing ship, with the sails listed, from Mystic Seaport Museum's 1856 edition of Richard Henry Dana Jr., *The Seaman's Friend: Containing a Treatise on Practical Seamanship, with Plates; A Dictionary of Sea Terms; Customs and Usages of the Merchant Service; Laws Relating to the Practical Duties of Master and Mariners* (Boston: Thomas Groom, 1851). Courtesy of Mystic Seaport Museum.

and Fox-Strangway's comment is one that resonates with my own reading of this tradition and forms the cornerstone for my own view of the origin of chantey singing.[36] Despite what I will outline of other scholars and despite the paucity of other examples in the period between 1400 and 1860, which I theorize occurs because of the lack of interest in the genre, it makes sense that chantey singing continued and even evolved as such oral traditions have a tendency to grow and change with time rather than die out completely or spring forth for only a finite moment.

Hugill references, in *Shanties from the Seven Seas*, this same piece by Broadwood and Fox-Strangways. He appears to place the origin of chantey singing within the same period that Broadwood and Fox-Strangways mention; however, this reading stands in marked contrast to other scholars who place chantey singing during a finite period of time in the nineteenth century, ending when wooden ships gave way to steam-powered ones. Others that venture a potential earlier dating of chantey songs are Duncan Emrich, in "American Sea Songs and Shanties," and George Hodge, in his memoir written between 1790 and 1833, though the memoir is not available to scholars as it was sold to a private collector.[37] Emrich notes that a version of "Haul

PLATE II.

A SHIP'S SAILS.

INDEX OF REFERENCES.

1 Fore topmast staysail.	18 Mizzen topgallant sail.
2 Jib.	19 Mizzen royal.
3 Flying jib.	20 Mizzen skysail.
4 Fore spencer.	21 Lower studdingsail.
5 Main spencer.	21a Lee ditto.
6 Spanker.	22 Fore topmast studdingsail.
7 Foresail.	22a Lee ditto.
8 Fore topsail.	23 Fore topgallant studdingsail.
9 Fore topgallant sail.	23a Lee ditto.
10 Fore royal.	24 Fore royal studdingsail.
11 Fore skysail.	24a Lee ditto.
12 Mainsail.	25 Main topmast studdingsail.
13 Main topsail.	25a Lee ditto.
14 Main topgallant sail.	26 Main topgallant studdingsail.
15 Main royal.	26a Lee ditto.
16 Main skysail.	27 Main royal studdingsail.
17 Mizzen topsail.	27a Lee ditto.

Plate II: "A Ship's Sails," from Mystic Seaport Museum's 1856 edition of Richard Henry Dana Jr., *The Seaman's Friend: Containing a Treatise on Practical Seamanship, with Plates; A Dictionary of Sea Terms; Customs and Usages of the Merchant Service; Laws Relating to the Practical Duties of Master and Mariners* (Boston: Thomas Groom, 1851). Courtesy of Mystic Seaport Museum.

the Bowline," sung by Richard Maitland, might be traced back to Henry VIII and even mentions a connection between the chantey "A-Roving" and a scene in *The Rape of Lucrece*, which lands the chantey tradition potentially in the 1600s.[38] My own argument for dating engages research in the ballad tradition that argues for a connection between some chantey texts and collected ballads. Essentially, the argument can be made that there is a cross influence between chanteys and early ballads as sailors engaged with the different songs in port and carried them back to ship with them for their own work.

An important critique of such dating, however, is ventured by ethnomusicologist Gibb Schreffler within several of his own publications concerning chanteys. Foremost, in terms of the connections to the ballad tradition, Schreffler notes first an overrepresentation of ballad-like songs in modern collections of chanteys as such songs were well positioned for popular performances. Seeing a connection between the early modern ballad tradition and collected chanteys might be a consequence of this overrepresentation. In Schreffler's important contribution to the field of chantey research *Boxing the Compass*, he argues that many publications, including Hugill's *Shanties from the Seven Seas*, privilege material that closely aligns with areas like ballad research and folksong tradition more generally. Capstan songs, which are much longer and contain far more narrative, lend themselves well to investigations like this as there is far more fodder for analysis. Too, they provide tantalizingly similar language and narrative to collected examples of ballad material that stretch back to at least the Restoration. With so many collections presenting and privileging capstan songs and other ballad-like tunes, there is a lack of representation for shorter songs, like hauling or heaving tunes. Additionally, Schreffler notes that many collections and repertoires of chanteys are mixtures of both true chanteys and other songs that are likely not chanteys at all, like landbound ballads and sea songs. For his own claim, and one that James Madison Carpenter supports, Schreffler places the tradition squarely in the 1800s. In "The Execrable Term," Schreffler supports this argument for dating by demonstrating, through a close analysis of the term "chanty," how the term made its way from the chanteyman of the "mobile cotton-screwers and their chants" in the 1840s to the sailing ship at least by the late 1850s.[39] Carpenter, who was working with the genre far earlier, raises this same reading and makes the argument that the chantey was largely sung between the years 1836 and 1877.[40]

It is likely, however, that chanteys *appear* to exist only within this finite period of time as the collection of such texts was not a focus of folksong and folklore research until that period. Research in the ballad tradition supports this view as modern ballad collection saw a renewed interest "stemming from the founding of the Folklore Society in 1878."[41] Legman more pointedly notes that, for erotic material, there is little to no collection during the period 1820–1927. He notes, "Beginning with the publication of *Immortalia* about 1927, a rapidly increasing group of American publications of erotic folksong, jokes, and obscoena [sic] of the 'novelty' kind, made an appearance, necessarily private and unfortunately rather amateur."[42] The rise in chantey collections dovetails with critical and scholarly interest in cultural artifacts like ballads and other folksong traditions, but it is apparent that much of the collected examples were impacted by obscenity laws during the period of collection. Schreffler notes, in *Boxing the Compass*, that the first published copy of a chantey arrived in 1858.[43] This same cultural interest in both ballads and chanteys, appearing to have been generated with the founding of bodies like the Folklore Society, began as collectors recognized the tenuous nature of oral materials. Paired with the recognition of oral material as potentially fleeting was also a new interest in the sea and seafaring, which was not palpable in the years during which sailing was so much a part of everyday working-class life.

Musicologist W. F. Arnold captures the almost plaintive cry to preserve these working-class songs in his short discussion of the chantey genre that opens Frank Thomas Bullen's *Songs of Sea Labor*. He laments:

> The Sea Chanties are songs of labour ; the crude symbols of much heavy toil ; oft times terrible experience and physical suffering ; of heroic battling with the wild, untamed forces of Nature—that we might have our daily bread. They form a kind of rude epic of those that go down to the sea in ships ; a tradition which should not be allowed to die out. . . .
>
> The Chanty therefore is a last surviving link with a class of ship now almost extinct ; the last will and testament of a type and sailor fast disappearing. Soon there will be no music of the ships beyond the discordant creak of steam winch, the frightful howl of the siren, and the monotonous, pulsating rhythm of the propeller. The roar of the gale, the thunder of the surf and the whole vast orchestra of the sea will be heard alone, undisturbed by the feeble piping of frail but unconquerable man.[44]

Arnold's description of the content included in Bullen's collection evokes a sentiment that folklore scholar Kimberly J. Lau notes collectors should be mindful of so as not to attach sentimental readings to collected oral materials. Lau ventures that much of folklore scholarship attempts to capture what is or might be lost to time, an imagined world that is shaped as different and sometimes better than the world we are a part of today. She notes it is an "idealized lost past . . . a past that we are none the better and probably worse for losing," which Arnold certainly transgresses.[45]

Despite this note of caution and Arnold's transgression of it, Arnold's forward to Bullen's collection of chanteys is noteworthy in that it points to some of the reasons why there was a rise in the collection of chanteys during the later parts of the 1800s. The Industrial Revolution arguably rendered these songs and the men who sang them obsolete and in need of protection.[46] There was a sentimentality connected to the songs and the work of the sailing ship, a sensation of nostalgia that was not extant during the span of time when chanteys were likely sung, a reading that Kelby Rose posits is clear in collected examples he surveyed.[47] Chantey collector Joanna Colcord notes this same reality in her collection of songs, in which she identifies that "ship building was too common an industry, seafaring was too ordinary an occupation, the country was altogether too nautical, for the data on which its maritime enterprise rested to seem to be of any especial importance."[48] Though it may seem to state the obvious, it is important to bear in mind just how integral seafaring was to life and commerce in the early modern period, and what Colcord captures is that it was so much a part of daily life that no one paid special attention to cultural objects from the sea. Objects like chanteys or scrimshaw or sailing memoirs were likely invisible in pop culture until the period in time during which modern inventions rendered seafaring of old unnecessary and thereby an almost curious relic.

Interestingly enough, when Schreffler tracks the emergence of the term "chanty" to describe the genre, he notes that it was not a term that was either applied to shipboard singing nor potentially used as a descriptive word by sailors until the later 1800s. Though he appears to be supporting his argument for a later dating of chantey texts, I contend that it lends further support to viewing chanteys as objects that were so much a part of sailing life that they were not recognized or categorized until much later and likely existed much earlier. Indeed, if we consider the fact that genre type and collection appear around the same time, it supports an argument that chanteys, as a collected genre, appear during a certain period wherein scholars are in the process of naming, collecting, and collating material. Before that period of naming and collecting, the songs were a part of the sailor's tool chest, and he would not have recognized a need to identify such songs under any particular category nor would collectors necessarily recognize the material as something worthy of note, collection, and scholarly treatment. Schreffler supports this idea of the chantey as a tool where "the knowing of chanties first and foremost as tools one learned to use at the same time as one learned to work a ship."[49] Folklore and folksong scholars, in contrast, require mechanisms by which to order and treat collected material as evidenced by the expansive Stith Thompson motif index or the Aarne-Thompson-Uther tale-type index. It makes sense that when modern collectors, especially those in the field of folklore, began taking note of the songs the sailor sang, they would use a descriptive category in order to sort collected content and would preserve what they could from informants.

What I am contending in terms of dating and the approach that I take here and throughout is that chanteys are not a blip on the radar of folksong: they are evolving and unfolding and arguably possible to trace back to a much earlier time. What my argument suggests is that chanteys are to be viewed similarly to other working-class song and folk traditions. Charles Conrad argues for a specific attachment between working-class life and song: "Because music permeates both work and leisure time, workers remain part of their mythical community regardless of their actual lifestyle, form of work, or geographical location."[50] Chanteys did not spontaneously appear on the scene; these songs were likely a part of the early modern sailing man's occupational space in the same way that has been observed in other working-class spaces. These songs were always there, though unnamed and unnoticed, and evolved and were applied to different things and different periods, different men and different locales. Percy Adams Hutchison appears to have supported this idea in 1906 when he argued, "If so many variations of one theme have come down to us, how many more, simply for lack of a recorder, must have perished?"[51] Important, too, is that these folk songs and folkways have been shared among a vast number of men across time and space, and that facet of the chantey is an important one in understanding my own approach to dating them.

In thinking about the chantey and its particular attachment to the work of the sailing ship, it is impossible to divorce them from continuity, indeterminacy, and something of a continuum. Indeed, it is a continuum similar to the one I use to consider gender and sexuality in the remainder of this project. I view seafaring and the waterways as intense contact zones where sailors have incredible opportunities to engage with men and women sharing in oral traditional culture, especially while at work, and it seems impossible that they would not make a connection to their own work on the sailing ship. Sailors are hardworking, intelligent, and witty, and encountering figures like the fishwife or mountebank in England's port towns would provide some fodder for sailing work songs that would be carried back to ship. Additionally, work songs, bonding songs, and indeed oral traditional culture have been traced through the centuries, and it would be difficult to believe that a working-class sailing man, bent to the sometimes-incredible tasks of the sailing ship, would be the lone space wherein song did not attend his work until the 1800s. It is fair to contend that making connections to the sailing man of the 1600s may be speculative, as a collected song from the 1800s may not match his exact expression of self, but there are enduring qualities of masculinity that match with the durable reality of work songs and working-class life. The chantey, as a part of sailing work and life, is an object attached to waterways that are unstable, expansive, and timeless. It rides along with sailors as they make their way across oceans and stop off at various ports to meet with vast and diverse peoples and cultures. They are songs that sometimes go down to the depths with those lost at sea, but they just as often survive to move on to different ships and even to different vocations and places because human beings are the conduit through which they are shared and deployed.

Tied with the argument concerning chantey dating is, of course, how to situate the chanteys within a finite period of time for analysis. Based on my own argument for a longer period during which chanteys were sung, *Cabin Boys, Milkmaids, and Rough Seas* draws on a number of historical periods and situations. At first, that choice might appear haphazard, like poor historical research and framing. The apparent haphazard approach is purposeful when considering chanteys to be a part of a period that stretches from the 1400s into the later 1860s. That is obviously a vast swath of time to cover, and I want to make it clear that the suggestions to come are not meant to be exhaustive or meant to place any one chantey on a very specific timeline or date. As historian Marcus Rediker notes: "The analysis of sea songs is rendered difficult by the problem of dating. Since the songs were a part of an oral tradition, in which they were continually modified, it is difficult to use them as specific evidence of maritime life in the eighteenth-century."[52]

What I see in the chanteys from Hugill are multiple comments on masculine culture that both have finite places in time and are timeless. Though some of the commentary or interpretation might be separated in time and space, the cultural gestures captured in these songs are indicative of a long-term core of masculinity that is illustrative. When I see castration anxiety inherent in a song like "Blow the Man Down," it is possible to draw on historical research that is both old and contemporary. Charles L. Briggs notes, "I have drawn on Bakhtin (1981, 1986) in suggesting that performances are not snapshots of a particular moment in time, but complex cartographies of the movement of discourses, subjectivities, and politics between contexts, genres, and texts."[53] I support this view in my own work where collected chantey versions contain within them narratives that are not static or necessarily tied to any one period and are also concrete and historically specific. When the sailing character's jibboom gets bent in the process of fornication in "Blow the Man Down," it evokes that sensation of castration anxiety that is deeply imbedded in conversations concerning both masculinity and virility, regardless of time and space. Just as researchers like Robert Darby are able to discuss the scene in *Tristram Shandy* during which Tristram loses his foreskin, as a moment of castration,[54] it is possible to apply similar thinking to the bent jibboom in a song that was collected much later than the publication of *Tristram Shandy*. Similarly, a scene like the one from "The Hog-Eye Man" gestures at similar masculine anxieties that have been captured in contemporary research into cuckolding as a pornographic phenomenon. Consider the following lines:

Oh, who's bin here since I've bin gone?
A big buck [n----r] wid a hard-on on.
If I cotch him here wid me Jinny anymore,
I'll tattoo his dusters, an' he won't fuck anymore.

They gesture at the same sensations captured in modern cuckolding scenarios despite the difference in time between the early 1900s and the 2000s.

On the surface, an ahistorical view of the different song narratives might appear sloppy or noncommittal, but the reality is that the songs capture something that is enduring about masculine identity and also about anxieties surrounding the construction of self. How I prefer to view the chanteys in time and space is to locate them within the din of voices as callouts in concrete language that might be investigated for what is timeless within them and also defined by time. Metaphors of castration and seminal power, for instance, can be located in scholarly treatment of texts like *Fanny Hill* and *Tristram Shandy* from the eighteenth century or even in medical discourse around spermatorrhea panic in the nineteenth century incorporated into discourse around cuckoldry in modern pornography.[55] These different contexts and content are separated by time, space, and even modality, but they sometimes gesture at the same materials that are extant in many of the texts from the manuscript.

I am, arguably, attempting to queer the very way that we see time in that it is at once finite but also unstable. By "queering time," I am thinking as Elizabeth Freeman does in her analysis of *Frankenstein, Orlando,* and *Sticky Fingers of Time* in which past, present, and future not only collide with one another but also are actively in the process of relating between each other.[56] Indeed, Freeman's work forces us to consider not only how time itself is constructed but also how encountering time is visceral, sensual, and even erotic. Certainly, there is a linear quality to time as moments can be viewed in sequence; however, time is also an episodic patchwork, not unlike Frankenstein's monster, where pieces of dead flesh or time are stitched together into a new constitution in time and place. The reality of the monster himself living on in the novel, being read outside of the time in which he was conceived, is a part of what it might mean to consider queer time. Freeman notes that an "erotohistoriography" is one that "does not write the lost object into the present so much as encounter it already in the present, by treating the present itself as hybrid."[57] There is a dialectics to history that is true when we think about what the chanteys communicate of a time but that are also divorced from time and even resonate into our present. She discusses, several times, the notion of an "*ars erotica* of historical inquiry" and an embodied process of historical research and analysis, and "then the writing of history is also figured as a seduction of the past and, correspondingly, as the past's erotic impact on the body itself."[58] In a way, thinking about history through a queer lens disrupts the linear quality that has attended historical inquiry to date and, in a way, reanimates it, reembodies it so that it might be possible to run one's fingers along experiences of the past. It is an approach in which history is not necessarily in the past but rather is a continuum that reaches out into the present, always connected and always sentient.

We think about time as being something out of reach, as moments that occurred "back then," which we recapture in our writing and research and thinking. What queering history does is permit space to think about history more in terms of something that is still here with us, functioning in the past but also informing the present. It is a constant presence that we can indeed touch and see in the here and now. Freeman notes, "We need a story of how discipline's temporalized body met with other bodies in modern social formations reducible neither to institution nor population, neither to identities nor genital sex—but in ephemeral relationalities organizing and expressing themselves through time."[59] She says in her *Beside You in Time* that the work "turns from the passions back to the body receiving sensations and puts the body at the center of analysis, but focuses on ways of using and tuning the body in relation to other bodies present, past, and future."[60] What she outlines of her own work is what is occurring in the blurring of historical lines in *Cabin Boys, Milkmaids, and Rough Seas*. Time is relational, culturally constructed, and arguably unstable in ways that if we think about history as something that we can physically bump into, it makes it possible to think about a cultural object like the chantey in both a very specific period of time and across time. I take seriously, too, Freeman's argument about reembodying and visiting attention directly to the body. She calls this approach a "sense-methods," which "can rearrange the relations between past and present, linking contemporary bodies to those from other times in reformulations of ancestry and lineage."[61] An example from the research of Jason T. Eastman, William F. Danaher, and Douglas Schrock helps to underscore this idea of certain earmarks of identity transgressing time and space, where "despite rather notable changes in the industry (i.e., de-unionization, etc.) and women's rights over the past 70 years, we surprisingly found little substantial change in the themes of these songs, which center on gendered imagery."[62] Arguably, despite songs arriving in different spaces and times, men in working-class environments appear to sing about roughly similar ideas. There is a similar continuity among chanteys, regardless of the repertoire, which suggests that some masculine ideals and images might be traced across time and space and across genre and therefore capture enduring qualities of manhood that engender a particular identity that is markedly different from those outside of working-class occupations.

As Charles W. Joyner notes, "the folklorist, like the historian, is faced necessarily with the problem of parts and wholes," and such an observation is particularly applicable to this project.[63] I am attempting to look at both parts and whole simultaneously, and at times, that will mean there is some seeming ahistoricity. He goes on to note that "folklorists would do well, even while using generalizations, to approach their subject with a deeper regard for the individual particulars of human experience," and in going directly to the texts, using different theoretical lenses, I am able to think about not only individual moments within the songs but also ways in which they attach to specific moments and examples in human history that are illustrative.[64] I do keep in mind, however, the caution that Lau outlines, which is that "published [and even unpublished] collections are often little more than essentialist, metonymic representations of the given culture or group, which is assumed to be an integrated, identifiable whole."[65] I bear in mind that collections like that of Hugill and Legman or even those of R. W. Gordon or James Madison Carpenter, located in the American Folklife Center at the Library of Congress, and others outside of these collections are representative of a particular collector, a particular time, and often a specific place. I recognize, too, that the readings that I produce of these texts might contribute to a view of chanteys as somehow capturing a larger whole, which potentially misrepresents the culture out of which they evolved and were circulated and even the genre as a whole. Despite some places where it appears that history is scattershot, "historical context is no mere ornament to folkloristic inquiry, it is of its essence."[66] Chanteys are certainly as individual as the men who sang them, and their historic specificity is important and does come to bear on readings of these texts more often than not.

Who Sung the Chanteys?

There is, much like in the case of the date of origin for chanteys, much disagreement concerning who originally sang the chanteys or "created" them as a genre. For some, the chantey is a purely American tradition that was taken up by British sailors who came in contact with singing American sailors. Schreffler shows that at least one early British collector, W. Clarke Russell, writing near the "fall" of chantey singing (which was around 1870–1880), argues for a purely American place of origin and apparently makes the distinction "that while forecastle songs were British, chanties were American."[67] The distinction that Schreffler makes is that songs sung in the fo'c'sle or when sailors are away from their shipboard employments are songs that were created by the British and circulated to other sailing men. Chanteys are to be understood, through this argument, as a purely American tradition.

Others, like humanities and social-science scholar Gerry Smyth, claim the opposite and argue that chanteys are British in origin, born out of the ballad tradition, and those chanteys were then circulated by British, Irish, and American sailors alike. Looking at a comparison between the ballad and the chantey tradition, it is possible to argue a British origin of chanteys in that contact with or having a relationship with the ballad and oral tradition of the early modern period might predispose someone to the communicative power of song. Many of the British port towns, too, were historically hubs for the mixing of sailors, cultures, and differing traditions. Historian Brad Beavan notes the transient nature of port towns and even attaches cultural readings of sailors as akin to the indeterminant nature of the port towns they visited. He writes that "the transient nature of sailortown and the notorious reputation of the sailor led many opinion-formers to believe that seaports lay outside of the justice system's quest for 'civilizing' the English streets."[68] In these port towns, sailors frequented taverns, brothels, street markets, and other diversions where they came in contact with lively cultural traditions, not the least of which was song. There is an argument to be made that early sailors—mixing with traditions like the Billingsgate fishwives' calls—might have borrowed and shaped materials they enjoyed into their own work songs.[69]

To the potential English origin of chanteys, Smyth, in his "Shanty Singing and the Irish Atlantic: Identity and Hybridity in the Musical Imagination of Stan Hugill," makes a compelling argument concerning the Irish origin of some chanteys. He also contends that "the shanty might be regarded as a typical product of the diasporic imagination—a riposte to the powerful conceptual framework which maintains 'a homology between a culture, a people, or a nation and its particular terrain.'"[70] He claims "that the shanty both partakes of, and contributes to, the formation of a counter-culture that shadows mainstream institutional modernity, and that Irish music represents a seminal element within that process."[71] In Smyth's view, the chantey, like other music, not only has a connective and electric power that stretches though time and space but also has the potential to connect and even evolve through its contact with other people, places, and periods. Situating the chantey in as specific a place as Ireland supports a plausible European origin for chanteys, which when tied to other viewpoints like that of Hugill and other European singers renders such a place of origin ever stronger, but it is equally as probable that the chantey originated in early America based on early and recent research into the African American influence of many chantey tunes.

Scholars writing to bolster the American origin argue that the chantey was born of the African American tradition and that the songs were taken and employed by sailors who came in contact with working slaves in American ports. There is a case to be made concerning the African American influence on sailor's chanteys; however, as with the question of whether the chantey is originally British or American, the influence of African American song meets with the same disagreement. Some chantey collectors, even Hugill himself, argue that sailors' songs can be traced to the hitching and chanting sounds used by African American slaves while at work and that sailors recognized the expediency with which work was completed while accompanied by song.[72] According to student Isaac Allen, who published an article about sailor songs in 1858 for his Oberlin College paper, the songs sounded similar to African American works songs, and he distinctly notes, "Then the conclusions of my speculation on the probable cause of this evident similarity between the chorus melodies of the sailor and the negro were something like these—First, the similarity of the object; that is, the unifying effort in labor, and thus to secure simultaneous action, as in rowing, pulling, hoeing, &c., &c., by the measured and rhythmical occurrence of vowel sounds."[73] In his short discussion of "sailors' songs," Allen remarks on similarities between the sailor's chantey and the work songs of African American men and women.[74] The chantey "Do Let Me 'Lone, Susan" from Hugill's repertoire contains the following annotation from Legman's unpublished manuscript: "From Hugill, who says, Haylard shaty [sic]. Of Negro origin and has never seen the light of print until now. Much improvisation was given to this shanty." The song reads in the following way:

Do let me 'lone, Susan, oh, do let me 'lone!
Hurrah! Me looloo boys, DO let me 'lone!
When I put me arm 'round Jinny's waist, Oh, Jinny jump away,
Hurrah! Me looloo boys, DO let me 'lone!

When I put me hand up Jinny's clouts, oh, Jinny jump about,
Hurrah! Me looloo boys!

Do let me 'lone, Flora, oh, do let me lone!
When I put me arm 'round Jinny's breasts, Oh, Jinny jump away,
When I put me hand on Jinny's snatch, Oh, Jinny jump about.[75]

The way in which the song reads lends itself to a possible African American origin. According to Gale P. Jackson, a scholar of interdisciplinary arts, in her "Rosy, Possum, Morning Star: African American Women's Work and Play Songs":

> African American women's work and play songs utilize characteristically African modalities of storytelling, improvisational "bantering," and historical documentation, pairing song and dance in percussive, multi-metered, polyphonic, call and response performance, to engage in circles of ancestry, articulation of journey, acts of witness, transformative pedagogy, and communal artmaking. These performances, in the African tradition, chronicle a specifically diasporic legacy, expressing both received values and cumulative historical knowledge.[76]

In Jackson's descriptions, there are some similarities between the African American traditional work song and the chantey. Mainly, the call and response, communal artmaking, improvising, and storytelling that each play a role in the African American tradition are traceable through many chantey texts and research concerning their creation and circulation on shipboard. In the example provided above, in "Do Let Me 'Lone, Susan," there is also a "percussive" and "polyphonic" sound to the text that elevates the possibility that at least this text may represent the cross influence between sailors and African American laborers. Just as with the question concerning the British or American origin of the chantey, there is another side of the argument that maintains that African American work songs were influenced by contact with the singing sailors who were met in port or on slaving ships.[77] Cross influence and cross-pollination sit at the nexus of chantey origin and evolution, and it is more advantageous to consider it a cosmopolitan genre than situated in any one space beyond the sea.

There is, though, a general assumption about the sailing world more generally and chanteys specifically that they are primarily white, Anglo-Saxon spaces and traditions. This conception of the sailing world and the folk items that attend it is born primarily of the reality that many early historians, scholars, and collectors whitewashed those traditions, pointing to American and European examples of sailing life and folklore traditions, often only mentioning other races and cultures that contributed to the landscape. Schreffler, in his critique of early chantey collections, shows of the collector W. B. Whall that "this implies [speaking of a rather caustic remark made by Whall in his collection] that, due to his low regard for them, Whall had left out (or failed to collect) most chanties that he thought were of Black origin."[78] He also notes that collector C. Fox Smith similarly made derogatory remarks concerning those collectors who included songs from the African American tradition; namely, she pointed her attack, including racialized language, at Frank Bullen.[79] It appears that some collectors actively attempted to whitewash representations of the genre, picking and choosing texts that perpetuated an idea of the tradition as being Anglo-Saxon, primarily of British and American origin.

There are many singing traditions that were and are attached to primarily Black singers that clearly influenced the chantey tradition. Roger D. Abrahams, in his research, demonstrates that "songs called shanties are found in association with coordinated work activities throughout anglophonic Afro-America from Trinidad and Tobago, Providencia and Belize to the mainland United States."[80] Black men, particularly from the Caribbean, have sung chanteys while they were at work fishing, moving houses called "shanties," or even rowing. In each of the examples of African American and Black work songs and collective singing, it is possible to see the earmarks of the chantey tradition as well as many other collective songs that have been discussed thus far. Schreffler points to the collections of Alan Lomax, who encountered men who sang chanteys while they fished with nets in Virginia. These "menhaden had a tradition that they also called 'chanteys.'"[81] Similarly, David S. Cecelski notes the use of songs like "Sally Brown" in rowing, observed by Moses Ashley Curtis in the 1830s.[82] Cecelski shares, "The version of 'Sally Brown' reminded me of other, more recent chanteys that I heard when I was a child: the raucous songs hoisted by black menhaden fishermen."[83] These later collections of chanteys, as employed in the Caribbean or even in North Carolina waterfronts, demonstrate not only the elasticity but also the longevity of the genre. It is possible to even extend the argument that the chantey grows, changes, and endures in places like the Caribbean because it is, in fact, where it originated.

Hugill points to the connection between what he calls West Indian singers and his own chantey repertoire, noting that he learned many of his own songs from fellow sailors who were from what was once understood as the Caribbean. Hugill also takes time to note that there is potentially a connection between African American work and slaving songs as they attach to chanteys. In a letter to Legman, Hugill indicates:

> I was shipmates with a Blackball sailor (of the 'Seventies) and later with Irishmen from the Colonies Trade (Australia and New Zealand emigrant sailing-ships). Also with a seaman who had been shanghaied on a whaler. From these men, mainly Liverpool and New York Irish I learnt my shanties, as well as from a coloured native of Barbadoes [sic], a wonderful shantyman who had served in Bluenose (Nova Scotia), Yankee and Limejuice (British) sailing vessels.[84]

Here, Hugill outlines a vast array of influences; most notable are those from the men of Barbados. In *Shanties from the Seven Seas*, Hugill indicates that chantey singers owe a great deal to their Black and African American comrades, noting a clear cross influence between sailors and Black workers who encountered each other in port towns.[85] He specifically cites Mobile Bay as being a primary place at which singing sailors mixed and traded with African American workers and slaves. R. W. Gordon, in "Folk Songs of America: A Hunt on Hidden Trails," underscores Hugill's claim when he shows that "with the sailor chanteys he did the same thing. The negro on the docks heard them sung by white sailors. He borrowed them with minor variations. Those he liked he rebuilt to suit better his own tasks, and later he invented new chanties on the old model."[86]

Each of these observations makes clear that the potential remains that Black singers influenced the repertoires of many sailors. Black men shipped before the mast just as much as Anglo-Saxon men, and the work of W. Jeffrey Bolster is especially key to understanding just how important the sailing world was for Black men. It was both a means of freedom and an exercise in a specific masculinity that was profoundly important to identity and personhood. Bolster's rich historical account indicates that ships were populated with "black men who often arrived in America not in chains, but as sailors or linguists on commercial ships."[87] According to Marcus Rediker, the nineteenth-century sailing ship was comprised of what he designates as "a motley crew," and in the case of Bermudian vessels, historian Michael J. Jarvis indicates that "Bermudian privateers were usually manned by mixed-race crews that blended free and enslaved labor and divided profits using the share system."[88] Clearly, history tells us that Black and Anglo-Saxon men worked together on sailing ships, often despite the lurking reality that Black men were still subordinated in those spaces, and many note that sailors not only borrowed from the singing traditions of Black men and women but also might have looked to Black men as ideal singers of chanteys, even potentially as the main chanteymen. Abrahams notes, "The shanty was taken up in the sea trades when sailors of every complexion became members of the crew of working ships, in all probability by the use of the West Indians as shantymen."[89] Abrahams, throughout his research, demonstrates that chanteying is still an integral part of work at sea and on shore for who he identifies as West Indian men and women. His *Deep the Water, Shallow the Shore* provides critical discussion concerning the unique place the chantey held, at least during his research in the 1970s, for men and women who worked the waters and shores of Nevis, Tobago, and St. Vincent.

An example of a chantey that might demonstrate cross influence between sailors and the African American tradition comes in "The Hog-Eye Man."⁹⁰ Legman shows in his notes on the song in his unpublished manuscript that "Hugill notes: 'This [the line "a bale down the hatch"] links this shanty with the white and coloured stevedore or hoosiers (cotton-stowers of Mobile and New Orleans), from whom many shanties stemmed.'" In Legman's annotation, it is clear that there is a cross influence between sailors and African Americans who worked in the cotton industry. It is not clear from the note, however, whether Legman or Hugill feels that one group influenced the other or created the chantey to begin with. One stanza of the song reads:

She was too late to hide her snatch,
An' the hog-eye [n----r] jammed a bale down the hatch.
He caught-her all aback, an' he caulked her little crack,
She wriggled like the divil [*sic*] but she couldn't shift her tack.

The "hog-eye" man is also described as having "a prick from here to Tennessee," thus locating the song in the American South.

Abrahams, in his work "Afro-American Worksongs on Land and Sea," provides several examples of songs that appear quite similar to at least two songs from Hugill's repertoire. In one example, from a corn-shucking event, Abrahams cites the observations of William Cullen Bryant as he listens to workers sing "Johnny Come Down de Hollow," which is incredibly similar to "Johnny, Come Down to Hilo," provided by Hugill.⁹¹ A further example, also from a corn-shucking event, is a song, "Oh, Jenny, Gone to New-Town," with the chorus "Oh, Jenny gone away!" which also bears a resemblance to Hugill's "Jinny jump away!" phrase in "Do Let Me 'Lone, Susan."⁹² The fact remains, however, that the chantey, regardless of who originally created the song, really belongs to all of them. On a sailing ship during the great age of sail, one would encounter a mixed crew in which British, American, Caribbean, African American, and African men were all singing the chanteys together as they pulled at the ropes with united strength.

Despite all the research demonstrating that chanteys were likely sung and influenced by Black traditions and even the reality that mixed-race crews have worked collectively on sailing ships, Hugill's songs and many others are often racist in both language and their representations of men and women who are Black, Indigenous, or people of color. Several of Hugill's songs are pointed in their racist ideologies and often violently target the bodies of racialized women. In songs like "Saltpetre Shanty," women from Chile are noted to be *putas*, the

Spanish term for "whores." Black men are referred to using the pejorative and deeply racist epithets "[n----r]" and "Negro." Exemplary of this type of terminology is the song "Sally Brown" and also "The Hog-Eye Man." Racialized figures are also cast as sometimes monstrous, violent, and untrustworthy and are othered to the point of complete subordination. In "Shenandoah," women are referred to as "little brown gals" and the "little black whore" in order to linguistically subordinate nonwhite female figures. Such a linguistic choice should immediately call to mind the process of othering that occurs within football chants and even rugby songs. The term *putas*, especially, was a part of belittling othered figures within football songs. In several of the songs from Hugill, the lyrics also cast nonwhite women as specifically carrying disease, which impacts our reading of those figures as being dangerous, disease-ridden villains.

One example that weds race and disease is from "Saltpetre Shanty," in which one line reads, "them barstards is poxin' us all o' the time." Other songs appear to draw on damaging cultural stereotypes of nonwhite figures; an example is in "The Hog-Eye Man," in which the song narrative focuses on an African American character who, as mentioned previously, has "a prick from here to Tennessee" and also violently invades the body of Jinny while her "fancyman" is at sea.[93] The song draws from a cultural depiction of Black men as having a dangerous sexuality that is especially targeted at white women. In each example, attention is drawn to the race of the characters, and the racial dimensions of these characters are often predicated on images of folks hailing from Black and Latinx cultures. The primary undercurrent to these depictions is that figures from these spaces are dangerous, hypersexual, disease ridden, and dishonest. They are figures to fear and revile and certainly those that the sailing characters should avoid despite their allure.

What is important about the dimensions of race within these songs is the reality that Hugill might have visited his own prejudice and bigotry onto the narratives that are contained in the manuscript. Despite the reality that he learned many of his songs from fellow sailors who were Black, many of these unexpurgated songs contain pointed violences against nonwhite bodies. The racialized narrative and language might be partially indicative of the period during which Hugill was singing these songs; however, it is a dimension that is worth noting. Schreffler appears to support a reading of Hugill as potentially harboring racist ideals in that "Hugill himself was evidently uncomfortable singing the more obviously culturally 'Black' songs."[94] Employing these racialized images and deploying language that is symbolically violent toward different races and cultures falls in line, however, with how other song traditions attempt to cast an us-versus-them comparison.

For my own part, I contend that chanteys, in all of their iterations, should be viewed as a cosmopolitan genre uniquely attached to the indeterminacy of the sea. The reality of the sailing world is that it is cosmopolitan in nature, and the waterways bring together a number of different men and women from all over the world. The sailing ship, specifically, is an ideal place to begin to understand the kaleidoscopic reality of the sailing world, where mixed-race crews, what Hugill called "checkerboard crews," have more often been the norm than an anomaly, and representing chanteys as a purely white tradition is inherently misrepresenting the reality of sailing life and the chanteys. In the summary notes for "Do Let Me 'Lone, Susan," Legman glosses that Hugill shared how "this shanty was very popular in the West Indian Traders, particularly aboard those with checkerboard crews—i-e-, one watch white, and one watch colored." I do heed Lau's warning, however, and venture that, in defining these songs as "cosmopolitan," I am centering the multicultural identity of these songs and their creators, highlighting the reality that this is, perhaps, a tradition that is more than any other representative of a collectivity of the fo'c'sle that stretches in time and place to different locales, cultures, and epochs. Dorothy Noyes writes, "We [researchers and folklore scholars] cannot leapfrog from the local into transcendent meaning," but I do argue that it is possible to engage the micro to the macro in some instances.[95] Where possible, I identify some of the informants and cultural notations regarding certain examples in the manuscript so as to ensure that informants and groups are fully recognized; however, I am challenging the reader to think about this genre and these examples from it as a uniquely diverse data set that sometimes defies time, space, and place and locates itself within the confines of a very specific group of diverse men.

Bawdy or Clean: Fixed Lyrics or Impromptu?

Cabin Boys, Milkmaids, and Rough Seas is particularly interested in analyzing the content of collected chantey texts. Just as there is disagreement concerning when, where, and who sung the chanteys, there is considerable disagreement concerning the content of collected versions of this genre. First, there is a distinction between fixed chantey lyrics, extant in collections, and the reality that songs were impromptu and informant specific. Chanteys are, by nature, almost living entities, growing and changing with the ship, the crew, the particular task, the particular chanteyman, or even the occurrences that befell the men on a particular voyage. The chantey collector and sailor Frank Thomas Bullen, in his collection of chanteys, supports the argument for the impromptu nature of texts and refused to print anything besides the opening lines of chanteys that he heard while he was at sea, contending that this representation of the genre is the only one that accurately depicts the chantey. He holds:

> The stubborn fact is that they [chanteys] had no set words beyond a starting verse or two and the fixed phrases of the chorus, which were very often not words at all. For all Chanties were impromptu as far as the words were concerned. Many a Chanteyman was prized in spite of his poor voice because of his improvisations. Poor doggerel they were mostly and often very lewd and filthy, but they gave the knowing and appreciative shipmates, who roared the refrain, much opportunity for laughter.[96]

There is much evidence to support Bullen's argument concerning the impromptu nature of chanteys as most collectors note the fixity of only the first few lines of song. The chanteyman was *prized* for, as he mentions, both his voice and his ability to extemporize lines. Such improvisation is traceable throughout other song traditions, in which men often alter and change songs so as to fit with a particular context. Chanteymen sung these impromptu songs across multiple oceans and within varying ships, spanning many periods in time and calling at diverse and multiple ports.

It is a genre that is diverse in the way that Frederick Pease Harlow identifies of "Blow the Man Down."[97] Though Bullen makes an important case to the contrary, many songs with set words made their way into the collections of numerous scholars and amateur collectors alike, not to mention there are many chantey "versions" that are found to be quite similar between informants. Likely, in considering Bullen's and others' claims, scholars interested in the chantey tradition should understand that collected examples of texts, like the Hugill songs, are evidence of one informant's repertoire of the genre and not necessarily evidence of narrative that was sung across multiple ships. The songs would likely ride with the sailor who conceived them on his separate voyages, but the songs belonged to no one sailing man and grew, changed, or were altered sometimes within the space of a single voyage and even by the same man. What I mean by the latter is that though one sailing man may have sung one version of a song at one time, he may alter or change lyrics as he sees fit during one voyage, in subsequent voyages, and even as he shared them with a collector. As James Madison Carpenter says of the genre, "It [the chantey] was the product of no one chanteyman, as resourceful as he might be. Rather it was a skein of many threads, a kaleidoscopic pattern to which numerous weavers of sailing songs contributed their art."[98] Though we must understand the genre as elastic—growing and changing and evolving not unlike other oral traditions—we do have at our disposal collected texts that are worth investigating for what they uncover about certain people, periods, and places.

Fixity of lyrics is only one facet of the dispute; there is also the reality that chanteys were alternately noted to be bawdy and relatively tame or clean. Throughout my early research, it became clear that many scholars and collectors noted a bawdy and salacious quality to chanteys, but they were not able to publish such examples because of strict censorship laws at the time of publication. The refrain of almost every published edition of chantey material was the lamentation that examples had to be wholly altered so as to pass the censors. Hugill often noted, in *Shanties from the Seven Seas*, that he was not able to print a version of a chantey in its full and original form in fear of the censors. It was Hugill's admission that content had been altered or changed that led me to search for unexpurgated examples and that forms the key argument for the importance of these texts for scholarly study. The songs that Hugill provided to Legman are those that would not have passed the censorship laws, and indeed, Hugill notes, in a letter to Legman, his own fear concerning the exchange of such content via the post system as well as the fear and even *reluctance* to share these texts more widely. He writes, "I, having been a shantyman myself and also, having learnt my shanties from old shellbacks, know many of the not-so-salubrious versions of the shanties as sung when the 'Old Man's' wife wasn't aboard, but, although many times I have declared that it is a pity the not-so-clean originals should die with the passing of the last shellback, I have unfortunately all the Englishman's usual reluctance in putting these versions to paper."[99] In this letter, Hugill demonstrates the tension inherent in the study of chanteys. There is the prevailing understanding of chanteys as containing bawdy and salacious lyrics, which would entertain the sailor in a similar fashion to other all-male singing traditions; however, there is also the reticence to circulate such songs outside of the confines of the sailing ship. Musicologist Harold Whates, in his "The Background of Sea Shanties," argues,

> No sailor would ever have dreamt of singing a shanty in his watch below. It cannot have been too easy to induce him to sing one properly when ashore, and I can imagine the difficulties of a collector, himself unacquainted with work aboard ship, in trying to gather material from shy and reluctant seafarers in a sailors' home or waterside tavern. A rope or capstan bar and hard work, either monotonous or immediately strenuous, were essential accompaniments to a shanty.[100]

Hugill sharing his songs with Legman helps, in part, to palliate the paucity of salacious chantey versions and succeeds in preserving such texts for later study. W. B. Whall, in his *Sea Songs and Shanties*, supports Hugill's note concerning bawdy chantey texts and argues, "Now seamen who spent their time in cargo-carrying sailing ships never heard a *decent* shanty; the words which sailor John put to them when unrestrained were the veriest filth." He goes on to say, "But another state of things obtained in passenger and troop ships; here sailor John was given to understand very forcibly that his words were to be decent, or that he was not to shanty at all."[101] According to collectors like Hugill and Whall, songs that were sung by the sailor at work were *vulgar* and *indecent*, even *filthy*, and were not meant for circulation in wider culture, especially in the presence of women. The primary interest of *Cabin Boys, Milkmaids, and Rough Seas* is to unpack what is communicated in chanteys as they were likely sung while the sailor was at work at sea, and if, as notable collectors lament, collections were changed and censored so as to remove the more salacious content, those songs do not represent the chantey genre as it was understood by the very men who employed them. Hugill's repertoire, then, is the closest to the original form of the chantey as it was sung among sailing men bent to their tasks on the ship as it is unexpurgated and reproduced as Hugill remembered them.

Connection to Work Songs and All-Male Singing Traditions

When working with chanteys, it is possible to draw connections to other, similar occupational songs that structure bodies and work. Most closely aligned with the chantey are logging songs and prison work songs in which music is aligned with the work being performed. Indeed, the music structures how the work functions. Ethan Blue notes that prison songs "set the timing and pace of agricultural prison labour and, importantly, allowed for a covert challenge to guards' authority."[102] In the latter, where prison songs generate space to critique or challenge those in authority, there are similar hidden transcripts to chanteys wherein the songs pull double duty. Of key interest here, though, is how the song functions as a structuring mechanism that connects the body, the breath, and voice to work. Similar to chanteys, the songs "would time their strokes [when chopping trees] so that no blade would fly out of control and maim another."[103] Songs are integral tools to ensure that the work is completed, but they are also a means to ensure safety, both in terms of one's individual body and the bodies of other workers involved. The timing of the song sets the tone for the work, structuring and coordinating movement so that multiple workers can function efficiently in sometimes dangerous and high-pressure situations.

Another form of song deployed to regulate bodies are the military cadences used for drills in military spaces. There is, arguably, a thread connecting prison songs, military cadences, and the work songs of African American slaves, and the latter appears to have influenced both genres. Schreffler, as mentioned, demonstrates that many chanteys are likely derived from African, African American, and Caribbean singers. Hugill himself notes the Caribbean origin of many songs in his repertoire. Military cadences, like the prison work songs mentioned as well as chanteys, work to regulate bodies as they are moving and are recited as call-and-response songs in much the same way that Blue recognizes.[104] Sailing work songs were call-and-response songs in their deployment, with the chanteyman singing out the first lines of song and sailing men falling in with their bodies and voices in answer. There are distinct connections, in fact, to African and African American work songs in regard to the call-and-response factor as well as the regulatory vein. David G. LoConto, Timothy W. Clark, and Patrice N. Ware argue, in an investigation connecting West African singing culture to the military jodies mentioned above, that songs are deployed by a prized singer and are "viewed as a measure for work performance. These songs were used throughout the workforce and were readily accepted by whites as a means to work faster and more efficiently."[105] LoConto, Clark, and Ware are specifically discussing the use of songs within the context of slavery here. Chanteys fit within this framework of work song or occupational song in that they are deployed within a specific space (the sailing ship), used as a tool in the execution of work (and are not sung outside of that context), and actively regulate the bodies of the men deploying them as the rhythm, time, and length of the tune directly applies to the action being performed. In this way, chanteys almost map onto the above-mentioned song types, even down to the lead singer and call-and-response form.

Occupational and work-song material is also specifically rooted in finite places. Though there are similarities across the different traditions (cadences are similar to chanteys are similar to logging songs), their use in specific places is an identifying factor worth driving home. In this way, occupational and work song becomes a part of an identifying marker for various working groups such that their songs attach specifically to them but also to the type of work they are performing. The lyrics, as will be discussed below, are key factors to this identification. In the finite places where work songs materialize, we might consider the groups who create those songs as "affinity groups," in which song functions as a means to solidify group identity. The songs are not only tools of work but also markers of a specific identity and even a celebration of that identity. That personhood is predicated on the dangerous, alienating, and sometimes "othered" status of the men and women who are a part of these different workplaces. If we consider where many of these songs bubble up—like prisons, sailing ships, and logging camps—we begin to note the relative insulation of these groups and even their outsider status. Kristen Bailey notes, in fact, that "loggers were often perceived as being outside of traditional American identity by virtue of the transience of their job and the fact that they traditionally worked in isolated circumstances away from the region's more permanent population."[106] Similarly, sailors are trapped on floating wooden vessels, which carry them far away from hearth and home. Collective song, which is tied specifically to a type of work one is performing, is a means to bond people together within an environment where they only have each other.

Songs might be viewed as akin to other ritualized practices that are used as a means to mark certain individuals as a part of the collective space. The crossing-the-line ceremony at sea specifically gestures at what I am suggesting in that it is a ritualized process that belongs to a specific group, accomplishes a specific rite of passage, and marks an individual as one who is wholly a part of something opposite to the world around him. When we think about occupational song, and work song more generally, we must consider the ways in which that object is intimately connected to the men and women who created it. There is cross influence among the different song types, to be sure, but an aspect of collective song that is often lost in conversation is the specificity of that cultural artifact to a group of people and its importance to that group as an object belonging solely to them as a structuring mechanism and an identity marker.

What differentiates occupational song and work song from other forms of folk song is the reality that these artifacts are a part of insulated spaces that are often uniquely tied to danger—both real and symbolic. Other forms of cultural ephemera, especially those created by men, demonstrate similar lyrical earmarks to items like chanteys; however, the key difference is their situatedness. A fraternity song, sung by young men within a college fraternity, demonstrates similar lyrical content, but the college campus does not carry with it some of the same occupational dangers that a vocation like logging or sailing does. In fact, this distinct difference between occupational work song and general bonding / songs of comradery helps to underscore why the miscategorization of something like a chantey does distinct damage to the perception of the song type.

Barre Toelken shows,

> [folksongs] tend to cluster around certain kinds of highly charged human values and activities. Some work songs (like chain-gang songs and some sea 'chanteys') are sung in such a way that a work leader can organize and pace the rhythm of the work being done, while expressing through the words a longing for folks at home, recollections of a lady friend, distaste for the work, hatred for the boss, or the anticipation of returning home.[107]

Added to this definition, of course, is the backdrop against which such songs are sung. On a sailing ship, life and death are predicated on an unpredictable sea. Legman notes this intimate connection among danger, chanteys, and obscenity in *The Horn Book*, in which he also notes, "Exposed to danger at all times by reason of their trade, the sailors sang songs that have always been notably obscene."[108] In Legman's critical perspective, bawdry specifically arises from those places where danger is an intimate aspect of daily life. In a logging camp, a slip of a saw or wrong move on a moving log means injury or death. What is underneath these songs, as they are reunited with their occupational space, is the distinct vulnerability that courts the singers who create the songs. They are, indeed, vulnerable to their environment, to the men in control and in positions of power, to the changing landscape of the economy and society, and even to each other. Stuart M. Frank notes of the chanteys "sung" in Herman Melville's novels that song "juxtaposes the 'cheerful' and 'cheering' atmosphere of chanteying against the gothic and fearsome image of pumping a leaky ship far out at sea."[109] Occupational songs do not only register real and present danger but also gesture at the symbolic dangers of changing tides of work. When we consider the backdrop of occupational song, both in terms of the workplace but also the culture, it is possible to reimbue the songs with what makes them so evocative and potent. Indeed, as is the case with something like Hugill's songs, the symbolic clashes between characters are no longer simply prostitutes and sailors engaging with each other. The songs might gesture at the sensation of a life in flux.

Functioning within a dangerous place requires that those toiling connect in some form or fashion. Occupational songs function to structure work, body, breath, and voice and, through that process, facilitate strong bonds among workers, sometimes across cultures. Susanna Trnka observes of military cadences, helping support the connection between cadences and their power to unite, "So 'potent' is its [the cadences'] power that it erases differences and barriers between soldiers, for it is precisely by learning these rhymes, and in turn the values they need to embody, that male recruits not only become soldiers but they all become 'men' again."[110] The same is ultimately true of chanteys, which unite men from varying places within the close confines of the sailing ship. Differently from some collective-song traditions, the uniting quality of chanteys is attached to the safety of the sailing men as well as the proper running of the ship. Archie Green captures it best when he argues that "the requisite bonds of stability and solidarity that operate at the campfire, molasses run, courthouse square, or fo'csle [sic] also operate in the hiring hall or labor temple."[111] In dangerous and demanding environments, song becomes a unique method to assuage feelings of vulnerability, but songs also serve as a means to foster lasting bonds that ensure a collectivity that affords a measure of trust and safety. LoConto, Clark, and Ware note of slaves' songs: "Music served a unifying function by demonstrating commonality amongst slaves. This unification was facilitated through the bondage of slavery and the daily grind of slave labor, especially that found in the fields and the songs that emanated from this context."[112] There is much cross influence among the different types of collective work song, and it is likely because each of the separate song types attaches to the specific realities of work where one's body is placed at the mercy of the job at hand. In terms of the lives of slaves, of course, this work was violently commanded, and autonomy was rent from them, rendering the backdrop of these songs far more charged than the chantey or the logging song; however, the suggestion made by LoConto, Clark, and Ware is applicable to other work songs used where bonding and comradery were paramount for survival.

William Main Doerflinger, in his *Songs of the Sailor and Lumberman*, makes the argument that the songs of the lumberman were influenced by the sailor's song and that sailors may have been, in turn, influenced by the songs of the lumberman. In a letter to Legman, Hugill claims that sailors influenced the songs of soldiers in the First World War and maintains that "then again it is possible that it [the song "Bosun's Wife"] went the way of much nautical stuff—slang, idioms and song—during the 1914–1918 War; the merchant seaman joined up as a 'Terrier' and gave a wealth of mich [sic] material to the Army, the latter, from recent Army Slang Dictionaries, apparently nowadays claiming it as its own. [sic] brain-child."[113] I am contending that the uniting factor among these different work or occupational groups, however, comes down to the embodied reality of their workspaces. In each, the person at work was at the mercy of powers beyond his control, and he was placed in a position where song becomes a potent means of collective bonding, potential safety, and certainly an opportunity for symbolic power and a degree of levity.

Collective song garners power through the particular lyrics deployed, and the lyrics of occupational song are at the heart of this inquiry. *What* the singers are articulating in their songs holds illustrative value in that they communicate a particular worldview formed within these finite affinity groups. Across different work-song traditions, especially those from all-male homosocial spaces, the lyrical content articulates a particular masculine identity that is predicated on the specific realities of working-class or even enslaved life. Regarding the latter, I am thinking about slaving songs, of course, but there are connections between the lives of slaves and working-class men. Indeed, the early modern sailor, as observed by Marcus Rediker in *The Slave Ship*, found an affinity with enslaved men and women and even fought alongside of them during abolition.[114] When it comes to the lyrics of occupational and work song, what consistently arises are symbolic images and language that function to combat feelings of longing, loneliness, and alienation as well as powerlessness, subordination, and frustration. Collective song employs language artfully so as to fight back against dangers encountered, whether actual or symbolic.

Chanteys are a part of the all-male singing tradition specifically for, during the great age of sail, ships were populated more significantly with men. Though some women did ship before the mast as passengers or under disguise, the vast majority of those engaged on the work of the ship and who deployed chanteys were men. Hugill's lyrics reflect what I see of the all-male singing tradition, in which sex and gender figure prominently. This is not to say that women did not sing collective songs in homosocial spaces.

Aligned to the material in Hugill's repertoire are the chants and calls that the Billingsgate fishwives engaged in while they were selling their wares. These calls and chants were notoriously filthy and Rabelaisian, fitting with the prevailing cultural sketch of the fishwife as a subversive figure. Part of the fishwife's transgression was that she utilized masculine language in her calls that created a reading of her figure as one that went against cultural ideals of gender presentation. Succinctly, the fishwife and her singing and chanting were both performed with facets of male identity that were unbecoming of a woman. Her singing and chanting, like the chanteys, were a part of her work and also her identity; the two were bound up together and functioned to demarcate her in public space.

Similar to the Billingsgate fishwife songs are the Scottish waulking songs that were an integral part of the process of milling cloth. Waulking and the songs that attended it were nearly identical to the chanteys in the sense that they were protected aspects of a specific work situation. The waulking songs in the Scottish Highlands were sung by women only while they worked in a women-only group, and the process of waulking was a full-day process that involved drinking, storytelling, and female comradery. The songs were a part of relieving boredom but also a part of a shared cultural tradition. The waulking songs were later taken up in Cape Breton as a part of milling ceremonies, which involved men. The work of Heather Sarsfield and Heather Sparling highlights the early and continued use of these waulking songs. Of note is that, in the protected space of women, the songs and stories often included narratives of sexual intrigue and engaged in some bawdy language not unlike what is observed in Hugill. A final example of the many female-singing traditions are the African American work/slaving songs discussed above.

Though there are a number of similarities between what has been observed in all-female singing spaces and all-male ones, there is a specific gendered vulnerability that I note in all-male singing that does not seem to be present in women's singing. The Scottish waulking songs and the Billingsgate fishwives' songs each appear to harness some of the masculine imagery observed in logging songs or chanteys; however, the difference lies in the backdrop or foundation of the singing. The particular vulnerabilities of male singers inject their song narrative with an interesting critical difference. For male singers in their workspaces, they are often navigating and are subsumed within a hierarchy that places one's male identity in a near constant state of risk, not unlike the working-class body as it is at the mercy of external forces. As Blue notes of prison songs, "Worksongs allowed for expressions of men's physical potency and these, it seems, were fulfilling for male prisoners in a situation that attempted to render them powerless, and thus feminized."[115] The lurking fear of being feminized, castrated, or otherwise subordinated is a sensation that imbues all-male singing with a significant difference and one that is palpable within a number of separate male song traditions. It becomes something of a connecting undercurrent wherein men use the lyrics of their songs in order to navigate and even combat sensations of powerlessness or potential feminization. That feminization occurs through overbearing bosses, the crippling drive to be the breadwinner, the powerlessness in the face of uncontrollable workplaces, and the breakdown of the body, among so many other points of vulnerability.

Peter F. Murphy's work touches on this alienation and fear specifically and supports how and why sexuality and work potentially are ultimately conflated. He writes, "Male heterosexuality conceived of as instrumental, as an encounter alienated from man's humanity, pervades the masculine experience, and labor as both alienated work and a highly disciplined regimen imbues masculinity with certain beliefs about what it means to be a man."[116] Work and sex become sites of alienation, fear, and discomfort as well as conduits for male identity and personhood. It makes sense that sex and identity would become integral parts of work-song traditions, in which men give vent to the parts of themselves that feel unstable and out of control. What is true across multiple examples of all-male occupational song is that virility and masculine power both become wish fulfillment and also rallying cries to combat these sensations of inadequacy and fear. They may not be able to control what happens to their bodies or identities, but they can control what occurs within the spaces of their cultural artifacts.

Songs across these different occupational traditions, especially collective songs within all-male homosocial traditions, are arguably connected through their use of hypermasculine language as well as hypersexual and hypermasculine narrative and imagery. It is possible, indeed, to trace a line between and among different all-male song types, whether occupational or a part of leisure activities, based on the similarities within the narratives and language used in the space of song. The similarities I am about to trace are part of the reason why so many song traditions have become intertwined to the point that it is difficult to differentiate a military cadence from a chantey from a schoolyard ditty. When I use terms like "hypersexual(ality)" or "hypermasculinity," I am thinking of what Elizabeth Freeman notes of the prefix "hyper-" as it is attached to inquiries using a queer lens. She contends, "I lean on the prefix 'hyper' meaning not only over, above, beyond, in excess, but also (in its more present-tense, truncated usage) a suggestion of excessive motion, as 'hyper' is slang for 'hyperactive.'"[117] Noting sailors and sailing men as hypermasculine or hypererotic suggests a movement or a state consistently in flux and never static. Such a perspective requires a reflexive approach to analysis, an ability to "shift tack," or move from one side to another quickly, as I discuss in chapter 3, which is unstable.

The lyrics of chanteys from Hugill's repertoire, like the songs from all-male environments like fraternities, freemason lodges, and even football (American and European), contain hypermasculine narratives, hypersexual and even erotically fixated narratives, and linguistic patterns that index a particular masculinity that is agentive, virile, and even violent. Folklorists Ronald L. Baker and Simon J. Bronner state that the song "Lady Lil" is repeated by "teenage boys and young men, and the performance settings are mostly all-male" and continue that those are "bars, pool halls, summer camps, military bases and ships, jails, bachelor parties and other 'stag' events, and fraternity and club houses," but of note is the connection between these all-male spaces and specific song content.[118] Throughout the different types of songs, images of women and sexuality as well as foul or coarse language all figure prominently and demonstrate that there is a particular way by which men (and sometimes women) express themselves in collective song. Folklorist Lisa Gilman writes, "The prevalence of these themes in oral tradition [like sexual relations or fear of disease] suggests the high degree of social anxiety that exists around gender relations and sexuality," and what is true across a broad range of song examples is the relationship between the chosen words and content of songs and the shared nature of those chosen narratives and terms.[119] Of chief import, of course, is what Gilman highlights in terms of the intersection of gender/sexuality and social anxiety/fear. These elements appear to align not only with Hugill's chanteys but also within the broader framework of collective song, especially among men.

The use of rough language in all-male singing accesses a particularly powerful and potent masculinity and is identifiable across song traditions, rendering this earmark of male homosocial singing a salient one. Mikhail Bakhtin, in *Rabelais and His World*, notes that "whenever men laugh and curse, particularly in a familiar environment, their speech is filled with bodily images. The body copulates, defecates, overeats, and men's speech is flooded with genitals, bellies, defecations, urine, disease, noses, mouths, and dismembered parts."[120] This same rough, hypermasculine, and erotic language is present in the Hugill songs, which specifically index a particular type of masculinity. Similar to research that has been conducted in contemporary rugby and football, in which collective singing and chanting is often deployed during and after games, songs are structured using rough language that privileges a strong and agentive masculinity, often at the price of other identity constructions that are cast as less than masculine—that is, as feminine or same-sex affiliated.

William Huddleston, in his discussion of Argentinian football chants, notes that collective chanting in the football arena is specifically structured so as to capture what is called *aguante*, or what "is tenacity, endurance and stamina, a moral and practical framework which demands total devotion to one's chosen club."[121] This *aguante* is often captured through both physical and symbolic violence perpetrated either by individuals against others or within the chants that are circulated during the game. These chants and demonstrations of *aguante* often lean on depictions of the other team as soft, womanly, same-sex affiliated; pointedly, the "other" is less than masculine. The chants often contain violent language that is "encoded with a paradigm of graphic sexual domination," in which tearing anuses or violent "fucking" are deployed as shows of strength.[122] Huddleston notes, "This discursive paradigm is profoundly violent, and places aggression and physical domination as a central tenet of male identity."[123]

Murphy, in his investigation of metaphors in male discourse, notes a particular connection between masculinity and war/sports. He contends, in fact, that war and sport are often conflated together, and the connections are palpable in language used.[124] The songs, regardless of the tradition, appear to be scapegoating and doing linguistic violence to an "other" in order to cast themselves, by proxy, as the more achieved male. In Hugill, it will be clear that the songs employ a similar scapegoating and aggressive language, sometimes doing violence to other characters in service of showing a masculine dominance; however, of interest is the fact that Hugill's songs will also admit moments of masculine failure and subordination, sometimes in the face of sexual exploit. Hugill's songs are rendered quite complicated in this light as they appear to grapple with both the expression of accepted masculine superiority and the tenuous nature of that construction.

It appears that male singers also attempt to displace any lurking fears of feminization or effeminacy through channeling those fears onto the erotically charged bodies of female or feminized characters. Along with the eroticizing of female characters, all-male songs appear to denigrate and linguistically do violence to gay characters or perceived queer individuals. In terms of erotic content, Trnka shows, of military cadences, that "prevailing themes in soldiers' songs and rhymes is sexuality," and these narratives are often quite graphic and sexually explicit, similar to that which is contained in Hugill's repertoire.[125] Trnka's observations of military cadence pairs with the erotic chanteys of Hugill, in which sex and eroticism are the main themes and women, especially nonwhite women, are often subordinated and objectified in service of connecting men to each other within a very specific all-male enclave.

Regarding homophobia within collective song, Eduardo Herrera quotes a number of songs that engage with language like "faggots" and "*putos*" to describe the other team.[126] What Huddleston and Herrera identify in Argentinian football chants is also recognized much earlier in British working-class songs, demonstrating a connection between male singing, violent sexual imagery, aggression, and the creation of bonds across time. Anna Clark argues, "During their single years, journeymen had celebrated their 'freedom' with ribald songs and crude rituals" and later highlights the reality that "it may also have been that their practice of singing misogynistic sexual songs and celebrating mistreatment of women helped them to form male bonds; present only symbolically, women's absence highlighted men's fragile masculinity."[127]

Violently consuming bodies, subordinating bodies, and using foul language and coarse imagery appear central to much collective singing, and I view this collective linguistic choice as a means to both privilege a perceived masculine voice and identity and to assuage a lurking fear of the frailty of male identity. The treatment of feminized figures in song is often violent to underscore both the differences between the singers and rivals and the incredible power and virility of the singers. Steven P. Schacht notes that male rugby players identify their own masculinity in both song and ritual through subordinating women and what are viewed as weaker or softer men. Indeed, Schacht views many traditions within rugby as "masculine rituals," in which, at each turn, players attempt to reinforce a particular type of masculinity that is predicated on an understanding of weaker and more passive individuals. When discussing injuries acquired during a rugby game, he notes, "For to admit one is hurt gives indications of being something that one is supposed to always guard against—being vulnerable, potentially weak, and feminine."[128] It is possible to take this observation and plant it alongside other all-male singing traditions in which using women and perceived weak male figures as scapegoats is a means by which to guard against those same accusations being thrust in one's own direction.

Collective songs, especially among men, appear to also leverage their singular masculine identity through specific comparisons that underscore an "us-versus-them" mentality. These comparisons are created, of course, through violent language and also through the gendered and sexualized scenarios discussed thus far; however, this specific identity-shaping mechanism is a distinct aspect of collective song that will come to bear on the understanding of Hugill's repertoire. The creation of an identity based on comparison to what one is not creates a dichotomy of power and lack regardless of the comparison under discussion. When it comes to the narratives of many collective-song traditions, the comparison often comes down to outsiders as they collide with the identities of the singers. In the all-male singing tradition, specifically, the comparison is often between the idealized masculine character and othered characters that fall into the categories of either women or failed male (who are arguably feminized). Such an us-versus-them comparison is identifiable in diverse spaces, like the chantey tradition but also trucking songs and football songs, whether American or European.

Though I will cover notions of what Eastman, Danaher, and Schrock identify as ways by which "masculine ideas are being reproduced," their theory of "*cultural masculinization of an occupation*" is salient through the ways in which they note how songs serve as mechanisms by which to circulate a particular cultural understanding of a vocation and identity.[129] They contend that song lyrics masculinize truckers, essentialize them, and also valorize them, and through circulating those narratives, both within trucking communities and the wider public, truckers succeed in cementing a particular ideal of this vocation that appears axiomatic—namely, that trucking is a masculine vocation alone. Eastman, Danaher, and Schrock note that some of this masculinization is achieved through lyrical comparisons between male and female truckers, in which women serve as gender deviants or sex objects and men are the true embodiment of the trucking vocation—in mind, body, spirit, and blood. Gendered space is created in song based on very complex boundary making that presents correct gender performance and assumed gender roles and positions, and these readings are then disseminated to fellow workers and also to the greater culture.

Trish Oberweis, Matthew Petrocelli, and Carly Hayden Foster note a similar reality in military cadences, in which songs like the jodies "differentiate that [the soldier] identity both from its opposite, or the 'non-soldier' identity, as well as from other similar but distinct identities, such as Air Force."[130] The similar uses of collective song demonstrate a connecting thread across song traditions, which suggests that the reading of Hugill's songs, in the chapters to come, might be reproducible in later investigations of other collective-song traditions. Because individuals come together to linguistically and symbolically combat perceived threats, alleviate boredom, and bond together within shared space, the world of collective song is drawing from something that feels almost aligned with the collective unconscious. The similar lyrics, uses, and applications of the different song types as well as the images that appear to draw from a communal well combine to generate a reading of collective song as connecting disparate people across time, space, place, and culture. What appears most distinct is that these songs seem to materialize specifically within places where men and women are participating in a shared identity, and their songs are ones meant to solidify those identity markers, celebrate them, and police the boundaries of those spaces—or, potentially, admit where they fall short.

Where language and metaphor are concerned, collective songs draw from a well of masculine discourse that is fixated on the elements of male identity that paradoxically confirm but might also deny male power. Cultural artifacts, like songs from all-male singing environments, provide a data set to consider the ways in which men grapple with what Murphy notes as a "discourse that reflects an objectification of self and sexuality, a phallocentric sexuality, a disembodied sexuality, and a great deal of ambivalence about sexuality."[131] Added to this, of course, is what I see lurking in the margins of these songs and all-male folklore traditions, which is nearly the opposite of these observations: a self-conscious presentation of sexuality and self, a fear of the failed phallus, a reembodied sexuality, and a deep-seated care and concern about sex and sexuality. The discourses of masculinity in their cultural artifacts are actually vulnerable admissions of what they wish to keep secret. The use of language that leverages Murphy's observation, and what is clear in collective song narratives, is actually an attempt to distance the singer or listener from what is perceived as feminized but what is deeply anxiety producing as it continues to haunt the periphery. Murphy goes on to say that "the discourse of male bonding is not only cultural but exists in direct relationship to the ways in which men think or reason about their sexuality, and these metaphors should not be seen as isolated examples of male oppression of women but as a part of a larger linguistic framework in which men conceptualize and describe their relationships with women and with other men."[132]

The point of demonstrating the position of Hugill's chanteys within the broader framework of occupational song and within all-male singing more generally is to underscore how this project serves as one data point in a much larger conversation. Though it might be argued that the similarities between these different song traditions is axiomatic and that what is observable in Hugill's repertoire has long been understood and even taken for granted (i.e., that there is foul language, sexuality, a particular masculine identity, etc.), it is this "taken for granted" that I seek to challenge. Underneath Murphy's observation is a charge to deeply interrogate cultural artifacts for what they might articulate about identity. Because we can trace a connection between and among so many different all-male and occupational singing traditions, what do these comparisons articulate about an imbedded masculine reality that is traceable across time, space, place, and culture?

Conclusion

Regardless of the tradition one is discussing, all are deployed within specific finite spaces that function to bond people together within a shared sense of identity and a shared space and experience, often using a shared language. The sailing ship is a close and confined space that is adrift for sometimes months or years at a time. The calls and collective chants of the sailor ensure that he is aligned with his sailing brethren to make the ship sail and also to alleviate tensions that might abound in a close space that collects men from varying and sometimes disparate places. The sailing ship requires collective work, men working literally together and in unison in order to move heavy ropes, capstans, and other sailing equipment to get the ship under weigh and sustain it across the length of the trip.

We have to understand the sailing ship in a similar way to songs like those from logging camps in Appalachia, as a "call to action," in which men are unified under and within sound, lyric, and occupational framework. There is a uniting factor in song that goes beyond simply uniting voices of those singing. The chantey's connection to other song traditions, like the trucking or even early modern freemason songs, is salient to an argument I am venturing concerning the connecting qualities of breath, body, and voice. Indeed, the collective nature of singing is such that its power reverberates across many separate song traditions, ultimately uniting to show how collective song and the lyrics that are a part of those traditions are meaningful not only to singular groups but also potentially across a broad range of genres. If we can think about lyrics of songs bonding men across the world engaged in the sometimes-dangerous spaces of long-haul trucking, it is possible to also consider the ways in which chantey lyrics might speak to an imbedded solidarity among men that the songs ultimately celebrate and also solidify. What I am contending is that the chantey functions in such a way that the sound of the voices together, the collective work of the sailing ship (all the same and together), as well as a particular thread of narrative sung throughout the chanteys themselves not only create a brotherhood but also solidify a group language and even a group identity through what is deployed within the framework of song.

In the chapters to come, I am viewing a continuity to masculine identity, a core set of values and ideals concerning the construction of masculinity; so, too, am I venturing the possibility that if we look into the songs that are often shared among men (and sometimes women), we will also see kernels of continuity and connection rather than difference. In looking at this set of songs from Hugill, I think it is possible to eventually compare his texts and my reading of them with other collected examples of collective song in a similar fashion. Though some scholars have done this work with some occupational work songs, no project to date has looked at a repertoire of songs like this in a manuscript format. One glaring reality of scholarship in work song is that few manuscripts and even articles seek to analyze the content that is expressed in collected versions of songs. Hugill's repertoire contains the same earmarks of these other song traditions, and though there are arguments to be made that what was collected by Legman from Hugill is one man's repertoire and potentially his own creative interpretation of the genre, there is enough within the songs that aligns with similar collective-song traditions that renders it valuable for study as well as comparison along a vast swath of song traditions. Hugill's songs, even if we were to say that they are the imaginings of only one chantey singer, reproduce the same type of language, imagery, and undercurrent of vulnerability that is identifiable among the corpus of collective song. If it is possible to trace a line of connection between and among these different collective song types, and it is, then what is presented in the body of *Cabin Boys, Milkmaids, and Rough Seas* opens the door for further plumbing of other song traditions for the complicated ways in which singers negotiate identity within the space of song.

CHAPTER 2

Hugill's Repertoire and Training an Interdisciplinary Lens on Expressions of Gender and Sexuality

Pointing to the idiosyncrasies of the chantey genre, noting the process of collection/collation, and defining the boundaries of the genre are all important facets of laying the groundwork for future academic inquiry. Scholars need to have that work in place so as to have materials available for study and processes through which to vet that source material and to recognize it within a framework of genre. Because the work of collecting and collating is now long complete, I want to investigate those sources for what they contain and what they might divulge. *Cabin Boys, Milkmaids, and Rough Seas* focuses attention on one repository of songs—arguably, one repertoire of songs—that comes from the combined efforts of erotic folklore scholar Gershon Legman (1917–1999) and chantey singer, sailor, collector, and self-proclaimed "last chanteyman" Stan Hugill (1906–1992). Of all the many erotic songs that might serve as a case study for deeper investigation, the songs collected by Legman from the Hugill repertoire are compelling for a number of distinct reasons, which each come together to generate a topic that forces scholars to think about what is internal and also external to song. I chose to focus on the unexpurgated Hugill chanteys because no one has as yet critically read these *particular* texts for what they say, mean, and do both historically and on their own terms, especially as it aligns with articulations of gender and sexuality. Hugill tells Legman that "here again, half-a-dozen of the songs I've given you, have never, even in camouflaged form, seen the light of print, so their music is only in my head!"[1] In focusing on Hugill's songs, specifically, I am both presenting content that has never been circulated to a wider audience, as the examples are still in archival form, and circulating them differently than scholars have to date.

Scholars such as Gerry Smyth and Kelby Rose attempt some level of analysis of collected chanteys, though they do not plumb the depths of particular repositories or repertoires. Rose contends that "the lyrical content of shanties, however, suggests an important secondary function," which is "stimulation, diversion and a chance for self-expression to the life of a sailor."[2] Rose investigates primarily published copies of chanteys in Hugill, Doerflinger, Colcord, Harlow, Richard Runciman Terry, A. L. Lloyd, Bullen, and Frank Shay, as well as several others, and ventures the argument that those collections of songs capture an air of nostalgia.[3] These investigations are of expurgated texts and therefore only provide partial analyses of the genre.

It is investigative work into unexpurgated and specifically erotic texts that needs to be broadened and deepened. Differently from Smyth and Rose, I perform close readings of specific chanteys in Hugill's repertoire to understand what is being said within the confines of the song especially as it is attached to questions of gender and sexuality. Indeed, this project answers the call that Legman ventured in 1962, which is that "the job of American folksong specialists, as in England and the rest of Europe long since, has now moved on to something more difficult: that the shotgun collecting phase [of folksong] has now to give way, and the indexing and actual study have got to begin."[4] In this way, the project palliates a seismic gap in chantey research that has been relatively neglected in scholarly conversation of this genre. The process of arguing between authentic and inauthentic versions or when songs where sung, how, why, where, and by whom have reached a point of impasse, and it is time to focus attention on what the examples we have *say* and what they *mean* as cultural objects. This chapter lays out the reasons behind focusing on this distinct repertoire and also the ways in which I bring a particular interdisciplinary lens to bear on the content.

There are other repositories in which bawdy and suggestive lyrics are extant outside of the Hugill manuscript, and it is worth taking the time to compare several examples from these spaces so as to underscore the reasoning behind the focus of this study. The R. W. Gordon Inferno Collection and the James Madison Carpenter Collection are two archival spaces where suggestive chanteys are located; however, none of the examples in these collections contain the level of bawdry and explicit sexuality that is a part of the Hugill repertoire. Like no other repertoire or collection, Hugill demonstrates the spirit of the genre roundly in terms of lyrical content. Ed Cray and Vance Randolph have published certain bawdy versions of chanteys that come closer to what has been outlined of chantey content in many collections (i.e., of an explicit nature)[5]; however, their publications fall in line with so many other publications dealing with chanteys that mix authentic chantey songs with other materials like sea songs and ballads.

The importance of Legman and Hugill's work is really twofold: they provide an opportunity to view chanteys in their original form, which is erotic, violent, humorous, and sometimes instructional; however, they also permit space for scholars to investigate the undulating qualities of identity that ebb and flow within the lines of song. These chantey examples provide concrete language through which to interrogate the long-held notions of sexuality and gender, especially at sea, through the particular type of narrative each song engenders. These narratives demonstrate a continuum of gender and sexuality that is powerful and even edifying for these texts contain curious idiosyncrasies that both help to support and work to trouble many narratives we have of identity formation. Sexuality and gender are only two potential identities of many on the high seas. It is possible to think about nationality, culture, race, and class, among so many other identity formations; however, gender and sexuality are the ones of chief import within the narratives from Hugill's repertoire as these are the topics that are most prominently displayed.

Why Study Hugill's Unexpurgated Texts and Not Others?

Hugill's repertoire is the obvious choice for a project investigating gender and sexuality. In no other repository are the chanteys as bawdy and salacious as they are in the Legman-Hugill manuscript. I am interested in investigating the dirtiest content possible, and Hugill's is, by far, the filthiest in the chantey tradition. In fact, the examples from this repertoire permit inquiries into the type of male discourse observed by Murphy, who notes that objects like dirty jokes "tend to focus on such male obsessions as physical endowment and sexual performance" and that their power is "reinforcing the role this kind of humor plays in fostering a shared set of values."[6] Though the songs to come are not "dirty jokes," they contain within them the same earmarks of male joking culture that Murphy, as well as Legman and others, note.

Hugill's songs provide finite space to interrogate the ways in which explicit sex functions within a specific repertoire, which is far different from other collections of chanteys or repertoires of chantey singers. Of course, there are other repositories of bawdy chanteys and even folksongs that are incredibly graphic in their depictions of erotic acts; however, as will be clear, these particular songs are the bawdiest of this genre (chanteys) and therefore both represent a more authentic reality of the songs (as evidenced by singers and collectors) and provide the opportunity to present such songs for the first time in scholarly publication. Hugill's chanteys offer a level of stark sexuality conducive to a deep reading of sexuality in song because there is no mistaking that there is sex involved.

Comparing archival and manuscript examples of "Blow the Man Down" from separate collections, like that of Gordon, Carpenter, and Hugill, underscores the differing treatments of gender and sexuality and supports the view that Hugill's manuscript is key to a project dealing with explicitly erotic content. In Gordon's Inferno Collection, he provides an example of the "false-parts-motif" version of "Blow the Man Down,"[7] which reads as:

> Oh blow the man down, bullies blow him away
> To my Way-Hay-ay Blow the man down
> Oh blow the man down bullies, blow him away
> Give me some time to blow the man down.
>
> As I was a walking down Paradise Street
> A pretty young damsel, I ha pened [sic] to meet.
>
> I said where are you going, my pretty maid
> I'm going a-milking, kind sir she said.
> Then I smiled at this damsel, so beautous [sic] to see
> And said—pretty maiden will you milk me.
>
> Oh no Sir she answered, oh no sir not I
> If I was to milk you I'd milk you too dry.
>
> I gave her 5 shillings, she took me in tow
> And away to her stateroom we quickly did go.
>
> As I stripped off my dunnage and jumped into bed
> This fair maid she scared me till I was nearly dead.
>
> Her catheads came off when she took off her dress
> Also with her bonnet came off her bright tress.
>
> Then she unscrewed her left leg—unhooked her right ear
> By that time believe me, I was feelin' dam [sic] queer.

When she spat out her teeth, and gouged out her right eye,
I grabbed up my dunnage, and left her to die.

Take warnin' my hearties, when you go ashore
Steer clear of false riggins & moor to a whore.[8]

The most suggestive lines in the song occur quite early and use metaphors of milkmaids and milking for erotic innuendo. The reader is entertained by the suggestion that the milkmaid will "milk" the interlocutor, though she teases that she might milk him "dry" or take all his semen.

I analyze the connection between and among milking, semen, and milkmaids extensively in my article "Engaging Imperfect Texts," which discusses, in part, the dating of chantey materials but also points to the ballad "A Merry New Dialogue" as the potential origin of the milkmaid versions of "Blow the Man Down."[9] Throughout, I discuss the attachment to milking and masturbatory or oral stimulation as it is produced in the image of the milkmaid and her milking tasks. Semen and sailors are also the express focus of "Semen, Seamen, and Virility," in which I trace the circulation among seamen, semen, and liquid, pointing to the crossing-the-line ceremony and its undercurrents of eroticism.[10]

Of course, these lines are interesting for how they align with early modern anxieties surrounding the loss of semen and the dangerous potential of "leaking" too much life force. The remaining parts of the narrative are focused on the frightful moment when the maid arrives at the bedroom, when she and the narrator are to erotically engage. She morphs from the beautiful maid to the monstrous other who is missing parts of her body: she is literally transformed into a frightful being.[11] Gordon's version of "Blow the Man Down," which includes the false-parts motif, is interestingly similar to a version of "Alouette" collected by Steven P. Schacht, which fragments a woman's body and also demoralizes her in front of the entire rugby team.[12] Gordon's version ends with the man urging others to "steer clear of false riggings & moor to a whore," suggesting that the entire song is meant to demonstrate the dangers of port and engagement with women. Gordon's version falls in line with many other "words-of-warning" songs, like those from Hugill that will be explored in chapter 3; however, what scholars are missing from Gordon are the unadulterated and concrete portrayals of sexuality that more poignantly tie eroticism with danger. Specifically, within Hugill's texts, there is a dynamic and complex dichotomization of space and interaction that colors the texts in ways that are missing from spaces like Gordon or Carpenter, to be discussed below. Hugill's words-of-warning songs concretely juxtapose the safety of the ship to the perils of land. The songs provide the suggested protection permitted of brotherly bonds as they collide against the trespasses of women and crimps. Sex and erotic scenarios not only are more vivid and tangible in Hugill but also accomplish more in their articulations.

In the James Madison Carpenter Collection, there are a number of versions of the same song. In fact, Carpenter presents several versions that fall in line with the suggested list of motifs that Hugill presents in *Shanties from the Seven Seas*: "The Flash Packet (from *Ratcliffe Highway*)" as version A, "The Sailing of the Blackballer," as version B, "The Flying Fish Sailor or Policeman Version," as version C, "The Fishes," as version D, "The Milkmaid," as version E, and "Bungyereye," as version F.[13] None of these versions, however, are as bawdy as the version provided by Hugill to Legman.

An illustrative example from Carpenter is a version provided by James Wright, and the inscription on the example reads that he "went to sea 1864—at sea 47 years." His version reads,

> I'll put on my boots and I'll blow the man down
> Way, hey, blow the man down
> I'll put on my—etc
> Gimmie [*sic*] some time to blow the man down.
>
> As I was a walking down fair London Street
> A charming young lady I chanced [*sic*] for to meet
>
> I hailed her in English and asked her the news
> This morning from Sally Port (in [Portsmouth?]) [handwritten under ~~Polly~~],
>   sir, bound for a curise [*sic*]
>
> Then I hove out my tow rope and took her in tow
> And away to the grogshop poor Jack he did go
>
> Then he wanted to board her without more delay
> Come along then, young man, if you're able said she
>
> Then she took me to a house of ill [handwritten] fame
> It was the sign of the ship in the water lane
>
> She had some whiskey and I had some rum
> She asked me if I would seee [*sic*] her home.

We went home together and to bed we did go
But what we did there I'm srue [*sic*] I don't know.

And in the morning when I awoke . . . .

[Note inserted under the lyrics:] Jimmie Wright, a packet [*sic*] rat, ten years between Glasgow and America, a tough crew—Liverpool the worst lot—(Harry Turner).[14]

The note, under the collected example, is included to demonstrate commentary concerning the often rough nature of sailing ships, which Charles Tyng notes in his own memoir of his time at sea, as well as to show shipboard tensions that might erupt between men.[15] In this version of the song, there are clear suggestions of sex and eroticism, but they are not blatant nor explicit. The narrator remarks that he "wanted to board her," using a nautical metaphor to communicate desire, and points to spaces such as "a house of ill fame," "her home," and the "bed." The singing narrator clearly admits, however, that he is unsure of what took place while in the woman's bed, and this is likely because of ingesting rum while at the tavern. Between Gordon and Carpenter, there are subtexts of eroticism that are clearly apparent, and the texts contained in these repositories are worth investigating further for not only how innuendo, metaphor, and suggestion are each deployed but also how narrative spaces are shaped and relayed. Additionally, songs like those from Gordon and Carpenter are worthwhile for other inquiries that might concern both the use of euphemism to mask bawdy language and the production of folksong content in the presence of collectors.

What examples like Gordon and Carpenter are missing is unambiguous and concrete eroticism that is often narratively tied to other important cultural perceptions and identities that arguably arrive in the Hugill repertoire. Hugill provided uncensored and fully unexpurgated versions to Legman. It will be clear that there is a degree of euphemism and nautical metaphor in his songs; however, rhetorical strategies, like euphemism and turn of phrase, are integrally and plainly linked to erotic realities that render such techniques almost fruitless or even potentially causes the content to become more provocative by the attachment to grandiose items like ship's jibbooms and bowsprits. Though Hugill's version of "Blow the Man Down" will be investigated at length in chapter 3, it is reproduced here in order to demonstrate the clear difference between it and the content contained in Gordon or the James Madison Carpenter Collection. The clearly bawdy and outright erotic nature of the material contained within the song is one of the primary reasons that the collection is ideal for a study of expressions of gender and sexuality in erotic chanteys; however, it is also important *how* such erotic situations are cast and *what* they often evoke or attach to.

>OH, where are ye goin' to, my pretty maid?
>>WAY-ay, BLOW the man down!
>
>Oh, I'm goin' a-milkin', kind sir, she said,
>>GIMME some time to BLOW the man down!
>
>Oh, have ye a sweetheart, my pretty maid?
>I'm lookin' for one, kind sir, she said.
>
>Then may I come with ye, my pretty maid?
>Well yes, since ye axed me, sir, she said.
>
>But I guess yer a bad un, kind sir, she said,
>Yer out for to fuck me, but don't wanter wed.
>
>Well, well, sez bold Jackshite, me thoughts ye have read,
>Let's look for a haystack, 'twill make a fine bed.
>
>Jack took her in tow, an' away they did go,
>The bull with a hard-on, the cow sayin' No!
>
>They came to a haystack, the maid she wuz shy,
>They backed an' they filled, Jack's jibboom stove high.
>
>The haystack capsizèd [sic], Jack's jibboom got bent,
>Straw hung from her arse-ole, her thing wuz all rent.
>
>So he left her a-sittin' with her bloomers all torn,
>He fucked her an' left her, that maid all forlorn.
>
>Now all ye young sailors that round the Horn sail,
>Don't take a young milkmaid away from her pail.
>
>Don't ye try an' fuck her a-top of a stack,
>Or ye might break yer jibboom, like did our poor Jack.

Look for a flash-packet what's got a nice bed,
Leave milkmaids to hayseeds, that's what poor Jack said.[16]

The milkmaid motif is still present in this version of "Blow the Man Down"; however, the erotic subtext that is suggested in Gordon and Carpenter is far more apparent in Hugill. Added, of course, are terms like "fuck," "arse-ole," and "hard-on" as well as clear descriptions of copulation, damage to the penis in the process of the haystack capsizing, and even some mention of female genitalia in "her thing wuz all rent." These added terms and narrative elements add layers to what can be interpreted in the text and solidify the critical importance of the Hugill songs. The addition of terms like "fuck" permits opportunities for linguistic analysis, while direct mention of intercourse opens conversations concerning hierarchy and sexual ordering—for instance, who is dominant and who is subordinate.[17] Colorful comparative metaphors, like the use of "bulls" and "cows," generate complex narrative action that requires multiple layers of interpretation, and such content is not extant in other spaces like the collections of Gordon or Carpenter. Hugill's work is raw, fleshier, and more nuanced, ultimately providing multilayered content that captures specifically erotic realities that are integral to understanding the ways in which sexuality may have functioned within some collected chantey texts.

This is not to say that content in Gordon and Carpenter is not important for scholarly conversation; it is only that the material contained in those repositories does not provide the starkly erotic material that is arguably a part of the chantey tradition, though removed because of censorship laws and informant reticence, as well as the main topic of inquiry in this study. If it is true what multiple collectors mention—that chanteys in their original form are so salacious that they might be "a penitentiary offense"—then these songs from Hugill are the only ones that meet that criterion. All other collected songs are either censored throughout or are only suggestive in their erotic nature. Published collections were censored in order to pass strict obscenity laws, and the publishers have admitted such. Archival collections are quaint in comparison to Hugill: both Gordon and Carpenter's collections are suggestive but not always outwardly obscene or aggressively sexual. When researching gender and sexuality, it makes a difference if one is looking at a text like "Blow the Man Down" as it is presented in Gordon or Carpenter or Hugill. In focusing on Hugill, I am privileging a *type* of sexual expression conducive to conversation surrounding all-male spaces that requires the fully exposed narratives of texts.

Perhaps the most important facet, then, of Hugill's songs is that he was able to provide Legman with examples that other informants were likely not able to provide to other collectors. Though they might have shared content that was close to the original version of song narratives, when providing content to researchers and collectors, singers who provided examples to Gordon and Carpenter likely self-censored content based on the audience they were addressing. Many scholars note that sailors have often been reticent to share their more salacious content with collectors as they did not feel that it would be appropriate to use base language in the presence of an academic. In the foreword to Richard Runciman Terry's *The Way of the Ship: Sailors, Shanties and Shantymen*, sailor Walter Runciman says, "In speech, the old-time 'shellback' was notoriously reticent—almost inarticulate; but in song he found self-expression, and all the romance and poetry of the sea are breathed into his shanties, where simply childlike sentimentality alternates with the Rabelaisian humour of the grown man."[18] Hugill was asked, in an interview for *Country Music World*, if chanteys had bawdy lyrics, and his response was emphatic: "'Yes, they did, but I won't repeat those, however much the folk fans ask.'"[19] It is clear, from this published comment, that Hugill's stance was one that he was unwilling to share such potentially salacious material with the general folk, the press, or others whom he deemed might be offended by such content.

In the same article, Hugill later shares an anecdote concerning Dutch shanties and how a Dutch man's clergyman son-in-law located the bawdy material and "was so shocked that he picked up the papers with a pair of tongs." It is altogether possible that so many of the collected materials we have at our disposal are those that were specifically and pointedly changed for the audience because the Rabelaisian material was deemed just as "defiled," as the article goes on to mention.[20] Folklorist Charles Joyner notes, "The response of the immediate audience may affect the performer in a number of specific ways, but the immediate context is less likely to *produce* performance than it is to *inhibit* or reshape performance—to cause a performer to bowdlerize or otherwise select from his folkloristic repertory."[21] What he identifies is that informants would, based on their perception of an audience, possibly choose different items to share in the repertoires or alter lyrics so as to conform to a particular understanding of the audience to which they are singing. What they would sing among friends and fellow comrades would be far different from what they would share with an outsider, viewed potentially as an interloper.

A similar reticence in informants is noted by Schacht when he investigates the folkways and rituals of male rugby players. He highlights how "they [the rugby players] did not, however, seem very open (they seemed almost secretive) about the informal activity that occurred during and after the matches," which he later demonstrates is often highly sexually charged and violently misogynistic.²² Schacht was arguably not able to see or participate in some of these events until he was viewed as part of the team. What is available in Hugill's repertoire is, essentially, an insider's view into the chantey. Because he likely viewed Legman as an audience open to the more salacious content (he was male, he was a scholar of specifically erotic folklore material, and he was just as antagonistic to the scholarly world), we have in Hugill's repertoire bawdier renditions than other informants might have shared with other collectors.

Hugill's repertoire not only is bawdy but also contains foul language, bold erotic descriptors, and the type of material that aligns with what has been observed in other working-class song traditions. To focus a project tasked with understanding gender and sexuality in chanteys, it is necessary that content is not only close to what was sung at sea but also captured using the type of language and rhetorical methods observed of other working-class folklore traditions. The expurgated versions of songs, whether they are admittedly expurgated or assumed expurgated (like in Gordon and Carpenter), do not provide the type of narrative material that is conducive to a close reading of texts from the all-male song tradition. They are missing a quintessential piece of content that is key to materials shared among men, whether it is a joke, a song, or a story. In no other place is the blunt admission and sketching of eroticism laid bare for analysis in the way that it is in Hugill. What we are not able to do with other content collected is unpack the ways in which sex and gender function in chanteys through a specific type of language and through similar frameworks that have been identified in other collective song. Susan G. Davis writes of Legman's particular interest in gender and sexuality when she observes that "the theme of a hidden history of gender organization and sexuality crops up often in Legman's later writings on folklore," and Legman sought the songs from Hugill's unexpurgated repertoire while he was engaged in one of his final projects, incomplete and clearly unpublished at the time of his death.²³

The fact that Legman was keenly interested in material that looked specifically at the construction of gender and sexuality supports the critical importance of Hugill's repertoire for a study such as the one attempted here and throughout. Legman obviously sought the work of Hugill for what he had to contribute to the study of erotic folklore and folksong. Indeed, he outlined as much in a letter to Hugill, in which he expressed:

> First, let me say how deeply—how really profoundly grateful I am to you for allowing me access to these truly remarkable texts. I have been under the impression for years (since 1940), and this has been increased by things said to me by famous folklore collectors, that "the sea shanties are all lost, insofar

as they were obscene, because no published collection ever included them." I see now that these laments were premature and erroneous, and that a whole slew, or raft, or sheaf of the most fascinating have not only been preserved—by you—but in full and annotated versions, for the greater part, and not in the usual pathetic fragments and misremembered lines.[24]

What is at stake, then, is understanding gender and sexuality through the language and metaphor that was arguably a part of this tradition but was erased from the record because of early modern obscenity laws. To date, scholars have only had the assumption of bawdy chanteys with access to song examples that do not come close to what collectors suggest. In Hugill, scholars have the bawdy texts themselves, and they are such that they align both with what is said about them and what is comparatively similar in other all-male traditions.

It should be noted that Hugill's repertoire is not infallible, however. The manuscript compiled by Legman and Hugill is clearly an outlier to some degree as the bawdiness and salaciousness of the lyrics render it far different from other repositories of chantey material. Hugill admits, in a letter to Legman, "I have gone 'nearer the bone' than any previous collector," meaning that, in his expurgated text *Shanties from the Seven Seas*, he was able to publish material that was much closer to the original rendering of chantey versions.[25] Hugill further explains later in the letter that "nearer the bone" regards the relative bawdiness of a chantey example. The unfortunate reality that comes with that admission is that either Hugill took liberties to fashion songs that were bawdier than many encountered at sea or his collection is the last remnant of the more salacious songs sung that died with the men who used them and enjoyed them during the great age of sail. It is impossible to know for sure.

A long-time friend of Stan Hugill, Tom Brown, in an email communication with me, underscored some anecdotal arguments from other scholars that Hugill invented lines of his songs so as to appease his audience. Brown detailed:

> For what it's worth, my own opinion is that Stan was a highly charismatic character. I think the folk revival forced him into a certain mould because of its expectation—he was not the only source singer to whom this happened. He undoubtedly was a rogue, loved a good yarn, and 'made things up'—as did all the source singers who actually sang shanties for work (as opposed to stage performers) so for me that is not a criticism.[26]

From this description, it is clear that Hugill had a penchant for creating lyrics and entertaining people with his personality and wit. Deeper than this, though, is the potential that Hugill created some of the content in his repertoire in order to satisfy a particular view of the genre that he felt was in line with the tradition. What I mean by this is that he recreated lines and lyrics based on his singular view of what the genre "should be" and not what it potentially was in practice. It is worth noting that historian Joanne Begiato comments, concerning men in the nineteenth century, that "old men's bodies were precarious" and therefore open to circumspection and pity.[27] Hugill reproduced many of his songs after he had (mostly) retired from the sailing world and sung them well into his old age. It is possible to speculate that he visited into his songs a hypermasculinity and a virile masculine ideal that masked his own anxieties around aging and decaying. Perhaps the songs, then, might only be Hugill's vulnerability as he faced a decline in his person, but to have so many other working-class song traditions that evidence such vulnerabilities and hypermasculinities supports an overarching reading of Hugill's repertoire as coming close to the chantey singing tradition as it was likely sung. Like Pauline Greenhill, I recognize that, "like any other collection of songs, they clearly reflect the collector's aesthetic."[28] There are competing arguments concerning the nature of chanteys, and without other examples of the genre that are closely related to what we see from Hugill, it is possible to open this manuscript to questions of validity.

Regardless of how the content from Hugill might be situated (authentic, imagined, or a mixture of both), the examples from this manuscript do afford a way to read all-male singing traditions differently through training a lens of gender and sexuality on one particular repertoire of song. In contrast to other repositories, the Hugill manuscript represents the source of one chantey singer's repertoire as it was collected by one singular collector, which allows for less complicated processes of authentication and the opportunity to trace connections between it and other song traditions akin to it.

Similar to the work Legman produces in *Rationale of the Dirty Joke*, this book focuses attention onto a group of material and parses out the connections between narrative content and the specific world in which it was generated. He writes, regarding investigating erotic and bawdy jokes, that "what is meant is that these stories [jokes and narratives within them] and individuals do personify what the tellers and singers well know to be real but inexplicable peculiarities of human behavior, which they are attempting somehow to fit into a rational view of the world, whether as horror or as humor."[29] By focusing on one particular repository and repertoire, I am taking the opportunity to deeply plumb and also think connectively through this one dataset about how men fashion a sense of the erotic and gendered world around them. If we can take a cue from Legman and consider something like joking culture as articulating a particular worldview or conception of self and the surrounding world, it is possible to also interrogate one repertoire in order to consider the singular perspective, as well as to think through its attachment to perspectives that function outside of it. I am detailing how this particular swath of song provides insights into what is already known and understood about sexuality but from the perspective of a particular group of songs and from a particular subset of men that has not, as yet, been investigated thoroughly. In pursuing this work, I am generating further analytical examples that create conversations between certain content and theoretical frameworks that we have at our disposal. The reality that this is a singular singer's repertoire is important enough to scholarly study as it provides a finite representation on one informant's view and knowledge of texts; however, Legman's tie to specifically erotic folklore and folksong collection is of particular note.

The first area of interest in these songs from Hugill is their tie to a particular form of masculinity. It has been established that all-male singing, joking, and storytelling traditions contain misogyny, sexuality, foul language, and other markers of hypermasculinity that fit with social renderings of male identity. Many interpretations of other all-male ephemera confirm the reality that cultural objects from these traditions contain narratives that support a particular ideal of masculinity. Foremost, in presenting the songs from Hugill and in interpreting their content, it is possible to confirm some of these same narrative elements that have been observed in other spaces. What is of primary import, then, is supporting a reading of all-male cultural objects that transcends time, space, and place. What the lumberjack sang at work or the narratives that carpenters share together might, through shared masculine elements, be connected to spaces like the Hugill chanteys. Succinctly, the songs potentially demonstrate an ideal masculinity that is transcendent and enduring, and we can begin that conversation through looking at one specific repertoire—stable or not.

The work of Begiato helps to support the reality that, especially for sailing men during the period 1760–1900, a particular masculine expectation was so imbedded in cultural reality that it surrounded men, women, and children. In *Manliness in Britain*, Begiato shows that images of hypermasculine men, like sailors and soldiers, were a part of children's toys, housewares, and art. She contends, "The objects [like art and toys] could evoke feelings associated with an idealized manliness and, thus, were not just storehouses of meaning, they acted upon those who encountered them, shaping notions of gender and self."[30] We have to understand that Hugill's songs, and others like them, were born within spaces where these exact notions of masculinity were drawn. The struggle to live up to those ideals—the ones ultimately shaped and circulated culturally—would have been and likely still is incredibly constraining and anxiety provoking. Begiato and others note that sailors in particular became not only a source of national pride but also a symbol of the nation more roundly. Living up to such a cultural expectation would breed concerns and frustrations in a man about whether he was able to measure up to such expectations. As for the bawdy nature of this set of texts, they arguably provide "more honesty and nobility—and immeasurably more life—in even the worst bawdy songs than [what is found] in the ephemeral slubberdegullion of so-called popular songs."[31] In portraying masculinity and the delicate negotiation of gendered performance and sexual experience, they gesture at a continuum of identity that arises across a vast number of cultural ephemera from all-male spaces.

The second, and perhaps more important, area of interest in these songs from Hugill concerns what is at stake in the particular reading that I am venturing: a recognition of both these foundational representations of masculinity and also a deeper reading of those narrative spaces that reveals something far more nuanced and potentially vulnerable. Reading these songs only for what they recycle about enduring masculine narratives is too much of a surface-level approach, and I argue that a more penetrative reading (pun intended) reveals a recognition of both social expectations of masculinity and the more vulnerable reality of performing those identities. Begiato demonstrates that, particularly in the nineteenth century, there was an "inherent paradox of masculine identity," in which excesses of vice and desire were viewed as "masculine failures" but that "many manly behaviors were also those which, in a managed form, were central to the performance of masculinity."[32] Hugill's songs were likely sung at the very moments during which these paradoxes were most prevalent and vacillating among cultural expectation, inborn desire, and the meeting of the myriad demands placed on the man, his body, and his position in the world, which were likely deeply alienating and frustrating.

I am, then, positioning these narratives as complex and creative objects that grapple with deeply emotional and sometimes philosophical issues at the base of human existence. It places at the center a recognition of the artful conjuring of interiorities, sometimes covered by metaphor and even distracting narrative, which sketch chantey singers and their close comrades as engaged in a delicate analysis of their own experience of the world that contradicts social perceptions of those same men. As David A. McDonald identifies of song and dance in Palestinian culture, "songs served to inscribe culturally appropriate practices, beliefs and values iconic of the way men ought to behave and interact with one another" and such songs are "citational" to "an engendered archetype."[33] Sailors are cast, both in popular culture and history, as being rough, uneducated, crass, and even potentially violent. In these songs, we are able to see both the cultural rendering of the sailor—almost like the sailor playing a sailor—and a deeper gesturing at the realities of playing that part.

Hugill's songs are clearly ideal for ongoing conversations in the field of erotic folklore and folksong. Gershon Legman focused the bulk of his own work, outside of this unexpurgated unpublished manuscript, on collecting and commenting on erotic folklore, folksong, and cultural ephemera. Indeed, *Rationale of the Dirty Joke* and *The Horn Book* are each painstaking collections and commentary on erotic ephemera, which, at times, include analysis of collected examples. *Rationale of the Dirty Joke* gathers together a vast number of limericks, jokes, and obscene barbs, and Legman notes, in the introduction, that the process of locating these materials for publication was onerous, citing the rarity of printed obscene ephemera.[34] *The Horn Book* also contains a lengthy passage on bawdy folksong and laments the enduring frustrations of working with erotic folklore and folksong and especially notes the paucity of bawdy chantey examples. He cites Hugill's work specifically, but his lamentations concerning expurgation and general reticence of publishers to circulate collected erotica nearly echo what I have pointed to thus far.[35] *Cabin Boys, Milkmaids, and Rough Seas* is the first to investigate erotic chanteys for what they might, similarly or differently, articulate to what has been observed in other oral-tradition culture. Legman pointedly takes aim at academics in his *Horn Book*, in which he states, "It may be shortly said that the entire history of folksong publication in the English language is one of falsification and expurgation for the last two hundred years, and that it has invariably disguised forgeries and dishonesties behind mealy-mouthed prefatory brags of sexual purity."[36] Throughout the chapter "The Bawdy Song in Fact and Print," Legman meticulously catalogs all of the available collections of bawdry and that which was bawdy and expurgated and scathingly indicts collectors, editors, and scholars for willfully decrying, ignoring, and even outright sullying the texts that he (rightly) views as inherently folkloristic. This project rectifies, in fact, what Legman views as one of the issues inherent in folklore research, which is that treatment of this type of folksong—song that is "uncontaminated by vulgar gentility"—has often been to ignore it, relegate it, expurgate it, or pass it over for other forms of folksong and folklore deemed somehow "more appropriate" or more salubrious.[37] Legman's indictment, in *The Horn Book*, of what has been done to erotic folklore is worth reading on its own.

A final motivating factor for focusing on the project between Legman and Hugill is that these songs are representative of the work of two men who have entertained something of a complicated relationship with the scholarly world. Just as the chantey tradition has yet to be explored deeply from an analytical perspective, so too has the work of these two men lacked adequate focus and attention, save that in the work of Gibb Schreffler and Susan G. Davis. Indeed, I am leveraging my own position as a scholar to bring more focus and attention to a text created through a collaboration between two men who have often encountered suspicion and even antagonism from the academy. These collectors and their work are primed for recognition in the chantey singing and folksong tradition and, outside Davis's biography of Legman, this project is the first to engage with content from Legman and Hugill in a more robust scholarly fashion. Legman and Hugill's work have each, at varying times, been brought under scrutiny in the academy. Their methods, backgrounds, and relationship to scholarship have each come to bear on the treatment of the content they collected, shared, and produced. Sarah Lash summarizes the voices of scholars who have interrogated Legman and his work, citing that many scholars' distaste for or criticism of Legman's work rests on issues with both Legman the man and Legman the researcher: his distinct distaste for the academic community, outright antagonism toward the academy, his own eccentricity, the reality that he was self-taught, his almost complete lack of organizational structure (which is arguably similar to the process of Hugill), and, finally, his apparent refusal to distance himself from the material he discusses. Lash shows that "Legman's approach, though unquestionably erudite, did not assume the scholarly veil of objectivity."[38] She contends, however, that "Legman's approach is perhaps not foreign to us now as it was in his time, and we have a great deal still to learn from his work"—a suggestion that I am supporting in the publication of this critical work.[39]

For a project that focuses on gender and sexuality in erotic songs, anecdotal comments about Legman's preference for heterosexuality and bias toward homosexuality are inherently interesting and add additional layers to the investigations within this project. Martha Cornog and Timothy Perper argue: "Unlike modern right-wing critics of Kinsey, Legman was a radical with a radical agenda to elevate heterosexual love over the violence he saw coming from male-male bonding. No matter how his dislike for homosexuality reads today, it echoes a period of world-wide horror."[40] His personal beliefs on same-sex relationships or sexual encounters do not seem, however, to have clouded his ability to collect folklore materials that describe, suggest, or deal with same-sex sexual encounters. What I suggest is that many of the songs from Hugill's repertoire contain same-sex erotics and even some queer subtexts, which render the material collected and collated by Legman from Hugill all the more intriguing for those who study sexuality in folklore. Succinctly, knowing Legman's reticence to engage with same-sex erotic texts and even his dislike of same-sex eroticism colliding with queer readings of collected texts in his manuscript implies either a willful dismissal of those queer subtexts on the part of Legman or a level of veiled curiosity.

As for Hugill, similar arguments have been made concerning his approach to collection and publication. As outlined, Schreffler is, perhaps, the only scholar who has taken the time to critique modern collections of chanteys, and he argues:

> Hugill aimed to be as inclusive as possible. Any song that he heard which might have been sung "as a chanty" (a dubious criterion, implying that a song becomes a chanty if someone sings it during work on a sailing vessel) was included. In reading his text, one has no idea which of the items were known by more or less every chantyman (say, 40–50 out of the total 400+ items in the book?) and which were one-offs and provincial songs that are really outliers.[41]

Similar to Legman, Hugill is cast as an uncritical, uncareful collector who lacks the skills or pedigree to offer examples that are trustworthy or authentic. Hugill leaned on his background as a sailor and his self-proclaimed status as the last chanteyman in order to prove his merit and the trustworthy nature of his sources. In some circles, Hugill is hailed as the "god" of chantey singing, and the examples of his repertoire, located in Legman's manuscript, are oft cited as the holy grail of chantey texts. Like Legman, Hugill is also cast as something of a character, described as a larger-than-life personage who became more interesting and even potentially provocative as his life progressed.

In a review of *Shanties from the Seven Seas*, Robert Lloyd Webb describes him as follows:

> With his hair pulled back in a queue, tattoos on both the inside and outside of his forearms, a goatee, a striped shirt, worn jeans and an earring, he was the picture of the Cape Horner we all envisioned in our mind's eye. Yet he was also a scholar, linguist, historian, educator, artist and raconteur. If education is 25

percent preparation and 75 percent theatre, as one wag claimed, he was every bit of both, only better prepared.[42]

In Webb's description of Hugill, it is clear that the sailor turned chantey collector might be considered almost an actor, playing the part of the salty, weatherworn sailor; however, Hugill clearly had much to contribute in terms of publishing material that, without his decision, would not be available to scholars today. Indeed, within the description, it is possible to see a similar tension that is inherent in the work of Legman. Though Hugill appears to be playing the part of the sailor, he is also cast as someone who acquired the many skills expected of an erudite scholar over his many years of work. Chris Roche, a long-time friend and correspondent with Hugill (as well as a chantey singer himself), admits in his obituary for Hugill, "His own standards were high and yet he was a man of immense ego, an ego that seemed to grow as he got older. Yet, he was a fount of so much knowledge."[43] There is a paradox inherent in both collectors that potentially serves as the crux of the scholarly issues with them. Hugill and Legman were resistant to the methods and required degrees that grant support for scholarly work, yet they dedicated their entire lives to deeply studying their content and worked tirelessly to produce and circulate material despite circumspect reception.

Underneath the critiques of both Legman and Hugill is a degree of scholarly presumption that because the men were not formally trained in collection, collation, and dissemination of folklore and folksong, they are not entities to be trusted in the academy.[44] Stuart M. Frank shows that Hugill "was educated briefly at the Church School, which he never much liked, and went to sea in 1921 at the tender age of 14, serving first in steam and later in a square rig."[45] Similarly, Cornog and Perper demonstrate that "Legman was self-taught, describing the New York Public Library as his university. He absorbed his intellectual grounding from psychoanalysis seen through a strong sense of sexual and social idealism."[46] Essentially, critiques are right to take aim at the level of education of both men and view their published and unpublished materials with a degree of circumspection, but I will posit that we need to be more inclusive in our view of content collected and created by those outside of the academy.

Scholar Charles L. Briggs offers the following approach to folklore work, which I believe is at the heart of the choice to focus on the work cultivated by these two men: "I suggest an alternative approach that fosters innovation by collaborating on theoretical issues with nonacademics who reflect deeply on the poetics and politics in vernacular culture—people scholars used to call 'the folk.'"[47] Though Briggs is discussing the need for a different theoretical approach to content—and one that privileges informant's own interpretations of texts—I see it as useful here, too, in considering the work of Legman and Hugill. This project seeks, in part, to demonstrate the erudite processes of these two men and also leverage this idea of engaging in conversations with texts that were produced or collected by "the folk," or nonacademics. The reality is, though, that both men worked dogmatically to collect and publish content that was meaningful to the landscape of folklore/folksong generally and chanteys specifically. Cornog and Perper show that "professor of American culture Bruce Jackson observed [that] 'Legman is the person, more than any other, who made research into erotic folklore and erotic verbal behavior academically respectable' and who made accessible to other scholars material that scholarly journals had long been afraid to publish."[48] For Hugill's part, Roche argues, "Had he in later years not written five books to his credit, then the folk music world would not have had these shanties to sing and cherish."[49] Roche is referencing Hugill's publications *Shanties from the Seven Seas*, *Sailortown*, and *The Bosun's Locker: Collected Articles 1962–1973*, as well as two other publications of chantey texts.

The songs from Hugill's repertoire are reproduced and analyzed here so as to bring them into scholarly conversation and treat them as cultural objects worthy of analysis and study. Researchers might choose to focus on the content collected by Carpenter or Gordon, who were both formally trained and even used some of their content to satisfy doctoral requirements. The reality is, though, that such a focus would continue to devalue the work of Legman and Hugill, who arguably might have secured better content because both men were not a part of the scholarly world. Robert Young Walser, an expert on the James Madison Carpenter Collection, mentions, "It is my hunch that working with a folklorist was a foreign experience for old sailors and that they were possibly hesitant to include off-color material in the presence of a well-educated stranger."[50] In many respects, Legman and Hugill were far closer to their content based on their connection to the working-class world and sometimes antagonistic relationship with the privileged realm of academia. Hugill captures the importance of their collaboration best when he outlines, in a letter to Legman, dated July 25, 1956, that "apart from joking, it is quite true that 2 copies in existence of each tune would help folksong posterity—particularly as one never knows what lies ahead in these quick-moving times!"[51] Hugill appeared to register that the material he and Legman exchanged, as a part of a voluminous epistolary relationship, was an important part of folklore history and would be lost had they not decided to embark on the collaboration together.

Training the Lens on Gender and Sexuality: Theoretical Framework

This project is predicated on the stance Pauline Greenhill takes in "Neither a Man nor a Maid," in which she exclaims: "My queer reading, particularly, is 'perverse' (Zimmerman 1993) in that it deliberately and willfully goes against the grain of conventional interpretations, which have assumed heterosexuality. I will also argue that scholars' heterosexist readings amount to silencing, ignoring, and suppressing the songs' multiple implications."[52] *Cabin Boys, Milkmaids, and Rough Seas* is chiefly focused on going to the texts first and making connections and associations with cultural images that arise from those texts. In that way, it is an exercise almost firmly grounded in new criticism, where the texts speak for themselves, and I am drawing on materials to bring those images into focus; however, the specificity of some materials in terms of time period and place helps to drive home a reading of these chanteys as representing the true cosmopolitan and timeless nature of the songs.

Close reading of materials like chanteys is supported by folklorist Robert McCarl when he argues that "the vehicle through which all this [verbal arts and workplace culture] takes place is *metaphor* and by starting with this aspect of occupational folklife, we can begin to develop the basis for a more systematic approach to the verbal arts in work culture."[53] Arguably, in considering the chantey as a workplace "verbal art," I am contending that a close reading of the metaphors involved in these texts provides insight into some of the inner workings of identity and life for the working-class sailor and even the working-class man. By placing metaphor at the center of the conversation, by performing a close reading of those texts produced by a particular man or men, we have the opportunity to potentially meet with this culture through their own language and cultural products. McCarl demonstrates, through a close look at firehouse culture, the ways in which metaphor is utilized not only in "linking two previously unconnected ideas" but also in shaping the landscapes and the identities of the men who are engaging with those metaphors.[54] I see enduring qualities to the songs that have specific times but are also timeless: they are evolving, growing, and changing but also sometimes static. I must admit that such a direction will prove frustrating to historians; however, this project seeks to do something innovative with a reading of finite texts. It asks the question as to whether or not we might free ourselves from specificity and see, instead, what might arise from the act of reading the texts as texts that evoke and provoke different and sometimes overlapping readings.

In drawing on queer theory and queer frameworks, "queer" here and throughout should be understood as a term that destabilizes category. Queer, in the contemporary world, has been aligned with identity more concretely; however, my use of the term is as a lens to interrupt categorical thinking. Theorist Sara Ahmed argues that "we need to complicate the relation between the lines that divide space.... After all, direction only makes sense as a relationship between body and space," and this project is one meant to complicate the fixed and the finite.[55] Ahmed's view helps to texture moments in song that appear out of line, or queer, and scenarios in songs rise as examples of "queer orientations," or "those that don't line up, which by seeing the world 'slantwise' allow other objects to come into view."[56] Queer and homoerotic narratives are readily apparent in other collected examples of folklore ephemera, suggesting both a curiosity about the confines of gender/sexuality and also the need for further investigation to uncover potential motivations for such repetition.[57] Hugill's songs provide entry into queering the working-class song tradition and are primed for an inquiry using queer theory, among other theories, as they are complex and multilayered in their narratives. Simply analyzing the heteronormative main framework of the songs would reproduce readings of these songs in line with what Greenhill pushes back against. Such readings do not penetrate deeply enough; they lean on heterosexist viewpoints and neglect the opportunity to see heteronormative narrative differently—*queerly*.

It is worth highlighting that when I am speaking about "masculinity" and "queer" theory, I recognize the tension inherent in the application of queer theory to masculinity and that when I use "masculinity" as a term, I am referring to an identity practice and not using the theoretical framework of masculinity studies. As Jonathan Allan notes, "Queer theory, thus, recognizes the complexities of an intersection that accounts for gender, sex, and desire. Queer theory plays and embraces the messiness of complexity," and it is in this "messiness of complexity" that the coming analyses target.[58] To the specific focus on masculinity, the practice of manhood, and maleness, Allan also importantly posits that "queer theory, thus, is an important intervention in the field because it might allow for critical studies of men and masculinities to focus on the unsaid, the non-normative, and the complexity and messiness of desire."[59] Here, again, is the focus on the complexity and messiness of desire; however, added to that is pointing to reading the margins of texts for what they might communicate in their silences. I am listening closely to the silences of these collected chanteys and interested in the sometimes buried and suggested ways that gender, sexuality, and desire present themselves singularly and often in overlapping ways.

The articulation of gender and sexuality in collective work song is all the more interesting for it is occurring within the framework of a hypermasculine homosocial environment. My use of the term "queer," as well as my use of queer theory as a lens, attaches to Allan's reading of the term in "Queer Theory and Critical Masculinity Studies." Allan notes, "Masculinities are not static, and to study the fluidity of masculinities requires a theoretical perspective that relishes in the slipperiness of identity."[60] In my analysis, I am interested in, just as Allan discusses, mining the silences, the unsaid, the margins of texts, to see what they might expose about the messy quality of lived existence. To "queer," for me and throughout, is to "question the normative" and read with sometimes seemingly disparate lenses in order to bring into focus the unsaid and suggested.[61] Queer theory is not only about queer identity; it is also about disrupting normative thinking and reading in order to privilege the discordant or the performances of self that do not fit within the confines of expectation. Queer theory is inherently kaleidoscopic in that it looks to how identities collide with one another and the world around, opening and changing and evolving, colors on top of colors, to the point where the collisions create something new or alter the image in such a way that old meanings are obscured.

Our way into the songs from Legman and Hugill and what they capture about gender and sexuality is to begin with the backdrop of the sea. Open waters are either expressly stated in the songs or are suggested throughout, and the tie to the indeterminate and unmoored quality of the water helps to situate the notions of identity formation I will be suggesting. In my reading, it is impossible to dismiss the queer nature of the sea and sea life: the moving, changing, ebbing, and flowing quality works in the same circular pattern identified by Natasha Hurley and Sara Ahmed.[62] The sea itself is an entity wide and foreboding, moving with a sentience all its own, living and breathing. The mysterious quality of that space lends it to readings that defy categories; it is powerful enough to register corporeally and emotionally on malleable bodies and takes with it and swallows secrets that may never breach the surface of the hungry waters. Indeed, Valentina Bold and Pauline Greenhill note that "du Maurier's creek again represents sexuality and sexual liberation" as based off a quote describing the novel by a "Roger Phequell."[63] Though they are discussing a small creek, it is worth recognizing the ways in which the sea has been aligned with the erotic and also the unstable. The sea is often described as a liminal space, where the dangers of the deep produce tests for a man in ways that the land could never manufacture. Literary scholar John Peck describes Herman Melville's *Moby-Dick* as grappling with "the unpredictability of the sea, the voyage and life in general, and the human impulse to try to assume command, to explain and understand," and this complex navigation of the self, against an unstable and ever-changing background, is at the heart of *Cabin Boys, Milkmaids, and Rough Seas*.[64] Imagine floating for months and sometimes years on a plane where the only human contact comes from the other men trapped in the same wooden workspace. Perhaps there is an occasional meeting with other men on other floating worlds while at sea or the intrusion of the captain's or mate's wives, but primarily, one has his fellow seaman, the sea, the infinite force of Mother Nature, and time. Such a powerful object like the sea, indelible and enigmatic as it is, would begin to go to work on the precarious facets of fragile man. A man must begin to make negotiations that help to confront the liminal quality of so vast a space. The hardened and hypermasculine identity that a man boasts must face and negotiate the difficult reality of his feeble body against the tides and rages of the water, the frustrating nature of desire and longing while trapped at sea, and the confusing and sometimes painful realization that he must function within a hierarchical framework in order to preserve his own life and that of his brothers. This difficult and delicate process, cast against the backdrop of an unstable environment that is both wooden and watery, is the pinnacle of a queer space and queer interaction. In fact, it is a "queer negotiation."

The notion of a queer negotiation relates to what Ahmed writes of orientations in her *Queer Phenomenology*. Her work serves as a lens to be trained on the chanteys included in this book in order to begin understanding how the narratives are fictitious renderings of the real and lived frustrations of the orientations that sailing characters encounter within their floating workspace. Ahmed's notions of bodies encountering each other, clashing, and opening up or moving toward new paths is roughly akin to the narrative turns of the chanteys from Hugill. The moment at which an actor encounters a situation, path, person, feeling, or notion, the body and the mind are forced down new paths of orientation: the being is opened to new possibilities and new frameworks because he has been situated in a particular way. As Ahmed notes, "the very proximity of pea to pea, as well the intimacy of the dwelling that surrounds them like a skin, shapes the very form of the peas. Likeness is thus not 'in' the peas, let alone 'in' the pod but rather is an effect of their contiguity, of how they are touched by each other and envelope each other."[65] For Ahmed, the orientation occurs because the body has been situated in a particular space, at a particular time, and surrounded by particular things. In the chanteys, we might begin to see these orientations as they play out in the constrained space of the ship.

Within chanteys, singers are able to fully vent experiences and elegantly negotiate, through embodied language, the idea that, at base, all socially constructed expectations of identity (whether dealing with sexual expression or gender construction) fail to capture the complexity of performances in reality. The pressures of performing properly, adhering to set standards of identity articulation, or confronting the moments at which socially constructed expectations and categories fail will likely build to the point at which the frustrations can no longer be held at bay nor remain contained within the vessel tamping them down. The continuous process of swallowing moments of shame (for failing to perform properly) or burying identifications of "doing something wrong" will slowly begin to pile, event on top of event, until the actor needs to vent or simply spill the experiences before he drowns in what is compressed down.

These songs collected by Legman from Hugill demonstrate at least one method of release that allow singers to unite breath, voice, and body but also vent the complexities of their lives through deploying images and backdrops that are just as liminal and queer as lived reality. The chapters to come ultimately reembody the songs with the lived realities of sailors (and other men) and focus on how the songs capture breath, voice, body, and experience: a circular relationship that always moves both inside and outside of the singer. By reading the analysis, too, the chanteys continue to live on, arguably providing a further way through which the songs themselves are embodied, alive, and evolving.

Cabin Boys, Milkmaids, and Rough Seas specifically queers the texts from Hugill, looking at uniquely heteronormative texts for what they say and also elide. Hurley, in her *Circulating Queerness*, importantly highlights the circulatory process through which identities emerge, specifically through a relationship and a collision between what is already circulating in the world and registration of those identities within a character or a person.[66] Hurley points to a similar process as that of Ahmed, who argues that we begin to shape a sense of self as it bumps into other things and identities that leave marks on us and fundamentally change us to conform to the new world that has opened up to us.[67] Hurley and Ahmed are key here to understanding the complexities that are at work in places like the chanteys from Hugill or in other works of bawdy songs, like rugby tunes, drinking songs, or even Mexican *pornocorridos*, because, in those spaces, we encounter crystallized representations of the undulating negotiation of identity. *Pornocorridos* are sexually explicit ballads that rose to cultural significance in the 1970s.[68] Sex and gender arrive so often in folksong and folklore because, in the same circular pattern that Hurley identifies in novels, humans use literary spaces as avenues through which to circularly grapple with the realities of their lives; these are not static and are, indeed, in a constant state of movement. Identity structures are foundational to our sense of life and the world around us and pockets of our interior worlds are accessible in those places where we deposit our innermost thinking and most vulnerable realities. The characters in the songs from Hugill, thus, are a means through which to trace a complex wrestling with identity formation that is intensely juridical, just as it is freeing. When I use the term "juridical," I am applying it based on Michel Foucault's conception of it in *Discipline and Punish*.[69] Victor Tadros, in "Between Governance and Discipline," outlines the use of the term best when he contends that "the juridical conception defines power in relation to a series of acts. It defines which acts transgress and which are permitted . . . what Foucault calls 'the juridical' is not equivalent to legal power. It describes any form of power which attempts to prevent a certain type of action through the threat of legal or social sanctions."[70] Throughout my analysis, I am chiefly interested in the later portion of this definition where an actor is exposed to the power of social sanctions and is disciplined away from transgressions; however, residue of the transgressive remains within cultural artifacts, like song.

I spoke of the connection between body and voice in Hugill's songs, but the work of both Hurley and Ahmed is key in uncovering the existential battle between following an unbound, uncategorized exploration of gender and sexuality and the very real and concerted juridical models that police structures of gender and sexuality from the outside. The weight of these unexpurgated song examples is that they register identity and personhood in a fleshy as well as a provocatively symbolic fashion, constantly in motion between finite objects and opaque suggestions that capture collisions and reverberations, vulnerabilities and strengths. All these negotiations are spectral and queer, sometimes barely tangible.

In reading Hugill's songs "slantwise," in peering through a queer lens, the primary message that hums beneath the surface of these songs, and arguably others in all-male singing traditions, is the notion of *masculine vulnerability*. Masculine vulnerability has been noted in research dealing with other all-male traditions and homosocial spaces, like the crossing-the-line ceremony, prison songs and brotherhoods, and songs and mores observed in logging camps and other spaces. There are, to be sure, far too many examples of where homosociality and comradery function against a backdrop of masculine vulnerability. It almost appears as if those brotherhoods exist and congeal so as to combat the outward appearances of those vulnerabilities.

Simon J. Bronner, in his study concerning naval crossing-the-line ceremonies both past and present, notes the undercurrents of masculine vulnerability within the ritual. He specifically notes that the ritual might be attached to "constructed gendered divisions of the land and sea" and goes on to paint the ritual as one "that alter[s] the perception of the vulnerable ship moving in 'placeless' open waters and give[s] it rootedness in tradition."[71] In this reading of the ceremony, the sailing man and the ship are conflated such that the vulnerabilities of the ship on the open waters are the same as those attending the man, his body, and his presentation of masculinity. Specifically, the "rootedness" of the ritual provides a space where the participant might find solace, connection, and a degree of control wherein control is often rent from him. Masculinity, like sexuality and race, is a social construct that is in constant need of being confirmed, reinforced, policed, and acted. The performance of this unstable and unfixed identity—especially against the backdrop of a moving vessel, within a confined space like the sailing ship, and with danger around every corner—is often tested, usurped, and even overturned.

Some of this same vulnerability is registered in research dealing with logging men "where they often recounted incidents of bravery and masculinity" especially because their work was so dangerous.[72] In fact, not only were their lives similar to the sailing man, but also, as Bailey and Doerflinger both note, logging men and sailors likely traded places quite often within the working-class milieu.[73] When life and identity are most at stake, it seems, the louder the cry within collective artifacts and spaces. What I mean by this "cry" is what Blue notes of work songs in prisons: "The revitalization of hypermasculine imagery and misogynistic narratives is a reaction to perceived threats to men's self-images under police control and invasive street searches, heightened by economic insecurity in flexible labor markets."[74] Of course, Blue is discussing prison and urban cultures, but his observation maps onto vulnerabilities courting the working-class sailor too, especially at the close of the age of sail as sail gave way to steam. The sailing man's struggle was not unlike what Bailey notes of loggers, who were similarly impacted by the industrial age.[75]

In Hugill's chanteys, masculine vulnerability is often registered through broken, diseased, and disabled body parts, more often than not damaged genitals, and these images demonstrate the vulnerability of the body as it is exposed to external forces and dangers. Symbolically, this vulnerability also attaches to other ways by which the particular sailing body is open to situations that may render him either injured, debilitated, or deceased and are akin to castration narratives like those that often circulated in other bawdy spaces, like limericks and bawdy songs. Legman notes, at least in terms of bawdy limericks, "It is the *rationalization*—the attempt to make understandable, or at least believable, even endurable, if only as a 'joke'—of some highly-charged neurotic situation into which the original folk-teller of the tale has stumbled, or has found himself forced to live, perhaps out of his own (or her own) psychological need."[76] Legman's observation concerning the "why" of bawdy material, notably Freudian in its tenor, is that the folk teller uses folklore objects as opportunities to capture and rationalize those parts of human existence that are painful, confounding, and life altering. In Hugill, perhaps the most vulnerable of all appendages is the penis, which is literally and also figuratively castrated by disease and damage. All that the penis endures, throughout many of these collected songs, functions as a cipher for the implicit and explicit realities of both early modern sailing life and the life of men more generally. The penis, in a word, becomes the point of rationalization, the joke, but also the truth telling of vulnerability.

Greenhill's work points to a vulnerability in gendered constructions and her observation is worth quoting in full:

> But ballads also implicate the fragile construction of sexuality and the fragility of assumptions that people are 'naturally' attracted only to those of the 'opposite' sex. And while lesbian, gay, bisexual, and queer identities are historical and contingent, these songs [cross-dressing ballads] indicate a persistence of same-sex orientation (and the need to deconstruct a presumption of heterosexuality as the only normal kind of orientation) that precedes the historical coining of terms like *homosexual, gay*, or *lesbian*.[77]

Greenhill's argument centers the type of reading that this project engages, which includes attending to the fragility and vulnerability of bodies and identities and thinking about the songs through a lens of *persistence* and even longevity. Too, I am thinking about these vulnerabilities as liminalities, as literally queering the lived life through damages that impact identity formation and change one's sense of self. Her use of the term "fragile" here resonates with my own reading of masculine vulnerability in the Hugill songs. The *fragile* and *vulnerable* gesture at instability, movement, and change as well as at fear, destruction, and dismantling. She notes that her work adds the idea of "performative character of sexuality" to the conversation of performative gender, and this project continues that type of inquiry in the space of folksongs.[78] In playing the role of the heteronormative, hypervirile sailor, it is possible to see vulnerabilities that haunt the margins of texts and also visit themselves quite profoundly in spaces, if one is willing to look closely and differently. This is especially true if we consider the number of mishaps and damages that are visited on the penises of sailing characters in Hugill's songs that castrate and thereby upend masculine identity.

Masculine vulnerability is traceable throughout a number of all-male singing traditions and, as such, contributes to the importance of a critical investigation that places male vulnerability at the center of the inquiry. Within working-class spaces, there are inherent paradoxes to those lives that generate emotions of alienation, frustration, and even defeat. Folklore objects in these vocationally specific places are ripe with material that help researchers understand both the materiality of those lives and how those who experience those lives grapple with the very real frustrations that often attend them. Such emotions generate a need to ease the stresses of everyday work and life and likely foster a desire to connect with the men (and sometimes women) who are actively involved in these distinct workspaces and experiences. Cultural items like song, jokes, storytelling, and even hazing or cajoling are integral to the creation of bonds among those at work. As Roger D. Abrahams poignantly notes, "one can predict that routined [sic], pattered, self-consciously rehearsed expressive means will develop and be transmitted as essential—if not always acknowledged—element of carrying out the job."[79] Essentially, wherever there is repetitive, sometimes-alienating work, a foreboding sense of vulnerability, and even outsider status, especially in confined and what Abrahams notes as "isolated settings" like sailing ships, we will find various means by which such vocations and experiences are assuaged by a collective folklore and folksong.[80]

Though each of the chapters to come will focus on chanteys and the experiences and lives of working-class sailors in the early modern world, this book will suggest that each investigation of this song tradition carries with it the application to other all-male, working-class situations and song traditions and, perhaps, to other male spaces as well. As Lisa Gilman outlines, "People use folklore to contest restrictive social norms around gender and sexuality and to create more equitable gendered spaces and alternate ways of being. It is through folklore that people gain a sense of self and connection with others, and it offers the opportunity for individuals to belong to multiple overlapping and sometimes conflicting networks."[81] Nowhere is this connection perhaps more important than in those spaces where one's body and identity are most exposed and vulnerable. These songs are a window into masculine worlds, relics that highlight the reality that categorical approaches to gender fail to capture the lived experience of performing those expectations in real time.

In terms of venting or releasing frustrations and vulnerabilities, consider that most collected song traditions from the working class are connected to vocations that are often quite dangerous and very often lead those employed in those vocations to serious injury and even death. Truckers, lumbermen, sailors, soldiers, and even football players are each engaged in some type of vocation that renders their bodies distinctly vulnerable. Collective song bonds people together, sometimes across space and place, and unites their voices and, ultimately, each other in such a way that the song becomes almost a balm for the subordination that surrounds them. David A. Carter argues that "songs become a means of uniting against and coping with a common enemy."[82] Critical studies in union songs, especially in the early 1900s, demonstrate the ways in which collective song, sometimes borrowed from known popular songs, has the ability to unite workers from across the world. These songs unite them under the common cause of seeking better pay, better working environments, and more recognition for the important work they produce. Their songs often register symbols of battle/war, injury, and sometimes death. The ability to bond with other men in these vocations in and through the texts that they share among them creates a comradery connected deeply with masculine vulnerability. They can share with other men, in protected spaces, the inherent dangers and fears they carry with them concerning their livelihoods. The undercurrent is that these spaces require a particular *type* of man, one who is able to withstand and even conquer the trials of these vocations. The shared nature of the songs means that men are gathering together around these shared ideas and celebrating their singular ability to be a part of a "crew of men" able to confront these trials. This ability is clearly lauded at the expense of other men, and women, who are unable to muscle through the same.

The intense emotions, experiences, and vulnerabilities inherent in working-class life and even the recognition of the liminalities and misalignments of identity performance generate the need for a release valve of some nature to deal with the pressures and stresses inherent in such environments. What I mean by "release valves" is that the pressures and anxieties surrounding the presentation of self build up to the point that they need to be vented. As Michel Foucault notes in his *History of Sexuality*, "Whether in the form of a subtle confession in confidence or an authoritarian interrogation, sex—be it refined or rustic—had to be put into words."[83] He then cites a profusion of discourse concerning sexuality and identity, the likes of which were unprecedented prior to that moment. It is the theory of confession, noted in chapter 5, that is both a release valve and a mechanism to be used for social policing. It is the release valve that is of most importance to the discussion to come. Where there is a sense of vulnerability and even liminality and instability, there is pressure built with the anxiety that surrounds these sensations. There is a fear that lurks in the song lyrics and an inherent vulnerability that hypermasculine language attempts to mask. That ability to mask, however, is ultimately undone by the use of proxy-type comparison. As Archie Green notes, "We are all absorbed in such stories [like those he describes of the dangers he learned of his own trade] because we could dissolve our fears in a comrade's tragedy or borrow courage from an heroic fellow worker."[84] What I contend is that in these same songs and stories, there are undercurrents that gesture at even more important facets of identity. These facets of identity are the ones hidden within the enjoyment we derive from dissolving fears and borrowing courage. They are the murmurings of our inherent need to be seen, to be a part of something. They are the vulnerabilities that are threatening underneath the fear that the fallen comrade could be us at any moment. They are the desires to be something more than we are, self-aggrandizing desires that hide below them a distinct and penetrating anxiety that our lives are meaningless and that we are powerless in the face of challenge.

These collective songs even betray our common need to belong, which is fueled by a sensation of being the outcast. Hugill's songs provide an opportunity to begin reading in the margins in this way, to see the sensations that are both clearly articulated and also suggested underneath. In approaching the songs in this way, in queering so as to expose the hidden parts of the narratives, we might get at some of the less palpable but ever-connected realities that attend song traditions that are uniquely a part of facilitating bonded space. They are funny, they are irreverent, they are bawdy, but they are also sincere evocations of human vulnerability and need. They are the release valve for intense feelings that are frightening and alienating. They are the fabric of our collective lives and the recycling, indeed, of some of the sensations that we all feel at one time or another.

Greenhill contends that "periodic cracks in the construction [of gender] occur, as they do with cross-dressing ballads, if readers are willing to see them," and I am noting these same cracks in the songs from Hugill's repertoire.[85] They are cracks that relate to other fissures in gendered performance, which we have to look closely to find. I see them, similar to cracks, as release valves for the tensions of performing gender in a certain way. Just as Greenhill points to the work of Judith Butler, so too do I see the juridical construction of gender colliding with the vulnerability of the body in certain places and contexts that ultimately breeds these fissures or creates the cracks in the veneer. Gilman notes, "Studying folklore in military spaces also suggests that this ideal of monolithic masculinity is inherently flawed," and she goes on to discuss the ways in which military men are often tasked with more "feminine" duties. She notes the same reality that attends sailors on sailing ships being asked to "fulfill roles that would typically be associated with women."[86] These different expectations clash with the prevailing cultural depiction of these "manly men" and create a pressure-cooker situation wherein there are competing social expectations of a presentation of self as it clashes with vocational expectations that might transgress the sense of self cultivated outside of the ship. It is a vulnerability tied to a recognition of this "flawed definition," and the songs are spaces where singers might release these anxieties and frustrations, albeit often under the guise of heteronormative narrative.

Obviously, it is not only gender performance that generates this need for release. Sexuality, especially that which runs counter to expected hypermasculine constructions, seeps into release valves like songs. Sex arrives in so many all-male singing traditions and seems to be a key facet to all-male singing, and such imagery is both the symbolic way through which singers grapple with external realities they encounter and simply a venting of the erotic within a shared (and safe) social space. Heteronormative sexuality figures most prominently in Hugill and other all-male singing traditions; however, the way in which this sexuality is cast often slides between the homosocial and the homoerotic. Masculine figures in Hugill's songs are powerful and agentive, imbued with phallic energy that is stirring and potentially enticing. It is true that men are sharing in these songs within a shared masculine space that is the pinnacle of phallic energy, but the degree to which these songs appear as both homosocial and homoerotic appears to let slip the deeply vulnerable admission of queer curiosity or even outright same-sex desire. Men singing erotic songs in the company of other men and doing so within all these different masculine spaces communicates both a desire to be and a desire to see in a scopophilic way. It is possible to argue that because our society does not permit men the space to fully experiment with or articulate desires that run counter to hegemonic masculinity, they manufacture ways by which they might vent these desires and curiosities, one of which is song. We can think about collective all-male spaces as pressure cookers of emotion and desire where the songs become something akin to a pressure valve: a place for release. The songs, however, are veiled in the ways by which they articulate these desires. If it is possible to trace enormous penises, epic sexual encounters, and virile, agentive male characters across a number of different all-male song traditions, it speaks to the potential that men are creating narrative in their shared song that celebrates and also consumes.

Though distilling materials down to one particular connecting factor might appear limiting and essentializing, I take Lau's comment that collections like

"*Favorite Folktales from around the World* reduces difference by emphasizing the fact that a number of different cultures might share a single tale type."[87] Though Lau is discussing folktales and is arguably critical of texts like *Folktales from around the World* for eliding difference, her view of collections and scholarship in folklore points to the potential positives of anchoring readings to a distinctive theme. In defining and viewing these songs as cosmopolitan representations of release valves for masculine vulnerability, especially concerning gender and sexuality, this project actually in no way elides difference or attempts to demonstrate that any one song is representative of all men everywhere at every time. What this inquiry *does* accomplish, though, is the privileging of a reading of masculine vulnerability and the sketching of how expressions of that vulnerability attach to certain texts, certain men, certain times, and even specific contexts. As Conrad notes of "country music's workers," "the concept encompasses a social collective unified by its members' acceptance of the inevitability of powerlessness, repression of their individual identities, and suppression of their aspirations for autonomous lives."[88] Not every worker is the same, but he is united in the toil, in the danger, and in the way by which his body is sacrificed for something outside of himself. Indeed, it is possible to view such an approach to materials as all the more inclusive in that by centering a certain theme, I am connecting a vast swath of different men from varying backgrounds and periods to something that universally unites them. Carter argues, "Evidence abounds demonstrating the use of songs to deal with 'hard times' and oppression."[89] And those oppressive regimes may arguably be the confining gender and sexual categories that structure and order bodies in real time.

In each finite example from Hugill, in contrast to other collected chantey texts, scholars are able to attach complex theoretical lenses to crystallized articulations of gender and sexuality, not unlike the work that has been done with *Fanny Hill* or other erotic literary texts. There is a similar structuring occurring in the Legman and Hugill texts that is comparable to other folklore material in which narratives are providing space for experimentation with realities that may be desirable, taboo, or improper but are very much a part of a shared reality.

Folklore materials are the registers of identity, whole and solid like the pinpoint image of a kaleidoscope, but they are also expansive and engaging, impacting those who collide with them so as to fundamentally change or impact their own sense of identity, much like the rings and colors that grow out of the central image in the glass. The metaphor of a kaleidoscope is an apt one through which to understand the different images and realities that come into focus during a close reading. Looking through the glass, it is possible to see multiple shapes and colors, sometimes fully defined and other times opaque. Each movement of the glass alters the images and colors within, allowing for new images and colors to come into focus. There is the focal point of the image, the finite person that appears to remain static and is at the center of the scope. That being is whole, weighty, and resonant as it tends to stay within the center of the visual field. What reverberates out from that one being, the colorful circles that migrate out and around the central image, constitutes the lived quality of identity. As the colors and shapes grow larger and expand out, they become a bit quieter, less defined, and certainly further away from the clear object that began the movement. This distance, quiet nature, and even the barely perceptible definition does not impact the recognition of both those rings remaining and their original connection to the body that sent them out. Too, these rings and colors have the ability, in their constant stretching out and away from the body, to touch other spaces and objects that would not have been possible for the focal object alone. In this, I am thinking about Sara Ahmed and the lines that define and divide space and of Natasha Hurley and circulations: each of these theories helps to capture the radiating quality of identity as it moves and changes. This shaping process is not static and is beholden to the things it bumps into, the realities encountered, and the forging of new paths impossible to avoid. The bodies of sailing characters and the tempting men, women, and situations they collide with are like moments trapped in amber to be excavated and interpreted, but they are also like this kaleidoscope. Though these characters are, admittedly, not real and sentient beings, their plights and triumphs are narrative situations that aid us in thinking about the realities around us that are always there but sometimes ignored, imperceptible, or, more often, inconvenient. Humans like answers, the finite; we always want what is easy, neat, and categorical. There is a level of tidiness in identity, like the shapes and colors that open out into the kaleidoscope's glass, but that compact quality is not absolute nor perfect. As the rings move out and touch other objects, as the images and colors shift and change further away from the place of origin, so too can we think about identities as they are presented in the Legman and Hugill manuscript and other folk ephemera.

    Laura Gowing, in her *Common Bodies*, captures the same idea I am gesturing at here. She argues:

> Sex stories were told and retold. They gave modest observers a way to put themselves into a sexual discourse that risked being compromising, and they enabled people to reflect on the rules of sexual behaviour. Perhaps they worked rather like murder stories, where the titillating stories of horrible, subversive

crimes licensed the exploration of transgression and disorder, before the criminal's hasty confession provided a suitable moral closure. In the same way, talking explicitly about their neighbours' sexual transgressions enabled both women and men with a claim to modesty to act and speak as voyeurs.[90]

Though she is writing specifically about stories told in the eighteenth century, the importance is palpable as it pertains to the subject at hand. Songs, like the ones from Legman and Hugill, are mechanisms through which composers insert themselves into events and also share them with a wider social world. The songs provide permission to be voyeurs as much as they also give space to assimilate oneself into the storyline, to feel the experiences of the characters included within the narrative situation. Most poignant in the excerpt from Gowing is, of course, the notion that they "were told and retold." In the sharing of collective song, in fashioning narratives that are meant to be experienced by multiple people, the examples from Hugill and Legman, as with other folksong and folklore, capture the need for continued sharing of narrative that is risky, taboo, titillating, and, potentially instructive. In the chanteys, what comes into focus is the instability of heteronormative gender and sexuality, and this comes into focus through deploying covers and ciphers that grant permission and mitigate risk. The songs use the cover of joke akin to what Gowing sketches here, even the cover of hypermasculinity and hegemony, to deliver narratives that represent a more unstable and vulnerable reality.

The first aspect of chantey narratives that I investigate concerns how opposite-sex-affiliated narratives, especially those which contain words of warning, communicate the idiosyncrasies of identity construction. Songs of warning in the Legman and Hugill manuscript help to set the stage for the instability of gender and sexuality categories that pervade the entire manuscript. Buried underneath humorous tales of sex gone wrong, narratives appear to cope with identity formation, which often slips between meeting expectations and also flippantly eschewing them for identities more predicated on desire and pleasure than cultural mandates. Many of the songs located in the manuscript use sexual encounters with women as the means through which to warn fellow sailors of dangers in port, especially where women and sex are concerned, but these appear more as opportunities to point to the hierarchical environment that sailors are embedded within and the frustrations with negotiating those frameworks. Though gender and sexual expressions are policed from within and outside of the sailing characters, especially through painful juridical punishments, the characters appear to recognize the discipline and order and then choose paths that highlight a far more complex sexual economy. Succinctly, sex is not always simply an erotic exchange and is, sometimes, imbued with deeper and more complicated nuances that transcend sex and identity itself. It is within these symbolic moments that scholars are able to interrogate the utility of the sex act in spaces sometimes outside of the erotic economy.

That the songs of warning set the stage for toying with identity categories is further supported through a close examination of other songs that demonstrate opposite-sex sexual interactions. Though cultural narratives abound concerning a sailor's penchant for same-sex erotic release, and there is some historical evidence to substantiate such experiences, the majority of the songs included in the manuscript detail a sailor's experience chasing women in port and the dangers they clearly sometimes bring with them. The book begins with a discussion of how these narratives provide an elegant, if funny, presentation of sailors in heteronormative economies and identify that these same narratives likely masked the true and complex nature of sexuality and power at sea. The same observation feeds into the chapter focused on heteronormative encounters more generally and further underscores the ways through which these songs deploy opposite-sex narratives in the service of giving vent to the reality of identity performance, even when it appears to meet cultural expectations. These songs demonstrate evidence of sailors reveling in expected masculine social scripts, in line with many other all-male, working-class song traditions, but these constructions are not pervasive or finite. They demonstrate, instead, an instability and a vulnerability in the face of undulating realities of identity.

Though many of the songs are hypermasculine in their subtext and confirm masculine social scripts, there are other songs that provide sailors the space through which to fetishize male bodies and even to explore same-sex erotics under the cover of heteronormative narratives. My book considers, after discussing the opposite-sex sexual encounters of chanteys in the Legman-Hugill manuscript, how some of the other chanteys included in the compendium contain narratives that appear to substantiate anecdotal, cultural treatments of sex at sea and, at the very least, provide opportunities to discuss the sliding of the homosocial into the homoerotic. I point to at least one chantey that contains a narrative in which the entire focus is on a same-sex sexual encounter throughout the duration of the voyage; however, other narratives in the manuscript contain subtexts that gesture at same-sex tensions and add an important layer to the discussion of gender and sex at sea, which is that identity and desire are really unbound.

This critical study closes with a meditation on the themes that emerge throughout the songs surveyed and how they might be applied to other archival and contemporary spaces. The Legman-Hugill manuscript presents a sailing identity and, arguably, a part of masculine identity construction that is not often the subject of conversation. The songs detail elegant negotiations of power and disempowerment, frustrating evocations of sex and sexual release, and the inborn, deep-seated fear of danger that followed every sailor throughout his life, whether he was at sea or in port. Through chanteys, the true nature of identity and erotic expression are each articulated, and scholars are able to contend with the frustrating realities that are a part of living life as an early modern man, as a sailor, or even as a modern man or woman. Even though these social realities lie, sometimes hidden and buried, under the protective cover of humor or narrative that presents a hegemonic construction of identity, chanteys are a mode through which we can begin to articulate the reality that there is more to gender and sexuality. Those categories do not really fit the lived human performance. These songs were and continue to be pressure valves for frustration, for desire, and for belonging; yet, and more importantly, they also capture the juxtapositions and idiosyncrasies of human life that reach back in time and reverberate even now, at the moment you are reading this. Though the songs now exist in two-dimensional form, sometimes with two-dimensional characters, they bring with them three-dimensional implications related back to the bodies and voices of the men who sang them and have bearing, too, on social realities that we are still mired in discussing today.

CHAPTER 3

Words of Warning and the Ebb and Flow of Identity

Song has the unique ability to bond people together. Voices and breath rise in unison as familiar words are belted together. Collective singing provides the opportunity for singers to insert group identity into song lyrics and bolster connections and solidarity through sharing in collective ideals, sensations, emotions, and even fears. Collective song is the space where frustrations are vented, where comradery is celebrated, and where sometimes deeply intimate experiences are shared in protected space. Perhaps nothing is more sacred than sharing one's vulnerabilities. Venting the unstable parts of oneself, those shadow versions of the self or spectral qualities that haunt the margins of identity, provides a level of power and agency for someone especially when battling against sensations that might feel wholly out of control. What we fear about ourselves and the way that we function in space are each aspects of our lives that we attempt to bury and hide, sharing perhaps only with those closest to us and only when we feel safe enough to share.

In Hugill's songs, it is possible to see hints of these vulnerabilities, these sensations and fears that lurk at the corners of identity. Indeed, in the first turn of the kaleidoscope, we must delve deeply into the unstable parts of the self in order for other, more solid revelations to take shape. Looking into the murky images of the self, the spectral and shadowy, it is possible to begin defining the confines of identity as it is negotiated. Specifically, in Hugill's songs of warning, characters encounter moments at which identity constructions are challenged or upset, sometimes completely altered, and they must navigate and then articulate these experiences to caution and also commiserate. The narratives of these songs appear as release valves for venting recognitions of the instability of identity construction, sharing narrative situations that capture the literal and also symbolic vacillating nature of lived reality. Within these songs of warning, there is a vulnerability and a liminality of identity construction that serves as the foundation for our understanding of all other articulations of self throughout the remaining songs contained in Hugill's repertoire. As was noted of the collective environment, working to assuage a vulnerability felt together in particular spaces in all-male singing traditions, the lyrics captured in several of Hugill's songs appear to specifically grapple with and fight back against a sensation of vulnerability as it attends the unstable construction of masculinity. These negotiations are, to a degree, the same *queer negotiation* that we will see in other songs, but the songs of warning specifically appear to navigate the push and pull of power and agency in the face of situations and characters that often usurp the position of the male character, generating an arguable symbolic attack on masculinity.

Research into collective singing traditions specifically demonstrates that some song, especially that sung in all-male spaces, is meant to solidify a masculinity that appears to hang in the balance. There is a perceived attack on hypermasculinity, forcing a new, softer masculinity in its place that threatens the nineteenth-century idea of the "solitary man." The paradox, here, is that it appears men are seeking to bond together so as to reinforce an idea of the solitary man. Bonding with other men is a way to bolster a masculine individuality and fight back against structures, individuals, and cultural evolutions that threaten to upset the accepted frameworks of ideal manhood.

The sailor has long been aligned with images of careless rabblerousing, excessive drinking, and having a woman in every port, becoming an archetype of manhood, indeed almost a paragon of masculinity, not unlike how contemporary society views others in working-class vocations or even sporting spaces. Many cultural images of Jolly Jack Tar show him as he is at leisure in port, and these visual representations of the sailing man help to produce an image of him as one who is and emulates the quintessential hegemonic male for the early modern era and even the contemporary period.[1] Historian Paul Gilje argues that many "British caricatures [circulated] of seamen dancing and drinking with heavy and full-busted women bulging out of their dresses."[2]

Hugill's songs of warning, at face value, reflect some of the popular renderings of sailing identity and appear to not only celebrate the rough, ready, and virile sketches that circulate of sailors throughout eras but, importantly, also relate the unstable reality of this construction. As Steven Dashiell writes of masculinity, "Men are actors in front of an immense social audience, attempting to master a part for which there is truly no one exemplar, as a perfected masculinity is driven by idealistic views rather than reality."[3] Under the hypermasculine

THE LIVERPOOL JUDIES

WHEN I was a youngster I sailed with the rest,
On a Liverpool packet bound out to the West.
We anchored way down in the harbour o' Cork,
Then we put out to sea for the port o' New York.
  Singin' ho! ro! Ho, bullies, ho!
  Them Liverpool Judies have got us in tow!

stet/

For forty-two days we was hungry an' sore,
Oh the winds was ag'in us, the gales they did roar.
Off Battery Point we did anchor at last,
With our jibboom hove in an' the canvas all fast.

The boarding-house masters was off in a trice,
A-shoutin' an' promisin' all that was nice.
An' one fat ol' crimp he got cottoned to me,
Says he, Yer a fool, lad, to follow the sea.

Says he, There's a job as is waitin' for you,
With lashin's o' liquor an' fuck-all to do.
Says he, What d'ye say, lad, will you jump her too?
Says I, Ye ol' barstard, I'm damned if I do!

stet/

But the best o' intentions they niver gits far,
After forty-two days at the door of a bar.
I tossed off me liquor, an' what d'ye think?
Why the lousy ol' barstard had drugs in me drink.

The next I remembers, I woke in the morn,
On a three-skysail yarder bound south round Cape Horn,
Wid an ol' suit of oil-skins an' two pair of socks,
An' a bloody big head an' a dose of the pox.

Now all ye young sailors, take a warnin' from me,
Keep a watch on your drinks when the liquor is free,
An' pay no attention to runner or whore,
Or your head'll be thick an' your prick'll be sore.

Sailing Ship Shanties, 1927-1956.

"The Liverpool Judies," a song collected from the repertoire of Stan Hugill. Scanned copy from "Sea Songs," unpublished manuscript of Gershon Legman. Personal copy sent by Judith Legman, October 10, 2014.

presentation of self in early parts of the songs lurks the full kaleidoscope of identity construction that is recognizable only when characters attempt to express this agentive masculinity and are then met with foils that expose the unstable reality of their constructions. Characters in these songs of warning are used specifically to navigate frustrating aspects of gender identity and performance expectations that not only are applicable across a broad timeframe but also articulate certain vulnerabilities and frustrations, even a liminality that might be traceable throughout other song traditions. What we are able to see is a distinct grappling with identity construction, presenting with agentive masculinity only to be feminized or subordinated in such a way that characters' identities ultimately run counter to the early modern ideal of a powerful man. This chapter interrogates the songs of warning as release valves that articulate the complicated reality of masculine life, which is that performing the ideal masculinity is subject to encounters beyond one's control.

Within the specific songs of warning, which were chosen based on closing lines similar to "The Liverpool Judies"—"Now all ye young sailors, take a warnin' from me"—Hugill shares song narrative that gestures at some of the same vulnerabilities that are observable in other all male-singing traditions. The characters in these songs are relayed in such a way that we are to look at them as objects of pity but also, and more importantly, figures through which to learn. Through venereal disease, loss of money and belongings, impressment on another sailing ship, encounters with women, and the navigation of juridical scenarios, the characters articulate tensions surrounding the presentations of self. Loss of a sense of manhood and control, struggle with the realities of sex and desire, and anxieties concerning the future and one's sense of self each as they crash into desires and pleasures just as strong and enduring register vulnerability, frustration, dichotomous realities, and a liminality of gender and sexuality. This chapter seeks to destabilize the hegemonic, hypermasculine covers of the narratives and queer the ways that we read songs from Hugill in order to uncover the vulnerabilities that are hidden beneath tales of violent sex, carefree rabblerousing, and the pursuit of dangerous vocations. The songs articulate that releases have consequences and that characters must confront the shifting nature of their own position in the world as well as their own changing sense of self as it clashes with their understanding of their own identity.

"But a Gal's a Gal, an' Sailors Is Men": Playing the Role of Hypermasculine Sailor

The songs of warning from Hugill's repertoire reproduce an expected hypermasculine narrative cover in order to attempt to bury vulnerabilities under a mask of agency and virility. In the song "Sacramento," the sailing man proclaims, "But a gal's a gal, an' sailors is men, / I'll still be a-cock when I see another hen," which suggests important sensations captured in these particular songs similar to the us-versus-them dichotomy recognizable in other song traditions like trucking songs and which has even been identified in porn discourse. As Dashiell notes, "Dominant theories of masculinity, while

SACRAMENTO

As I wuz rollin' down the street,
    Hoodah, to me hoodah!
Two charmin' bitches I did meet,
    Hoodah, hoodah, day!

    Blow boys, blow, for Californ-eye-o!
    There's plenty of grass, ter wipe yer arse,
    On the banks o' the Sacramento.

I chose the one with the curly locks,
She wuz the one that gave me the pox./
Off to the doctor I did go,
Prick an' balls I had to show.

In came the nurse with a mustard poultice,
Clapped it on but I took no notice./
In came the doctor with a bloody big lance:
Now, young sailor, I'll make yer dance. . . .

I had to pay for me bed an' room
By gettin' a knot on me ol' jibboom./
But a gal's a gal, an' sailors is men,
I'll still be a-cock when I see another hen.

An' when I'm well an' free from pain,
If I meet that whore, I'll fuck her again./
Sing, me boys, oh, heave an' sing,
Heave an' make yer arse-ole spring.

                      Sailing Ship Shanties, 1923-1956.

"Sacramento," a song collected from repertoire of Stan Hugill. Scanned copy from "Sea Songs," unpublished manuscript of Gershon Legman. Personal copy sent by Judith Legman, October 10, 2014.

inconsistent, support a sense that masculinity is a space that is oppositional to femininity, as the one way to lose masculinity is to be seen as feminine or taking a feminine role."[4] Within the dichotomous relationship between men/women or dominant/subordinate, there is a very clear distinction, and in the songs from Hugill, it is possible to see the same divisions between men and women and even sailors and other men.

Bound up within this evocation is both gender and sexuality but also a distinct identity and its attending expectations. A woman is understood as every woman, while a real man is a sailor, different from other men who are not sailors. Further, when a sailing man sees a woman, he will do what is expected of him, which is to copulate with her and, arguably, do so animalistically. The cover of the cock and hen in the example from "Sacramento" suggests barely veiled eroticism, as "cock" produces a reading of penis, as well as the assumption of cocks relentlessly pursuing copulation with hens. Within these lines there is an agentive masculinity that is powerful, in control, clearly different and distinct from all other iterations of masculinity, and obviously repeatable. The presentation of this form of self will be enacted each time the singer encounters another woman. This line reproduces an understanding of sailing masculinity that it should be distinct, always ready, and dominant. In the other songs of warning from Hugill, the expression of this type of masculinity is captured in characters who seek quick and ready pleasure, pleasure at any time and through any space, and such erotic configurations are explored using language that is potentially impenetrable to those outside of the vocation. What will be clear is that songs of warning, from the outset, sketch an expected mode of sailing masculinity that dovetails with historic representations of Bachelor Jack and even aligns with some aspects of masculinity in the present day. The songs of warning, however, demonstrate the instability of this identity construction through juridical punishments that visit themselves on the bodies of hapless sailing characters.

Surface readings of the songs of warning draw from a particular view of sailing masculinity from the early modern period. By "surface readings," I am considering what Marcus Rediker writes about the need for a history that penetrates more deeply and considers perspectives and insights from an alternative vantage point. Specifically, he writes that "history, in my view, [is] seen from the wrong end of the spyglass," and interpretations of artifacts tied to vocations like early modern sailing require perspective that not only works from the bottom up but also specifically thinks about the nuances and complexities that surround any given artifact.[5]

It is possible that many of these narratives align with what Valerie Burton recognizes of early modern sailing life, which is that the industrial age brought about changes in working-class life that destabilized the position of the sailing man. She contends that sailors navigating the new social and domestic expectations of the nineteenth century drew on old images of the hypermasculine Bachelor Jack in order to regain a sense of masculine control in a world where their recognition of their own power and authority was being usurped from them. Indeed, Burton points specifically to the liminal construction of sailing sexuality as being one site of vulnerability for the construction of sailing identity. Burton argues that "as one authority has it, [part of the push for marriage was predicated on] bearing guilt and anxieties resulting from shipboard homosexual liaisons (real or potential)," which pairs with the reality that sailing men were constrained by social readings of their all-male world and were actively working to shape constructions and presentations of their identity that would run counter to potentially feminizing narratives.[6] They were forced to make emotional and domestic choices that, in part, sought to ameliorate prevailing images of them but also functioned to adhere to new notions of masculinity. Both realities were at odds with the old formation of masculine identity, especially sailing masculinity, and placed the sailing man in a vulnerable position where he was functioning within competing drives: the expectation on land and the desires that were pulsating within him.

In fact, in Legman's observation, "monogamic marriage, as practiced in the West, is actually the principal focus of male sexual anxiety" and potentially why relations between the sexes make their way into joking or song culture.[7] From the historical perspective, Burton goes on to show: "Behind him was the homosocial world of the fo'c's'l [sic] where male norms were unchallenged and supreme. That world was recreated on shore in the brothels, lodging houses and public houses of port towns which were patronized by a seafaring clientele and by other working men."[8] In the songs of warning from Hugill, there is a clear push and pull within the narratives. Songs recycle some of these same mythic renderings of Jack Tar, like his penchant for quick and ready sex, but within those expressions, it is possible to see the beginnings of instability that harbor expressions of anxiety. These songs often vacillate between the hypermasculine presentation of the horny sailor, open to "any port in a storm," and the shifting foundation beneath those constructions.

One of the first ways in which Hugill deploys a sense of hypermasculine identity is through using language that appears to borrow from military imagery in order to bolster a strong, collective, and violent masculinity, viewing militaristic spaces as male preserves that contain only the hardiest of men. Joanne

Begiato contends that early modern British cultural artifacts utilized military metaphors when discussing sailing men, connecting sailing, battle, and manliness. She argues, "Such military metaphors linked ordinary workers to the heroism and utility of military masculinity and material culture that helped disseminate these manly ideals of behavior."[9] In this observation, she is specifically reading the May 20, 1862, speech delivered by Edward Glyn to miners who had rescued fellow men. In terms of the songs from Hugill, there is also a distinct use of military language and metaphor, especially when capturing sexuality, that underscores a particularly agentive and even violent masculinity that is similar, too, to contemporary research into American college football as well as actual military artifacts, like military cadences in which lyrics leverage a particularly violent masculinity that is predicated on conquering, power, and a violence that is unmatched. Male sexuality is often blended with images of war and domination to the point that sexuality and violence appear conflated.

Hugill's version of "Ratcliffe Highway" includes some of this violent imagery: "Then I manned me gun an' I caught her at large, / Fired into her stern-port a filthy discharge." In these lines, the sexual encounter is relayed using images of water-bound warfare with the two characters being cast as ships engaged in combat with the phrase "caught her at large" and the male character conquering the other by manning his gun and firing into her "stern-port." The penis and ejaculation are each melded with guns and fiery and filthy discharges.

In American football, John Michael McCluskey notes that songs sung during football games and even songs chosen for the opera that is American football attach to militaristic images and movements. He argues, "While most college football programs are not as nearly connected to militarism as the Aggies, martial associations are central components to college football culture."[10] The attachment to militaristic images provides a landscape of aggressive masculinity that is prepared for battle in both body and mind, regardless of the foe and, seeming, the time period. American football ethos draws on a particular ideal of masculinity, one that is *rough* and *tough*, as McCluskey further notes, and the powerful and agentive images of firepower and war are the pinnacle of masculine fortitude and endurance. American football seems a stretch from work songs like chanteys, but football songs attach to other primarily masculine spaces, like the sailing ship or the fraternity or even the military where shared folkways are coded as hypermasculine and appear like "fratriarchies," which Ben Wadham notes function through "rule of the brother[hoods]."[11]

Of course, military cadences more fully elide sexuality with violent imagery, sometimes conflating the two to the point where sexuality and war are one and the same. Susanna Trnka highlights the violent imagery inherent in military cadences, arguing that the cadence "This is my rifle, this is my gun" leverages a conflation of sex and violence and "equating the penis with a 'gun,' the rhyme functions to acculturate the military recruit into a frame of mind that equates sex with violence, and killing with 'manhood.'"[12] There is a distinct focus on ensuring recruits are indoctrinated in an expression of masculinity that is tough, nearly impenetrable, and virile. Sex is battle, battle is eroticized, and the men at the center are masculinized through their association with both the imagery and their fellow men engaged in the cadence or the environment.

The second way through which the songs gesture at hypermasculinity is through articulating an unbound pleasure that has sailing characters seeking quick and ready sexual release through any available orifice. Throughout the songs, sailing characters penetrate nearly any receiving "'ole" (mouths, vaginas, and anuses). This communicates sexual proclivities that are pleasure seeking alone and illustrative of men who champion their appetites over societal expectations, which in the period, included that sex was procreative in its aim. Within several of the songs, the sailing characters desire pleasure in whatever way they may garner it, whether it is starkly mentioned as "up the front in Callyo" or "up the back in Lima," as the sailor explains in "Serafina," or if it is more veiled and vague, as it is throughout most of the other selections that utilize sailing and sea metaphor to communicate erotic encounters. In "Serafina," the sailor notes, "She's the queen, me boys, of all the whores, that do a *rump the coolo*," which glosses to mean "anal sex."[13]

Anal sex is also suggested in "Sacramento," in which the singers remark, "Sing, me boys, oh, heave an' sing, / Heave an' make her arse-ole spring," thereby engendering a reading of collective violence focused on the anus of the woman not unlike what has been observed in football songs from Argentina.[14] In both, there is an agentive violence, with the singer placed in the position of penetration, that ensures both power and also pleasure. Too, there is a level of misogyny inherent in the lines from Hugill's songs that is palpable, especially in the songs of warning. Burton notes of the nineteenth century that "there was a difference between the 'bachelor' culture which gave rise to tales of whoring, drinking sailors around the mid-19th century and an equally ebullient, but more aggressively misogynist culture of the seafarers in the early 20th century."[15] The new strictures placed on men in the era during which Hugill was singing his songs were reflected in the misogynistic images relayed in the songs. They were militantly fighting back against the constraints being placed on them and hearkening back to what they imagined as a period in which men, especially sailing men, were captains of their own identities. Using Burton's observation, it is possible to read the lines from "Serafina" and

```
                          SERAFINA

    IN Callyo there lives a whore, her name is Serafina,
         SER-afina!   SER-afina!
    She sleeps all day an' works all night on the old Cally Marina,
         SER-afina!   SER-afina!

    She's the queen, me boys, of all the whores, that do a rump the coolo,
    She used to fuck for monkey-nuts, but now she fucks for vino./
    At robbin' silly sailor-boys, no whore was ever keener,
    Y'could stow a barge inside her cunt, 'tis like a concertina.

    She'll suck yer prick, yer balls an' all; that's how her mum did wean
    She likes a prick like a chimney-stack, or the funnel of a White Star
        steamer./
    Serafina's got no drawers, I've been ashore an' seen 'er,
    She's got no time to put 'em on, that hard-fucked Serafina.

    When I was young an' in my prime, I first fucked Serafina,
    'Twas up the front in Callyo, an' up the back in Lima./
    But the finest sight I'd ever seen was the cunt of Serafina,
    Till I got a load, a right full-house, then I wisht I'd never bin
                                                              bin ther

                                         Sailing Ship Shanties, 1925-1957
```

"Serafina," song collected from repertoire of Stan Hugill. Scanned copy from "Sea Songs," unpublished manuscript of Gershon Legman. Personal copy sent by Judith Legman, October 10, 2014.

"Sacramento" as capturing a particular agentive masculinity that is both violent and also evocative of cultural depictions of sailing men for the era. They were viewed as men who were hardened by the work of the sailing ship, erotically voracious from months trapped at sea and ready to spend their hard-earned money in port to release the tensions of working away from land.

Arguably, the songs specifically register what has humorously been observed about sailors in fictitious renderings of them, like the sailing character in *Fanny Hill*, where sailing men are so desirous of and aligned with sexual gratification that they do not care where their pleasure is garnered. John Cleland writes of the sailing man encountering Fanny that "with the other canting up my petticoats and shift, bares my naked posteriours [sic] to his blind and furious guide; it forces its way between them, and I feeling pretty sensibly that it was not going by the right door, and knocking desperately at the wrong one, I told him of it: 'Pooh!' says he, 'my dear, any port in a storm.'"[16] The sailing man is sketched as being so desirous of sex that he will put in "at any port," the storm communicating that the sex is so necessary that he must seek cover for his embattled penis. In the songs of warning, the use of any orifice attaches to readings of hypersexual sailing men; however, it also reproduces a reading of the vulnerabilities inherent in such a construction. The use of a queer space like the anus for sexual pleasure destabilizes heteronormative expectations and registers that sexual need is so great that the man might seek whatever he can to satisfy his urges. "Queer," here, is deployed to point to the anus as a shared and genderless space—though a term and an orifice obviously loaded with symbolic meaning. Additionally, admitting that need subordinates the construction of masculine control to the unbridled feeling of erotic urges that cannot be contained or trained vents a vulnerability as submitting to this need runs counter to the prevailing expectation of masculine control and order in the sexual economy as well as the cultural sphere.

This vulnerability is palpable in "Maggie May" when the sailor laments that he, the next morning, woke "not knowing if I'd shagged or shove up shite," which implies that the sailing character awakes unsure of whether or not he copulated vaginally or anally. He was so desirous of the sexual encounter that he lost control of his faculties (partly because of inebriation) and also his penis as he has no recollection of where he copulated with the woman, only that he did. The only thing that he takes from the event, he remarks, was that he did not ejaculate, as evidenced by the word "blueball," and had "two chancres for me pay." "Maggie May," importantly, dually captures the seeking of and anxiety around pursuing quick and ready sex, but it also points to the subordination of the man to his desires. The "not knowing" in "Maggie May" portrays a discomfort and anxiety in the life of the apocryphal Jack Tar, who seeks pleasure at every turn without any concern for what may befall him in his hedonistic pursuits. The discomfort potentially registers the instability of such an identity formation that is predicated only on a spectral ideal of gender.

It is not only the seeking of "any port in a storm" that communicates an unbridled sexual need; songs of warning also express that erotic encounters occur within spaces that are quick and ready and ultimately viewed as potentially queer as they fall out of line with normative expectations of erotic encounters. Queer spaces are being read using Ahmed's framework of colliding with alternative spaces, or "seeing the world 'slantwise.'"[17] Within the erotic economy of Hugill's songs, male and female characters engage with each other through transient or queer spaces, like a keyhole in the door, alight through queer sites, and enjoy sexual release on nonnormative planes that appear to both capture the agentive sexuality inherent in male sailing characters and destabilize the erotic act so that it gestures at a liminality and even vulnerability. Removing

MAGGIE MAY

COME all ye sailors bold, an' when me tale is told
I know ye all will sadly pity me.
For I was a goddamned fool in the port of Liverpool,
On the voyage when I first paid off from sea.

Oh, Maggie, Maggie May, they have taken you away,
To slave upon Van Diemen's cruel shore.
Oh, you robbed many a whaler and you poxed many a sailor,
But ye'll never cruise 'round Paradise Street no more.

I paid off at the Home, after a voyage from Sierra Leone,
Two-pounds-ten a month had been me pay,
An' as I jingled in me tin, I was sadly taken in
By a lady of the name of Maggie May.

When I steered into her I hadn't got a care,
I wuz cruisin' up an' down ol' Canning Place,
She wuz dressed in a gown so fine, like a frigate of the line,
An' I, bein' a sailorman, gave chase.

She gave me a saucy nod, an' I like a farmer's clod,
Let her take me line abreast in tow,
An' under all plain sail we ran before the gale,
An' to the Crow's-Nest Tavern we did go.

When I got full o' beer, to her lodgings we did steer,
She charged me fifteen shillings for all night.
I wuz so ruddy drunk, as I got in her bunk,
Not knowing if I'd shagged or shove up shite.

Next mornin' when I woke, me prick all bent an' broke,
I hadn't got a penny to me nyme.   stet/
So I had to pop me boots, me John L's an' me suit
Down in the Park Lane pawnshop Number Nine.

[continued.........]

> Maggie May --continued -2-
>
> Oh you thievin' Maggie May, ye robbed me of me pay
> When I slept wid you last night ashore.   stet/-
> Guilty the jury found her, for robbin' a homeward-bounder,
> An' she'll never roll down Park Lane any more.
>
> A week it passed away, an' in me bunk I lay,
> A-cursin' the day that I'd met Maggie May.
> I'd got a dose o' clap, an' it ran just like a tap,
> With a blueball and two chancres for me pay.
>
> She wuz chained an' sent away from Liverpool that day,
> The lads they cheered as she sailed down the Bay.
> An' every sailor lad, he only wuz too glad
> They'd sent the ol' whore out to Botany Bay.
>
> <u>Sailing Ship Shanties</u>, 1926-1957.
>
> BALLAD NOTES.
>
> <u>Maggie May</u>. Weir, p. 112. Forebitter (chantey), often used at Capstan in Liverpool ships. SEE: Manifold 6,26, a mild text with tune giving chorus line 3: '<u>For you robbed so many sailors, and dosed so many whalers</u>;' <u>Rugby Songs</u> 94, <u>Snatches & Lays</u> (1973) 89 In 6:3 <u>cop</u>, pawn; <u>John L's</u>, long woollen underpants, so called from the well-known oldtime boxer, John L. Sullivan. <u>TUNE</u>: "Darling Nelly Gray."

"Maggie May," song collected from repertoire of Stan Hugill. Scanned copy from "Sea Songs," unpublished manuscript of Gershon Legman. Scan also contains some explanatory notes and stray marks. Personal copy sent by Judith Legman, October 10, 2014.

the marriage bed first from the exchange and turning instead to haystacks, boardinghouses, and women's rooms creates a backdrop for queer erotic exchanges that will become doubly queer in what they lead to. Sailing men are subordinated to the erotic drive and desire to the degree that they seek out spaces that subvert the sexual economy and hierarchy, which ultimately opens them up to a level of vulnerability. "Johnny, Come Down to Hilo" and "Can't Ye Dance the Polka?" engage the queer site of cuckoldry, an image to be discussed in greater detail in the next chapter; however, the repeated mention of nonprocreative spaces recognized for quick and ready sex generate a reading of sailing characters as aligned with sex that is unbound to expectations, certainly procreative ones.

These queer erotics relay at least the tension inherent in the songs, in which the sailing characters are seeking pleasure in its own right and remain unconcerned with social expectations tied to domesticity. Indeed, in showcasing the erotic act in these various places that are completely removed from the marriage bed, we see a seeking of pleasure that is in direct opposition to the marriage contract, embracing instead a relationship with erotic outlets that are entirely aligned with pleasure. The characters are meant to be viewed as those who eschew the virtues of the domestic man and seek instead sexual gratification in any way in which it presents itself. The marriage bed symbolizes fixity, settling into a domestic structure where the man would be required to fulfill the new qualities of a married man with a family.

Burton, in fact, notes that there was a distinct cultural change occurring during the nineteenth century, when Hugill likely encountered his songs, where sailing men were experiencing a new relationship with domesticity. Indeed, domesticity was tied to their ability to gain employment. Burton notes, "Images of physical power and scripts of primitive drives were drawn upon by seafaring men as they negotiated between the world of men at sea and the world shared with women on shore."[18] The songs from Hugill arguably register these tensions and instabilities as men navigated the changes between land and sea. In the domestic world of marriage and family, the husband would be viewed as an outsider of sorts, and the narratives of these songs perhaps register the pressures inherent in the demanding new world of domesticity as it collides with a particular sailing identity. That sailing identity, whether fully true or culturally manufactured (arguably a bit of both), encouraged a roving nature, even though historians have begun to recognize the sailing man's attachment to land, home, and family. In terms of sailing characters in these songs, seeking nonprocreative pleasures potentially assuages domestic demands and even liberates a man's identity, even his sexuality, so as to symbolically celebrate pleasure and flout a potentially constraining custom. Metaphorically, the quick and ready sex becomes a symbolic stolen pleasure that provides a taste of a life unencumbered by domestic responsibility. Attaching to what Burton calls the "Jack Tar myth," the hypermasculine, hypervirile sailing man perhaps provided space to celebrate a rough masculinity that was on its way out of fashion. The deliberate turning away from the marriage bed and noting sex that is quick and completely divorced from domestic spaces indicate at least an oppositional relationship with conventional expectations.[19]

Underneath these expressions of quick and ready sex lurks the shifting nature of sexuality. Queer orifices and queer spaces underscore the liminality of sex and eroticism, which align with other unstable identity structures that court the sailing man. These instabilities are registered through nautical metaphors used to articulate and explore the sexual scenarios and wed the pleasures of sex with the indeterminacy of the sea, bringing further to light a liminality of sexual expression—something that is already a shifting construct.[20] Sex becomes a place that is unmoored, like the ship adrift at sea, which is itself a symbol of queer realities. Within each of the songs, the main way through which the sailor penetrates the sexual object is often queer in its deployment, lending to the reading that the main focus is sex in and of itself and not a sex act tied to any particular expectation of category, especially procreation. The penetrative act of sex in songs of warning, and indeed throughout many of the songs in the Hugill repertoire, is often glossed by images like "I caulked her seams," "stove his toggle up her ol' deadeye," "into her paint-locker I stuck me jibboom," or "shoved it up her hatch."[21] In any of these phrases, it is possible to read the erotic focal point as either the anus or the vagina, rendering the lines not only open to interpretation but, more importantly, queer, interchangeable, and purely focused on pleasure. Readers look on as the sailing character in "Ratcliffe Highway" "fired into her stern-port a filthy discharge" to complete his intentions, but the means by which he arrives at his sexual crescendo is without any real connection to a specific category or, arguably, even a place on the body.

Using sailing jargon and images of the sailing life specifically function to separate sailing men from those who are outside of this identity construction. Burton notes, "The customs and rituals of an 'old-fashioned' seamanship raised their consciousness of what they shared and what distinguished them from landsmen," which attaches to the reading of certain sailing metaphors as capturing an old sense of sailing masculinity that championed hard men who kept softer domesticity at arms' length.[22] In "Ratcliffe Highway," in fact, the entire song is relayed using nautical metaphors in place of both the female and male characters, and the sexual encounter becomes opaque through the symbolic masking. The sex act is described as follows: "She clew'd up her skirts, boys, we had much sea-room / I raked her from forard [sic] wid a greasy jibboom. / Then I manned me gun an' I caught her at large," right before the "filthy discharge." The erotic act is not masked enough that it is completely elided, but the nautical metaphors succeed in queering the experience for it is unclear where the discharge is deposited except for the vague "stern-port." Additionally, the "jibboom" and his "gun" are trained to "catch her at large," where "her" is understood both as a woman and a ship. Where the character manages to "catch" the object, whatever "she" may be,

RATCLIFFE HIGHWAY

COME all ye young seamen an' listen ter me,
I'll sing ye a song all about the high seas.
Now it 'tain't very short nor it 'tain't very long,
'Tis of a Flying Fish sailor jist home from Hong Kong.

    Singing, too-relye-addie, too-relye-addie,
    Singin' too-relye-addiee, aye too-relye-ay!

Oh, as I wuz a-rollin' down Ratcliffe Highway,
A flash-lookin' packet I chanct for to see.
Of the port that she hailed from I cannot say much,
But by her appearance I took her for Dutch.

Her flag wuz three colours, her mast-head wuz low,
She wuz round at the counter and bluff at the bow :
From larboard to starboard an' so sailed she,
She wuz sailin' at large, she wuz runnin' free.

She wuz bowlin' along with the wind blowin' free,
She clew'd up her tawps'ls an' waited for me.
I fired me bow-chaser, the signal she knew,
She backed her main-tawps'l an' for me hove to.

I hailed her in English, she answered me clear,
I'm from the Black Arrow, bound to the Shakespeare.
So I wore ship wid a, What d'yer know!
I passed her me hawser an' took her in tow.

(In a snug little corner, oh soon we did moor,
I bought me some rum for this young Highway whore.
She told me her fancyman wuz at sea for a spell,
So I gave her me flipper an' we wuz both bound to Hell.)

I tipped her me flipper an' took her in tow,
An' yard-arm to yard-arm away we did go.
She then took me up to her lily-white room,
Into her paint-locker I stuck me jibboom.

She clew'd up her skirts, boys, we had much sea-room,
I raked her from forard wid a greasy jibboom.
Then I manned me gun an' I caught her at large,
Fired into her stern-port a filthy discharge.

```
Ratcliffe Highway -2-


We closed alongside, boys, I hauled in me slack,
I busted me bobstay -- she busted her crack.
Now me shot-locker's empty, me powder's all spent,
Me gun needs repairin', it's choked at the vent.

She then dropped her courses, I lashed up and stowed,
I gave her some shillings 'fore I left her abode.
But it 'twarn't quite enough, boys, she wanted some more,
She cursed me an' called me a son-o'-a-whore.

She blazed like a frigate, at me she let fire,
Oh nothing could stem, boys, that Irish tart's ire.
She kicked me, she farted, she spat in me jaw,
An' I beat retreat through her open back-door.

I've fought with the Russians, the Prussians also,
I've fought with the Dutch and with Johnny Crapaud,
But of all the fine fights that I ever did see,
She beat all the sights o' the heathen Chinee.

Now all ye young sailors, take a warnin' I say,
Take it aisy, me boys, when yer down that Highway,
Steer clear o' them flash gals on the Highway do dwell,
Or they'll take up yer flipper an' yer soon bound to Hell !

                              Sailing Ship Shanties, 1925-1956
```

"Ratcliffe Highway," song collected from repertoire of Stan Hugill. Scanned copy from "Sea Songs," unpublished manuscript of Gershon Legman. Scan contains some stray notes and marks. Personal copy sent by Judith Legman, October 10, 2014.

is open to interpretation but is clearly not meant to be a procreative space. Note the use of war metaphors, too, which was discussed above in terms of military cadences and other songs from all-male singing traditions that are employed so as to create a rough masculinity.

Chasing Women Left Me "Gettin' a Knot on Me Ol' Jibboom": The Vulnerable Male Body

Though the narratives of pleasure that open the songs are titillating and attach to cultural renderings of the early modern sailor as cavalier and pleasure seeking, the main purpose of the songs is to *warn* listeners of the dangers that are all around them. Illustrative of these warnings is the ominous closing line from the "The Liverpool Judies":

> Now all ye young sailors, take a warnin' from me,
> Keep a watch on your drinks when the liquor is free,

> An' pay no attention to runner or whore,
> Or your head'll be thick and your prick'll be sore.

This line captures the male singer as a benevolent figure whose intentions are to relay to those listening what might happen were one to embrace the life of pure pleasure and frivolity. Whereas the primary narratives articulate the Jack Tar myth as he carouses port towns and violently infiltrates orifices wherever and whenever he pleases, the warnings articulate the vulnerability of the sailing man as he embraces an identity that is both unstable and also potentially destabilizing. What the attending warnings concretely articulate is that not all women are as they appear and sex in port carries immediate consequences, and the misadventures of the narrators are meant as cautionary tales to protect the delicate balance of male power and agency in the face of encounters and obstacles that are sometimes out of their control.

What is symbolically suggested in these warnings is the vulnerability of the body and the liminality of identity constructs. When sailing characters clash with objects they desire or when they fulfill social constructs of their sailing masculinity, they often find their bodies broken and bent at the end of the encounters. What these narratives demonstrate is that constructions of masculine identity are far from absolute and arguably capture the shifting masculine structures that were evolving on land. These destabilizing and potentially alienating realities are registered in the juxtapositions between agentive sexual pursuits and the injuries that are visited on the bodies of sailing characters. Joanne Begiato notes, "Although all representations of heroic, noble, or dignified labour used manly muscular arms and bodies, the reality of excessive hours of toil and unsafe workplaces and practices was that workers' bodies frequently failed."[23] These same paradoxes arrive in the songs from Hugill, in which the presentation of self is virile and masculine, but the façade also registers the opposite: the potential for failure, disfigurement, and emasculation.

The songs of warning evoke what Foucault recognized of policing structures generally. In the songs from Hugill, listeners and singers look on as penises are bent, broken, or suffer debilitating venereal disease; in each, the affliction rends sexual function from the sailing men and thereby disciplines their bodies after pursuing gratuitous sex. Sailing men are also subjected to loss of money and freedom at the hands of prostitutes and crimps. Pain and suffering, delivered to male bodies and male psyches, especially directly after sex acts, appear akin to what Foucault recognized of punishment and discipline:

This means that the "pain" at the heart of the punishment is not the actual sensation of pain, but the idea of pain, displeasure, inconvenience—the "pain" of the idea of "pain." Punishment has to make use not of the body, but of representation. Or rather, if it does make use of the body, it is not so much as the subject of pain as the object of a representation: the memory of pain must prevent a repetition of the crime, just as the spectacle, however artificial it may be, of a physical punishment may prevent the contagion of a crime.[24]

Narrative inclusions of pain, buttressed against the pleasure lately enjoyed, actively function in a similar fashion to discipline listeners into recognizing the potential trouble with not recognizing the limits or with testing boundaries.

The songs capture, especially in their juridical punishments, the cultural growing pains of living in two distinct worlds: the mythic representations of Jack Tar and the new push toward domesticity. For the period, men were experiencing a shifting masculine reality where the hypermasculine male was all at once a beacon of identity to reproduce, as Begiato notes, an identity to eschew or grapple with, as Burton recognizes, and a means to fight back against the strictures put in place that policed the emerging sense of the breadwinner.[25] The sailing characters in Hugill's songs, especially when they meet with juridical policing mechanisms, embody the cultural reality that men were embroiled in during the industrial age and even later into the First World War. The sailing characters who experience the pain and punishments after unburdened sex become the spectacles that Foucault outlines here, and their suffering is symbolically attached to both the struggle to meet competing expectations of manhood and the real pain likely felt when one fails to meet with any of these expectations. Their bodies are the focal point of the warning and communicate both the desire to follow well-trodden paths and the confusing and potentially liminal new reality that they were wrestling with.

In the case of the sailing character in "Sacramento," he literally becomes a spectacle both by his injured body being laid bare and through literally being objectified and humiliated by an attending male character. The lines below relay a sailing character who is literally placed on display, and the pain inflicted on his body is held up as a cautionary tale to ensure, it is to be assumed, that others will be so in fear of encountering the same fate that they will turn away from the temptations of women like the "one with the curly locks" and perhaps discipline themselves to the new manly expectations that curtailed sexual exploits outside of marriage. It is clear that the man is made out as a spectacle:

Off to the doctor I did go,
Prick an' balls I had to show.

In came the nurse with a mustard poultice,
Chapped it on but I took no notice,
In came the doctor with a bloody big lance:
Now, young sailor, I'll make yer dance.

"Sacramento" engages multiple levels of spectacle, taking aim at both body and manhood through the various characters that engage with the inflicted sailor. The humiliation related has to do with subordination of the sailing man to the doctor and even the nurse. His penis is the target of this humiliation, the spectacle we are to view, and he is subordinated through the venereal disease, the infliction of the lance to release the pressure from the chancre, the focus on the "dance" initiated by the lance-wielding surgeon, and also through the almost forgotten application of the mustard poultice.[26] The gendered nurse (likely female), for her part, infantilizes and also erotically teases the sailor despite him taking "no notice." In their interaction, the injured penis is doctored by the nurse, a transaction heavy with erotic suggestion and also power, but serving the same purpose of creating spectacle as the disease and the lance. Cures and ailment become one in this juridical situation.

It is worth noting that Margaret S. Creighton argues how "caging women up meant keeping them, of course, but it also meant restraining them. Women were an ascending power in the nineteenth century, not only in the home, but through church and social organizations, in the world at large."[27] Caging women in song, like the nurse who patronizes the ailing seamen, functions as an image that both captures masculine failure and feminizing, but it also gestures at the real cultural change in the nineteenth century that would have actually subordinated the man to his female counterpart. These examples are, thus, not only accessing social scripts but also, in doing so, disciplining the bodies and minds of those listening to follow the patterns that might keep them out of the path that would lead them toward suffering similar to that of characters. Scenes of injury to the penis access memories of pain or stir registration of potential pain and, in turn, discipline the listening audience and, arguably, the characters back to accepted forms of performance that would protect them from such encounters. They would become what Foucault calls "docile bodies," falling in line with gendered script in fear of the pain and humiliation displayed.

The penis in the songs of warning is in a near constant state of conflict between desire and the boundaries of culture. Indeed, the penis is the nexus of reality and symbolism.²⁸ A main-narrative scene in "Blow the Man Down" captures this argument elegantly:

> [The characters] came to a haystack, the maid she wuz shy,
> They backed an' they filled, Jack's jibboom stove high.
>
> The haystack capsizèd [*sic*], Jack's jibboom got bent,
> Straw hung from her arse-ole, her thing wuz all rent.

Within these two stanzas, it is possible to see the first blush of desire seeking nothing except for ready pleasure. The rush to a haystack instead of a bed underscores the desire for immediate gratification, and the vague "backed and filled" suggests a shared ("they") sexual experience not tied to procreative sex nor to a specific orifice. This scene obviously supports the unbound pleasure that each of the songs begins with and appears to support Burton's observation that sailor's sought an identity of which "libidinal energies could be reclaimed for pleasure and enjoyment against the persuasion of political economy to harness them to work"; however, the immediate punishment comes swiftly, painfully, and with a clear juridical message.²⁹ Quick, thoughtless, pleasure-driven sex and sex that is not tied to procreative outcomes carry only pain and damage to what has been repeatedly cited as the seat of male identity.

In fact, the entire song is predicated on this one heedless act as the song closes with a warning worth expressing in its entirety:

> Now all ye young sailors that round the Horn sail,
> Don't take a young milkmaid away from her pail.
>
> Don't ye try an' fuck her a-top of a stack,
> Or ye might break yer jibboom, like did our poor Jack.
>
> Look for a flash-packet what's got a nice bed,
> Leave milkmaids to hayseeds, that's what poor Jack said.

In the closing stanzas of the song, the juridical model is distinct and focused directly on key aspects of masculine identity and expectation. The singing narrator expressly warns against neglecting masculine duties of work, symbolically tied to taking "a young milkmaid away from her pail," urges eschewing quick and ready sex for fear of encountering the same painful outcome,

BLOW THE MAN DOWN

OH, where are ye goin' to, my pretty maid?
<u>WAY-ay</u>, <u>BLOW</u> the <u>man</u> <u>down</u>!
Oh, I'm goin' a-milkin', kind sir, she said,
<u>GIMME</u> some time to <u>BLOW</u> the <u>man</u> <u>down</u>!

Oh, have ye a sweetheart, my pretty maid?
I'm lookin' for one, kind sir, she said.

Then may I come with ye, my pretty maid?
Well yes, since ye axed me, sir, she said.

But I guess yer a bad un, kind sir, she said,
Yer out for to fuck me, but don't wanter wed.

Well, well, sez bold Jackshite, me thoughts ye have read,
Let's look for a haystack, 'twill make a fine bed.

Jack took her in tow, an' away they did go,
The bull with a hard-on, the cow sayin' No!

They came to a haystack, the maid she wuz shy,
They backed an' they filled, Jack's jibboom stove high.

The haystack capsized, Jack's jibboom got bent,
Straw hung from her arse-ole, her thing wuz all rent.

So he left her a-sittin' with her bloomers all torn,
He fucked her an' left her, that maid all forlorn.

Now all ye young sailors that round the Horn sail,
Don't take a young milkmaid away from her pail.

Don't ye try an' fuck her a-top of a stack,
Or ye might break yer jibboom, like did our poor Jack.

Look for a flash-packet what's got a nice bed,
Leave milkmaids to hayseeds, that's what poor Jack said.

<u>Sailing Ship Shanties</u>, 1927-1956.

"Blow the Man Down," song collected from repertoire of Stan Hugill. Scanned copy from "Sea Songs," unpublished manuscript of Gershon Legman. Personal copy sent by Judith Legman, October 10, 2014.

and instead pushes for the listeners to seek accepted and expected modes of pleasure that adhere to male identity structures.

Sex and work, in terms of Burton's research, were key anxieties that attended the early modern sailing man during the industrial age. As social and economic changes were occurring and impacting sailing men's ability to find work, sailing men found a relationship between and among work, identity, domesticity, and duty. Begiato, too, demonstrates that the nineteenth century was a time during which there was an express focus on tempering the desires and libidinal energies of working-class men. She writes that "unmanliness was imagined through such unrestrained appetites and feelings, and their impact upon bodies, minds, morals, and, therefore, gender" and goes on to discuss how vices such as heavy drinking, masturbation, and seeking general unbound pleasure were marks of a man out of control and therefore to be avoided.[30] Such unbound pleasure was used as a model in cautionary pamphlets to warn others against the vices that would render them weak, effeminate, and unmanly.

The paradox that Begiato recognizes, though, is that men were also expected to enjoy these same pleasures, within reason, in order to demonstrate their masculinity. The bent penis is a spectacle of suffering, held up for the listening audience to consume and assimilate and, potentially, for them to recognize as the desire that could conceivably confirm their masculine identity but also upend it. This spectacle maps onto what Begiato is identifying in nineteenth-century Britain, where the purely pleasure-driven individual (almost always working class) found his way toward injury, death, and disgust and was also held as a literal spectacle to his fellow men as a cautionary tale.[31] Sex followed swiftly by such an incredible and likely lasting pain is meant to discipline and order responses back to "safe places," where sex might not undo the symbol of masculine identity. For the sailing man in the nineteenth century, this could either translate to the ship or his landbound home or, as Begiato notes, a culturally supported ideal of masculine comportment.

"Blow the Man Down" is not the only song that directly targets the penis as a site of punishment, where the penis itself is bent in the process of illicit sex and rendered a spectacle of warning. The penis is the receiver of any number of calamities that are directly tied to the illicit and unbound sexual desires and pursuits of the character, sometimes becoming unusable in subsequent sexual encounters because of the severity of the injury. In several additional songs, the penis is bent, burned off, or damaged in such a way that it renders the act of sex impossible in the short and, potentially, long term.

"The Fire Ship (II)" concludes with the warning "Steer clear of lofty fire ships, for to me they brought bad luck, / For one burnt off me ol' Jibboom, an' now I cannot fuck." The song accesses the image of historical fire ships, actual wartime naval strategies where a ship was set ablaze and launched toward an enemy ship, and in the use of this nautical metaphor, the song further underscores the juridical mechanisms aimed at curtailing free and wayward sex. Casting the woman as a fire ship and the sailing man as the "enemy ship," the metaphor employs language of war, raising the act of sex to a battle ground between man and

```
                    THE FIRE SHIP (II)

. . . We went up to her bedroom, an' soon all sail was stowed,
Upon the brassbound bedstead, boys, to the bitter end we rode.
I caulked her seams with red-hot pitch, which made her jump for joy,
She cried that I had just the gun for a fire ship to employ.

Now all ye bully sailormen that sail the Western Sea,
An' all ye jolly 'prentice lads, a warnin' take from me:
Steer clear of lofty fire ships, for to me they brought bad luck,
For one burnt off me ol' jibboom, an' now I cannot fuck.

                         Sailing Ship Shanties, 1930-1956.
```

"The Fire Ship (II)," song collected from repertoire of Stan Hugill. Scanned copy from "Sea Songs," unpublished manuscript of Gershon Legman. Scan contains some stray marks. Personal copy sent by Judith Legman, October 10, 2014.

woman, genitals and venereal disease, control and disempowerment. Readers are not clued into the identity of the woman until the sex act is complete: after "I caulked her seams with red-hot pitch, which made her jump for joy, / She cried that I had just the gun for a fire ship to employ." Attention is immediately drawn to the comparison between a gun on a fire ship and the penis of the sailing character, collapsing the two so as to become one and the same, as has been observed in other all-male song. The gun on a fire ship would be consumed by flames and likely destroyed in the process of attacking an enemy ship; thus, the metaphor primes the reader to imagine the imminent demise of the sailor's seat of pleasure. By the end, that catastrophe is realized when the sailor admits that his penis has been "burnt off" and he has lost his ability to seek further sexual gratification. Indeed, he has lost his penis entirely.

In "Ratcliffe Highway," the sailor character warns, "Me gun needs repairin', it's choked at the vent" after sex with "a flash-lookin' packet." Similarly, in "Maggie May," the sailing character wakes to several ailments, most importantly here he finds that his "prick [is] all bent an' broke." Damage to the penis takes on a level of castration anxiety, where the seat of masculine pleasure and identity is literally and figuratively removed, forcing the characters and, arguably, readers to come to terms with the reality of masculine vulnerability and how open they are to damage when they pursue sex and pleasure that is unmoored. Judith Butler, in *Bodies That Matter*, contends, "Castration would not be feared if the phallus were not already detachable, already elsewhere, already dispossessed; it is not simply the spectre that it will become lost that constitutes the obsessive preoccupation of castration anxiety. *It is the spectre of the recognition that it is always already lost, the vanquishing of the fantasy that it might ever have been possessed—the loss of the nostalgia's referent.*"[32] Butler emphasizes the final sentence here and her view of specters and their attached anxieties gesture at the specter of loss I see conjured in the space of the songs. The specter, in Hugill's songs, appears as a means to discipline and police bodies back in line with expected masculine performance. Lurking beneath unbridled hedonism are painful reminders of delicate masculinity, and these suggestions urge the need for vigilance in the face of temptation. Heedless seeking of pleasure can damage the seat of masculinity to the point that the once agentive man becomes the subordinated other, even feminized.

Venereal diseases, as a juridical object, are also important for the ways in which they directly impact a male character's ability to perform his masculine sexual duties and become a mark on his identity as a male out of order. According to Raymond Stephanson, "Its diseases, too—chancres, lues, gleets, stranguries, priapisms—were easily converted into social and moral tokens, evidence of the failure of masculine will, of social or political immorality, or even a national decline," which demonstrates that the penis ravaged by venereal disease, bent in the process of sex, or otherwise rendered impotent is one that is out of order and therefore counter to masculine expectations, something that an actor would want to avoid.[33] Images of damaged and poxed penises create the conundrum of whether it is worse to fall out of line through pursuing pleasure in its own right or to receive the painful discipline that punctuates such acts. In "Sacramento," the singer makes clear that he is not able to engage with women until he is "well an' free from pain," underscoring the notion that the penis damaged by venereal disease is one that renders the man incapable of fulfilling his masculine expectations of penetrative sex. A similar idea is relayed in "The Fire Ship (II)" when the singer belts out "one burnt off me ol' Jibboom, an' now I cannot fuck," which shows that the fire ship, a woman, discharged a venereal disease so awful that the sailing character was not able to use his penis again.[34]

Similarly, in "Sacramento," readers watch as the sailor is asked to bare his naked body, submit to the gentle prodding of a nurse (his only comfort), and accept the pains delivered by the surgeon and, finally, the embarrassment of paying for the entire affair by "gettin' a knot on me ol' jibboom." The narrative of injury relays that "in came the doctor with a bloody big lance: / Now, young sailor, I'll make yer dance," which suggests that the surgeon gleefully punctures the knot with the enormous lance. The lance and the man's penis are likely meant to be compared. The phallic imagery of the lance articulates that the surgeon is now in a position of dominance, wielding the phallic object toward the subordinated and injured penis, and the poor sailor is not able to use his member because of both the venereal disease and the new injury created by the lance.

The myriad images of injured sailing men as they are juxtaposed against other characters place in stark relief a comparison between dominant and subordinate figures. Indeed, through the injury to the seat of male identity, the sailing characters in songs of warning become the subordinated figure they often appear to distance themselves from. With an injured penis that no longer works, the sailing figure becomes feminized and othered, and the characters who stand before them wielding poultices, lances, or even their money (as will be clear later) rise as more agentive and masculine than the suffering sailor figure. The warning produced in the songs is one that cautions against the potential reality that heedless following of desire or pleasure may force the unhappy character into the realm of not being able to fulfill erotic expectations in the future. As Stephanson captures, the penis damaged by venereal disease to the point where it cannot be used is a readily apparent symbolic character that captures this "failure of masculine will." The sailing character is thus meant to show that men are expected to pursue their erotic desires but only to the point that they can control and only as is regulated by social norms. Otherwise, it is possible to sacrifice one's own masculine identity on the altar of pleasure, losing power and status in the process.

Punishments directed at the penis create a symbolic means through which to return listening audiences back to expected masculine comportment, but they also gesture at the vulnerability of the body and the man himself. Harnessing and deploying fear of castration, both actual and symbolic, communicate the reality and vulnerability of male power and identity. Through the turgid image of the penis, singers, listeners, and even readers are forced to focus on the paradoxical power and vulnerability of the organ and, by extension, the man, and those engaging with the image are disciplined back to expectations through the recognition of what might befall them. What the penis does and what happens to the penis are each integral to understanding the inherent push and pull of unbound desire and juridical reprimanding: it places the man himself in a liminal space between them both, and the nexus, literally and figuratively, is the penis. It is not only that the physical member might be impacted, as castration anxiety conjures in its literal sense, but also that the figurative idea of manhood might be assaulted, destroyed, or castrated.

Creighton appears to gesture at what is occurring within the space of song: "Seafaring represented, for many men, the means of owning a home with a wife and children, but it also represented a way to avoid living there."[35] There is a push and pull between land and sea and duty and desire, and the sailing man and his penis appear at the nexus of these separate drives and expectations. When some of the narratives urge that listeners should "look for a flash-packet what's got a nice bed" or "steer clear o' them flash gals" or even not to "ever fool around wid gals, yer safer off Cape Horn," the subtext is that such quick, ready, and always inherently non-procreative sex leads to unwanted and painful maladies. The "nice bed," in fact, directly suggests that the listener should look to finding women that are meant for procreation and long-lasting heteronormative coupling as balms against the pain described.[36] Through the lines of song, the warnings point listeners to the painful realities of the sexual scenarios and to ultimately discipline their bodies back to accepted modes of gender and sexual performance, but the songs also register an attachment to older forms of masculinity of which agentive sexuality and virility are paramount, sometimes to the detriment of the man himself.

"Goodbye to the Gals and Our Money as Well": Women Usurp Power

Vacillation in the songs isn't only registered in the competing drives of pleasure and domesticity; it is also symbolically relayed through narrative situations in which the gender order is subverted, demonstrating the tenuous hold on power and authority where gender is concerned. In fact, in this subversion more than anywhere else, the liminality of categorical gender is registered. Sailing characters are seen, at least in the beginning of songs, to act in ways facilitated by adherence to categorical gender, but the later narrative situations reveal a penchant for men deferring to the women they once sought. In the songs, men often follow women toward erotic pleasure, women are in control of the sexual experience, and punishment for the transgressive sex acts are associated with the women whom the sailors follow. Sailing characters note that they follow as they "let her take me line abreast in tow" or "she then took me up to her lily-white room" or even "up the stairs we climbed." Each of these lines suggests that the sailor subordinates himself to the desires of the woman he is pursuing. The sailors follow "like a farmer's clod" ("Maggie May") toward the different places for sex and appear to eschew the heteronormative scripts that would expect men to be in control of the sexual encounter.

Gender theorist R. W. Connell maintains, in *Masculinities*, that "heavy manual work calls for strength, endurance, a degree of insensitivity and toughness, and group solidarity. Emphasizing the masculinity of industrial labor has been both a means of survival, in exploitative class relations, and a means of asserting superiority over women."[37] Working-class men, a group to which the sailing characters of these songs belong, are viewed as masculine actors who not only boast the strength and power glossed above but also, and more importantly, execute their relationships with the othered, primarily women, in such a way that their dominance and control is paramount. Chanteys from Hugill's repertoire sometimes run counter to this sketch of working-class masculinity, which suggests an admission of the true instability of gender hierarchies and organizations. In the songs of warning, women leading men toward their sexual pleasure indicates a relationship with the erotic continuum in which male characters are willing to turn away from confining categorical expectations of control and order and move instead toward any means by which they can secure erotic release. Such a subversion of gender norms queers the opposite-sex erotic scene and potentially raises the subversive male character as a representation of what can occur in the event that one chooses to transgress the accepted order while seeking pleasure or, perhaps, registers the same cultural shifts recognized historically of which women were already usurping some masculine positions and upending old gender scripts within new rules of domesticity.

David Brandon Dennis notes a similar gender subversion as it relates to sailors and prostitutes in port in his study dealing with German merchant sailors during the period 1884–1914. He notes that the German sailor came to be viewed as something of a prodigal son, and "as a transnational figure, the prodigal son can be interpreted as a counter-image for a more stable, rooted 'German' ideal of manliness." When these mobile sailing men would succumb to the temptations on land, "the prodigal son threatened to undermine the patriarchal gender order."[38] It was this very gender subversion, as well as the sailor's cosmopolitan nature and reality, that precipitated interventions, such as warning manuals, that sought to bring German sailors back to their homeland and a distinct sense of masculine duty.

In a way, Hugill's song narrative sometimes reads akin to a warning manual as characters embrace masculine power and agency at the outset but articulate, through various encounters with women, that this position easily unravels. Many of the songs begin by describing female characters as "charmin' bitches," "flash-lookin' packet[s]," or "pretty maid[s]," among other descriptors that create a sensation that the women are beautiful, well formed, and positioned as sexually subordinate. Also, having the sailors describe the women from the beginning appears to generate a narrative power for the men as they are able take control of the women through naming them. "Bitches," "maids," and even the nautical term "flash-packet" suggest a subordinated status beneath the sailing character describing them. Hiding beneath these exteriors, however, are realities that narratively unseat masculine identity, subverting the assumed subordinated role through the venereal disease and control over the sexual economy. In seeking pleasure with the women in these songs, sailing characters render themselves vulnerable and confront the reality that their conception of gendered frameworks is unstable and easily altered, sometimes within the space of a moment. That quick slip is evident in songs like "Blow the Man Down," in which the maid is cast as demure and subordinate and the sailing man, agentive, and then the quick capsizing of a haystack leaves the two characters hierarchically equal.

Gender transgression does not only happen in terms of linguistic denotations and realities of characters; it also occurs through the use of nautical metaphors that function to underscore the unstable quality of gender performance. Distinctly, such metaphors permit the space for female characters to best their male counterparts, usurping the position of power and threatening the performance of masculinity as it is expected. The first narrative stanza of "Ratcliffe Highway" reads:

> Oh, as I wuz a-rollin' down Ratcliffe Highway,
> A flash-lookin' packet I chanct [sic] for to see.
> Of the port that she hailed from I cannot say much,
> But by her appearance I took her for Dutch.

As noted earlier, the woman and ship are interchangeable, and this reading is supported by the next stanza, which describes all parts of the woman as if she were a ship. Such a narrative choice suggests a sliding in terms of gender performance where identity construction is not finite and is always in danger. In "Ratcliffe Highway," the woman goes from this "flash-lookin' packet" that the sailor follows for sex to "blaz[ing] like a frigate, at me she let fire, / Oh nothing could stem, boys, that Irish tart's ire" to the point where the sailor "beat retreat through her open back-door."[39] The woman as ship was fearsome enough that she vanquished a list of different nationalities the sailor had fought and sent him running from the room. Such a cowardly flight does not capture an agentive male character and instead casts the woman as a hellishly powerful figure that subordinated the sailor with her ire. The warning, similar to what Dennis outlines of German sailors and interventions meant to turn them back to their homeland, demonstrates that gender subversion and masculine failure are immanent in the face of such hellish and monstrous figures and that the sailing man must seek spaces of respite and safety to keep hold of gender constructions and protect their own vulnerable identities.

It is specifically female characters that function as the foils to agentive male characters, and they arguably force a recognition of unstable identity constructions. Female characters in these songs present, on the surface, as titillating and accommodating—the pinnacle of desirable women who privilege male desire and pleasure. Underneath, though, their motivations appear to leverage these presentations as an opportunity to combat male superiority and ultimately unseat male agency. Such a continuum between presentation and underlying motivation is apparent in "Maggie May" when the singer describes how "she wuz dressed in a gown so fine, like a frigate of the line, / An' I, bein' a sailorman, gave chase" just before the notorious Maggie May gets the character drunk and robs him, and he awakes the next morning with his "prick all bent an' broke." Within the space of an evening, the encounter between a sailor and a woman goes from heteronormative expectation, with the beautiful and willing woman and the man primed to chase as he is wont, to a very different reality in the morning: the woman has robbed the man of not only his money but also his manhood. How his penis broke and by whom is open to speculation, but it suggests that he was not in control of the scenario enough to protect his most precious organ. In this setting, reminiscent of other experiences in songs of warning, expectations are subverted, and identities slide in ways that run counter to the accepted script. The male character is subordinated to the wiles of Maggie May—even though she is eventually imprisoned later in the song—and is left dominated by her in both mind and body. He laments, "A week it passed away, an' in me bunk I lay, / Accursin' the day that I'd met Maggie May" for she not only robbed him, injured his penis, and fled but also left him with venereal disease. Maggie May still haunts him a week after engaging with him.

In this narrative, too, the female character presents, at first, as beautiful and as one adhering to the gender script. By the end, she has revealed that she is scheming, and her hidden identity is one that ultimately impacts the identity of the sailor. These characters morph and change and impact the sailing characters in ways that explode notions of categorical identity and demonstrate the dual quality of identity that plays out even outside of fictitious situations.[40] In terms of lived experiences for sailing men, the turn to domesticity undoubtedly forced a collision between a man's sense of position in the world and the new expectations he met at home.[41] Perhaps the true reality of identity is predicated on both parts of the continuum and on neither: the beautiful maid with the venereal disease and the hypermasculine sailor a step, or slip, away from losing his hold on that performance. It is possible that the vitriolic language used to describe women in these songs of warning serves as a release for this tension of recognizing that categorical performance—that is, maintaining the façade—is an impossible venture. The wielding of a term like "whore" or aligning women with inanimate objects like the ship, which is arguably driven and therefore controlled by men, demonstrates the process of linguistic subordination needed as a tool for regaining masculine agency in the face of vacillation between expectations and reality. There is an anger at the disconnect and the potential disempowerment that lies at the bottom, but its arrival also heralds a recognition—an admission—that the sailing character and his identity are not as different from the two-faced Maggie May, among others.

In terms of language, these female characters appear to control the deployment of their erotic capabilities and even, in at least one example, control their own erotic enjoyment without the help of a man. Indeed, their erotic potentials almost seem more hypererotic and powerful than the men who seek them out throughout all the songs of warning. Women, like the one in "Can't Ye Dance the Polka?," state "if you want to dip yer wick, ye'll have to rock 'n' roll," tempting sailors by voicing their own sexual desires and communicating that the sailor needs to act on her word immediately. She is structuring how the sailor reacts, orchestrating and controlling the erotic situation.

In other songs, the female characters are cast as sexually ready and willing, with songs like "Serafina" cataloging all of the erotic pleasures the titular character will perform, all of which appear in greater detail than the erotic actions of the sailing man seeking her promised pleasure. In "The Fire Ship (II)," the female character notes that the sailor "had just the gun for a fire ship to employ," suggesting that the sailor would be in service to her, the woman cast as a fire ship. The female character in "Johnny, Come Down to Hilo" takes complete control of her own erotic pleasure and does so without the aid of the man who looks on. We encounter the scene where "she'd just grabbed hold o' a piece o' plank, / Shoved it up her hatch (crack), an' gave herself a wank." In this description, the man is not required at all and is left out of the erotic economy, except in terms of scopophilic consumption. This female agency appears akin to what Kathleen Lubey discusses in terms of eighteenth-century pornographic texts, where "accounts of women's genital experience ... go so far as to fantasize a penetrative sexuality that excludes men altogether and, with them the inequitable subject positions that were sustained by eighteenth-century practices of heterosexuality."[42] Such acts, Lubey importantly remarks, reinscribe a level of power and agency for women, genitally, where before their generative organs were viewed as sites of male ownership, property, and privilege. Over and above those claims of ownership were the ways by which women were defined by their genitalia, in the eighteenth century and onward, especially when they had been penetrated. The women in "Serafina," "The Fire Ship (II)," and "Johnny, Come Down to Hilo" arguably contain what Lubey contends are "queer resistances," especially within heteronormative economies.[43]

Throughout each of these examples, it should be apparent that expected modes of opposite-sex couplings are subordinated to the seeking of pleasure, and readings of the different characters and scenes reveal a penchant for highlighting instability and queer realities. Pointedly, in terms of women taking on a more powerful and agentive role, sailing characters are subordinated and appear to eschew the expectation of masculine control in the sexual situation so as to achieve the pleasure they are seeking. They will, succinctly, do anything necessary, even if it is transgressing the gender script, to assuage their longings.

The Clash of Land and Sea:
Songs of Warning Embracing Liminality and Vulnerability

The queer spaces of these songs of warning and the juridical narrative elements that immediately collide with such hedonistic pursuits aid in creating space to consider how identity truly functions. Discipline and punishment happen when an actor falls out of line, and use of the spectacle disciplines the body to become what the social world expects. Songs register the confusion, frustration, vulnerability, and liminality of the actor: a man or a woman is policed from within and from outside, and they learn how to navigate the world so as to avoid pain, whether physical or emotional. Such categories and expectations are, however, arbitrary. I do not mean that they are arbitrary in that they do not matter—they are distinctly important, real, and often felt very deeply. What I mean by arbitrary is that they are categories that many queer theory scholars note as being changeable, needlessly constraining, and open to failure. What the songs reveal is something that is uniquely human, which is that on the path to locating desire, pleasure, and feeling good, we recognize the strong social

CAN'T YE DANCE THE POLKA?

AS I rolled down the Bowery one evening in July,
I met a maid who axed me trade : A Sailor John, sez I.

Then away, you Santee, my fair maid (dear honey),
Oooh ye New York gals, cayn't ye dance the polka ?
(Oooh ye New York gals, ye love us for our money!)

To a fancy store I took her, I did not mind expense,
I bought her two gold earrings, and they cost me fifteen cents.

Sez she, You Limejuice Sailor, now see me home ye may,
But when we reached her own back door, she unto me did say :

My fancyman's a Yankee, wid his hair cut short behind,
He wears a pair o' long sea-boots, an' he's bosun in the
  Blackball Line.

He's homeward bound tomorrow, an' he will want his 'ole,
So if you want to dip yer wick, ye'll have to rock 'n' roll.

So I grabbed her right and proper, afore her flash man docked,
An' up the stairs we climbed right smart, an' soon her snatch
  wuz cocked.

I rode her long an' hard boys, she wriggled like an eel,
An' when I rammed it home two blocks, this maiden sure did
  squeal.

When I awoke next morning, me head wuz sore as hell,
She'd hit me with the piss-pot boys, and skint me pay as well.

I wrapped me glad rags round me, and to the docks did steer,
I'd never court another maid, I'd stick to rum and beer.

I joined a Yankee blood-boat, and sailed away next morn,
Don't ever fool around wid gals, yer safer off Cape Horn !

Sailing Ship Shanties, 1928-1956.

"Can't Ye Dance the Polka?," song collected from repertoire of Stan Hugill. Scanned copy from "Sea Songs," unpublished manuscript of Gershon Legman. Personal copy sent by Judith Legman, October 10, 2014.

expectations that discipline us, but we also yearn for what we desire and cannot contain. The metaphoric way in which the songs of warning register this pressure is by the return to sites that have caused pain and also by pointing to unique seafaring tensions that communicate the battle between self and constraining categories. A return to sites of pain is a literal pushing back against the warnings that the songs engender, and this flippant return happens in only three of the selected songs, but there are also juxtapositions between land and water and façades colliding with reality that capture the same struggle between the projection and the reality. Indeed, in thinking about the duality of female characters, it might be possible to consider the mirror image of the man who is projecting a social front to the world but hides within himself a reality that does not meet social mandates. In all, there is an undulating movement back and forth, just like the sea.

Despite the painful realities that attend the sailing characters and even the recognition of the futility of agentive masculine performance, admissions in three of the songs of warning demonstrate a masochistic compulsion to return to the sites of pain and suffering. Where listeners are expecting to see a level of restraint after the cautionary tales relayed in the songs, they are instead treated to an almost willful turn back to the place of suffering. This vacillation between pleasure and pain, even in thinking about pain and pleasure being inextricably linked in the songs, aids in capturing a continuum of existence more broadly. Running toward pleasure in spite of pain represents a distinct combatting of the juridical model, a sliding back and forth between pain and pleasure in the service of gaining and maintaining power. There is power in speaking truth to the identity performance, and there is also power in literally choosing to return to sites of pain. In choosing to return to places where pain and pleasure are mingled, sailing characters deliberately transgress expectations, leaving the narratives to reveal the true complexity inherent in these songs (really, in all the songs from Hugill's unexpurgated repertoire). Such complexities are that life, identity, and desire can be policed from the outside and such policing can be recognized, but the body and the mind will seek the paths that are fulfilling, and this is often in spite of the disciplinary and juridical mechanisms that would attempt to persuade otherwise. When songs relate that "a gal's a gal, an' sailors is men, / I'll still be a-cock when I see another hen" and "when I'm well an' free from pain, / If I meet that whore, I'll fuck her again," there is a powerful wedding of both recognition and ownership and also of pain and pleasure: bound up within each is the admission that following pleasure is more powerful than convention but that both are necessary parts of negotiating identity.

A similar sentiment is relayed in "Johnny, Come Down to Hilo," in which the singer closes with "An' he swore he never would touch another bloomin' whore, / But was back on the job, next time he came ashore," which again highlights the intersection among recognizing the pain lately experienced, the reality that desire will pull with far more strength, and that all is bound up in navigating a world constrained by expectation and internal drive. The real relationship between the pleasure and the pain in the songs is ultimately a negotiation of sexual desire and juridical policing such that the actors are engaged in the constant process of recognizing expectations, being tempted by their own desires, and experiencing the pain of discipline but then choosing to return to their temptations even after incurring suffering. The songs

JOHNNY, COME DOWN TO HILO

NOW, who's bin here since I've bin gone?
Some big buck nigger wid a hard-on on.
    Johnny, come down to Hilo! oh, poor old man!
    Oooh! wake her! oh, shake her!
    Ooooh! wake that gal wid the blue dress on!
    When Johnny comes down to Hilo, oh, poor old man!

I won't wed a nigger, no I'm damned if I do,
He's got jiggers in his bollocks and his arse-ole too./
He travelled all around till he came to the shack
Where his Sally made a livin' oh, a-lyin' on her back.

Went upstairs an' he looked through a crack,
Sally lyin' on the deck with her mains'l aback./
She'd just grabbed hold o' a piece o' plank,
Shoved it up her hatch (crack), an' gave herself a wank.

He opened the door — she gave a little cry,
An' then he stove his toggle up her ol' deadeye./
He was hard as a rock, an' he soon was two-blocks,
But in five days' time he had a dose of pox.

An' he swore he never would touch another bloomin' whore,
But was back on the job, next time he came ashore.

<u>Sailing Ship Shanties</u>, 1930-1956.

"Johnny, Come Down to Hilo," song collected from repertoire of Stan Hugill. Scanned copy from "Sea Songs," unpublished manuscript of Gershon Legman. Personal copy sent by Judith Legman, October 10, 2014.

demonstrate that desire cannot be contained within finite categories, and the masochistic return relates to the human reality of transgression against essentializing categories. In this way, the songs act as release valves for sensations that arise in the near-constant state of negotiation: they are bodies in explosive and agentive movement.

Taken as a whole, the songs of warning underscore a vacillation between pleasure and pain, between expected masculine ideals and agentive women, and even between desire and warning. These vacillations ultimately attach, figuratively and literally, to sailing life and life on land. Indeed, the distinction between land and water appears as a sliding scale attached to pleasure and pain. Land and water become the symbolic vessels transporting the realities of gender and sexual performance inherent in songs treated in later chapters. The tension between land and water unquestionably exists in other songs located in the manuscript and are arguably a part of larger conversations concerning the sailing life, but what is poignant here is the inherently unstable quality of the water as it vacillates between extremes of danger and safety, the fixed and the in flux. Life on the high seas is certainly dangerous, more so than any other vocation, and that reality is hinted at in places where Cape Horn is mentioned as being a safer place than with a woman on land, but the songs of warning appear to predicate their narratives on the idea that land might be more dangerous in some respects. Water is tied to other sailing men, to worlds that are far from land (especially one's own land), to exoticism, to sensuality, to the capriciousness of Mother Nature.

The continuum between land and water is actually most poignant and telling in the absence of any warnings that speak to dangers on ship. This absence helps to support the vacillation I am suggesting because what is not said is something that immediately clashes with what is shared. The ship, at least in these songs, appears to be a place where someone might look back at land and consider the dangers he has weathered, learned from, and now from which he turns away. It is the moving away and looking back in hindsight that are important here because they suggest a movement, sometimes toward and sometimes away. If we are to think of the songs of warning as those tunes that detail the pitfalls of seeking that which is expected of you, it is possible to imagine the queer underpinnings of the songs as urging the listener to consider erring on the side of the unstable, pushing the listener back to the water, back to safety, and back, at least in terms of the song, to other men instead of women. The presentation of women as being housed on dry land and bringing with them all the diseases and maladies that might befall a hapless sailor carries the symbolic weight of demonstrating the pain and danger inherent in the absolute, in the firm.

Marriage and procreation, too, are tied to the land in a similar way as the temptations described. One's home carries with it loved ones, friends, and familiar places but clearly also enticements and enduring responsibilities, such as maintaining a family. Parts of the fixed and firm provide comforts and have a distinct draw, but they also seek to lure the sailing character away from his watery vocation and his sense of unbound freedom: he vacillates between desire and duty, the changing and the static. The warnings, thus, appear to recognize the continuum between these two spaces but also seek to rectify the pull and note that the interstices between land and sea are the spaces in which the characters appear most at home.

Just as will be clear in later songs, many of the songs of warning close with musings like "I joined a Yankee blood-boat, and sailed away next morn, / Don't ever fool around wid gals, yer safer off Cape Horn," which illustrates the collision of dangers on land and the safety of water. This line is particularly queer for the singer notes that one should not *ever* seek the arms of a woman and should instead look to the water for safety and comfort. The subtext is, at least in this line, that being at sea with other men is more advisable. The finite descriptions of venereal diseases, injury to the sexual organs, and thievery that befall the sailing characters set the stage for a reading of life in port as one that is fraught with danger but no less important to his construction of self. Juxtaposed against land is, of course, the waterway, which is not static. Though the waterways hold the same power and danger as land, if not more so, the watery expanse appears to provide some level of freedom and comfort that land does not. It is, thus, impossible to understand the full scope of identity unless one attends to the watery workspace always functioning in the background in the songs, which encourages a performance that is more in flux and adaptive.

The movements between land and sea perhaps capture the categorical confines of gender and sexuality more roundly than other narrative elements. In considering the manmade vessels of identity—the categories that attempt to capture and control lives—it is possible to see how they succeed only to a degree when they are brought to bear against nature and her powers of temptation. The vessel of identity is so much like the sailing vessel as it collides with the rages of the natural world. The choices of using sailing characters within the songs and deploying nautical metaphors to capture both the characters and the actions bring the realities of sailing life into sharper focus, but the symbolic quality of these characters and nautical metaphors does the most work in forcing us to consider the ways in which life on the water shapes the existences of even fictitious nautical characters. Pointedly, the unmoored nature of the sea and the reality of life at sea clashing with the finite realm of land does work on the characters, the actions, and the reading. Sailing life is predicated on unpredictability, the ability to shift tack at a moment's notice, and the reality that one should trust more in what cannot be controlled rather than what can be controlled. The controlling and ordering process of categorical structures is exactly what these songs appear to combat. In the songs, this shaping of identity takes it cue from things like Mother Nature, intangible qualities of masculine relationships, trappings of constrained life on a sailing ship, and the distant hope of seeing home or port. These aspects actively shape an identity structure that aligns with something like a continuum that vacillates and adapts to the realities that are not fixed or predictable. The nautical metaphors, then, are a path into understanding a sex and gender structure that defies attempts at holding it down or controlling it.

The critical way into these songs is to imagine them as floating vessels that herald identity formations predicated on the environment, relationship, and situation and not on finite categories that do nothing more than constrain and attempt to fix lived qualities of personhood, which are unpredictable and not easily controlled. It is possible to think about the finite as being impossible. There will always be a movement toward and away from expectations and realities. Such movements—leaving, returning, and sliding—attach to the idea that "the differences between how we are orientated sexually are not only a matter of 'which' objects we are oriented toward, but also how we extend through our bodies into the world. Sexuality would not be seen as determined only by object choice, but as involving differences in one's very relation to the world—that is, in how one 'faces' the world or is directed toward it."[44] Ahmed suggests that identity is not static: it moves and changes and evolves. I am advocating for water and land to rise as symbols of this same process of movement and evolution; indeed, both alter and change as they collide with one another as land erodes with the tides and water circulates and shapes itself against the hardened soil. In this conception, water and land may be considered as not completely separate but rather connected through the way in which they undulate and collide together. The continuum of pleasure and pain succeeds in this relationship, too, through the way in which they relate to one another and to the bodies impacted. Water and land, pleasure and pain, bodies and identities—they all vacillate between the hard or static and perpetual change and movement.

What songs of warning reveal is this continuum; they register the lived reality of "doing things right" and following "what feels good" as it brushes with disciplinary structures. They, at several turns, confirm categorical expectations of identity as well as register the queer nature of lived existence, which is unsettled and constantly in the process of negotiating sometimes impossible scenarios. If there is anything finite, it is the admission that the foundation is always shifting. Narratives, in these songs, appear contradictory because they relate a reality that was rife with contradictions, then as now. The outside covers the real self underneath. The songs of warning help to channel the frustrations of negotiating a world in which desire does not always meet with social expectations. The drive within cannot be disciplined and ordered despite the power of juridical forces that seek to ensure that very process, just like the façade of female characters.

The frictions and contradictions I have been teasing out up to this moment are captured best in the final line of "Blow the Man Down," where the singer urges listeners, after the damage to his penis, to seek "a flash-packet what's got a nice bed." The specific double suggestion is an integral part of hegemonic expectations of male identity structures, but it also captures the anxieties that exist beneath the surface. Covered by nautical metaphor, the singer urges that listeners dually seek out other women besides milkmaids and, specifically, "flash-packets," or ships, that have safe and comfortable lodging. Though the singer's penis was damaged in his encounter with a milkmaid, he does not discourage sex roundly. He pushes the listener to find pleasure and relief in the arms of any women other than milkmaids and, to some degree, suggests that the best place for safety and comfort is on ship with other men. Because the suggestion is vague and seems to slide in contradictory ways, it is possible to connect the line to larger implications within the songs of warning. There is, here as in other songs, a continuum and sliding scale between pain and pleasure, land and sea, identity and desire that evokes Ahmed's reading of the negotiation of gender and sexuality against the backdrop of identity-policing mechanisms. The body and the mind are at the mercy of competing sensations: the reactions that police and the desires that motivate. These are often "on a slant" and are very rarely as perfect as identity categories would like to appear.

Conclusion

Songs of warning and others in the manuscript force readers to collide with the liminality of the sea, and through that collision, readers are asked to confront other spaces that are just as liminal and unmoored. In the main premise of the warnings, the world of the sea and the realities of the land are rendered in stark opposition. All the maladies that befall a sailor occur when he is in port and not when he is at sea with his fellow sailors. This dichotomous narrative point serves to create a framework that reverberates across all the selected songs from the Hugill repertoire. Land is finite, real, tangible. There are realities there that are painful and ever present. The water is, alternately, a space more unmoored. The identity of the sailor might even be viewed as something as liminal as the sea. In his character, we are able to think about the complexities that play out in the everyday. In the songs of warning, seeking out queer pleasure and existing within the background of queer spaces produce a reading of identity as something unstable. It is capable of being policed, of course, but it is possible to fight back against such constraints. These songs rise as representations of release valves that push back against constrained and restrained identity expectations. They create curiosity about other spaces where writers and singers negotiate the projected image as opposed to the one buried within, though the one buried often betrays itself.

It is possible to imagine that the warnings in these chosen chanteys help to fashion an approach that tempers categorical representations of sexuality and gender to come in later songs and the chapters that focus on them. The warnings give pause to the reader that they should take note of the narratives that precede the warning; however, they also function to facilitate the if/then and us/them reality that is unstable, queer, and runs more in line with the idea of continuums rather than absolutes. Lived reality resides within the interstices between if/then, either/or, and us/them. The warning acts as a means through which to differentiate between the fantasy and the reality, but the deeper importance is that it symbolically captures the fantasy and reality. The symbolic fantasy is that the world is a place where categories work and actors fulfill the expected qualities of the categories that make sense to us. The symbolic reality is what the remainder of the book will show. We imagine both that the sailor characters are fulfilling the reality of sailing mores for the early modern era and that they are capturing the qualities of hypermasculine men and their sexual desires. Indeed, the early parts of the narratives create this storyline and recycle expected ideas of gender and sexual expression. The reality is visited both on the character and on the reader through painful warnings deployed at the end of the songs. The true warning to internalize is the fact that, in the face of the world itself—the real world with its venereal diseases, thieving women, crooked crimps, and enduring desires—the categorical ideal of life is met with challenges it cannot overcome. We can take heed of the warning only if we understand how that warning reverberates into the other narratives and into the wider social sphere.

CHAPTER 4

Heteronormative Economies and Shadow Admissions

It is apparent that gender and sexuality are unstable categories and that negotiating those categories can sometimes prove as liminal and dangerous as traversing the high seas. Just as songs of warning permit space to see unbound performances of sexuality and gender, juridical punishments, and flippant disregard of those mechanisms, other songs with a heteronormative framework recycle and deepen these same complexities. In songs where relationships between men and women take center stage, we can think about these characters as vessels that hold and carry some of the same elements captured in the songs of warning. This chapter, though, is tasked with complicating the conversation in order to highlight the clashes between the different vessels and what those clashes mean as they meet with notions of liminality. In the previous chapter, I considered liminality through thinking about negotiations of lax and fixed categories, but other songs in the manuscript demonstrate other layers that emerge in opposite-sex erotic clashes. In songs where men and women figure, it is clear that these characters function as release valves for performing identity, but this turn of the kaleidoscope's glass reveals that reactions to these constraining performances are anger, aggression, and further tension, much like other singing traditions. Just as it is clear that songs of warning suggest the failure of performance in the face of expectation, the same surfaces again as the investigation turns more deeply to specific characters. In this chapter, the liminalities are fleshier and more attached to the point that crystallized scenes register nuances generated through continued unbound desire and the frustrating negotiation of categories that appear always already pregnant with the possibility of failure. Venereal disease, injury, and some level of warning arrive again, but in this additional swathe of song, heteronormative economies grapple with performances that are much more unstable.

Women, in this chapter, arrive in sharper relief and, in the chanteys surveyed, rise as vessels through which to *imagine* feminine desire for men. They act as foils to masculine identity formation and appear as symbolic objects through which men attempt to regain some level of agency in their constrained environment. Alternately, the male characters are the legion "we" and function to stimulate collective identification, act as symbolic representations of the ideal male, and, if a lone man, open the interpretation of utilizing him as a means through which to create and situate a masculine performance. When these gendered vessels collide, however, their juxtapositions are just as, if not more so, illuminating and intricate than what has been made clear of the gestural push and pull between desire and category.

This chapter focuses discussion on eight songs located in the manuscript that register a wholly opposite-sex affiliated narrative quality. These songs are "Saltpetre Shanty," "Shenandoah," "Sally Brown," "Do Let Me 'Lone, Susan," "Cheerily Man," "Billy Boy," "John Brown's Daughter," and "Jinny Keep Yer Arse-'Ole Warm." Though there are other songs in the manuscript where opposite-sex scenarios are present, the songs listed do not hold the same focused warnings as those in chapter 3 nor the louder homoerotic subtexts that are the focus of chapter 5. The songs that are identified for discussion here are exclusively tied to sailors' interactions with women, making it prudent to deal with these narratives within this finite category. All the songs to be covered narratively focus on sailing characters' relationships with women, whether they are wives, girlfriends, prostitutes, or, in some specific situations, daughters to other characters. I will begin by attending to the singular characters of the songs and discussing how men and women arise as anonymous vessels through which to think about frustrating aspects of gender identity. I will then turn to a focused discussion of what arises when these vessels clash. Specifically, the songs betray a vulnerability and a liminality delivered through a particular joie de vivre, which articulates that even though the songs contain violence, vulnerability, desire, and disease, the reader is meant to view these narrative elements as similar or, perhaps, equal.

Men and Women as Vessels in Legman-Hugill Chanteys

Vessels hold and carry. They have the ability to contain, protect, and potentially transmit objects to other places or even periods in time. Even the sailing ship is a vessel that carries men, women, and mercantile objects from place to place. Historian Marcus Rediker expressly ties chanteys to vessels when he argues that "such songs, in all their variety, were the very vessels of a collective consciousness at sea, the media through which tars expressed their common fears, hopes, needs, and social realities. The bonds that slowly and fitfully emerged from shipboard cooperation often found their way into song."[1]

Though the vessel itself is an important object for what it does and achieves, it is often the material found inside of the vessel that holds even greater weight. In thinking about a vessel like the Egyptian canopic jar, the external vessel itself evokes the images of the gods sent to protect earthly remains and, as such, holds importance in and of itself. For the afterlife, however, the organs protected by the ornate jars are what remain as fragile and vital. Indeed, these vessels and what they contain have managed to be transported in time and space and propel stories and interpretations of a world now long gone. The image of the vessel is a powerful one in its application to the characters encountered in the songs surveyed in this chapter. Just as a vessel, like the Egyptian canopic jar, might carry and protect hidden items and catapult them into other times and spaces because of the impenetrability of the container, so too is it possible to imagine characters and images as vessels that transport protected messages and representations.

In speaking of male characters, Jeana Jorgensen notes (when discussing fairytale characters), "These men are literally a blank slate."[2] Her reading is similar to open vessels, to which we may apply any number of readings and foist any number of feelings, impressions, and anxieties. In the case of the chanteys from Hugill, the vessel-like quality of the male and female characters contains and transmits insights into complicated questions concerning the construction of gender and sexuality. The external vessel itself, which, in the case of the songs, arrives in the form of relatively anonymous male and female characters, holds just as much weight and narrative value as what it conducts within it.

The male characters encountered in the songs selected, though they are relatively two-dimensional, appear as agentive narrators, the collective "we," and sometimes, like in "Billy Boy," as named characters whose role is to respond to an anonymous narrator. Male characters are assumed to present and organize the narrative of every song. Though a gender is not assigned to any of the narrators encountered within each of the songs surveyed, the song narratives are fashioned in such a way that readers are meant to assume a controlling male perspective. The singular narrative voice operates as an anonymous vessel of masculine desire and experience as, through his mouth, the stories are shaped and relayed. He manipulates the viewer's experience as well as the positions and actions of the extant characters. His view shapes both what is encountered in the narrative and how viewers are meant to consume it. The anonymity of the narrator, his use of the collective "we," and the express focus on hypermasculine, hypersexual narrative render a reading of this male character as an authoritative and gendered structuring device. The collective "we" within the selected songs is imbued with impulses of hierarchical influence, individuality, to some degree, dismissive entitlement to those deemed subservient to them, and a registration of a working-class comradery predicated on the notions of work or duty as well as collective entitlement to the bodies of women, similar to other all-male singing traditions. Despite the fact that female characters present their own degree of agency, it is evident, based on the structure of the songs and the organization of the narratives, that the male characters are at least controlling the narrative framework and material and doing so with fellow men in mind. Though masculine power and agency are each important aspects of the songs surveyed, narratives reveal tacit recognition of vulnerability, subordination, and failure in the performance of masculine identity. Their clashes with the female characters function as the symbolic means through which we may continue to unravel the complexities of masculine identity performance within a constrained narrative event.

Compared against the male characters of the songs, female characters are deployed in complex and myriad ways. These characters are, at times, fleshier and more vivid than their male counterparts even despite what Jorgensen notes of male and female characters in fairy tales, who embody characteristics and constructions similar to that which is observed in the chanteys from Hugill. Directly, she opines that, in fairy tales, "male characters take up more space than female characters do. Their increased three-dimensionality is part of the construction of men as more substantial, more human, than women."[3] Their weightier quality is not surprising when considering their likely origin in an all-male, homosocial space; however, their function within the narrative is multiple and largely uninvestigated as of yet.[4] Whereas male characters fulfill the qualities we expect of them (agentive, bonded, flippant, and cavalier), the female characters pull double duty in the narrative and are really the heart and soul of the material deployed. All interactions begin and end with the male characters encountering certain women, and it is through these female characters that deeper symbolic qualities of the songs arise.

The women are largely anonymous, with the exception of a few women being referred to by name, with the vast number of female characters identified more often by their race, sexist epithets, and collective characteristics and desires. In a way, the female characters serve a roughly similar function to the sailor characters within the songs in that they are empty vessels that are ultimately filled with desires, fears, and experiences, but their identities are stamped onto their bodies through the language used to describe them. Very little is divulged of the women outside of their distinct tie to sex and genitalia or, at least in the case of "Billy Boy," to all the comforts expected of a wife to be, but these narrative elements are telling and evocative. On the surface, they are hyperbolic representations of the perfect woman for they are described as having penchants for nonnormative sex, are always ready for sex, openly desirous of sex, and long for the sailor and his epic manhood. Certain *types* of women are also privileged as those with whom to create a family and are juxtaposed against women with whom the only interest is copulation. What is markedly different from the male characters in the songs, however, is the fact that women are the focus of a disproportionate amount of sexual rage, general debasement, and almost flippant disregard for well-being outside of the few pockets of narrative that betray a level of female agency leveled to combat their subordination.

Male and female characters offer space through which to grapple with frustrating aspects of living gendered lives; the frustrations and gendered experiences are channeled into and through the vessel of the two-dimensional character. Small earmarks of identity help to at least differentiate characters within the songs; however, the more important work that they accomplish is arising as ciphers for felt tensions imagined of the sailing life, but they are also indicative of all human life. These songs ferry the echoes of the working-class past and usher indelible marks of the human experience. Funny and entertaining as they are, it will be clear that the humor masks a frustrating reality that life and manifesting one's sense of self are each painful and confusing, but perhaps what is best is to apply the sailing adage "grumble ye may, but go on ye must" to all of life's identity-forming processes.[5]

When Vessels Clash

One of the first and most evident frameworks that the male and female characters confirm is expected presentations of hypermasculinity, especially in terms of acting definitions of working-class men. Working-class song tradition conjures the expectation that one will encounter narratives of male prowess, virility, strength, and fortitude, even as it is delivered with humor and revelry. At first glance, all the songs selected for this chapter present some level of these hypermasculine, working-class expectations of manhood and manliness, just as was evident in songs of warning. Throughout, the songs register a degree of violence, especially sexual violence, examples of male authority and dominance, especially regarding those viewed as subordinate, and expected sexual voracity, desirability, and virility that access the male sense of agentive and dominate self. Through looking at linguistic and narrative violence, male control as it specifically aligns with ideas of the male gaze and voyeurism, and male desire as a narrative focus, initial readings of the chanteys in the manuscript appear to confirm working-class male identity such as what was outlined by R. W. Connell. Connell indicates, "Hegemonic masculinity can be defined as the configuration of gender practice which embodies the currently accepted answer to the problem of the legitimacy of patriarchy, which guarantees (or is taken to guarantee) the dominant position of men and the subordination of women."[6] Later, when elucidating women's agency in the songs, the instability of this identity will be laid bare. Just as songs of warning demonstrate gendered vessels that appeared fixed, similar characters function in this swath of songs to exhibit the vulnerable and shifting nature of the identities contained within such categorical coverings.

An expected working-class masculinity is apparent within the violence that emerges in many of the lines produced in song examples from Hugill. This violence is foremost apparent at the word and language level. Linguistically, the songs do violence to the women described by referring to them as *"putas"* (whores) and "barstards" in spaces like "Saltpetre Shanty."[7] Elsewhere, such as in "Shenandoah," women are directly referred to as "whores." The linguistically dismissive treatment of women is in service of narratively positioning these characters as less than the men describing them, and use of terms like *"putas"* or "barstards" demonstrate how language engenders violent and agentive masculine dominance. The sexually charged epithets are hurled at the women, shape the reading of them, and produce a framework in which the sailor is cast as superior to the lowly "whores" and "barstards" he encounters.

The song "Sally Brown" reproduces a similar linguistic violence when the narrator describes the titular character as "a big buck [n----r]," using the pejorative term for Black men and women. The use of this racist appellation serves a similar linguistic violence as the use of terms like *"putas"* or "barstards" within other songs contained in the manuscript. "Shenandoah" is another song in the manuscript that demonstrates additional linguistic violence when the lyrics point to the "little brown gals" and the "little black whore." Similar to other songs discussed, the women are pejoratively denoted by the color of their skin and also distinctly referred to as "little" and "whore." The choice of language controls and orders the relationship with the female characters deployed as the words function as ordering mechanisms to relate how the characters should be viewed and interpreted.

Chapter 4

```
           SALLY BROWN

OH! Sally Brown's a big buck nigger,
    Way, hay, roll an' go!
Her arse-ole's big but her snatch is bigger,
    Spend my money on Sally Brown.


Sally Brown, I love yer daughter,
I love the place where she makes her water./
Sally Brown, I fucked your daughter,
Gave her twins an' stopped her water.

              Sailing Ship Shanties, 1928-1956.
```

"Sally Brown," song collected from repertoire of Stan Hugill. Scanned copy from "Sea Songs," unpublished manuscript of Gershon Legman. Personal copy sent by Judith Legman, October 10, 2014.

Cast alongside of the sailing characters in the song, the women are conveyed with a level of aggressive disdain that succeeds in highlighting an earmark of working-class song tradition and masculine identity more generally. The work that such violent language accomplishes in the song is akin to what linguist Scott Fabius Kiesling recognizes in the space of modern fraternity houses, arguably similar to other all-male homosocial spaces, in which "we have evidence that 'bitch' is associated with this subordinate role through another derogatory terms used by the men: 'bitch boy.' This term is loaded with dominant-subordinate meaning: first through 'bitch,' and second through the term 'boy,' also used to refer to a servant."[8] In a similar fashion, male characters hurl insulting names at the women described, and these titles impose a new identity on the female characters. The act of denoting women as "*putas*" or "barstards" functions to replace any other identities with epithets that position and reconstitute them as something othered in contrast to the male character deploying the terms; through this linguistic act, the women are symbolically placed in subordinate roles similar to the fraternity-house linguistic process of denoting othered males, usually pledges. The songs thus present an element of masculine identity structure such that those who are deemed "failed males" or othered are relegated to a space beneath those who are identified as fulfilling masculine qualities; women are always already positioned at the same level of these "failed" and othered males.[9]

Affirming expected masculine identity through subordinating women continues at the general narrative level as well. Women's bodies are the focus of violence and rage, supporting the theory of masculine identity as one that produces violence, especially at the cost of women. The general treatment of women in these songs accesses Connell's notion of working-class male identity as one that brings a "degree of insensitivity," though the narratives are far more aggressive than Connell observes of working-class comportment more generally.[10] An example of this narrative violence is apparent in the entire refrain of "Saltpetre Shanty," which reads "Arse-ole! Slap her arse (tits)! / Ram it two-blocks up her arse-ole!"[11] Clearly, the weaponized "it" is rammed into the anonymous woman's anus hard enough that it forces the orifice apart in a similar fashion to spreading two tight, wooden blocks apart. The same violence directed at the anus has been observed in football songs from Argentina and was noted in the chapter concerning songs of warning.[12] This agentive violence surfaces as a crystallized narrative interaction between a man and a woman, in which the woman is violently subordinated to the physical and sexual power of the man. The expected "degree of insensitivity" is confirmed, while the line also points to an aggressive securing of hierarchical positioning. The victim of the weaponized penis is physically subordinated similarly to the linguistic process of debasement, in which women are ordered through sexist and racist epithets. Such aggression betrays an element of fear within the sexual situation as the singer chooses to have the male violently engage with the woman rather than approach her in an egalitarian fashion.

A further example of this aggressive violence is apparent in the song "Shenandoah"; though the sailor "loves" Shenandoah's daughter, he wishes to *fuck*, both literally and symbolically, the daughter of the Old Man, an intimate act that is much more violent than "loving" implies. The Old Man's daughter, which should be understood as the captain's daughter, is the site at which sailing men would recognize their subservience to the captain. The line from "Shenandoah," then, becomes loaded with a narrative violence trained on and through the body of a female character in service of bolstering an expected working-class male power structure, while also assuaging a masculine frustration with performing the primed script. Similar to "Saltpetre Shanty," the use of an agentive and weaponized penis aligns with the "asserting superiority over women" as the violent intrusion into women's bodies produces an ordering mechanism.[13] The woman's orifices are at the mercy of the impeding male genitals, and the woman is thereby subjugated to the man and extensions of him.

SHENANDOAH

```
                SHENANDOAH, I love yer daughter, A-way! ye rolling river,
                Wish I wuz a-fucking of the Old Man's daughter,
  stet/             An' away we're bound to go, 'crosst the wide Missoura.

                When I wuz a young man in me prime, A-way! &c.
                I'd shag them yeller gals two at a time./
                Foretops'l halyards, the mate he will roar, A-way! &c.
                Lay along smartly, ye son-o'-a-whore!

                Them little brown gals ain't got no drawers, A-way! &c.
  stet/         They covers their things with bits o' straws./
                Them Liverpool gals I do adore, A-way, &c.
                But I'd sooner shag a little black whore.

                                        Sailing Ship Shanties, 1933-1956.
```

"Shenandoah," song collected from repertoire of Stan Hugill. Scanned copy from "Sea Songs," unpublished manuscript of Gershon Legman. Personal copy sent by Judith Legman, October 10, 2014.

The linguistic and narrative violence subordinates the female characters described in order to articulate and secure a sense of power, control, and domination, which is necessary to the masculine identity structure. This subordination is especially apparent through the fact that women often serve as punchlines to larger narrative frameworks. In "The Gals o' Chile," singers express that "Rosita, Anna, an' Carmen too :2: / They'll greet ye with a hullabaloo, / An' they'll drop their drawers for a nice fuckeroo." In "Jinny Keep Yer Arse-'Ole Warm," the sailors sing, "An' soon we'll be off the ol' Rock Light, / An' I'll be up yer flue tonight" as well as "Oh, 'tis way down below an' pack yer bloody gear, / An' I'll soon be two blocks up you, me dear." In both lines, the rhyming couplets come at the end of narrative content, acting as punchlines for the stanza, which place the women in question at the very end. Serving as punchlines, the women are narratively subordinated to the things that are done to them, but they also arrive as a final and forceful thought. The humor and cavalier quality of the line is delivered through the female character, erasing her agency and relegating her to the space of a narrative tool doing violence to the character figuratively. "Punch," as a term, conjures images of aggressive violence and aligns with the reading of working-class men as rough and ready for the dangerous requirements of their particular vocations. Women acting as punchlines, coupled with linguistic and narrative violence, confirms expected scripts of sailing masculinity. In fact, mariner Charles Tyng remarks, as regards a set of sailing men, that they were "about the roughest looking set of fellows as I had ever seen. There were eight of them. All of them had been drinking, and some of them were intoxicated, feeling more ready for a fight than to work."[14] The suggestion of "punching" as an act of violence or placing a woman as a "punchline" of a narrative aligns with this nineteenth-century description of rough and aggressive sailing men not unlike those described by Tyng. Moreover, the larger narrative choice of subordinating women, both through language and general narrative content, orders relationships within the songs so that men appear to achieve the characteristics described of sailors in the early modern world and working-class masculinity more generally. In a way, when these male characters are ultimately juxtaposed against the moments of vulnerability and masculine failure to come, these narrative choices of violence and aggression appear more as posturing or performance mechanisms that shield the viewer, at first, from seeing the reality of their identity performance. Indeed, it is possible to see the violent language and even the punching and punchlines as vulnerabilities in and of themselves, a preemptive strike against perceived weakness. If one is ready to fight and leads with violence, that presentation of self contains within it a vulnerable need to protect oneself from a perceived threat. The tough outer shell protects the vulnerability beneath it.

Masculine identity in the songs is predicated on a particular sense of superiority, shaped through the linguistic and narrative treatment of women; however, these creative mechanisms are markedly more distinct in relation to nonwhite female characters, who are doubly othered. Narrative treatment of these characters, though similar to the violent language and narrative content focused on other female characters, is disproportionately more pointed and debasing than what is encountered with other female characters in the songs. The doubly othered body is needed for securing masculine superiority by proxy.[15] Unlike other female characters in the songs, nonwhite women are aligned with excrement, which dually humiliates and subordinates as well as lends a level of desirability and titillation. Borrowing from Julia Kristeva, we might consider these characters as the pinnacle of *abjection*. In humiliating and subordinating them, the song captures how "the abject has only one quality of the object—that of being opposed to *I*."[16] Indeed, in focusing specifically on excrement—literal defecation—the song positions nonwhite characters as opposite to the singer as well as symbolic of death, the purging the body, filth, decay, and putridness: each the lowest and even most deplorable. Kristeva muses, "If dung signifies the other side of the border, the place where I am not and which permits me to be, the corpse, the most sickening of wastes, is a border that has encroached upon everything."[17] The abject, as well as abjection, for Kristeva are haunting or lurking realities, but they are also specifically embodied realities: one's identity as the abject becomes both *what* one is and *who* one is; the depiction, indeed, is taken back to the body where the abject is pure signification. Nonwhite bodies are recognized as fetid in the songs through their general personhood but also in their inherent corporeality. These figures are always already embodied as their abject status is reinscribed by their presentation of self as well as the singer's recognition of his difference from them. In drawing attention to corpses and waste, Kristeva provides the opportunity to consider the ways in which nonwhite bodies are akin to waste, death, the ego, the debased, and the debasing. For the singer to pursue the pleasures of nonwhite bodies, with Kristeva in mind, is to pursue the abject or to seek abjection through their bodies. There is, too, a circular association between the debased bodies, the excremental, and even the desiring figure.

The distinct attachment to excrement and, thereby, anality further solidifies this abject quality within the songs. The association between nonwhite bodies and excrement is apparent in the song "Sally Brown," in which both characters are Black, and the song reads, "Sally Brown, I love yer daughter, / I love the place where she makes her water." Within this line, the narrator bonds both the sexual possibility and bodily function of the daughter's vagina, mingling the two so as to make them almost interchangeable. In fetishizing and describing the daughter's vagina, base sexual and common human urges are combined: her sexuality and erotic allure become scatological and relegated to the realm of human excrement, the lowest part of human functions. The focus on urine is Rabelaisian, and the conflation of excrement and sexuality—or, at least, pleasure—is a point of focus in the work of Mikhail Bakhtin. He writes, "We must not forget that urine (as well as dung) is gay matter, which degrades and relieves at the same time, transforming fear into laughter. If dung is a link between body and earth (the laughter that unites them), urine is a link between body and sea."[18] Bakhtin is, of course, discussing what he sees of Francois Rabelais; however, his insights fit with what is occurring within chanteys, especially here in the focus on the excremental. He identifies the same paradox at play as Kristeva where the abject contains within it both pleasure and debasement; moreover, there is an identification that is tied to the body and what it produces. Nonwhite bodies, like those of Sally Brown's daughter, are embodied and exist within a dialectic between shame and desire, death and life, laughter and dejection, filth and desire. Worthy of note is the distinct connection between urine and the sea, which Bakhtin later underscores by adding to it blood, which, when applied to nonwhite bodies in chanteys, conjures images of miscegenation and other racist practices based on linking race to biology—to blood.[19] Too, the image of blood aligns with blood lost as men and women alike were brutalized during the height of the slave trade. The chanteys, sung while at sea and containing narratives that often appear to capture the abject, generate an intriguing circularity where the sailor and the nonwhite women he encounters become wedded together in abjection. They are connected by salt water and blood and urine, especially here, but they are also connected in their status as abject subjects. Nothing was more debased, indeed, than the sailing man who shipped out on a slaving vessel. True, the singing narrator is attempting to distance himself from those he describes, but there is a pull toward them that gestures at the compelling and porous reality of the abject that Kristeva notes.[20]

In considering nonwhite bodies as abject, the other side of the paradox, then, is the attendant titillation and intoxicating desire and pull toward the abject. There is both a repulsion and a yearning. In a way, many of the songs from Hugill capture what has been identified of other spaces: the nonwhite body is repudiated but also fetishized. Of particular note is the work of Katrina Dyonne Thompson in which she highlights both the libidinous desires of the men writing descriptions of African dancers in their travelogues and the spurning of those desires as the women are cast as monstrously sexual.[21] Their "significance is indeed inherent in the human body" to the degree that the women are defined by their bodies and what they do with them.[22] An example of desiring and also repudiating the abject arrives in "The Gals o' Chile," in which non-Anglo-Saxon women are cast as preferring nonnormative sex, specifically anal sex, when the singers remark that these women proffer "romper-la-cola."[23] The line roughly translates to "break the tail," which would immediately draw connections among sex, violence, the anus, and excrement, not to mention exoticism, for the line is delivered in rudimentary Spanish.

Songs like "The Gals o' Chile" recycle embedded narratives of Latina bodies as hypersexualized and available, much like the narrative violence done to nonwhite bodies more generally. They are, as Isabel Molina Guzman and Angharad N. Valdivia mention, "excessively sexualized and eroticized by U.S. and Europeans cultures" to the point that they are identified with "everyday needs of the body to consume food, excrete waste, and reproduce sexually."[24] What Latina bodies in the songs accomplish is to further imbed the relationship among nonwhite bodies, the abject, and specifically the sailor's dual desire for and debasing of the woman described. Within this line, there is an inherent fetishizing of the anus as well as a violent intrusion of it, almost a deflowering of the anus, which supports a reading of the nonwhite figure as one to use and subordinate. The implication of virginity here in the anus being broken calls to mind the breaking of the hymen and symbolic loss of

THE GALS O' CHILE

TO Chile's coast we are bound away,
    Timme arsy-ole, bungolero!
To Chile's coast we are bound away,
    We'll shag an' all drink pisco (get pissed, boys)!
To Chile's coast we are bound away,
Where them little Dago gals hawk their tripe all day,
    Timme arsy bungolero,
    Sing olé! for a well-cut whore (a two-way whore).

An' when we gits to Vallipo :2:
They'll grab yer round the middle an' they won't let go,
To the whorehouse, bullies, with a roll 'n' go!
(To the casa-de-puta with a roll 'n' go!)

Them gals o' Chile they are hard to beat :2:
They shag like a hen when a cock it meets,
Oh, a rumper-la-cola is a sailor's treat.

Them señoritas are smart an' gay :2:
They drink an' shag till the break o' day,
Then pitch ye out like a bale o' hay.

My trim little packet is a very smart craft :2:
You can have yer choice of a hole or a crack,
A peso up the front an' two fer up the back.

Rosita, Anna, an' Carmen too :2:
They'll greet ye with a hullabaloo,
An' they'll drop their drawers for a nice fuckeroo.

                                      [continued.....]

"The Gals o' Chile," song collected from repertoire of Stan Hugill. Scanned copy from "Sea Songs," unpublished manuscript of Gershon Legman. Personal copy sent by Judith Legman, October 10, 2014.

```
           The Gals o' Chile -continued -2-


                Them señoritas, as we know well :2:
  stet/        They're red-hot divils from the other side of hell,
                Keep yer hand on yer money when ye shag a Chile belle.

                When the time comes for to say farewell :2:
                Goodbye to the gals and our money as well,
  stet/        With a dose of the pox from ol' Corynel.

                                            Sailing Ship Shanties, 1925-1957.

  BALLAD NOTES.

  Gals O' Chile. Note from Hugill: " The sailors' usual name for
  Valpariso was "Wallop-me-arse-with-a-razor" [!]". The rumpoculo
  phrase (arsebreaker), referring to anal intercourse, also exists
  in Italian. An edition of the Dubbi Amorosi or "Amorous Doubts"
  attributed to Aretino, printed in 1792, gives the printer's mock
  name as 'Florindo Rompiculo.' (Bibliothèque Nationale, Enfer 204/6;
  Pascal Pia, Les Livres de l'Enfer, 1978, I. 203.)
```

virginity. Moreover, however, is the attachment to what has already been discussed in terms of both Bakhtin and Kristeva, which is that the anus, anality, and excrement are each a part of the larger assemblage of abjection. They are defining characteristics as they are repulsive: equally, they are desirable and contain a pull that succeeds in also defining the one who seeks them. They are also a border, a connecting element, and the anus is arguably the portal through which the abject is expelled, but desire is also pulled. When the sailing man violently inserts his penis here, the border between the two figures is eradicated and the two become one.

Siobhan Brooks, in "Hypersexualization and the Dark Body," discusses how Black and Latina women navigate issues of race in the contemporary strip club, and her observations pair with what is occurring in the space of chanteys, especially concerning the subjugation of nonwhite women, both Black and Latina. Far removed from the age of sail though it is, the observations of women linguistically and socially navigating race evoke some of the same mechanisms apparent in songs like "The Gals o' Chile." It is clear that the darker skinned a woman appears, the more she has trouble garnering male attention, and she is often recognized as expendable or even open to violence. Indeed, some women attempt to play up lighter-skinned attributes in order to attract white men, garner more attention, and place themselves in situations where their status does not open them to violence. Brooks argues that nonwhite women "are perceived by male customers, both White and Black, as worth less sexually, thus being more sexually available than White women."[25] There is a denigration of women of color, whether Black or Latina, and the same disposable quality is inherent in the narratives from Hugill, suggesting both a potential bias and racism on the part of Hugill and a clear use of racial epithets, categories, and treatment in order to establish an us-versus-them narrative structure predicated on nonwhite bodies. There is a clear linguistic power observed in Hugill. In aligning nonwhite women's sexual desires and sexual organs with excrement, many of these narratives suggest not only a desire to expel—to rid the body of waste material—but also a violent dismissal of the racialized women described.

Linguistic and narrative violence is an integral part of the chantey narratives, but it is the degree of male control that further promotes the interpretation that the songs capture a particular hypermasculine identity formation. This male control is evident from the position of the narrator to the male characters as they interact with women. Having a male character as the basis for the song narrative establishes a power and influence from the beginning, a masculine expectation that is indicative of not only song tradition but also general masculine social comportment. In terms of the ordering of the narrator, as he is juxtaposed against the interactions within the song, viewers and listeners recognize a privileged male perspective to the song narrative deployed, which is intriguing against the backdrop of what was raised concerning the transgression of heteronormative frameworks in songs of warning. Beginning songs like "Jinny Keep Yer Arse-'Ole Warm" with rallying words like "Now, m'lads, be of good cheer" opens the song with an agentive male perspective where the narrator presents as "just one of the guys" but is also clearly in control from the beginning. Other songs in the manuscript begin in a similar fashion and reproduce a controlling male gaze, which shapes the narratives later deployed.

The dominating masculinity inherent within at least a surface reading of the chantey narratives falls in line with the historical expectations of the men for the era when chanteys were arguably sung. Historian Karen V. Waters supports the reading of male scripts as engendering a measure of control when she argues of nineteenth-century English masculinity that, "in order to control the world around him, the Victorian gentleman had, first and foremost, to control himself."[26] These particular earmarks of a man clearly celebrate the ability to restrain both self and those around and privilege the masculine ability to act as conductor of self and social space. The same is ultimately true of early American masculinity, though greater weight is placed on individuality, which is its own kind of discipline. Historian Rosanne Currarino shows that a working-class man in America was a "powerful figure [who] represented self-employed, property-owning craftsmen and embodied the republican virtues of hard work, frugality, self-denial, and personal independence."[27] Virtues of the American working-class man were such that a degree of control, both of self and others, was necessary in order to fulfill the expectations of manhood. These same earmarks of control are evident throughout the frameworks of the songs and help to affirm that expected male scripts are positioned in relation to women; however, it will be apparent that one's ability to direct the situation is sometimes thwarted by experiences wholly out of the male characters' command. What the controlling male voice demonstrates, especially when it collides with situations and characters that emasculate the man, is that there is an attempt to posture a masculine authority even in narrative situations in which a man might lose his masculine position. As Margaret S. Creighton notes of sailing men, "When we ask, then, why these sailors might have objectified women, one of the answers is that they wanted to hold on to them better," or as is the case in song, they were looking for ways in which they might control or lord over female characters in ways not afforded to them outside of song.[28] Such a desire for control is likely predicated on the sailing man's own feelings of subordination in the face of shipboard hierarchy as well as lack of control over external forces, like weather and even seafaring attacks. Controlling and ordering women fulfills the need for masculine authority, but it likely also captures the sailing man's need to control another in the face of his own recognition of futility.

The narrative choice of a controlling male perspective in Hugill's songs appears akin to what Laura Mulvey recognizes as the cinematic "male gaze," the camera angles and visual focal points in film ordered based on the imagined male viewer. Power is assumed of and given to men in this framework, and the songs are delivered to confirm this male gaze. Mulvey argues that a female character is "fragmented by close-ups, is the content of the film, and the direct recipient of the spectator's look."[29] She recognizes a hegemonic male perspective, deployed with male viewers in mind, that shapes the course of the film as well as the experience of the viewer. This narrative-shaping male perspective is similar to the process inherent in the chanteys from Hugill, where song narratives highlight the desires of the primary figures, usually at the expense of the women described, and this narrative choice seeks to celebrate expected masculine identity scripts. Though all the sexual encounters within the songs fit with this primary masculine gaze, an example from "The Gals o' Chile" demonstrates the agentive male perspective. One stanza reads, "My trim little packet is a very smart craft :2: / You can have yer choice of a hole or a crack, / A peso up the front an' two fer up the back." Within the lines, the sailing character secures his pleasure from a woman through purchasing her attentions, and the "trim little packet['s]" experience of the erotic endeavor is erased. "My" insinuates that the woman *belongs* to the agentive narrator, and proffering her to other men reproduces an erotically charged male script in which the narrator is in control of not only the narrative situation but also the woman deployed. Song examples like "Sally Brown" and "John Brown's Daughter" more roundly tie to Mulvey's theory of the gaze, where the woman's body becomes the means through which to access male sexual scripts. Hypersexual and scopophilic narratives, at the surface, recycle a reading of male characters as agentive and fulfilling the expectations of manhood as the characters perform the work of posturing desiring men and willing women.

The male perspective of the songs also engenders an identification with the men sexually enjoying the women in the songs, which accesses a further point that Mulvey ventures concerning male sexual scripts being reified in and through the bodies of women. She argues, "Each is associated with a look: that of the spectator in direct scopophilic contact with the female form displayed for his enjoyment (connoting male phantasy) and that of the spectator fascinated with the image of his like set in an illusion of natural space, and through him gaining control and possession of the woman within the diegesis."[30] Applying Mulvey's view to the sexualized narratives of the songs, as communicated through the voice of a controlling male narrator, it is clear that they do the work of articulating a dominant male identity through mandating a male storyteller, by including male characters set in the expected likeness of the agentive narrator, and by positioning characters in sexual scenarios in which the expectation is male control and pleasure. The scopophilic consumption of women's bodies is no more apparent than it is in "Sally Brown" and "John Brown's Daughter," mentioned above, in which the bodies of women are of chief focus and are essentially penetrated both by the gaze of the viewer consuming the narrative and through the narrative voice of the man deploying the song.

"John Brown's Daughter" exemplifies this. Within each line, the genitals of John Brown's daughter are penetrated, arguably raped, by the trained vision of the agentive narrator, which confirms the expected male scripts for her body is at the mercy of both the narrator and those consuming the narrative.[31] She is immobilized, breached, and subordinated. Similar narrative elements are apparent in the Hugill's version of "Sally Brown" when two women's vaginas and anuses are placed on display for visual consumption and their bodies are overpowered by the commanding male gaze. In "Sally Brown," the genital

JOHN BROWN'S ~~BODY~~ DAUGHTER.

JOHN BROWN'S daughter is a virgin, so I'm told,
Her arse-'ole's decked with diamonds and her cunt is
   decked ~~with~~ with gold.
John Brown's daughter's got a wart upon her snatch,
John Brown's daughter's got a wart on her main-hatch.

<u>Sailing Ship Shanties</u>, 1928-1956.

"John Brown's Daughter," song collected from repertoire of Stan Hugill. Scanned copy from "Sea Songs," unpublished manuscript of Gershon Legman. Personal copy sent by Judith Legman, October 10, 2014. Note that the title has been changed in the manuscript. "Body" has been changed to "daughter," potentially reflecting an error in transcription, but it is a curious juxtaposition between the male body of John Brown and that of his "daughter" described in the song. This change is loaded with interpretive potential. Does the female body belong to John Brown? Is it John Brown's male body?

images are not set as the primary focal point, but they are situated in such a way that a penetrative gaze is still deployed. Arguably, the female genitals are "estranged" from the bodies of the women described and through that "estrangement mark this peculiar separation of women from their bodies, a process that undermines their autonomy and transforms their social status."[32]

Through deploying songs like these, it is possible to imagine the collective visual subordination of the woman's body, which would succeed in presenting a juxtaposition of power and agency as it clashes with subordination and disempowerment. The female characters are each laid bare to the intended male audience without articulating clear consent, leaving the men in positions of power and the women's bodies as penetrated and powerless sites of subordination. Such a visual reality attaches to the discussion earlier concerning women as punchlines. The importance here is that the woman's body rises as a cipher for male identity. Her fragmented parts, in this look, assuage multiple levels of masculine need and lack, and they are accomplished through subjugating the female characters both in terms of their lack of consent and in how they are objectified and consumed. Cathy Lynn Preston's work is salient in thinking about a woman's body as it figures in collective song, where female characters become the site through which to recognize male agency and authority and function as a means by which to appease men's unrealized sexual desire.[33] Trapped in the narrative, these women are specimens in service to shaping a masculine identity, and the subordinated images rally a male recognition of order and control within the sexual economy. Placed as they are on display, the women's bodies are not their own, and narratives appear to align with opposite-sex erotics that are deeply hierarchical and predicated on men's imbedded notion of entitlement to women and their bodies.

Kate Manne discusses consent and the complicated and disjointed reality in which "men are deemed entitled to consent."[34] Her work comes to bear on readings of many Hugill songs in the that women's bodies are always already on display as well as open for sexual gratification, whether corporeally or visually: men's entitlement to those views and pleasures occurs without question and without protest from the female figures consumed. For Manne, there is a silent and implied consent, thus no real consent at all, wherein "relevant inequalities are a product of a patriarchal structure leveled at girls and women who resist and challenge the will of male authority figures."[35] When her insights are applied to the songs from Hugill, the degree to which the women in the songs are devoid of control further supports the overarching reading of them as containers for male sexual entitlement and power. Women demonstrate a degree of control in the sexual economy through weaponizing venereal disease and robbing sailing men; however, there are a vast number of narrative incidents in which female characters are subordinated to the desires of the singer/listener and also to the male characters within the texts, sometimes without their knowledge. Indeed, in the narrative of "John Brown's Daughter," the primary figure, John Brown's daughter, is described at a distance and is not a part of the interaction at all. Her absence from the action within the song, as she is only the scopophilic focus of the song, suggests the woman's absence from and therefore potential ignorance of her consumption as an erotic object. Her body is sexualized and objectified, placed on display for those listening, potentially without her consent, but her ability to interact in the description of herself is certainly absent. The description of this woman, then, is the height of male power and authority as the singer has chosen for the woman and shared her with a consuming audience.

Mulvey's "male gaze" binds within it a voyeuristic quality that impacts both the male and female characters present in the song, drawing both in to suggest the fulfillment of male identity performance: women desiring men and men participating in and consuming narratives in which their virility and prowess are the primary focus. Throughout the examples discussed so far, the controlling male gaze specifically trains the audience's focus onto the sexual escapades and capabilities of the male characters ventured, even though it will later be clear that the sailing characters are not always desirable or able to fulfill their roles. Both male and female characters succeed in accessing a male identity expected of working-class men that suggests men are voraciously eager to copulate and women are endlessly excited to deliver; the subtext of this is a voyeuristic celebration of the virile successes of male characters. The line "to the whorehouse, bullies, with a roll 'n' go!" in "The Gals o' Chile" fully captures this idea of masculine virility and decisiveness, along with expectation. Arriving near the beginning of the song, the line primes the audience for later narrative content that expounds on what the sailor meets when he arrives at the whorehouse: expectant women who are willing and eager to serve and abounding male energy to enjoy them all. There are also more pointed depictions of male virility, such as in "Saltpetre Shanty" when the women are "awaitin' us Jackshites to flush out their 'oles" or in "Billy Boy" when the "charmin' Nancy Lee" "can strop a block, an' she'll take a fathom o' cock" or in "Jinny Keep Yer Arse-'Ole Warm" when "she's hungry for the cock."

These narrative elements confirm a masculine expectation of women desiring sex with the sailing characters to the point that they are almost insatiably ready for the arrival of male genitalia, but they also register the male imagination of his own desirability and virility bound up within the material, each confirming agentive male identity scripts and arguably betraying a masculine voyeurism interested in consuming the male body. The same narrative elements of desiring male bodies are observable in "Cheerily Man" when the "widow Skinner, likes cock for dinner, Long, thick or thi[n]." In other lines of the song, singers celebrate the degree to which these women not only enjoy sex with men and are voracious enough to enjoy sex with inanimate objects but also engage in coprophilic acts, tying defecating in buckets to the question of whether or not one might like to engage erotically with the woman. The song appears, in fact, as a cataloged list of women encountered and is almost like the contemporary notion of the erotic "body count" touted by men as a mode by which to measure their virility and desirability.

The next chapter expounds on this homoerotic desire in greater detail, but voyeuristically celebrating male virility is further clear in the example from "The Saltpetre Shanty," in which the women are cast as waiting for the sailor's agentive and powerful sperm capable of "flushing" multiple orifices. The women are simply cast as the deviant characters desirous of the men's virile seed, which titillates but also confirms an expectation of male performance.[36] Within the song "Shenandoah," a similar narrative of powerful virility is apparent and placed on display when we encounter the line "when I wux a young man in me prime, A-way! &c. / I'd shag them yeller gals two at a time." Here, the promotion of masculine virility is at the expense of the racialized "yeller gals," who become almost punctuation in the sailor's tale of his own sexual agency.[37] Remarking on his ability to have sex with women

```
Oh, Nancy Dawson, ai-o-eeyo — Cheerily man!
She's got no drawers on, ai-o-eeyo — Cheerily man!
An' likes it head-on, ai-o-eeyo — Cheerily man!
Oh, olly-high-ee-o-o — Cheerily man!

Oh, Sally Hackett, Who'd like ter shaggit, An' get a packet?
Oh, Flora Fernanah, She likes a banana, Stuck up her vagina.
Oh, Widow Skinner, Likes cock for dinner, Long, thick or thi
Oh, Missus Duckitt, Shits in a bucket, Who'd like to fuck it

Oh, Sally Riddle, I saw her piddle, Through a cinder-riddle.
Oh, Betty Baker, Lives at Long Acre, I'd like to rake her.
Oh, Jinny Walker, Fucked by a hawker, Who had a corker.
Oh, Jennifer Bell, She fucks as well, 'n' never will tell.

Oh, Kitty Carson, She spliced a whoreson, Who likes it stern
Oh, Polly Hawkins, In her white stockings, Has had some fuck

                                    Sailing Ship Shanties, 1927-19

NOTE: Completing Hugill 312, who notes use of word 'cherrily' to urge
sailors on at their work, in the Bosun's opening speech in Shakespeare's
The Tempest (1610?) I.i.6.
```

"Cheerily Man," song collected from repertoire of Stan Hugill. Scanned copy from "Sea Songs," unpublished manuscript of Gershon Legman. Scan includes explanatory note concerning "cherrily [sic]." Personal copy sent by Judith Legman, October 10, 2014.

"two at a time" creates a narrative sense of his own capacity to pleasure two women at once and roundly ties his personhood to epic sexual capacities, an imagined male trait. Such a narrative image immediately calls to mind *Jack in a White Squall, amongst Breakers—On the Lee Shore of St. Catherine's*, a caricature of a sailing man in between two prostitutes demanding money, and supports this idea of hyperbolic male power, which will eventually be dismantled to a degree. Indeed, in the caricature, the sailor remarks, "I am hardup—not a Quid left, or Shot in the Locker—to pay the Fiddler—'mi eyes—what a Squall."[38] It is clear that he attempted to engage with two women, or more, but was unable to manage the demands of both, placing him in an intense "squall," where he was arguably out of money and, potentially, semen ("Shot in the Locker"). The "shot locker" calls to mind lines from "Ratcliffe Highway," discussed in chapter 3.

In each example of virility above, the sailing character's erotically charged imagination is positioned to be consumed by the audience, controlling the readers' or singers' experiences, requiring them to imagine epic male power as the characters become the paragon of masculine

Jack in a White Squall, amongst Breakers—On the Lee Shore of St. Catherine's, 1811. Library of Congress, Prints and Photographs Division, Cartoon Prints, British.

performance. The women and men, throughout surface readings of the songs, fulfill the quality of what Inger Lövkrona identifies of gender in premodern Swedish folklore, in which women are a way by which men demonstrate their sexual prowess and desirability in the service of underscoring, through song, their achievement of a privileged form of masculine performance. Though not discussing song, Lövkrona provides a framework to understand the arrival of gendered bodies in the narrative spaces of folklore, especially as they attend to questions of expected constructions of gender and sexuality. Regarding Swedish erotic folklore, Lövkrona says, "The politics of erotic folklore served to legitimize and sustain male power structures," which occurred in similar ways to what is communicated within the songs surveyed for this chapter.[39] Some characters either confirm "positive masculinity or femininity" or "negative masculinity or femininity." Using this framework, the narratives of the chanteys discussed thus far confirm a "positive masculinity" in that the characters are all outlined and aligned with, for the most part, expectations of masculine performance. Men are to be understood as "virile, potent, smart, and decisive," "always ready to seduce somebody, whether his object is a young woman, a wife, or an old woman or widow."[40] As should be apparent, the male characters are denoted by their sometimes violent, often controlling and decisive, and virile natures, confirming these social expectations of the agentive and successful working-class male.

Female Agency

What troubles the presentation of the agentive working-class male, however, is the fact that the songs contain a level of female agency, which tempers the masculine authority that stands most prominent upon first glance. In fact, the female characters often take on a degree of control that sometimes subordinates the male characters in question. This facet of the female characters is what helps to shape a reading of the chanteys as handling identity construction in all its kaleidoscope capacities and demonstrates the subtle ways by which vulnerability is admitted.

One of the first ways through which female characters posture authority is when they narratively kick men out of doors once the sexual encounter is complete or, at least in the song "Do Let Me 'Lone, Susan," actively impede the process of sexual satisfaction. Within examples of narrative situations where women actually throw men out once the sex is complete, there is a hint that sailing prowess is less than desirable and, once the women have secured their own pleasure or compensation, that the men are relatively useless. In "The Gals o' Chile," the narrator remarks, "Them señoritas are smart an' gay :2: / They drink an' shag till the break o' day, / Then pitch ye out like a bale o' hay." In rendering the "bale o' hay" as a symbolic representation of the men, the lyrics engender a reading of sailing men as easily moved and removed, which the term "pitch" suggests, and as useful only in terms of what purpose they will ultimately serve. Hay is for feeding animals; the men as hay may be understood as feeding the woman's need for pleasure and, perhaps, offering some level of financial support. In "The Gals o' Chile," despite racist and subordinating undertones lobbed at nonwhite female characters, it is clear that the same female characters thwart their subordination and essentialize, to a degree, the role they are fulfilling, but they also control it. In "Do Let Me 'Lone, Susan," female characters similarly thwart hegemonic convention when Susan, Flora, and Jinny actively work together to stifle the desires of the sailor, ultimately frustrating him in his pursuit of garnering pleasure from Jinny. The refrain "do let me 'lone" conjures the reading that Susan and Flora are foils to male pleasure. For Jinny's part, she refutes the sailor's desires in the physical removal of her body from the exchange. The sexual prowess of the sailor is no match for the invasion of Flora and Susan, but it is also clear that Jinny does not view the sailor as a titillating means for her own sexual fulfillment. This agency, as slight as it seems, expresses the denial of masculine sexual advances, thereby frustrating the pursuit of fulfilling masculine expectations. The women, in these pockets of narrative, represent an articulation or admission of the struggle to reproduce masculine identity scripts and register moments of masculine identity failures, especially when they encounter women.

Women also gain a degree of agency when they knowingly give characters venereal disease as well as steal from them, two realities that the male characters remark upon with a measure of anger and also resignation, as was explored in the previous chapter. The punchline of almost every chantey surveyed has the sailor either battling venereal disease or pointing to the diseases infecting the desired women. "John Brown's Daughter," in its simple elegance, both captures the desirability of the woman's body and highlights the dangers that lurk behind the enticing façade. The beauty of the daughter's genitals is dashed with the admission that she also has a wart on her "main hatch," which arguably could serve as a blemish or a misrecognition of her clitoris. As beautiful, desirable, and arousing as she may be, reading the wart as a blemish portends the likelihood of venereal disease, which could fundamentally impact the body of the sailor. It is possible to imagine the body of John Brown's daughter as a harbinger of what might intrude into the body of the sailor who desires her: though his body is the portrait of masculine agency and strength, a wart could penetrate his virility and render him ruined, as is clear in songs of warning, discussed previously. Read as a misrecognition of the clitoris arguably contains an attack on the sailing man's ignorance of both the woman's body and her pleasure, each remarking against his own capabilities in the sexual economy. Recognizing her clitoris as a wart stands as a symbolic registration of the sailing man's own confusion and disempowerment in the erotic scenario, as well as fear and anxiety about his ability to know a woman's body and meet her needs.

In terms of venereal disease, it is true that it is only agentive to a point—the woman is infected just as she will infect the hapless sailor—but even in its awful reality, the woman is able to choose whom she infects, targeting the sailor to exact a level of power. This is not a pleasurable moment of agency, though pleasure is potentially bound up in the act; however, the *choice* renders the transference of infection agentive. A similar wielding of disease occurs in "The Gals o' Chile," in which singers remark that they leave Chile "with a dose of the pox from ol' Corynel," and in "Saltpetre Shanty," the sailors lament the fact that "them barstards is poxin' us all o' the time." Though the songs begin with a cataloging of sexual pleasures derived from the women encountered in port, the final lines of the narrative underscore the painful realities of sex that ultimately send sailors out to sea sexually defective, and the women are potentially victorious, though both the men and women are clearly infected. The men's bodies, similar to the women they encounter, are vulnerable and therefore subordinated to the disease. Men and women, here, are rendered on equal and painful footing.

Venereal disease as a weapon of agency functions because it is brandished within a gender economy, in which damage to the male sexual organ would mean that the man has lost his ability to perform his masculine sexual duties. Leaving the sexual situation and remarking that he acquired venereal disease, the male character injects the chantey narratives with a recognition of his own undoing and even the penetrable and vulnerable quality of his body. The arrival of venereal disease in the songs immediately connects to the idea that a poxed penis is one that symbolically presents a man as out of order or as out of control of his own body: the man, his body, and his identity are each objects that can be invaded and reconstituted. Acquiring the disease and bringing it to narrative light in the songs discloses that the masculine hold on control in the sexual situation can be usurped by a woman's power, especially when she wields a damaging and potentially life-altering weapon. Weaponized venereal disease in these songs collides with the, at first, weaponized male penis and wrests power away from the male figure through disarming the seat of his manhood. At least in terms of the sailing world in the early modern period, acquiring a venereal disease had potential economic implications as it left the unlucky man infected, further defiled, and therefore vulnerable through his additional loss of money.[41] All these unfortunate realities—vulnerability, loss of money, and loss of control—position the man roughly akin to his female counterpart, conjuring images of any body as a vulnerable one.

Female characters, too, often appear willing to engage in anal sex with sailing men, and this predilection arguably melds with the wielding of venereal disease as a complicated way through which women recognize and actively combat their subordination. Women, in the choice of anal sex, ultimately control the sexual economy, ordering the mode by which sexual release is achieved. There is agentive action in structuring the sexual scenario and also in further imbuing of the erotic scenario with desirability. The infrequency with which women report, according to contemporary research, desire for anal sex generates a further empowering mechanism in that to choose it is to both leverage male desire for it and rise as something of a female anomaly. Deploying anal sex in this way renders the women rare and even more desirable, and recognition of their own rarity, and leveraging it for power,

```
                    DO LET ME 'LONE, SUSAN

       Do let me 'lone, Susan, oh, do let me 'lone!
            Hurrah! me looloo boys, DO let me 'lone!
       When I put me arm 'round Jinny's waist, Oh, Jinny jump away,
            Hurrah! me looloo boys, DO let me 'lone!

       When I put me hand up Jinny's clouts, oh, Jinny jump about,
            Hurrah! me looloo boys!

       Do let me 'lone, Flora, oh, do let me lone!
       When I put me arm 'round Jinny's breasts, Oh, Jinny jump away,
       When I put me hand on Jinny's snatch, Oh, Jinny jump about.

                              Sailing Ship Shanties, 1932-1956.

BALLAD NOTES.

Do Let Me 'Lone. From Hugill, who says, "Halyard Shaty. Of Negro
origin and has never seen the light of print until now. Much im-
provisation was given to this shanty. This shanty was very popu-
lar in the West Indian Traders, particularly aboard those with
checkerboard crews - i-e-, one watch white, and one watch colored.
```

"Do Let Me 'Lone, Susan," song collected from repertoire of Stan Hugill. Scanned copy from "Sea Songs," unpublished manuscript of Gershon Legman. Scan includes "ballad notes." Personal copy sent by Judith Legman, October 10, 2014.

functions to combat their general subordination, albeit through the choice of sexual engagement that contains hierarchical realities.[42] An additional reading, even further charged with power, is that the repeated use of the anus ensures that the woman is not burdened with an unwanted pregnancy stemming from the sexual interaction. In "Saltpetre Shanty," anal sex is so important to the song that it becomes a part of the refrain, where "arse-ole!" is repeated two times through. Though the line was discussed in terms of its narrative violence against women, there is the alternative reading that the use of the anus ensures that the woman is not left with a child and provides her with a sense of control in the sexual economy. Historian Katherine Crawford, in her *European Sexualities, 1400–1800*, argues that, in early modern Europe, "women were always more susceptible to sexual dishonor because they were more vulnerable to violence, dependent on the good opinion of others, and likely to display indications of sexual missteps on their bodies, such as pregnancy."[43] In relenting to forced anal sex, the female characters are tolerating sexual penetration that at least protects them from an unwanted pregnancy, one that could be potentially damaging to her position in society.

Lines such as "you can have yer choice of a hole or a crack" in "The Gals o' Chile" wed anal sex with another potential nonprocreative option, with "hole" understood as the mouth of the woman. Choosing the mouth as a site of erotic release would be a further mode of sexual interaction that carries with it no chance of unwanted pregnancy. The refrain of "The Gals o' Chile" underscores these women's desire for multiple sexual outlets: "Sing olé! for a well-cut whore (a two-way whore)." The alternative line provokes a reading of a woman willing to take sexual intercourse vaguely "both ways," insinuating a willingness for either normative or nonnormative sex. These fail safes permit both the securing of pleasure on the part of the male sailor and the protection of the women with whom he engages. Likely, if it were up to the choice of the male character, all sexual outlets would be ideal, but because there is a focus on these nonprocreative outlets, it is possible to read the scenarios as ones in which the women provide pleasure as desired by the men but controlled and ordered by the women. In bringing these sexual realities to the fore, the songs slowly weave a narrative attuned to the complicated realities of identity and personhood. No one person is in complete control at all times, and the moments during which the narrator chooses to detail women usurping male authority are those glimpses into the complexities of more vulnerable and evolving realities.

Wielding venereal disease as a weapon and actively choosing anal sex as a mode of protection are each certainly indicative of female agency in the sexual situations within the songs, but women's potency is also apparent when the female characters rob sailing characters of their money. Women stealing from sailing men is a symbolic way by which the gendered field is leveled: whereas a male's sexual gratification is considered hierarchically more important, a woman might unman him by robbing him, succeeding in both regaining power and symbolically castrating the man. Thievery is mentioned in "The Gals o' Chile" in the lines "keep yer hand on yer money when ye shag a Chile belle" and "goodbye to the gals and our money as well."

Stealing from the men symbolically castrates them, altering the hierarchical position of the female characters described by bringing a real act, such as thievery, to the sexually symbolic. Imagining an undercurrent of castration anxiety produces a reading of the narratives as registering a real and intense fear of the loss of the symbolic extension of the man. The suggestion of male castration injects the narrative with a degree of anxiety, even if the tone remains light and humorous—the same way it functioned in songs of warning.[44] Throughout many of the songs, sailors are cast as largely helpless victims in situations presented as precarious, especially when characters like "Pedro the pimp" are tangentially related to the "*putas*" and "whores" of Chile. Within the narrative, Pedro "a-primin' his vino, an' dopin' his beer, / To the Chinchas he'll ship us if we don't take care." Though the women look inviting, the sailing characters identify themselves as not only different from these characters on land but in danger when encountering these people; their masculine hold on control would be at stake in their presence, especially as they are potentially drugged. These warnings and juxtapositions hearken back to the realities of port experiences of early modern sailors and serve the narrative purpose of relaying the precarity of an identity predicated on control and symbolic extensions of male superiority.

Though, on the surface, it would seem that men control the sexual situation since the sexual encounters are ordered through the male gaze, women primarily orchestrate the sexual situation and control the type of sex that they deliver largely to their own benefit and not only through the choice of anal sex. Almost all the songs surveyed reproduce female characters, imbued with an inherent carnality, as objects that sailing characters desire for their anecdotal penchant for erotic pleasures. The women actually fulfill what Lövkrona sees of women in premodern Swedish erotic folklore, which is that "to be lewd, wonton, sexually active, etc. gives the female actors power and scope for agency. They not only pose a threat to masculinity, but also turn men into objects of ridicule."[45] These female characters orchestrate the sexual encounter through manipulating the sailing characters, even prior to their arrival in port, to desire their ultimate encounter with them. Framing the women in this way, the sailing characters become more like lovesick and hopelessly aroused boobs anxiously waiting for an engagement with the characters described.

A clear example is in "The Saltpetre Shanty," where the female characters described are so desirous of sex, specifically with sailors, that they are cast as anxiously waiting for the prospect of sex, regardless of what orifice the sailors choose. Similarly, in this version of "The Gals o' Chile," women are lecherous and desiring as well as willing and open to all types of sexual outlets, even and especially those which were deemed taboo. In each of these songs, the women fan the flames of erotic desire and even go to the extent of preparing their bodies for the arrival of the sailors to be pleasured. By posturing in the way that female characters do, sailing characters believe that they are titillated by the prospect of their arrival when, truly, the women are manipulating the male characters, taking the male script and using it for their own power and agency.

The concept is similar to what Mark Bracher outlines of nineteenth-century pornographic scripts, in which "fabrication of the desire of the woman is one of the major means by which pornography arouses desire in heterosexual men and provides satisfaction for them."[46] The excitement arrives through imagining the female's desire for the male love object; however, it is possible to extrapolate what is happening for the female character, one reading of which is that she recognizes his imagined desire and uses it for her own designs. Male power and agency are, then, undermined, and the songs register this reality alongside of the production of masculine identity structures; indeed, they each appear intertwined.

What the Clashes Mean Together: Anger and Aggression Speak to Vulnerability

This push and pull of power and control, deployed through the male and female characters as they clash within the songs, ultimately reveals a sense of vulnerability in the navigation of identity. Though sailing characters present a hypermasculine front and produce song narratives that confirm a particular hegemonic script, there are clearly some facets of the narrative that disclose how presentations of categorical gender sometimes fail in the face of lived performance. In pockets of narrative that fall outside of the "stiff-upper-lip" or "devil-may-care" attitudes that cultural narratives of sailors have recycled, we are able to see that the clashing of gendered vessels troubles presentations of self to the point that characters are rendered vulnerable and even demure. Where songs demonstrate agentive masculine violence (linguistic and narrative), subordination of women, especially nonwhite women, and the attempt to lord control, we see that much of that performance clashes with and is in response to female agency that troubles masculine superiority. Struggles with such confrontations elicit narratives that often appear as release valves that temper understanding of gendered performance.

Creighton argues, "The portrayal of seafaring as a combat engagement and sailors as warriors opposed to the tame female style of the shore, reflects in part middle-class gender ideals of the late nineteenth and early twentieth centuries, to which these historians were clearly attached. These ideals stressed the 'natural' polarities of male and female and celebrated a rugged, physical masculinity."[47] In a way, the liminality and vulnerability that are expressed in several song narratives capture the reality that true identity performance is something that is categorical expectation but also recognizes and even potentially embraces the failure of those performances. Differences between land and sea, similar to what was identified in chapter 3, certainly help to capture liminality and vulnerability, but what this kaleidoscopic landscape brings into sharper focus is the more embodied struggles that are a part of what Creighton notes in her research. Admissions of desire to be on land, suggestion of hope for intimacy with fellow men, expressed fear of emasculation, and a tinge of humor all combine to create a subtle undercurrent to the songs involving male and female characters. Brash and agentive violence and feelings of superiority evaporate when they are met with equally agentive women. The pockets of vulnerability in the songs, at base, admit a measure of suffering, and the violent rages and attempts at lording control are only mechanisms that fight to assuage confusing confrontations.

The vulnerability of male characters is evident during the several narrative moments when characters appear to yearn for time spent back at home, on land. The desire to remain on land is palpable when the narrative of "Jinny Keep Yer Arse-'Ole Warm" reads, "Now I'm safely on the shore, / An' I don' give a fuck how the windx [sic] do roar, / Oh, I'll drop me anchor an' I'll go to sea no more." The characters jointly point to the idea of dropping the literal anchor in port and vowing to never return to sea. This is a refrain often heard from sailors—that they wish to remain in port and leave the dangers of life on the open water. Symbolically, the songs access the idea of finding a wife and building a life on land such that landing the anchor means realizing the hope of starting a family and placing roots. In either reading, the narrative generates an interpretation that despite the foul language that subordinates women and the narrative lording of control in the sexual scenario, the characters release cries concerning the enduring pull toward the comforts of land.

The songs, in this way, navigate the cultural falsehood that sailors enjoyed their time at sea and chased water vocations based on an inborn need for adventure and instead turn our thinking to the comfort, safety, and affection that can be found in domesticity.[48] Clearly, *safety* is a facet of the shore life that the sailing character turns attention toward, and such an attachment to safety over adventure, violence, and dangerous feats of masculinity runs counter to the hegemonic script that appears as the primary narrative framework. No other song is more bent on the presentation of the comforts of home than "Billy Boy." This chantey is entirely focused on describing the prospective wife Nancy Lee, and the song captures the strong pull to anchored land and the love of a woman. Though it is true that the song progresses from the delightfully chaste to the erotic, the narrative contains within it a representation of the comforts of home that many sailors likely longed to have when they were adrift at sea and admits a level of vulnerability in its painting of the domestic landscape. Indeed, the song also registers what Burton notes concerning the turn toward domesticity in the nineteenth century, which impacted the sailor's own ability to secure gainful employment. The sailor was vulnerable both to his own need for a tie to love and kinship and to the need to fulfill the role of breadwinner for his family. Throughout, the narrator confirms that "me charmin' Nancy Lee" fulfills the qualities of a wife that anyone would hope to find. For instance, one stanza of the song reads:

> Can she make an Irish stew, Billy Boy, Billy Boy?
> She can make an Irish stew, aye an' singin' hinnies too.
> Does she sleep close unto thee, Billy Boy, Billy Boy?
> Aye, she sleeps close unto me, like the bark is to the tree.

This list of the comforts of home denotes the softer side of sailing characters or, at the very least, shows that there are vulnerable parts of men that need comfort and normative social expectations that are likely found only on land.

"Billy Boy" is not the only example of sailing characters hinting at this hearkening to hearth and home as a space of stability and safety. There is mention of certain "daughters" who are the focal point of desire, sometimes for love but often for sex. This tie to specific women, usually connected to some kind of family, which the word "daughter" evokes, in three separate chantey examples conjures a relationship with kinship ties back on land and divorced from the perils of the water. Mention of daughters represents the power and importance of familial connection, even a desire for an eventual familial connection, which would be strained by time at sea. These pockets appear to clash with some of the earlier discussion of agentive masculine violence and hierarchical vocations. Arguably, sailors were dependent on their families, wives and all, near the time when Hugill encountered or experienced these songs.

Male vulnerability is clearly a key undercurrent of the narratives, as evidenced by the admission of desires to remain on land, but it is also palpable in the ways through which many of the examples register intimate male desires that lapse into something almost coquettish, especially as they appear next to women they encounter in port. These narrative renderings of sailing characters are quite different from theoretical readings of working-class personhood and betray cracks in the façade of expected gender performance, even as it plays out in the examples from the manuscript. For one, narratives articulate a desire to be wanted by women encountered and described, even in the face of rejection. "Do Let Me 'Lone, Susan" is an example of a narrator describing a desire to be wanted by a woman but experiencing both rejection and an impediment. Though it is possible to read the entire chantey as akin to a rape narrative, it is interesting to consider an alternative reading of the text such that the sailor is cast as the vulnerable lover. Though he longs for Jinny's reciprocation, it is clear that she has no interest in the lecherous man.

The character Jinny appears again in "Jinny Keep Yer Arse-'Ole Warm," in which she figures in both the refrain and the main narrative. The same sense of longing and vulnerability are present even despite the more hypersexual and gender-script-confirming narrative. In the refrain, the sailor wishes for Jinny to "keep yer arse-'ole warm," with the interpretation being that her anus needs to stay warm for the coming sailor, but the underlying vulnerability of the line is the desire for Jinny to be both present for the sailor's arrival and sexually ready and willing. In fact, the line betrays the idea that the sailor is hoping that he is Jinny's only thought to the extent that she prepares for his arrival far in advance. This idea of preparation is confirmed in the later narrative line that reads, "An' there's my Jinny, oh, she's hungry for the cock."

A similar sentiment is apparent in "Saltpetre Shanty," discussed above. Within each of the examples, the male characters are vulnerable to the reciprocation of love and desire by the women they long to see. They are at the mercy of the women described. Such a narrative element communicates the impossibility of perfect gender performance, especially as it clashes against objects outside of real control. Though the expectation might be that a male character would control and order the sexual situation, the lived reality is far more complex.

Male vulnerability is also clear in that the songs register an almost violently paranoid concern that a character will be aligned with the feminine or that they might be viewed as penetrable or easily emasculated. Pockets of admission that betray a desire for hearth and home or the love of a woman might actually stoke some of these loaded responses that are meant to keep masculine identities intact. The narratives of the songs produce a hierarchical rendering of men and women, as was discussed above, and appear to do so both in order to assuage situations of which male characters recognize their own futility as well as their own vulnerability in the face of their desires and performances. Simon J. Bronner, in his study concerning "Barnacle Bill the Sailor," argues:

> It is more important for them [men] to separate from the mother than from the father, and a folkloric way to do that is to declare sexual, violent dominance over women or the mothers of peers. The independent sailor figure is an appealing one in this form of psychological projection, because he is clearly separated from the land of home and mother and he has a reputation for lustful, boastful behavior.[49]

Examples abound within the songs from Hugill that reproduce similar narrative treatments of women such that they are both the main narrative focus of the line, usually at the very end of a rhyming couplet, and on the receiving end of direct and weaponized male sexuality, which acts in service of separating the agentive male character from the soft, receiving female character. The reading of the chanteys as something akin to pressure valves for anxieties surrounding their masculine identity underscores Connell's argument that men

BILLY BOY

stet/

WHERE have ye bin all the day, Billy Boy, Billy Boy?
Where have ye bin all the day, me Billy Boy?
I've been walkin' on the quay with me charmin' Nancy Lee,
An' sweet Nancy kittl'd me fancy, oh me charmin' Billy Boy!

Is she fit to be your wife, Billy Boy, Billy Boy? Is she, &c.
Aye, she's fit to be me wife as the fork is to the knife./
Can she cook a bit o' steak, Billy Boy, Billy Boy?
She can cook a bit o' steak, aye an' make a griddle cake.

Can she make an Irish stew, Billy Boy, Billy Boy?
She can make an Irish stew, aye an' singin' hinnies too./
Does she sleep close unto thee, Billy Boy, Billy Boy?
Aye, she sleeps close unto me, like the bark is to the tree.

Can she make a feather bed, Billy Boy, Billy Boy?
She can make a feather bed, fit for any sailor's head./
Can she heave the dipsy lead, Billy Boy, Billy Boy?
Yes, she can heave the dipsy lead, but she's lost her maidenhea

Can she strop a block, Billy Boy, Billy Boy?
Aye, she can strop a block, an' she'll take a fathom o' cock./
Can she toss a bunt, Billy Boy, Billy Boy?
Aye, she can toss a bunt, an' she'll let you feel her cunt.

Sailing Ship Shanties, 1926-1956.

"Billy Boy," song collected from repertoire of Stan Hugill. Scanned copy from "Sea Songs," unpublished manuscript of Gershon Legman. Personal copy sent by Judith Legman, October 10, 2014.

look for opportunities for "asserting superiority over women," but the important and added layer to this reading is that there are cracks and fissures in the production of masculine identity in real time as they both recognize the need for women and register that such a need renders them vulnerable.

The choice of anal sex in a number of the songs underscores readings of vulnerability, but it also captures the complex and evolving ways through which power is negotiated. As an orifice that serves as a connecting factor between men and women, meaning that it is a cavity both genders share, it is possible to think about it as a neutral but highly complex space wherein identities might vacillate and connect. Though pleasure is the obvious initial reading of sexual engagements with the anus, it is possible to view it, too, as a complex way to negotiate and also regain control in a sexual situation, ultimately for both women and men. What anal sex attaches to, at least in this reading of the songs, is the navigation of the vulnerabilities of the body and identity, functionally a hole through which power dynamics slip and emerge.

The male body in the sexual scenarios outlined is vulnerable because it is invaded by the venereal disease wielded; in a similar fashion, the woman's own body is vulnerable to the male gaze, as discussed, as well as pregnancy and forced sex.[50] In this way, the male and female bodies are leveled: the female character succeeds in placing the man on the same plane as herself, which is in marked contrast to earlier parts of the song narrative. Venereal disease and the male character's alignment with the vulnerable female body help to temper the original image of male characters as strong, decisive, and virile. Anal sex rises as a tool used by both male and female characters to regain agency and protect the body from potential harm and invasion; however, salient to the discussion at hand is that women ultimately gain a greater measure of control within this particular sexual economy, and men potentially abdicate some of their power in this choice of orifice. Pointedly, through the choice of anal sex, female characters continue to subvert the heteronormative hierarchy and men relent some of their own control.

Anal sex is the potential balm for the vulnerability of the body, for both male and female characters, but it is complicated because of its loaded hierarchical reality. Indeed, anal sex proves a site through which to think about vulnerability, power, agency, and movement back and forth. Though many of the songs catalog the beauty and erotic possibility of the vagina, there is a distinct focus on the anus and other nonprocreative means of sexual pleasure, which serve as examples of female agency but also male control to a degree. Anal sex in particular is recognized as at least one intervention for staving off the threat of infection and could work as a means through which a male actor might attempt a degree of control in cases where he feared venereal disease.[51] Narrators point to the pleasures of anal sex in at least three of the songs surveyed for this chapter, and in this first reading, anal sex provides the opportunity for male characters to combat the threat of female agency exacted through knowingly infecting lovers with sexually transmitted diseases.

For the male characters in the songs, choosing anal sex, even in order to combat venereal disease, is loaded with potential hierarchical consequences, however. In the hegemonic male economy, the anus would be viewed as a site of submission and vulnerability and thus might signal that the male character in the song is dually subordinated through the venereal disease and through resorting to anal sex with either men or women. Jonathan Branfman, Susan Stiritz, and Eric Anderson note that "gay and bisexual men [are] frequently denigrated as dirty, emasculated, or deviant precisely for their cultural association with anal eroticism."[52] In choosing anal sex, characters run the risk of being associated with the penetrable; "men have an anus, and the possibility

```
            JINNY KEEP YER ARSE-'OLE WARM!

NOW, m'lads, be of good cheer,
For the Irish land will soon draw near,
In a few days more we'll sight Cape Clear,
      Ooooh! Jinny keep yer arse-'ole warm!
      Oh, jamboree, oh jamboree,
      Ai-i-i! ye big-pricked black man, sheet it home behind,
      Oh, jamboree, oh jamboree,
      Oooooh! Jinny keep yer arse-'ole warm!

Now, m'boys, we're off Holyhead,
An' there's no more casts of the dipsy lead,
'N' soon we'll lie in a fuckin' fevver-bed, Ooooh! &c.

Now the Bar Ship is in sight,
An' soon we'll be off the ol' Rock Light,
An' I'll be up yer flue tonight, Ooooh!&c.

Now we're haulin' through the dock,
All the pretty young gals on the pierhead do flock,
An' there's my Jinny, oh, she's hungry for the cock.

Now we're tied up to the pier,
Oh, 'tis way down below an' pack yer bloody gear,
An' I'll soon be two blocks up you, me dear.

Now I'm safely on the shore,
An' I don' give a fuck how the winds do roar,
Oh, I'll drop me anchor an' I'll go to sea no more.

Now I've had two weeks ashore,
I'll pack me bag an' I'll go to sea once more,
An' I'll bid goodbye to me Liverpool whore, Ooooh! &c.

                        Sailing Ship Shanties, 1933-1956.
```

"Jinny Keep Yer Arse-'Ole Warm," song collected from repertoire of Stan Hugill. Scanned copy from "Sea Songs," unpublished manuscript of Gershon Legman. Personal copy sent by Judith Legman, October 10, 2014.

of getting fucked always haunts phallic ideology."[53] Despite choosing anal sex so as to combat the power of the agentive woman, the character succumbs to the reading of anal sex as being potentially subordinating; indeed, it may hide a lurking desire to be anally penetrated. Admittedly, the sailing character is always invading the anus of the female character, securing a cursory reading of the act as an opposite-sex affiliated one, but it is impossible to dismiss the shadow of homoerotic implications. Too, in ejaculating into the anus, the male character is not able to fulfill his role as progenitor and his semen is essentially wasted on the pleasure. Though he could secure his power and authority through impregnating a woman, he chooses instead to vacate his sperm and let it die without seeking to fertilize an egg. During the nineteenth century, such a choice was the subject of medical and cultural anxieties as the loss of sperm was equated with loss of life for the man.[54]

Clearly, the songs from Hugill arguably capture a complex erotic reality for men where anal sex is concerned. They provide a cultural artifact through which we might consider men's desire for the anus and how a relationship with anal sex, both individually and externally to the man, might function. The conversation concerning desire for the anus is one that has only recently gained traction in scholarship dealing with gender and sexuality. Kimberly R. McBride and J. Dennis Fortenberry note, "Research is quite rare that specifically differentiates the anus as a sexual organ or addresses anal sexual function or dysfunction as legitimate topics."[55] Along with this observation is that the motivations for desiring the anus, especially on the part of opposite-sex interested men, have enjoyed scant little scholarly attention. Despite the paucity of scholarship on the subject, it is clear that anal eroticism and anal sex were important enough to become narrative focal points in many of the songs provided by Hugill, and recent scholarship points to a preponderance of anal fixation and curiosity for men who do not primarily identify as interested in the same sex.

It is possible to view some of the songs from Hugill as capturing what Stephen Maddison recognizes as a circular desiring for and disavowal of the male anus, generating a reading of the anus in the songs as "a site of contestation and anxiety," akin to what Maddison recognizes as occurring in contemporary pornography.[56] In attaching Maddison's reading of anal fixation in pornography to Hugill's songs, it is possible to see a violent displacement of male desire for anal pleasure, forcing female characters to endure the sensation that has been denied to men. There is an argument to be made that contemporary desire for the anus is spurred by the preponderance of anal sex in pornography; however, the existence of anal fixation and interest in Hugill's songs generates the potential that this desire has been articulated in other spaces. As Liam Wignall, Ryan Scoats, Eric Anderson, and Luis Morales note, "men must penetrate women, not stimulate or penetrate their own orifices, or allow their orifices to be stimulated or penetrated by others," but there is a clear curiosity and interest inherent in consuming, penetrating, and even destroying the anus in both observed contemporary spaces as well as within the songs.[57]

What is interesting about the linguistic configuration of masculine desire for the anus is that there is a positioning of the desire as one that is inherently opposite-sex affiliated and even one that might reify masculine superiority and agency. Penetrating women, or even effeminate men, as will be clear in "The Bumboy," still reads as opposite-sex affiliated for the experimentation is occurring in such a way that the penetrating man is in control of the erotic scenario and is in the position of dominance. This is not always the case in the songs from Hugill, as has been made clear. Women often choose anal penetration as a means to garner more control in the sexual economy, but underneath this agency is, potentially, some level of female subservience to men as well as acquiescence so as to protect themselves from pregnancy and disease.[58]

It is impossible to miss the sheer number of anal encounters in Hugill's songs, and the admissions suggest an interest in experimenting with not only the taboo (under the cover of an opposite-sex sexual configuration, of course) but also anality more generally. A similar method of "understanding, defining and rationalizing in order to maintain feelings of pride and stability" occurs within the framework of contemporary pegging discourses, where pegging is understood to be an erotic scenario in which a man is penetrated by a woman with the use of a strap-on dildo.[59] In these erotic situations, men seek to remasculinize themselves in the process of receiving anal pleasure and even anal penetration, and as is clear in the songs, "men's bodies remain the site of emphasis."[60]

What is of key import as far as the songs are concerned is that there is a vacillation of identities, power, and pleasures that renders the sailing characters as provocative ciphers for thinking through sexuality and gender. As characters announce anal sex as "a sailor's treat" and violently "ram it [a penis] two-blocks up her arse-ole!" readers encounter a crystallized and even potentially vulnerable admission of a desire that carries with it an association with same-sex affiliation and even their own subordination. Anal sex contains clear power dynamics, and it is a scenario always already loaded with phallocentric readings of invasion, penetration, and domination, but for men, it is also a very complicated and contested site of pleasure. There appears a drive and urge to ensure that anal encounters are read as opposite-sex affiliated in scholarship dealing with anal sex as well as within the narratives of Hugill's songs, and this sensation is attached to a potential anxiety around male penetration and loss of masculinity. Though anachronistic, the term "homohysteria" is an apt descriptor for the anxiety that potentially lurks beneath the surface as it "constructs anal stimulation as a homosexual affair, even if performed in the absence of another male."[61] Characters, at least in the songs, might displace this desire for their own anal stimulation through visiting that desire on the bodies of women. The violence inherent in that visitation has been observed in contemporary research on heterosexual anal sex; women are often violently subordinated to the desires of the male counterparts.[62]

It is worth considering the question posed by Jonathan Allan, which is, "What does the anus mean and do in fiction. . . ?"[63] Within the confines of Hugill's songs, the answer to that question is that it accomplishes a complex negotiation of gender, sexuality, desire, and personhood such that a character's lived reality is one that slips back and forth, ahead and behind, and even above and below within the space of a few short lines. The anus is the orifice through which, potentially, we can consider the slippery nature of desire and identity. Allan writes: "What is so shocking is that the anus is endowed so much meaning. Through it, shattering occurs—the phallus can penetrate any hole, as it were, and retain its power. But when Rusty's ass is penetrated [here, he is speaking of an anal rape scene in *Myra Breckinridge*], the possibility of symbolic unity is called into question."[64] In the songs, I can see a similar recognition of penetrability, of phallic power, but also loss of that power and, through that loss, a self-shattering and even a reordering of self. To desire the anus, here, is a registration of a desire that cannot always be spoken aloud for within in it is the recognition of one's own penetrability, one's own self-shattering, and the reality that the man can trade places with a woman in a moment. What I mean by self-shattering is that the male character is often undone by the female character who uses anal sex as a tool of power, but he is also shattered, to a degree, in his position as an agentive man, even when he is violently penetrating the anuses of women. There may be, underneath these intrusions, a vulnerable desire to trade places with her. I think the anus might become, at least in these songs, a place to read the sailor as a desiring character, one who is curious about and interested in anal eroticism, as well as a symbolic representation of the slippery nature of sexuality and eroticism, especially for men.

What is striking about all the elements outlined above is the fact that the songs deliver a continued recognition that this push and pull of power and subordination, fulfillment of masculine expectation and also failings, as well as liminalities lived between life at sea and life on land and desire and reality are each functions of life and there is not much that can be done about them. Throughout these songs, like songs of warning, both narrators and general male characters produce and situate themselves within the narrative using a casual and humorous tone, even in the delivery of narrative elements that include violence, pain, and deceit. There is a cavalier quality to the pronouncement of lines, and this approach to lyrics echoes working-class expectations of masculinity, especially sailing masculinity. The narrative also appears to align with extant research on other folklore materials from homosocial spaces. Succinctly, working-class men both present and articulate a masculine performance that registers and even embraces danger, sometimes through laughter, and this particular masculine expectation is echoed within their jokes and songs. Richard Henry Dana Jr. shows that, in terms of sailing men, "whatever your feelings may be, you must make a joke of everything at sea; and if you were to fall from aloft and be caught in the belly of a sail, and thus saved from instant death, it would not do to look at all disturbed, or to make a serious matter of it."[65] In fact, sailors were very often expected to make a joke of even something as serious as death. It is then interesting to consider something like the line from "Jinny Keep Yer Arse-'Ole Warm" that reads, "Now, m'boys, we're off to Holyhead, / An' there's no more casts of the dipsy lead, / 'N' soon we'll lie in a fuckin' fevver-bed [*sic*]." The song leverages, with equal weight, the prospect of heading toward land and the completion of work with the notion of lying sick in a "fevver-bed," underscoring the final prospect with the signifying and dismissive "fuckin."

Similarly, "Saltpetre Shanty" outlines, "Them *putas* o' Chile they're hard to beat :2: / With a blow-through an' a *rumper* an' a skinful o' wine, / But them barstards is poxin' us all o' the time."[66] Just as with the line in "Jinny Keep Yer Arse-'Ole Warm," there is a general comfort and even humorous disregard of situations that must have been painful and even deeply upsetting. In both examples, lines clearly denote sickness and even lasting venereal diseases, but these maladies are presented as almost routine, seemingly in an attempt to render some of the vulnerable admissions as not as important as they actually are, which is identical to the recognition and masochistic returns in songs of warning. Historian Brian J. Rouleau's work helps to elaborate on a particular sailing penchant for viewing large and small diseases and catastrophes alike; he argues, "Observers frequently commented on the relative ease with which mariners appeared to transition from moments of grave danger to those of an almost cheerful, even blasé complacence."[67] The same "ease . . . [of] transition" is apparent throughout each of the songs, and such a narrative choice betrays a particular masculine identity construction that seeks to downplay the suffering that the lines truly divulge. In fact, the songs present a registration of the realities of social space and elegantly deploy humor to grapple with painful vulnerabilities and social failings, like confronting agentive women that could possibly emasculate. Unlike expected male bravado and posturing,

```
                        SALTPETRE SHANTY

        TO ol' Callyo we are bound away — Arse-ole! :2:
        We're bound away at the break o' the day
        To where them putas o' Chili will grab all our pay.
              Arse-ole!  Slap her arse (tits)!
              Ram it two-blocks up her arse-ole!

        Ol' Pedro the pimp, boys, he knows us of old :2:
        He's a-primin' his vino, an' dopin' his beer,
        To the Chinchas he'll ship us if we don't take care.

        Ol' Madam the Judge stands her tarts in a row,:2:
        She wants all her gals to put on a good show.
        They're a-powderin' their fannies, they're scentin' their 'ole
        Awaitin' us Jackshites to flush out their 'oles.

        Them putas o' Chili they're hard to beat :2:
 stet/  With a blow-through an' a rumper an' a skinful o' wine,
        But them barstards is poxin' us all o' the time.

        We'll wash down saltpetre with pisco an' wine :2:
        When we're loaded an' ready for to sing a farewell,
        Them young Chili whores, boys, we'll wish 'em in Hell.

                              Sailing Ship Shanties, 1926-1957.
```

"Saltpetre Shanty," song collected from repertoire of Stan Hugill. Scanned copy from "Sea Songs," unpublished manuscript of Gershon Legman. Personal copy sent by Judith Legman, October 10, 2014.

the songs contain pockets of reality delivered with a wry and knowing tone, accepting that expectation and reality will never truly coexist.[68]

Sailing characters and the men and women they encounter in these narratives are vessels through which to articulate the frustrations and vulnerabilities attached to the delicate process of identity formation for a group of working-class men that are equal parts mythic, complex, and misunderstood. This chapter has trained an analytical eye onto the ways through which male and female characters, two-dimensional as they sometimes are, clash and collide occasionally with cavalier humor but more often and tellingly with nuance and complexity. All characters, male and female, function as a symbolic means through which we may understand identity formation and expression as less categorical and more kaleidoscopic. Throughout, these characters carry a weight and a communicative power that the expression of finite and expected gender norms, whether male or female, are subject to the painful and confusing realities of the social world. Bent as one may be on the process of reproducing the gender and sexual scripts expected, negotiating identity, personhood, pleasure, and ambient culture are each processes that are far too complex for only one mode of performance or intervention. Powerful and strong men will find that they are unable to maintain control in the sexual situation, are usurped by a wily and more agentive woman, or might encounter a situation that completely robs them of authoritative voice and ability to navigate. Pleasures, too, may misalign with expected gender scripts. Desires may leave a man appearing vulnerable and even soft. What should be clear is that when we place finite categories on identity, personhood, and self, a situation will ultimately clash with our deeply held beliefs that fundamentally alters our understanding of our social position and forces us to move and evolve—even reverberate out. The songs from Hugill require that we recognize the continuum of human identity and suggest, perhaps, that we take the same cavalier approach to moments at which we might fail to measure up.

CHAPTER 5

Looking Queerly and the Pleasures That Defy Category

In the final turn of the kaleidoscope's glass, it is possible to see the queer elements of these songs as more alive and potent, further bringing the continuum of identity into focus. Throughout, the suggestion has been that the chanteys from this manuscript gesture at ideas of gender and sexuality that are more real and more predicated on the messy, unstable quality of these identities, which means that they are performances that fail to meet categorical expectations. I venture here that the queer undercurrents of the songs motion toward even deeper parts of human experience that we often like to bury or dismiss: the recognition of the inherent inability to adhere to identity scripts and the seeking of spaces where we can alleviate the longing for erotic release that defies expected categories. What I mean is that the real quality of sexuality, pleasure, and desire is not really captured in finite categories and that song might be a space through which actors hint at the negotiation of and struggle with social categories beneath the surface. The songs deeply register the constraining and stringent realities of such confining categories and demonstrate that humans will seek spaces to vent their desires that defy restrictive expectations. The last chapters grappled primarily with gender, often as it was tied to sexual scenarios; however, this chapter more deeply investigates sexual desire as something just as, if not more, unstable than categorical gender. It bears repeating that though these instabilities appear axiomatic, venting these fluidities of gender and sexuality in song supports the view that cultural artifacts register complex human negotiations of self that are then, very often and importantly, shared with others in social space under protective guises that sometimes elide or dismiss the mutability.

The songs from Hugill's repertoire, especially those with something of a queer gaze, fully depict the experience of desire and pleasure, which is one that is unbound and predicated only on what feels good. The continuum of gender has enjoyed most of the analytical discussion, and a continuum of sexual desire and pleasure has been something whispering behind the lines. Here, the gaze is turned on those pockets of narrative that hint at experiences of eroticism that run counter to heteronormative scripts despite and even within and through heteronormative narrative. The main focus of this chapter is to take the suggestions of liminalities, discussed at length in earlier chapters, and apply those liminalities to the texts that train the gaze on the bodies of male characters. The unmoored quality of the sea, something that is attached to the bodies of sailing characters, visits itself on gazes and narrative moments that align more with a sexuality that is curious and flexible than one that is rigidly heteronormative and therefore contained and restrained by category.

This chapter specifically investigates "Reefy Tayckle," "What Shall We Do? (Drunken Sailor)," "Yaw, Yaw, Yaw!," "Miss Lucy Long," "The Hog-Eye Man," and "The Bumboy" for what they each articulate about the complexities of male desire and eroticism. Within the songs, there is permission granted to consume the erotically charged bodies of men through turgid members and virile testicles: songs acting akin to the keyhole in the door, which ushers a queer scopophilia and voyeurism. Throughout this chapter, I lean on work in literary theory, especially that which deals with material like *Fanny Hill* and the erotically charged literary war between Colley Cibber and Alexander Pope, the sociology of homosocial environments, critical work dealing with male hardbody films, and scholarly investigations in modern pornography in order to suggest that the narrative material located in the Hugill manuscript ultimately invokes similar relational patterns observed in these fields.

Erotic materials, like the Hugill songs, represent that there are multiple sites through which men appear to articulate a sexual desire or curiosity that falls outside of normative expectations. Almost everything in exclusive male culture, like joking, songs, poetry, and storytelling, contains not only a clear focus on sex and erotic expression but also an intentional gaze trained on male bodies, which communicates a continuum of desire and curiosity that runs counter to strict hegemonic codes. Because male genitalia arrive in so much ephemera from all-male culture, there is space to consider that these different but overlapping cultural objects capture the reality that men seek spaces through which to vent desire and curiosity that is not afforded to them in general culture. Indeed, their experimentation is relegated to spaces that are protected or are hidden from view. Just like in the case of constructions of gender, it will be clear that erotic desires and outlets often defy the confining and constraining categories fitted to them, and the narratives within the songs surveyed for this chapter imply that humans look for pressure valves and releases that protect and encourage the exploration of the taboo, usually through heteronormative covers that permit the gaze to occur sometimes imperceptibly.

Queer Narrative Elements Provide the Gaze

Though much of the narrative in Hugill's songs seems to support cultural renderings of a hypersexual, hypermasculine "man's man," there are elements buried underneath the narrative that work to erode the first impressions of the characters within. What is presented in the bulk of the chantey narratives collected in the Legman-Hugill manuscript, particularly involving the sailor and women in port, is a complex relationship with women, sexual expression, and longing and desire. While the irascible and lecherous old salt is someone encountered in cultural depictions and historical commentary, the lived reality, as it connects to the subtext of the chantey narratives to be discussed, is something far more intricate and interesting.

Hugill's songs slip from a simple hypermasculine celebration of agentive male bodies to an erotic and scopophilic consumption of those bodies through the narrative use of female impersonation as well as the repeated act of *watching* and *looking* at body parts like penises and testicles. Same-sex-desiring elements in Hugill's repertoire are most apparent in songs like "The Bumboy" and "What Shall We Do? (Drunken Sailor)," but the other songs surveyed here hint at desires for fellow men almost as plainly. The duty that the song narratives perform, ultimately, is to satisfy the urge to look at the bodies of other men within a relatively protected space, and that protection is primarily achieved through the narrative concealments and sleights of hand that render the celebratory and heteronormative frameworks as the superficial focal point. What is apparent is that song narratives present as celebrations of sexual virility and prowess, but these focal points work to cover the deeper realities of the songs as they are written. The surface-level reading of narrative material as a means to celebrate agentive masculinity carries within it a homoerotic fixation to *see* and *experience* the hyperbolic capabilities of other men. Because the man is viewing and consuming within a protected and expected framework, he is able to engage with the images and assuage even a small tinge of desire for the homoerotic without fear of exposure. Placing prideful awe as an entry point into homoerotic desire and fixation will demonstrate the trajectory from simple celebration to the reading of men manufacturing spaces and ways through which to experiment with same-sex erotics. Song is only one of the many male spaces wherein this sliding continuum occurs.

The Desire to Look

One of the first ways through which songs in the manuscript fashion a same-sex-curious subtext is through shaping a narrative gaze that is trained specifically on the bodies of men. These songs are training a look in similar ways to that which has been identified in other homoerotic texts. Not only is the gaze trained on the parts of male characters but also the language of lines encourages a manipulated look based on the ways in which the parts are described and narratively arranged.

This manipulation of the gaze runs in a similar fashion to Herman Melville's extended description of Billy Budd's body, in which descriptive lines blur between the complimentary and the desirous. Melville takes the time to describe each minute detail of Billy, highlighting small aspects of his body that further underscore his beauty and virility:

> The ear, small and shapely, the arch of the foot, the curve in mouth and nostril, even the indurated hand dyed to the orange-tawny of the toucan's bill, a hand telling alike of the halyards and tar bucket; but, above all, something in the mobile expression, and every chance attitude and movement, something suggestive of a mother eminently favored by Love and the Graces; all of this strangely indicated a lineage in direct contradiction to his lot.[1]

Melville fragments Billy's body so that the reader is forced to view each intimate piece in a similar manner to the hyperfocus on penises and testicles in the songs.[2]

In "The Hog-Eye Man," the reader is immediately drawn to the lines "his bowsprit was hard, his bowsprit was long, / He tickled her innards while he sang this little song." Within these lines alone, there is a clear interplay between scopophilic consumption of genitalia and aggrandizing hyperbole, which is achieved through a close and palpable description of the man's genitals. There is even, to a degree, a fixation on the anal and internal, evoked through the focus on tickling innards. The nexus of the gaze, of course, is the bowsprit standing in as his engorged penis, but the connection to the same homoerotic fixation identified in Melville is clear, especially when we consider that the bowsprit is invading innards, a queer erotic space because of its opaqueness. Other songs encourage a similar scopophilic consumption of bodies such that the reader is tasked with hyperfocusing on testicles, engorged penises either standing ready for the cause or invading the body of another character, and some celebration of the collective capacity of men, like what is seen as one sailing character of "Miss Lucy Long" extols "brass-bounders of the Blackball Line." Similar to how Melville lingers on Billy's foot, mouth, nose, and so on, the songs run a narrative finger over the contours of the genitals described: the metaphors can be seen, felt, tasted, and even heard.

The similar scopophilic consumption I am contending of songs from Hugill is apparent in literary criticism of *Fanny Hill*. In fact, much of *Fanny Hill* is predicated on the idea of *looking* and *seeing*, as if surreptitiously peaking at the sexual encounter in a similar way to the songs under consideration. Calculated watching occurs in such places as "Miss Lucy Long," where the narrator "view[s] the view an' take[s] the air" and "I showed her me knob." Likewise, in "The Hog-Eye Man," the singer "saw her" and "he tried to ring her bell," and then the cuckolded husband, later, "saw his Jinny a-lyin' in the grass." The song closes with "the hog-eye man, he's lookin' for a ride." That "ride" immediately conjures the image of the engorged penis of the hog-eye man, which "caulked her [Jinny's] little crack." "Yaw, Yaw, Yaw!," for its own part, includes a moment when characters "shit (piss) down on de peoples," which would involve peering down on characters below in order to train the excrement onto these unfortunate souls.[3] This line, of course, brings to mind Kristeva's "abject" and the discussion of excrement in chapter 4.

Literary critic Cameron McFarlane argues of *Fanny Hill*, especially in terms of how this watching might become aligned with the homoerotic, "the presence of Fanny as the 'I' of the narration and as our 'eye' into the textual world maintains and guarantees the look as 'natural' even as it simultaneously enables the solicitation of the homoerotic gaze."[4] Similarly, the look of the viewer in many of the songs is directed toward something "natural" or expected, like the opposite-sex sexual interaction, through the look of a narrator who is never fully identified in terms of gender and sexuality, and that narration is protected through both ciphers. What is allotted through that gaze, similar to *Fanny Hill* as well as *Billy Budd*, is a same-sex looking that is trained on male bodies or a forced looking on that is implicit and implicates the viewer in the act.

Joanne Begiato, in fact, notes that looking at male bodies, specifically working-class bodies, was an important aspect of early modern culture. Indeed, "for some socialists, the male working body was explicitly eroticized, even fetishized" and figured prominently in works of art that were often meant to instruct viewers in what a man should look like and embody.[5] Of course,

THE HOG-EYE MAN

Oh, the hog-eye man is the man for me,
With a prick from here to Tennessee!
Oh, hog-eye O! <u>Row the boat ashore for her hog-eye,</u>
<u>Row the boat ashore for her hog-eye O,</u>
    <u>She wants the hog-eye man!</u>

He came to the shack where Jinny she did dwell,
As soon as he saw her he tried to ring her bell./
O, Jinny's in the garden a-pickin' peas,
An' the hair of her snatch hangin' down to her knees.

She was too late to hide her snatch,
An' the hog-eye nigger jammed a bale down the hatch./
He caught her all aback, an' he caulked her little crack,
She wriggled like the divil but she couldn't shift her tack.

stet/

Soon he had her like a schooner on the rock,
She was a little maid who had never seen a cock./
His bowsprit was hard, his bowsprit was long,
He tickled her innards while he sang this little song.

An' then he went away, 'cause he'd had his little fun,
He left her on her back, with her fanny in the sun./
Oh, her sweetheart (fancyman) came for to court his lass,
An' he saw his Jinny a-lyin' in the grass.

Oh, who's bin here since I've bin gone?
A big buck nigger wid a hard-on on./
If I cotch him here wid me Jinny anymore,
I'll tattoo his dusters, an' he won't fuck anymore.

Oh, the hog-eye man, he's lookin' for a ride,
When he's ashore, lock yer gals inside.

<u>Sailing Ship Shanties</u>, 1930-1956.

"The Hog-Eye Man," song collected from repertoire of Stan Hugill. Scanned copy from "Sea Songs," unpublished manuscript of Gershon Legman. Personal copy sent by Judith Legman, October 10, 2014.

"the result [of these images] was idealized virile workers who possessed an erotic charge for both male and female consumption."[6] In much the same way, the nature of the songs is such that readers and listeners would be charged with envisioning the narratives they encounter; indeed, they are charged, through language, with the expectation that they will visually consume the material. In the songs, we experience a similar looking and watching to readers of *Fanny Hill*, in which the male writer dons a female persona to consume a sexual experience that becomes queered through the gaze deployed. When the narratives of songs note a moment when characters are watching or spectating, those scenes relate back to an overarching visual consumption, which, as should be clear at this point, contains a homoerotic subtext. In fact, even some of the watching and looking on that happens within the chanteys betrays queer elements. Natasha Hurley, in *Circulating Queerness: Before the Gay and Lesbian Novel*, captures the way "queer" is deployed in this view of the songs when she argues of Melville's *Typee* that it is "queer in the variety of overlapping ways that *queer* has come to mean in the time since *Typee*'s publication (sexually nonnormative, socially strange, homosexual, and just plain perverse)."[7] Added to this, of course, is also the opaque, the suggestive, and even the spectral. Viewing these songs queerly means that there are overlapping implications, such as the outright depiction of same-sex erotic desire as well as a more subtle and suggestive desiring that exists along the same-sex- and opposite-sex-affiliated continuum. In the latter, looking at songs queerly uncovers the potential for opposite-sex erotic engagements to attach also to same-sex-desiring subtexts.

The *watching* and *seeing* included in the narratives raise the act of visual consumption to the level of perceptibility, meaning readers are actually involved in perceivable sensations that register corporeally. We are reminded about the *watching* through the language employed and that watching is extended out from the narrative into the experience of the viewer (himself involved in the watching as is suggested in "view*er*"). Several songs in Hugill's repertoire take this looking and watching to the level of interactive touch. For instance, the scene of defecating or urinating onto people in "Yaw, Yaw, Yaw!" weds looking at a scatological moment when characters soil people beneath them and the sensation that the act carries with it. This scene is tangible and, of course, calls to mind the discussion of nonwhite bodies and excrement, discussed at length in the previous chapter.

There are other tactile moments of the songs when the watching and seeing becomes interactive to the point that it appears akin to point-of-view pornography, approximating touch. A particular scene in "What Shall We Do? (Drunken Sailor)" trains the gaze on a character as he scrapes hairs off a man's scrotum, an intimate act that requires someone to remain quite close to the genitalia in order to execute the action fully, all while ensuring that the man's genitals are shaved and not harmed. The character is clearly careful to ensure that he scrapes the hairs and does not chance a slip of the hoop-iron razor. To cut the drunken sailor's scrotum, potentially completely off, in the process of shaving would impact the virility of the character, and the narrative is specific in noting that the scrotum is shaved and unharmed. Note that the scrotum remains intact, unlike the broken and bent jibbooms in songs of warning. Such a narrative quality encourages a reading that there are equal parts juridical punishment—for the shaving is called on because the man is drunk—and calculated and almost sensual reverence for the scrotum. This distinct difference suggests that there is a desire to look onto the fully functioning and virile genitalia of the character.

Genitals are also in touchable relief in "The Hog-Eye Man," in which the cuckolded husband takes the time to level the threat that if the hog-eye man returns for more from his Jinny, he will "tattoo his dusters an' he won't fuck anymore." "Dusters" are meant to be understood as the testicles and scrotum, and to imagine a cuckolded husband holding down another man while tattooing his genitals conjures a queer and intimate, albeit violent, moment. In the narrative, such an act requires that the husband invent a punishment that would permit him a closeness to the genitals of the hog-eye man, both visually and tactilely, in the service of revenge, but there is also a notable degree of calculated care. The experience, as it is described in the song, would necessitate that the cuckolded man touch the other man's testicles in the process of this "revenge" and hold them delicately enough so as to tattoo them, which weds revenge with careful artistry and handling. There is certainly a level of retribution inherent in the narrative, unlike many contemporary representations of cuckoldry to be discussed in further detail below, in which the cuckolded man often joins in. Important to highlight, of course, is that in the delicacy with which the testicles are held, there is also a level of violence, especially as it attaches to something like tattooing as a form of ownership or branding against someone's will: painful for both the body and the mind. Viewing this narrative element as retaliatory and embodied is made all the more salient when considering the race of the man described for, at several turns, the man is denoted using the pejorative term for African Americans. The implication is that vengeance would come through Jinny's "fancyman" controlling the hog-eye man in the sexual economy, loading the tattoo imagery with historical significance and also erotic tension. That said, however, tattooing requires care and attention to be paid to the genitals and, indeed, draws further focus on the genitals in its tie to artistic expression and thereby connects the visual and tactile as well as the erotic.[8]

In both "The Hog-Eye Man" and "What Shall We Do?," there is a curious tension between potential violence and harm as well as caring scrutiny and exactness to refrain from injury. There is an intimacy involved that betrays vulnerability and desire to care for the genitals of other men. A later scene from "What Shall We Do? (Drunken Sailor)" contains one of the queerer narrative moments of the songs from Legman and Hugill, which captures the watching and seeing noted so far. Listeners watch as the collective "we"

YAW, YAW, YAW!

OH, mit mein niggerum, buggerum, stinkum,
    Mit mein yaw, yaw, yaw!
Mit mein niggerum, buggerum, stinkum,
    Mit mein yaw, yaw, yaw!
Vell, ve'll climb upon der steeples,
And ve'll shit (piss) down on de peoples,
    Mit mein yaw, yaw, yaw!

                     Sailing Ship Shanties, 1933-1956.

BALLAD:NOTES

Yaw, Yaw, Yaw! Hugill MS., noting in his book, p. 504, that the song 'was obscene throughout,' and there printing [giving] a 'camouflaged version,' but giving only this '"rudest" verse" in his MS. — SEE: Doerflinger 86, noting that it is a pseudo-Dutch or imitative Squarehead 'ditty at the expense of the "Dutch." In the lingo of the old-time sailorman, a "Dutchman" was anybody, regardless of nationality, who "said ja for yes" — except subjects of the Netherlands. They were especially identified as "Holland"Dutch",' also as "God-damned Dutch." So also the "Pennsylvania Dutch," from Deitsch or Deutsch, meaning German. (— Compare "THE PRISONER'S SONG.")

"Yaw, Yaw, Yaw!," song collected from repertoire of Stan Hugill. Scanned copy from "Sea Songs," unpublished manuscript of Gershon Legman. Scan contains "ballad notes" and some stray markings or notes. Personal copy sent by Judith Legman, October 10, 2014.

"stick[s] her [Queen o' Sheba] in a cage, an' let[s] a monkey fuck her." The line obviously ventures a narrative line of bestiality; however, what is relevant to the discussion at hand is the acts of both *facilitating* and then *watching* the sexual display, and there are also the implications of the monkey standing in for his human viewers.[9]

There is a level of the uncanny inherent in the idea of watching a monkey copulate with the woman as the monkey is a humanoid character; however, there is also a projection of the wills of those watching onto the display in front of them. This projection permits the viewers the opportunity to both erotically control and order the woman in the cage, but because of her status as a queen, the viewers are also able to reinforce their dominance through orchestrating her subordination at the hands of an animal.

```
                        DRUNKEN SAILOR
          WHAT SHALL WE DO? WITH A DRUNKEN SAILOR?


WHAT shall we do with a drunken sailor :3:
     Earlye in the morning?
     Way, hay, an' UP she rises :3:
     Earlye in the morning.

Scrape the hairs off his bollocks with a hoop-iron razor,
The hairs off his bollocks with a hoop-iron razor,
Scrape the hairs off his bollocks with a hoop-iron razor,
     Earlye in the morning, &c.

What'll we do with the Queen o' Sheba? :3:
Pull the hairs from her snatch with a pair o' tweezers./
What'll we do with the Queen o' Morrocker? :3:
Stick her in a cage, an' let a monkey fuck her.

                    Sailing Ship Shanties, 1930-1956.
```

"What Shall We Do?," song collected from repertoire of Stan Hugill. Scanned copy from "Sea Songs," unpublished manuscript of Gershon Legman. Personal copy sent by Judith Legman, October 10, 2014. The title "With a Drunken Sailor?" is crossed out and "Drunken Sailor" is added over the typed title. Song title becomes either "Drunken Sailor" or "What Shall We Do? Drunken Sailor."

The scene, then, reifies masculine power and agency through ordering and controlling the sexual situation, but in terms of the consumption of male bodies, it is worth noting that the line specifically focuses on watching "a monkey fuck her." By focusing the gaze explicitly on the now-agentive monkey, the line accomplishes the task of underscoring a desire to watch the erotic exchange, but it also raises the observation that the watching of such sexual intrigues almost always includes an intensely trained focus on the actions of the male figure. Indeed, the monkey copulating with the Queen of Sheba reproduces something of a caricature of the scenes that have, to this point, already been discussed.

Further examples of queer narrative moments that demand the gaze linger on a blatantly queer erotic encounter are those located in "The Bumboy."[10] In fact, this text is the only song within Hugill's repertoire with the entire narrative focused on a purely same-sex erotic fixation.[11] The gaze lingers on hyperbolic descriptions of the mate's penis, but it also demands that viewers consume the hierarchically ordered sexual encounter between the mate and the young sailing boy.[12] The fact that male genitalia and queer elements arrive within the narratives of many of Hugill's songs—as they do throughout multiple different examples from the song traditions of primarily male spaces— helps to venture an argument that men and boys look for release valves through which to channel deeply felt desires and curiosities about other men.[13] The *look* occurs because there is *desire*—an intentionality.

What is observable in these same-sex suggestive narratives is quite similar to what is noted by Thomas P. Oates in terms of the erotic consumption of male bodies in the NFL draft. He argues, "Looking is often linguistic as well as visual," and "although these fans do not generally concede this erotic subtext, 'voyeurism is voyeurism, acknowledged or not.'"[14] Eyes linger on the bodies of hypervirile and masculine men, ogling them. Additionally, their bodies are verbally commented on with an erotic tinge, which is impossible to dismiss. There is a similar wedding of the verbal and visual within these erotic songs, where the consumption is both celebratory, like in the NFL, and distinctly desirous and desiring.

Female Impersonation and Queer Narrators as Covers

The way in which the narratives often achieve the looking and watching is through the protective cover of the narrator *doing* the watching. The songs in this chapter evoke similar readings to those aligned with female impersonation narratives, which have been recognized as narrative tools that provide permission for consuming same-sex bodies. Many scholars have remarked that male writers will don a female cover so as to relay erotic situations as though they were from the female narrator's perspective. Venturing the narrative in this way, male writers are able to focus in on certain facets of the storyline that, through the female cover, are rendered less homoerotic on their surface; however, when unpacking the deployment of the narrative, the homoerotic subtext is readily apparent.

Though men likely shaped the songs, a female perspective or vague, nongendered, omniscient narrator serves as the voice to guide our reading and experience. "What Shall We Do? (Drunken Sailor)," "Miss Lucy Long," and "Reefy Tayckle" are each predicated on a queer perspective relayed through a nongendered narrator, while "The Hog-Eye Man" is equal parts queer and something like a female impersonation. The gaze is queer here because it is nondescript and interchangeable, male or female. For its own part, "The Bumboy" not only is told from what appears to be a male perspective but

THE BUMBOY

WHEN I was a tiny little boy,
I went to sea in Stormy's employ,
I shipped away as a little bumboy.
When I was just a shaver, a shaver,
Oh, I was weary of the sea, when I was just a shaver.
When I wwas just a shaver.

Oh, they whacked me up and they whacked me down,
The mate he cracked me on the crown,
He wanted me for his bit o' brown, When,&c.

When I went aloft by the lubber's hole
The mate he cried, Goddam yer soul!
An' he rammed his prick right up me 'ole, When, &c.

And when we lolloped around Cape Horn,
I wished to Christ I'd never been born,
The ice it froze the chief mate's horn, When, &c.

Oh, we left behind the ice an' rain,
An' once more to the tropics we came,
And the mate he was back on the job again.

When we made port, oh I skipped ship,
I'd had enough cock for one bleedin' trip,
With a boy-shaggin' mate, oh I'd never more ship.

Sailing Ship Shanties, 1925-1956.

"The Bumboy," song collected from repertoire of Stan Hugill. Scanned copy from "Sea Songs," unpublished manuscript of Gershon Legman. Personal copy sent by Judith Legman, October 10, 2014.

also contains within it a same-sex narrative. Literary criticism concerning *Fanny Hill* points to how a female narrator, written by a male author, not only describes sexual situations but also homes in on elaborate descriptions of male genitals. There is a celebratory and often lecherous perspective invoked, training the gaze onto the bodies of men as they are engaged in intercourse with various female characters via the protected narrator. This protected narrator is not unlike the "cover" of NFL commentators' gazes observed by Oates, such that the queer underpinnings of descriptions of bodies are safeguarded by the context of the description. Oates notes: "The NFL draft positions men as objects of desire, but the implied viewer remains the traditional straight male. This taboo desire is covered by intense homo- and femiphobic discourses and the discourses of capitalism, while serving to position prospects as the objects of the male gaze."[15] The female cover, observed in novels like *Fanny Hill*, runs similarly to what arises in songs like "Miss Lucy Long," in which the narrative turns from male to female or even in places like "The Bumboy," where a subordinated, feminized subject narrates the sexual encounter. Julia Epstein calls the narrative voice of *Fanny Hill* one "that thinly disguises a masquerading homoerotic male voice," and her assessment of this novel is akin to what is occurring within stanzas located in the manuscript, indeed in many songs from the male song tradition.[16] Where the primary narrative postures as positing a male-centric, opposite-sex-affiliated desire, the real object of consumption is the hypereroticized male body. Just as in the case of *Fanny Hill*, the audience is understood to be male, as is the original creator; therefore, the characters and objects that come to the fore articulate something more than the unreflexively heteronormative.

There is a flexibility to the erotic subtext that licenses a broader definition of excitation and desire when we consider the vague narrator and the elements that come into focus as opposed to others. In applying a reading like this to the songs from Hugill, it is possible to imagine that they capture a similar freedom of sexual expression by donning the cover of a female narrator, feminized narrator, or even one that is unidentified and omniscient. Only "The Bumboy" contains a reference to the gender of the narrator, and he is, by the end, understood to be a feminized subject through his submission to the mate; the narrators in all other songs are either vaguely attributed femininity, potentially female, or unidentified to the degree that they align with a "queer gaze," meaning one that troubles binary understandings of gender and sexuality. In "The Hog-Eye Man," the song begins with the line, "Oh, the hog-eye man is the man for me," an evocation that drops the gender of the singer, and then closes with the line, "She wants the hog-eye man!" which functions to gender the initial sing out and displaces the queer desire onto a theoretical female narrator. Later in "The Hog-Eye Man," the narrator provides the coquettish admission that "she was a little maid who had never seen a cock," which reads like a veiled admission of a similar desire in the singer so that the maid and the male viewer might be interchangeable. In imagining the songs as coming from an already "queered" gaze, either a nongendered narrator or a female narrator, the songs begin to fall in line with literature that uses something like female impersonation, an extension and broadening of the female narrator. Impersonation takes the visual cover of the female narrator into the lived quality of impersonation. *Looking*, in this way, steadily morphs into *doing*.

Narratives That Hint at Same-Sex Curiosity

It is not only the way that looking and watching occurs, or what comes into focus with the consuming gaze, but it is also the number of narrative events that provides clues to erotic curiosities that are nonprocreative, nondescript at times, and therefore queer. The song "Yaw, Yaw, Yaw!," though primarily a xenophobic song with nonsense and swear words meant as an attack on the Dutch, contains a narrative line that suggests a movement of characters from one side to another and, metaphorically, from potentially one sexual desire to another, all predicated on the continued repetition of "yes, yes, yes."[17] The term "yaw," used in both the title and the refrain, should be understood as "the quick movement by which a ship deviates from the direct line of her course towards the right or left, from unsteady steering"; however, it can also be understood as the corruption of the Dutch "*ja*," which means "yes."[18] The fact that the line always begins with "*mit mein*," which roughly translates to "with my," betrays an identification between the narrator and the sudden movement to another direction because of "unsteady steering."[19] The evocation of "yes, yes, yes" indicates a relative pleasure with such a movement, almost erotic in its ejaculation. Symbolically, the narrator appears to be aligning himself (or herself since the gender of the narrator is not revealed) with a ship that moves away from one direction to another, and within that implication lies a connection to steering from one sexual outlet to another, all with apparent shouts of pleasure.

If the symbolism appears too much of a stretch, there are narrative elements within the song that align with the idea of homoeroticism or even deviant behavior that steers off course from normative expectations. The repeated line "mit mein niggerum, buggerum, stinkum" contains the term "bugger," which is a same-sex sexual term with quite a long and colorful history.[20] The suffix "-um" is added to the end of "bugger," which linguistically calls to mind "them" and elicits a reading of the term as pointing to a buggering of one person or multiple people. Two additional phrases expressly contain deviant behavior, especially as they are tied to religion: "Vell [*sic* throughout], ve'll climb upon der steeples, / And ve'll shit (piss) down on de peoples." Historian Alan Bray was one of the first researchers to critically investigate same-sex sexuality in the early modern period, and in his seminal *Homosexuality in*

Renaissance England, "sodomy" is identified as a "catchall" phrase for anything that was deemed improper, potentially damaging to the cultural fabric of the particular society, and any deviant behavior to which the term could be applied, such as bestiality or nonprocreative sex of any kind.[21] Thus, not only the "buggerum" but also defecating or urinating from atop a steeple onto the unwitting people below would be considered sodomitical. With the movement of the narrator from one side to the other, by an understood unsteady navigation of the ship, along with the deviant behavior outlined within the subsequent lines, there is room to speculate that the song provides strength to the reading of some songs as betraying an alternative approach to categorical expectations as well as potentially even more taboo erotic desires and outlets, like urolagnia or coprophilia. When we consider the "yes, yes, yes" evocation as it is paired with images like "shitting" and "pissing" on the people beneath them, the song is injected with an even deeper sexually transgressive potential that aligns with desires that fall outside of normative expectations and stretches into the realm of fetish.

Another small nod at the homoerotic arrives in "The Hog-Eye Man" when the line reads, "She wriggled like the divil [sic] but she couldn't shift her tack." Legman glosses "shift her tack" to mean "to change position for a ship, to go from one side of the wind to the other." Though a surface reading of the phrase suggests that the woman was hoping to move in such a way as to accommodate the sailor or to spurn his advances, an alternative interpretation of the line, imbued with the idea of "moving from one side to the other" like in "Yaw, Yaw, Yaw!," suggests a lateral movement along lines of sexual expression and release. The fact that Jinny "couldn't shift her tack" implies that she could not change the direction of the sexual advances, though she may have wished to, and indeed, it appears she attempted to change the direction.

The queered line, though opposite-sex affiliated on the surface, contains a subtext that blurs the intentions of the characters involved. The nautical metaphor offers necessary cover to express a struggle between the polarities of sexual expression. The female character is read as the symbolic representation of a push and pull of sexual desire that moves back and forth rather than remaining static as expected. In fact, the female character, especially, is rendered almost out of control of the situation at hand, as if she is being moved in a particular way despite her efforts to the contrary. Employing a metaphor that specifically requires wind imbues this line with a movement that extends from outside of the bodies on which it acts and thereby solidifies a reading of characters' desires as being largely outside of their control. As it attaches to bodies, it is difficult to not read wind as potentially tied to flatulence, the anus, and, broadly, spaces that are contested and out of control. Taking it back to the ship, in the same way, that wind would be out of full control of bodies, and combating the desires of wind in nature would require that ship's sails were adjusted to accommodate the desired direction and path of the wind, melding bodies and ships to the wayward desires of the natural world. This is a crystallized metaphor for the epic struggle between identity and unbound presentations of self. Characters in the song express a desire to act in a certain way but also register situations within which those desires get directed to places outside of their control—moved, as it were, by uncontrollable forces. This queered reading of the line bolsters the idea that the songs contain release valves for erotic possibilities that fall perhaps outside of heteronormative expectation and ties sexual realities to parts of sailing life that support a reading of identity as vulnerable, unstable, and constantly changing.

These movements from one space to another call to mind Ahmed's argument concerning orientations, specifically sexual orientations. As mentioned earlier, she argues, "We need to complicate the relation between the lines that divide space. . . . After all, direction only makes sense as a relationship between body and space."[22] For Ahmed, bodies are pushed and moved down paths that ultimately align them with new orientations and open them to new spaces unknown before the direction changed. In much the same way, the inability to "shift her tack" as the character in "The Hog-Eye Man" so desires is an admission of a yearning to move in a new direction, to potentially shift to a sexual interaction that falls outside of the one occurring in the moment. The line is a symbolic representation of when characters "complicate the relation between lines that divide space" in the same way that it appears much of the primary narratives in Hugill attempt to do in redirecting the gaze to the bodies of fellow men and, potentially, to erotic outlets that are outside of normative categories. In "Jinny Keep Yer Arse-'Ole Warm," the sailing narrator ejaculates, "An' I don' give a fuck how the windx [sic] do roar," seeming to suggest that whatever way the wind blows, takes the ship, or challenges the sailor, he will fearlessly and agentively shift so as to accommodate what is required to keep the ship afloat and his fellow men safe. Reading that same line slantwise, however, suggests the same ability and even aggressive challenge to change positions (and erotic outlet) based on external forces outside of the sailing character's control.

The provocative suggestion I am encouraging is the existence of implicit homoerotics in that song narrative often blurs the line between the desire to be like and the desire to be with in much the same way that Eve Sedgwick recognizes of triangular relationships among two men and a singular woman.[23] Taking Sedgwick one step further, I actually see a homoerotic desire active in and through the bodies of women such that the opposite-sex sexual encounter provides the protected space through which to engage with the bodies of other men, even if by proxy. What I mean is that opposite-sex encounters permit actors to engage in taboo desires because they are within the context of accepted forms of erotic release. Characters are able to experiment with the taboo, with pleasure unbound, because pleasure is deployed within an accepted erotic space and through using ciphers like female impersonation and a trained gaze within an opposite-sex sexual scenario. Such an erotic triangle and taboo consumption of the same sex are markedly clear in "Miss Lucy Long" as Miss Lucy actively provokes the narrator to compare his own penis with that of "brassbounders of the Blackball Line," who have both money and more impressive genitals. The "dirty Limey" finds himself in a triangle relationship among himself, the men of the Blackball Line, and Miss Lucy, whom he desires.

It is not only a sharing of a dirty song or the scopophilic consumption of heterosexual narratives with homoerotic undercurrents; the sexual situation is also the way by which we might recognize an unfulfilled desire predicated on and protected by narrative covers that displace the queer narrative only slightly. What these examples from Hugill suggest, as they are placed within the continuum that is the male folksong tradition, is that opposite-sex sexual narrative, framed as it is like a celebration of heteronormative prowess, hides within it a deeper possibility. Lingering gazes, hyperbolic descriptions, and narrative repetitiveness of male sexual organs betray a reading that those parts are highlighted for two very separate reasons. The narratives show a celebrating as well as a desiring, and the queer nature of the songs' focal points requires more inquiry into other male folklore traditions and what they articulate about masculine longing, desire, and curiosity.

Male Bodies on Display

What the gazes are primarily trained on, as suggested above, are the erotically charged bodies of male sailing characters. Throughout the songs surveyed, the consumption of hyperbolic male body parts suggests a latent desire for those parts as men are watching as a character "jammed a bale down the hatch" or viewers take the place of a "little maid who had never seen a cock" so as to experience the erotic capability of the male body under cover. The descriptive lines of many songs from Hugill bring to mind the scholarship on works like that of Herman Melville or E. M. Forster, in which accounts of men, their bodies, and their feats were all poetic and sensual, sometimes erasing all other

MISS LUCY LONG

WUZ ye never down on the Broomielaw,
When the Yankee boys wuz all the go?
    Timme way-ha-ay-hay, hay-hay, hay-hay,
    Ah-ha, me bully boys, ah-ha!
Why don't ye try for to shag Miss Lucy Long?

Oh, as I walked out one mornin' fair,
To view the view an' take the air./
Oh, 'twas there I met Miss Lucy fair,
'Twas there we met, I do declare.

I axed, 'Ow much? Will five bob do?
Is that enough for a quick blow-through? —
You dirty Limey, you stink o' tar,
Besides, I know what Limeys are!

With brassbounders of the Blackball Line,
I only spend me whorin' time./
They've got good cash, they treats ye well,
Their knobs are big for to ring the bell.

I showed her me knob, an' she changed her mind,
As one of her crew I was very soon signed./
The moral of this, when a-whorin' ye go,
stet/   If ye've got a big knob, ye will git a good tow.

Yer pockets, me son, can be empty as hell,
But with a big bowsprit, ye'll do yerself well./
For a whore is a woman, an' better than cash
She likes a big sailor, that's got a big lash!

Sailing Ship Shanties, 1931-1957.

"Miss Lucy Long," song collected from repertoire of Stan Hugill. Scanned copy from "Sea Songs," unpublished manuscript of Gershon Legman. Personal copy sent by Judith Legman, October 10, 2014.

characters from view so that the male body is paramount. The steady gaze permitted to pass over the lines and contours of the men's bodies elicits an uncanny feeling in the reader that they are being forced or expected to linger in the same ways as the narrative gaze on the hyperbolic beauty and power of the male form. There is an awe in the look, especially as it is expressed by writers like Forster or Melville, and certainly that is the case in the songs as they are directed at the jibbooms and bollocks of various characters.

Though authors like Forster and Melville certainly have more narrative space than is permitted in lines of short folksong, the same sensation A. A.

Markley points to is palpably present in the songs where each stanza is punctuated by some aspect of the male body. An example of this continued punctuation is located in "The Bumboy"; each stanza ends with a remark about the chief mate and his encounter with a young boy, and his body and desires are the focus of each line. The song includes punctuating lines such as "he wanted me for his bit o' brown," "he rammed his prick right up me 'ole," "the ice it froze the chief mate's horn," "the mate he was back on the job [intercourse] again," and finally "with a boy-shaggin' mate, oh I'd never more ship."[24] By punctuating the stanzas in this way, readers are constantly drawn to the body and erotic actions of the mate; arguably, the position of the phrases, within the stanzas too, situate the narrative objects so that frozen members, homoerotic desires, and violent as well as constant penetration reverberate. Where Markley sees a synergy between Forster and his erotic objects and where it is possible to read such descriptions as merely narcissistic identification or awe-fueled celebration of the virile power and potential of the male body, there is a vibration of the homoerotic because the eye is constantly drawn to the same erotic places. The same is true in the songs and not only in the sole homoerotic text "The Bumboy." It seems impossible not to read some level of homoerotic fixation, in Forster and in the songs, when encountering the number of repeated moments of placing male bodies on display.

Before discussing the specific male parts that are the focus of many songs, the important foundation of the narratives is that women function within these songs, sometimes as narrators and sometimes as characters, but are largely elided by the more powerful images of penises and testicles. Epstein writes that *Fanny Hill* "does not focus, as one might suppose from its plot, on the aroused female body. It offers instead a celebration of male genitalia, of the aroused male, and of idealized and invincible male sexual prowess: the phallus is everywhere and is everywhere worshipped."[25] The same is obvious in the songs surveyed in this chapter. Across all examples, women and their pleasure are essentially erased by male genitalia, and those male sexual organs are described in grandiose and expansive ways to the detriment of any female character displayed.

There are few examples of women's bodies in the songs. In "The Hog-Eye Man," instances include the lines "the hair of her snatch [was] hangin' down to her knees," "caulked her little crack," and "her fanny in the sun." And "What Shall We Do? (Drunken Sailor)" has a line that reads, "Pull the hairs from her snatch with a pair o' tweezers." "Reefy Tayckle," for its own part, includes a stanza that has readers thinking of "hairy [cunt]" and a "fine pair of [tits]"; however, in those examples, the actual words for the body parts are dropped from the line for titillation. Within each of these stanzas, women are referenced usually only based on the hair covering their genitals; however, it is the sailing character's penis that is at the center of the discussion in the larger parts of song. Arguably, the mention of hair on female genitalia functions to demonstrate the covering or concealing of those bodies, further underscoring the prominence that male genitalia take.

This absence or eliding of women's bodies is similar to what Markley identifies in his discussion of Forster's *The Longest Journey*, arguing that "the virtual absence of physical description of the female characters" contrasts "to detailed descriptions concentrating on the appearance of men."[26] Markley is contending that male writers use the heterosexual narrative framework sometimes as a means through which to cover their own homoerotic desires. In many passages located in *Fanny Hill*, women are similarly described, and the sexual scenario is the point of focus; however, male genitals are almost worshiped through the incredible detail provided. In descriptions of penises, testicles, and ejaculation, there is an air of respect and even lecherous desire.

What will be clear of songs from the manuscript, as I analyze the distinct figures that populate within the texts, is that the image most paramount and that carries the most weight and power is the male penis, just as scholars have noted in novels like *Fanny Hill*. At the surface, such a narrative choice would engender a reading of celebration or of identifying with the prowess and power of the male genitals, clearly capable of incredible sexual feats; however, the reality is that such narrative content betrays a degree of erotic fixation and homoerotic curiosity, even if only celebratory. Such celebration and fixation will be most apparent in songs like "The Hog-Eye Man" as well as others like "Miss Lucy Long," with entire narratives dedicated to the comparison between enormous penises and those that cannot pack quite the punch desired.

Bowsprits, Jibbooms, Knobs, and Bollocks

The number of penises and testicles located throughout the songs selected, sometimes symbolically shrouded as they are, is remarkable. Of the six songs surveyed, there is only one song that does not directly reference male genitalia, "Yaw, Yaw, Yaw!," but it still manages to observe emissions that are tied to the penis and also provides erotic treatment of the anus. "Yaw, Yaw, Yaw!" appears to contain a veiled reference to masturbation based on the similarity to what mariner Philip C. Van Buskirk refers to as "going chaw for chaw," a term that is decidedly close to "yaw" and means "masturbation."[27] The song also uses the term "buggerum," with "bugger," as discussed, obviously calling to mind anal sex. Some songs, like "Reefy Tayckle," expect that singers

```
                    REEFY TAYCKLE                        stet/
                       ....                               ....

          EVERY good ship has an anchor, every anchor has a stock,
          Every boy that loves a flash gal has a bloody great —
stet/     Slack away yer reefy tayckle, reefy tayckle, reefy tayckle,
 ....     Slack away yer reefy tayckle, me bollocks are jammed!

          Every good ship has a lifeboat, every lifeboat has some rollocks,
          Every boy that loves a flash gal has a fine pair of —
          Every good ship has a sidelight, every sidelight has a wick,
stet      Every boy that loves a flash gal has a few fathom of —
 ....

          Every good ship has a mainsail, every mainsail has a bunt,
          Every gal that loves a sailor has a nice hairy —
          Every good ship that goes alongside makes fast to the bitts,
          Every gal that loves a sailor has a fine pair of —

                    Sailing Ship Shanties, 1932-1956.
```

"Reefy Tayckle," song collected from repertoire of Stan Hugill. Scanned copy from "Sea Songs," unpublished manuscript of Gershon Legman. Personal copy sent by Judith Legman, October 10, 2014.

are going to complete the dropped lines with the corresponding rhyming word, usually terms related to genitalia, while other songs expressly vocalize the sexual organs that figure prominently in the narrative. In any of the ways that male genitalia are presented, they arise as narrative focal points that are impossible to dismiss.

In fact, they often displace other characters and narrative occurrences such that their larger-than-life characteristics become the main action of the song. Highlighting the frequency with which male genitals surface in the narratives of these songs is salient to the discussion to come in that the manner of the arrival of these parts of male bodies suggests that male bodies are the entire inspiration for the songs. Though the songs are heteronormative in their narrative structure and women do appear in some songs, it is apparent that the primary storyline serves only as a cover for the homoerotic content that ultimately overshadows the heterosexual scenario. Where a reader might expect hyperfocus on the genitals and bodies of women, they meet instead a concentrated focus on the sexual organs of the male characters through the use of the protected covers discussed. This point-of-view narration succeeds in generating a participatory consumption, where singers, readers, and narrators engage directly with the parts described.

The penis, in particular, enjoys a spotlight in many songs from Hugill, unlike other characters and fragmented body parts, and the frequency with which the penis is described is telling and even Rabelasian.[28] Peter F. Murphy notes that, in all-male discourse, the "primary focus is on the penis" and "synonyms for the penis represent a metonymy for the man."[29] Throughout the songs selected for this chapter, Murphy's insights are salient as there is a keen focus on the engorged and sexually charged penises of characters, and they often reach gigantic proportions that demand attention and even a degree of envy. The view of male genitals here is reformulated to draw attention not to what they mean or reflect about the man himself but rather to what their presence in the narrative space communicates about the consumption of male bodies by other men.

In "The Hog-Eye Man," for instance, readers are expected to look numerous times upon the titular character's penis, which is described as a "prick from here to Tennessee!" This penis is a hyperbolic character in and of itself, but more importantly, the gaze of the viewer is trained on the appendage and what it does to and for various characters it encounters. The man's penis, described as reaching from the man all the way to Tennessee, is also glossed as something like "a bale down the hatch" when it engages with an orifice, painting the penis as a figure that is so large that it is comparable to a bale of hay. Alternately, readers encounter another description as the bowsprit of a ship. Each description of the penis is larger than life and certainly more immense than any one person could sexually accommodate. It is not only the size of the hog-eye man's penis that demands continued attention; the appendage is directly referenced five separate times throughout the narrative, and what he does with his penis forms the main focus of the song. Such a choice forces the penis into stark relief, pressing it off the page and into the minds of the reader, dominating the gaze and orchestrating the consumption of material.

Other songs reproduce male genitalia in a similar fashion. Sections of "Miss Lucy Long" explain that "their [Blackballer sailors] knobs are big for to ring the bell," "if ye've got a big knob, ye will git a good tow," and "she likes a big sailor, that's got a big lash!" The incredible size of the penis and the desire to find a penis of imposing size force the gaze onto the appendage in a similar way to what is observed of the hog-eye man. Though genitals are not expressly stated in the narrative of "Reefy Tayckle," the expected rhyming words created by the structure and general narrative provoke the evocation of male sexual organs in the same way as the songs discussed thus far; for instance, one line reads, "Every good ship has an anchor, every anchor has a stock, / Every boy that loves a flash gal has a bloody great—[cock]." A later line reads, "Every good ship has a sidelight, every sidelight has a wick / Every boy that loves a flash gal has a few fathom of—[dick]." In "The Bumboy," the narrative gaze is trained and frozen on "the chief mate's horn" and the experience of having "enough cock for one bleedin' trip."

Within each of these examples, the penis leaps up, complicating the view of the opposite-sex narratives. The sheer number of references to the penis and the attention to minute details of the organ in action generate equal parts celebratory rehashing and an element of homoerotics. Though lines of song in the manuscript like "soon he had her like a schooner on the rock, / She was a little maid who had never seen a cock" from "The Hog-Eye Man" draw the eye, at first, to the woman pinned helplessly like a grounded ship, the line ends with an immediate shot of the *cock* that does the pinning. The image that is most paramount in the grouping of lines is the male penis, and reference to it carries the most weight and power. At the surface, such a narrative choice engenders a reading of the line as celebrating the prowess and power of the male genitals, clearly capable of impaling a woman and keeping her in place, but the subtext of lines like the ones above are also imbued with a level of erotic fixation and homoerotic curiosity. Women, as has been discussed, almost become the backdrop to the sexual scenario, and the true focus—that of turgid, large, and imposing members—comes into view.

The male penis is not the only sexual organ that arrives within the narratives of the songs surveyed. Testicles are also inserted into the narrative, though the presentation of them vacillates between pleasure and pain. In a sense, the narratives appear to present to the consuming audience the entire package that is the male sexual system and often do so in such a way that it is impossible to turn away from the undertone of desire. "What Shall We Do? (Drunken Sailor)," discussed above, exemplifies training the gaze onto specific erotic parts, almost forcing a microscope onto the scrotum and testicles in the example. As noted, the first stanza of the song reads, "Scrape the hairs off his bollocks with a hoop-iron razor, / The hairs off his bollocks with a hoop-iron razor, / Scrape the hairs off his bollocks with a hoop-iron razor."[30] The repetition of "bollocks" alone compels the reader to cast an eye onto this particular body part; however, it is the addition of the shaving or scraping of the hairs off the scrotum that engenders the idea of a more trained gaze. The reader is required to get as close as needed to successfully scrape the hairs off the character's genitals. The small hairs of the man are almost burned into the mind's eye with each repetition, and as discussed earlier, there is a degree of intimacy and care involved too. The singer is careful to not cut the scrotum in the process, and we linger on the contours of the body part with almost surgical precision.

Shaving male body hair, or "manscaping," is the subject of much contemporary scholarship in which homoeroticism, same-sex desire, and male identity figure prominently. There is a degree of anxiety, in fact, surrounding the maintenance of heteronormativity as it collides with male grooming.[31] Of particular note is the use of the hoop iron for the task of shaving this character's bollocks, which directly compares to the hair noted on the body of the female character in "The Hog-Eye Man" but also attaches to specific cultural aspects of the sailing man's initiation into the fo'c'sle. A contributor to the online forum Mudcat Café indicates that the hoop iron was used as a part of the crossing-the-line ceremony, which has a history of homoerotic undertones; it is certainly a ritual that is imbued with hierarchical readings.[32] In wedding the image of crossing-the-line ceremonies, erotically charged hierarchies, and the shaving of the scrotum here, it is possible to bring into view the homoerotic interpretation and, more specifically, the desire to view male genitalia unencumbered. Added to this reading, of course, is the process of shaving the scrotum in order to make the penis appear larger. In considering "when there's no underbrush the tree looks taller," a further scopophilic possibility comes into focus.[33] Specifically, there is more of the male penis to see and consume, and Matthew Hall's work specifically ties male groin-grooming practices to eroticism and desirability, especially for the partner engaging with the male genitals.[34] At the nexus of desire, ritual, and calculated care are the testicles of this character. With so many other potential parts to train a gaze during a ritual act, it is provocative that the narrative lands on the bollocks.

"Reefy Tayckle" also contains a trained view of testicles; the line reads, "Every good ship has a lifeboat, every lifeboat has some rollocks, / Every boy that loves a flash gal has a fine pair of—[bollocks]," which uniquely discusses the fine quality of some men's testicles. "The Hog-Eye Man" contains a veiled reference to testicles: "If I cotch him [the hog-eye man] here wid me Jinny anymore, / I'll tattoo his dusters, an' he won't fuck anymore." Recall that Legman glosses "dusters" as testicles, which evokes an image of them as, perhaps, being so large that they dust the floor beneath the man. Additionally, in the same song, there is even reference to the sperm that is emitted from the testicles of characters in that the hog-eye man "caulked her [Jinny's] little crack."[35] Such keen focus on the part of the reproductive organs of the man, especially as they are relayed as primary characters, belies an attention that is tinged with a weight heavier than simple narrative necessity. Why focus a song narrative on picking hairs off scrotums, an intimate act indeed, or tattooing a pair of dusters, which also requires a great deal of focused attention and gaze? Why not turn the gaze, as expected based on the sexual engagements, on the bodies and genitals of women?

Contemporary research on pornography, specifically that which is consumed by a largely male audience, serves as an entry point into understanding the ways in which men experiment with same-sex curiosity in a similar fashion to that which I identify in the Hugill songs. Tellingly, in both pornography and song narrative, there is an intense focus on what is done to the penis along with a lingering on the ejaculatory completion of the male enjoying sexual pleasure. Lingering on the ejaculate calls to mind the work of Lisa Jean Moore in her chapter "Overcome: The Money Shot in Pornography and Prostitution." Worthy of note is that Moore discusses modern pornography as "a means to experience male bonding, as often films are watched by groups of men. Such acts clearly give rise to homoeroticism, or the experience of being sexually aroused by one's own sex," and this is especially true when spectating "impressive display[s] of ejaculation."[36]

The work of Thomas Waugh identifies, in a comparison between same-sex (specifically, male-male) pornography and opposite-sex pornography, that focal points appear to intersect in both forms of pornographic material.[37] He notes that the straight man "fucks and is sucked by one or more women" and "relations between women are usually a prelude to entry of phallus"; and, as compared to gay pornography, the man meets with "roughly the same with ejaculation coda more compressed because of scarcity of ejaculators (the gay taboo) and limited positions; straight men come outside too. Same for loops and shorts."[38] In both the gay and straight pornographic examples, there is an intense focus on the penis to the point that the camera angle is trained on what is being done to the penis and what the penis then does as a result. Waugh's comparison of such similarities between gay and straight porn has bearing on what is occurring within the song narratives found in Hugill as such contemporary similarities speak to an enduring male desire to consume the bodies of other men, even if only at a distance. Indeed, regarding gay male pornography, Waugh shows that there is a "phallus obsession, the close-up a metaphor of corporeal fragmentation and alienation." He goes on to identify the same "phallocentrism" in heterosexual pornography.[39] The song "What Shall We Do? (Drunken Sailor)" opens with the suggestive "Way, hay, an' UP she rises :3: / Earlye [sic] in the morning." Such an opening line calls to mind a nocturnal penile tumescence, with "she" understood as a penis, rising early in the morning, and readers are meant to look at this vulnerable man's body in a similar fashion as Waugh. There is a corporeal fragmentation and even a hyperfocus on the penis, and the same narrative realities are clear in other songs like "Reefy Tayckle" and "Miss Lucy Long."

Worth noting is that Waugh closes "Men's Pornography: Gay vs. Straight" by pointing to a potentially new form of pornography "that enhances our pleasure in our sexuality by starting from the raw place we're in right now and by responding to that place, without defensiveness or complacency." Waugh predicates this idea on an informant's summary of his own experience making pornography: "I can't understand my films when I first make them. It feels like I'm making them out of a real raw place."[40] The raw place is, I think, the moment at which we face the true nature of erotic pleasure, that it is undefinable, uncategorical. The informant cannot understand the film he has created at first because he cannot place it in any identifiable box: it explodes the categories that we use to define space, and it refuses to be contained or captured. I see this same "raw place" in the confines of the songs highlighted by Hugill. We can see pockets of cultural admissions of an eroticism that overlaps and defies categorical descriptions within these songs. Though largely collected within the early 1900s, far removed from this informant's experience, they capture the raw place that is confusing, unintelligible to a degree, but real and deeply felt. In the same way that it appears contemporary audiences are looking at and becoming sexually excited by the bodies of same- and opposite-sex partners, having their own sense of identity and desire tested, so too is it possible to see the same nascent admissions floating within the narrative space of places like song.

Contemporary niche pornographies also display a similar liminality of sexual desire and pleasure that appear in song, not to mention a likewise invoked homoerotic gaze specifically as it attaches to male genitalia. Geoffrey Lokke, in "Cuckolds, Cucks, and Their Transgressions," shows that "men were 58% more likely than women to search for cuckold porn," with "'bisexual husband' being the most popular searches before a viewer searches 'cuckold.'"[41] Lokke's work focuses specifically on white male desire for cuckold porn wherein Black men figure prominently. Lokke identifies a desire that runs counter to heteronormative expectations where bodies of women are used as protective covers to conceal the true desire of viewers: the bodies of other men. Disproportionately, it appears that contemporary men are interested in films that have them cast as cuckolds to well-endowed men, which attaches to the homoerotic desire evident in the songs from the manuscript, especially "The Hog-Eye Man." Lokke's distinction attaches to the sexual scenario detailed in this song of the more powerful and agentive male figure and the one who copulates with Jinny, who is awaiting her "fancyman." The male figure is denoted using the pejorative term for Black men and women. There is a fixation on the incredible size of the Black man's penis and his sexual prowess that "tickled her innards" that aligns with what has been recognized in contemporary cuckold porn.[42] It is possible to extrapolate the same homoerotic desire on to other song narratives located in the manuscript and certainly to other ephemera from the all-male, homosocial tradition. Lokke shows that desire for such pornographic material might help to articulate and assuage masculine fears and anxieties surrounding white men's own power and virility. His work more poignantly grasps at how such erotic fixations further point to an undercurrent of homoerotic desire that is given vent in taboo spaces like pornography, but key to this research is the reality that men are seeking opportunities for experimentation with those of the same sex and specifically with those who have been identified, racially, as more endowed and even predatory. Men are *looking* for material that grasps at a dual desire for both women and other men, usually more powerful ones.

Closely related to this notion of desire by proxy in films like cuckold porn is in gangbang pornographies, in which male power is multiplied and the women "are presented as responding inviolably ecstatically and orgasmically to multiple penetration (often to a gangbang), as if challenging normal rules of physiology."[43] In "Erotic Assemblages," Maryna Romanets discusses how a woman's body becomes the site through which we are able to view men's complex relationship with their genitals, at one point noting that the female character might be the site of male anxiety concerning the size and capability of the penis.[44] Here again, the eye is drawn to the male genitals at the expense of and sometimes even through the genitalia of women. It is clear that the hog-eye man's penis arrives as the agentive harbinger of masculine power as well as a weaponized masculine virility, invading the body of a woman with such force that it renders the singer an enraged cuckold, but the important message of the song is that there are erotic fixations apparent that focus on both men and women, often more disproportionately on the bodies of the men in question, just as is clear in research on cuckold and gangbang pornography.[45]

Women do function as part of the narrative, as Lokke also recognizes within cuckold pornography, but are "a proxy or catalyst for this contact, desire, and fluidity of identification."[46] Lokke's observation is nearly identical to Sedgwick's note in *Between Men*: "The sexually pitiable or contemptible female figure is a solvent that not only facilitates the relative democratization that grows up with capitalism and cash exchange, but goes a long way—for the men whom she leaves bonded together—toward palliating its gaps and failures."[47] The female body in niche pornographies serves in a similar way to what I recognize in the songs—that is, she functions to create a homosocial desire that aids in soothing both the delicate presentation of masculine identity, for the man in question is protected by his brothers (homosocial space) and the heteronormative space, and a homoerotic desire. The homoerotic and homosocial in Sedgwick's work, even, to a degree, in Lokke's and others', slip together to the point that they are almost imperceptible. Within songs like "The Hog-Eye Man," the husband is bested by a man who not only is more endowed but also appears to satisfy the desires of his wife better than he could ever manage, and such a narrative undercurrent functions to capture male displacement of erotic anxieties but clearly also entertains erotic curiosities for other male figures.

In terms of research outside of pornography, inquiries into the gaze deployed in hardbody action movies, an area of study in men's cultural consumption, confirm some of the same homoerotic desire that is apparent in the songs, especially in terms of lingering gazes on male bodies. Within these films, created for a primarily male audience, there are elements of the homoerotic that are a part of celebrating the capabilities of the male body—celebrations that are cast alongside of lingering camera angles that lapse into the visually stimulating. Regarding hardbody films, Drew Ayers argues that male characters exist as liminal figures, equally inside and outside of culture, which arrive on the scene "through excessively lingering shots, pans along the length of the body, and close-ups of specific body parts." Predicating his commentary on the work of Steve Neal, he further argues that "the male audience member represses his erotic desire for the male body by displacing the eroticized look onto the scenes of action that motivate the male spectacle."[48] Though I agree that there is a level of displacement in the look here, as there is a similar displacement in the songs to the act of opposite-sex sexual interaction, the truth of the matter is that the *look* is still a part of the process. The look is still trained on the body of another man, and the action, whatever it may be, is only the protective covering through which the gaze is permitted to be exercised. If we address the look through the queer framework, which is obviously deployed, we can perhaps provide a bit more agency to men in that they are *looking* at such images because there is a level of *liking* and desiring what they see. Pricks, bollocks, bits o' brown, and buggerum (and buggering), as well as myriad moments of violent penetration all appear to align with what Ayers notes about hardbody films. The songs appear to narratively address these unspoken desires for male bodies, especially with the near absence of women's bodies except as props. A cultural prism like hardbody films provides a way by which viewers might mask their desires through viewing content acceptable by social frameworks. For instance, a man may view such films because they evidence an agentive masculinity, but it is possible to consider how within that look and within that cultural prism lurks also the admission of an underlying desire or, at the very least, a homoerotic interest, like the one that escapes from within song narrative. Like the camera angles of film, the linguistic way by which the bodies of men come into focus betrays a certain underlying desire that is both wanting to be and, perhaps, wanting to be with.

All-male, homosocial spaces provide room for some of the same-sex experimentation I note in the songs, too. In fact, David Brandon Dennis notes, "Like other working-class men of the period [1884–1914], sailors probably were not limited by a strict hetero/homosexual dichotomy," and he goes on to argue that their sexual predilections were more in line with hierarchies and who maintained the dominant position and role.[49] Indeed, despite the fact that same-sex erotic encounters were punishable offences on naval sailing vessels into the 1800s and perpetrators were subject to the death penalty, few convictions were made, and "shipmates might have been loath to snitch on their comrades," generating a shipboard environment that was at least permissive of same-sex erotic outlets.[50]

Research abounds concerning how the sailing vessel became associated with same-sex predilections and how sailors were, to a degree, singled out as sexually transgressive individuals who sometimes erotically engaged with their fellow shipmates. Historian Barry R. Burg was the first scholar to conjecture about the same-sex inclinations of sailing men in his *Sodomy and the Pirate Tradition: English Sea Rovers in the Seventeenth-Century Caribbean*.[51] Burg argues, similar to Alan Bray and Katherine Crawford, that there was a general "ambivalence" about same-sex relationships during the golden age of piracy (a period that runs roughly along the same years as the great age of sail: 1500–1860).[52] Burg's research in *Boys at Sea* demonstrates the sheer number of trial transcripts in naval courts-martial hearings that capture, sometimes in vivid detail, same-sex interactions between men and ships' boys.[53] Within these descriptions, it is often clear that boys were raped and that more powerful men would use them as they desired.

There are even memoirs of some sailing men, like that of Philip C. Van Buskirk, which detail the realities of same-sex erotic outlets on sailing ships.[54] Van Buskirk, writing of an exchange with a fellow seaman concerning the use of sailing boys on ship for erotic pleasure, notes how a sailor, identified only as White, exclaimed: "what can a feller do—three years at sea—and hardly any chance to have a woman. I tell you, drummer, a feller must do so [have sex with boys]. Biles and pimples and corruption will come out all over his body if he don't."[55] Essentially, White contends that when one is at sea for so long, the only option he has is to engage with fellow sailors, especially young ones, in order to ensure his own health and well-being are maintained.

As was captured in the discussion of the sailor from *Fanny Hill*, it is apparent that the same erotic laxity of the sailor was visited into cultural spaces, meaning that what was captured in courts-martial records seeped into the cultural consciousness to the degree that the sailor became aligned with sex that was sometimes same-sex affiliated. It makes sense that there is an undercurrent of same-sex sexual interest in these songs as it ties with a prevailing reality on early modern ships: both the intense connections between and among men, simply by dint of their time spent together in danger, and the likely reality that some men sought sexual release with fellow sailors.

Contemporary research shows that this same curiosity is extant in other all-male spaces and that men, arguably, manufacture same-sex rituals as balms for longing, connection, and belonging, as well as sexual desire. Jane Ward, in her book *Not Gay: Sex between Straight White Men*, identifies specific (contemporary) all-male environments where men who identify as heterosexual are able to erotically explore male-male sexual encounters within a protected and, sometimes, sacred homosocial sphere, with the ultimate desire to be part of the group. Ward, in her chapter "Haze Him!," reiterates what sociolinguist Scott Fabius Kiesling locates in college fraternities, and she discusses how erotic contact between men occurs within homosocial spaces, usually as an initiation rite to become a respected part of the group.[56] She argues that "homosexual contact is such a common feature of male hazing scenarios that we might question whether hazing itself is a hetero-masculine fetish, one that allows men access to homosexual activity without the stigma of gay identity."[57] Worth noting is that her primary subjects are young white men; thus, there is an important racial dimension to her findings.

Rituals in which a heterosexually identified man sexually engages with someone of the same-sex, often in the presence of other men with whom he desires a connection, suggest the same undercurrent of same-sex desire I see surfacing in the song narratives. "The Bumboy" is an obvious example of this erotic ritual and hazing, sustained over the period of the voyage, and the relationship between the bumboy and the mate is one of dominance and subordination.[58] Though contemporary fraternity houses obviously afford real-time sexual engagements with fellow men, the song narratives betray a similar desire to appease a longing and curiosity, such as when men collectively share in a refrain that reads, "slack away yer reefy tayckle, me bollocks are jammed," demonstrating need of relief. There is an almost knowing admission that the men all feel identically, and the one way to remedy the jam is to ejaculate, together and within a protected homosocial sphere, whether that ejaculate is semen or lines of song (or both).

Ward further contends that "homosocial homosexuality is increasingly offered as a possibility for adult men who may have, in psychotherapist Joe Kort's words, a 'deep longing to experience the physical intimacy with other men that they are denied in a sexist and homophobic world.'"[59] In terms of the songs, whereas a man might experiment with the homoerotic in something like an elephant walk at a fraternity house or participate in a pledge ceremony wherein he is expected to receive anal sex from another man, the narrative emergence of penises and testicles in the songs along with the ways in which they are positioned and couched betray similar levels of erotic curiosity, admission, and experimentation.[60]

I am not intimating that any of these acts assign the men involved a particular identity: nothing could be further from the reality I am suggesting. Fraternity house rituals and other manufactured same-sex situations provide space for heterosexually identifying men to experiment with the homoerotic in a safeguarded sphere, and the songs, in a similar fashion, present a shield through their existence as song as well as in the shaping of such narrative within the homosocial sphere. The homoerotic becomes, as Ward argues, "not gay" by the heteronormative covering deployed and certainly through the situational context within which it is enacted.[61] The same sensation of rendering anal sex as "not gay" is apparent in contemporary conversations surrounding "pegging," the practice of men experimenting with being anally penetrated by a female partner via a strap-on. Discourses around pegging often highlight the masculine endurance necessary to engage in being penetrated, and "both women (peggers) and men (peggees) highlight the masculinity/power of their respective positions."[62] Lurking homoerotic readings of male anal-sex curiosity are distanced from same-sex affiliation through the use of masculine descriptors, opposite-sex erotic configurations, and a process of reentrenching heteronormative ideals into a penetrative practice. We might view some of the violence inherent in the selected songs as a similar protective cover that renders the fixations "not gay" by dint of their linguistic deployment and treatment.

I argue, then, that songs and other homosocial spaces and ephemera hold the key to understanding sexuality from an unbound perspective, from that raw place. We experiment with the taboo because it has been forbidden to us for some reason. The taboo is a part of our shared reality, and it combats, at times, the governing structures of sexual identity that have been prescribed and policed. Perhaps these homosocial examples demonstrate an easing of the categories, of "the lines that divide space," and we are witnessing an experimentation that is all at once playful, hopeful, curious, deeply provocative, and sometimes dangerous, almost always with a guarded layer that ensures an actor can experience suggestive homoerotic homosociality at a safe, barely perceptible distance.[63]

Conclusion

We may begin to view song narratives and other male ephemera (even pornography and homosocial ritual) as something akin to Michel Foucault's theory of "confession," which is detailed in the first volume of his *History of Sexuality* and has, within recent years, found a new trajectory within the theoretical framework understood as "disclosure." Succinctly, actors are either *compelled* to speak identity into existence, as we understand from Foucault, or they *choose* to vocalize personhood through the notion of disclosure. Either way, hidden parts of one's identity, certainly those parts that might bring a level of shame or vulnerability, are captured and brought to light ultimately coming to bear on identity and one's sense of self in relation to the wider world. Implicit within these effusions are either-or dichotomies whereby actors measure their own sense of personhood and identity against the wider cultural expectations inherent in their current situation. These theoretical frameworks help to shed light on what I see occurring in the Hugill songs as well as the wider social phenomena and ephemera from all-male spaces.

The important crux of this argument is the tension in the either-or dichotomy in the fashioning or vocalizing of self. In terms of the songs under discussion at the moment and their erotic fixation on eroticized male bodies, we must understand them as they are embodied both within the narratives themselves and outside of them. They exist within a cultural framework of gender and sexuality such that to speak a same-sex desire or act upon it, whether it is outright desire for male-male penetration or simply the curiosity to look more closely at the body of another man, carries with it a juridical implication that would be immediate and potentially devastating. Judith Butler's gender policing immediately comes to mind.[64]

By capturing sometimes literal examples of erotically charged objects, like a "hard-on," and in symbolic actions that suggest agentive erotic encounters, like the hog-eye man who "jammed a bale down the hatch" or other examples contained within the confines of songs, lyricists are able to satisfy the unspoken same-sex desire and also succeed in vocalizing that desire even if it is only under a protective cover. Just as in the case of erotic economies of all-male homosocial institutions or the camera angles and gazes of pornography, it is possible to look at songs, jokes, and stories shaped by men as quiet and symbolic ways this confession or disclosure takes place. In *Rationale of the*

Dirty Joke, Legman goes as far as to say, "It may be stated axiomatically that: *a person's favorite joke is the key to that person's character.*"[65] We have to be willing to hold our ears and eyes closer to the text for such disclosures as such admissions seep out in barely perceptible ways, but they are there and appear as whispers of erotic realities that could potentially emancipate men for further erotic exploration.

As I hope has been apparent throughout, the small narrative moments highlighted demonstrate a potential view of sexuality and sexual expression that is complex and nuanced. Though opposite-sex sexual encounters are the main narrative focal points, the narratives also leave space for the viewer to shift his (or her) tack and consume elements of the sexual encounter that defy categorical representation. These songs, indeed, "complicate . . . the lines that divide space" and encourage readers to imagine the world as it really functions: not within finite categorical expectations, but rather through a kaleidoscope of possibilities, with pleasure at the center.[66] Ahmed thinks about bodies, space, and collisions that complicate the way in which we view the world and social interactions. In fact, she identifies collisions as holding the possibility for opening whole new realities that we may have never imagined were possible or that were not a part of our identity makeup prior to our impact with new ways of being.

The work that the Hugill songs perform is to force the consideration that men entertain an inner sexual dialogue that potentially explodes our normative definitions of male sexual expression. These songs present a process akin to Foucault's confession, though in an obviously more subtle way than he outlines in his theory. Though there is no outright admission of a sexual desire that runs opposite to normative male sexual expectations, except for within the narrative of "The Bumboy," the gaze observed in the songs acts as something like a disclosure or confession, albeit one that requires analytical unpacking in order to unearth. If we can think about male social traditions, rituals, and cultural objects as containing pockets of disclosure, we might begin to seriously reconsider the rigid normative frameworks that have functioned in our social space since their inception. Just as in the case of men performing homoerotic rituals, song and joking cultures permit the same ability for disclosure but through a protected vehicle and only so far. Men do not come out and articulate, necessarily, "I desire my fellow man," but they do hint that they are curious. The small glimpses into the inner workings of male desire betray a cautious though hopeful attempt at communicating with other men, especially in homosocial situations, concerning their own curiosities and desires that are different from external, cultural expectations. The songs, poems, and rituals become symbolic disclosure, protected confessions that show the range of human sexual expression. Just as chapter 3 pointed to a liminality in terms of identity, the same liminality is apparent in terms of sexual expression. The fact that such deviations exist in both fact and fiction lends a level of validity to the claim that the sailing man ascribed to a sexuality that transgressed sexual mores of the time. Indeed, the contemporary world may take a page from the sailing man's book for our own approaches to gender and sexual expression.

CONCLUSION

"What Shall We Do with a Drunken Sailor" and His Comrades?

Cabin Boys, Milkmaids, and Rough Seas has been an investigation of kaleidoscopic movements. Each chapter was predicated on turning the glass one click further, penetrating down into the narratives just a bit deeper. What emerged is a constantly evolving understanding of gender and sexuality—a reality that the lived practice of identity is one that is opaquer, shifting, colorful, and open to melding and changing depending on the will of the one turning the tool. Images clash in the kaleidoscope's glass just as characters clash, and in so colliding, they receive indelible marks that fundamentally alter our perception of those characters; such collisions often alter the perception of the characters themselves within the space of the narrative. These turns and collisions function, too, to create a reading experience that challenges us to think about narrative elements, even lived realities, differently.

As Ahmed argues and I have suggested throughout, through taking on a "queer orientation," or engaging a reading that is radical in its interpretive force, we are guided toward "seeing the world 'slantwise,'" which "allow[s] other objects to come into view."[1] Indeed, it is worth noting that the origin of the term "queer" is the root *terkw-* from the Proto-Indo-European language, which roughly translates as "to twist," wedding the turns of the kaleidoscope with queer readings—readings that are turning and moving.[2] The images in a kaleidoscope certainly sometimes come in slantwise and are always shifting and altering so that other things come into view with each agentive motion. It is impossible not to see things differently as you are peering into the glass. If we allow ourselves to be swept up into such an experience, playfully toying with the boundaries of space and categories, much like manipulating the images we see in the glass, we might at first be surprised by the things that come into focus but will ultimately find comfort in seeing our own experiences reflected back to us. What I mean is no one leads a perfectly categorical life. Our existences are always at the mercy of the tension between what we have learned we are supposed to be and the quiet voice within us that tempts us to try that which falls outside of expectations. If we look, there are more pockets of admission, like these chanteys, than we have considered to this point.

In drawing *Cabin Boys, Milkmaids, and Rough Seas* to a close, I want to leave the reader with a summary of the way we muddle through the struggles of identity in a safe space and how lived experience unfolds circularly, like the colorful images in the glass that opened each of the analytical chapters.[3] Indeed, now that I have sifted through various readings of these chanteys, I want to touch on what is to be done with the drunken sailor, his fellow comrades, and the instabilities of identity that men visit in the spaces of their collective folklore, especially when we think about the liminalities and vulnerabilities inherent in the songs.

This particular identity construct (gender and sexuality), as I have shown throughout, is not static, and each chapter dealt with unpacking this notion especially as it attaches to a group who is often at the mercy, sometimes stringently so, of categorical frameworks, juridical policing, and expectations. The chantey is clearly attached to human experience, and the kaleidoscopic and complicated way in which the narratives unfold helps to evoke readings of songs like chanteys as pressure valves and pockets of release for the frustrating negotiation of emotions, desires, and expectations.

It is possible, based on my interpretation of Hugill's songs, to understand why songs like chanteys enjoyed a renaissance of sorts in popular culture during the later parts of 2020 and even into 2021, which will be covered in greater detail below.[4] I also want to point to the many repositories of folksong that have yet-untapped objects through which to continue this investigation of song as a release valve, even song as this reverberation of identity. For these, I want to suggest paths forward for the continued investigation of a rich, though complicated, genre.

Why Is This Work Important?

The framework that I have provided throughout is one that I hope will generate this deeper investigation of collected chantey material specifically. It is clear that the genre is an enduring one as 2020 brought them back to the forefront of our collective attention.[5] Throughout 2020, a global culture attempted to navigate the COVID-19 pandemic, confronting isolation, uncertainty, and contagion, which required some kind of release valve in order to grapple with such an incredible collective experience. Singers created and circulated songs they called "shanties" in places like the virtual world of TikTok in order to assuage sensations of disconnection, longing, and fear. Obviously, these songs are not chanteys in the strictest sense, and Legman would likely call them "fakelore," but they do, in many ways, attach to the historical genre that came before them.[6] The songs that men and women, from all over, are singing together in the virtual world are gesturing at the same global and cosmopolitan culture of the sailor and are succeeding in connecting the sometimes disparate places during a time of intense uncertainty. We are seeking communal spaces, a respite of sorts, wrestling together in song concerning notions of identity, desire, and longing, gravitating toward these homosocial traditions because they are predicated on connection. In seeking out collective song, and actually participating in singing together, our contemporary world is sharing in song narrative that evokes all that is uniquely part of the human experience.

In the digital world, our connections have become vast and sometimes paradoxically disconnected to some degree, and tapping into folklore material and sharing in the digital world recaptured the drive toward community, especially in moments during which we are at our most vulnerable. Foundational to these songs—chanteys and other folksong alike—is, of course, narrative material that echoes and endures, and if we can begin deconstructing collected examples, a working thesis on the lasting power of folk material will continue to take shape and we might begin to understand, in applying these notions to our world now, how song acts as a social balm in the most trying of moments.

Mary Ellen Brown, in her "Placed, Replaced, or Misplaced? The Ballads' Progress," makes the argument that "many things are called ballads. In fact, 'ballad making' is probably a continuing practice, an accessible artistic vehicle—at once local, regional, national, and transnational; popular ballad, broadside, and literary."[7] What is true of ballads is also true of the chantey tradition in that it is a genre that has continued to grow, change, and be applied in places sometimes outside of the sailing tradition. It is a living genre, and perhaps the chantey is back because it never really left our unconscious—indeed, the articulation of gender and sexuality in these songs, too, has been a similar evolving part of our cultural reality for eons. The chantey is at least one representation of something that humans continue to do and perform as a means of making sense of things and experiences that sometimes defy articulation or that might make someone feel isolated. What I think we might find more often is that material like Hugill's manuscript connects us far more than it divides us, and throughout the investigation, I have sought to show that the chantey is a folk object that captures those provocative and timeless connections to identity construction.

The songs gesture at human juridical realities that are deeply felt, enduring, and transcend time and space. All around, there are disciplinary processes, real and symbolic, lending themselves to both control and social order. We find pockets to express tamped realities that are buried because they are transgressive. They do not fit within the confines of social expectations or even category. The suggestion inherent in this investigation is that songs, like the ones from Hugill, are the pockets through which unbound identity seeps out. What is stunning about the revelations throughout is that they attach to human experiences regardless of the time period in which they were created and sung. It is possible to see some of the same sentiments radiating out into other folklore and song traditions, lending to the argument that archival songs give vent to collective human frustrations and curiosities.

Policing of gender and sexuality occurred in the nineteenth century just as it has in our own modern time. It is true that the expectations and the policing processes change from period to period; however, the foundational ideas remain static to some degree. Even though we are likely seeing less policing of sexuality now than in the nineteenth century, disciplinary processes are still in place that resemble the same sites of contestation that were clear in the early modern era. We can historically trace what I am gesturing toward in discussions of same-sex erotic experiences. The notion of an identity predicated on desire for the same sex did not have a title or category, really, until later parts of the eighteenth century to the early nineteenth century.[8] There were policing mechanisms in place, even without identity structures, but as time wore on, there was almost a pressure to release buried identities and desires, which then created further and new policing mechanisms to address the transgressions.

As Foucault notes, in his *History of Sexuality*, "Whether in the form of a subtle confession in confidence or an authoritarian interrogation, sex—be it refined or rustic—had to be put into words."[9] He then cites a profusion of discourse concerning sexuality and identity, the likes of which was unprecedented to that moment. It is the theory of confession, noted in chapter 5, that was both a release valve and a mechanism to be used for social policing. In their introduction to *English Masculinities, 1660–1800*, historians Tim Hitchcock and Michelle Cohen argue, "While earlier in the eighteenth century, sodomy had been seen as a part of a broader libertine sexuality, later in the eighteenth century and into the nineteenth century it appeared increasingly as a perversion of a new 'naturalized' heterosexuality."[10] While this was occurring, we begin to see pockets of release arising in spaces like the molly house subcultures and even in the cultural representations of figures like the fop and dandy. These spaces and figures were in direct opposition to the juridical push to conform to heteronormative ideals and took place despite the incurring of punishment for transgression. Here, the tensions among performances of transgressive identity, outlets for those identities, and the policing mechanisms that made such performances taboo and even dangerous are plain. The drive to control ultimately forces identities to seep into other places—they cannot be contained.

Such historical realities are clearly captured in chapter 3, which showed sailing characters attempting to navigate the sometimes-confusing messages of identity and desire. Characters are pushed toward sexual release, and the pleasures of performances that do not adhere to a set expectation are met with painful and real punishments that seek to return the character back down expected paths of obedience. It is possible to see something like the bent jibboom in "Blow the Man Down" as registering a competing push and pull that is similar to the creation of something like a molly house subculture. The penis is injured while seeking pleasure, the sailor wants to continue seeking pleasure, and he creates the song of warning to highlight both his attempt at seeking unbound pleasure and the juridical model. The song is like the molly house, the roving moral gangs that sought to eradicate them are the bent penis, and at the center is the frustrated and desiring male figure who is trying to rectify two competing drives.[11]

Earmarks of these same struggles with gender and sexuality are still palpable today and, to a degree, might even appear in starker relief. At this moment in time, men are still deeply fearful of how they are perceived, which demonstrates the continued and complex relationship with gender and sexual identity that I pointed to in research on same-sex sexual desire.[12] Throughout time, men have competed with expectations concerning their demonstration of self, battling to align with cultural expectations and recognizing how vulnerable they truly are in those ventures. As linguist and gender scholar Scott Fabius Kiesling mentions, "one of the most paradoxical aspects of masculinity is that while men are supposed to be powerful and dominant, very few men feel that they have power."[13] This sense of powerlessness at a foundational level stems from the recognition that performances of gender are not static and are indeed fallible. In fact, we are in the constant process of recognizing expectations, attempting to meet those requirements, and registering those times when we miss the mark either in our lived existence or in the quiet whispers within us.

Literary scholar Jonathan Allan notes this same phenomenon as one of "cruel optimism," in that "we believe and continue to believe that it [successful performances of masculinity] is attainable even though we continually fail at masculinity."[14] Importantly, in terms of attachment to the narratives of chanteys and their ability to speak in the contemporary world is the reality that "men are set up to fail, but are told that failure is distinctly unmasculine because masculinity favors success. It is in this spirit that I feel drawn towards 'cruel optimism' as a model through which to think about masculinity, precisely because it recognizes the failure not as a reparative gesture, but as a reality with which we live on a daily basis."[15] What I see is that the formation and performance of masculinity explodes into spaces outside of the actor and even produce a specific discourse that tries to grasp at this palpable struggle that Allan captures. This tension is clear in the chapter dealing with the clashes between male and female vessels.

One look into research involving something like sperm donation shows the fragility of masculine identity and the ways by which language is utilized as a release valve for those fears and anxieties. In *Sperm Counts*, Lisa Jean Moore notes that the explosion of sperm banks appears to impact notions of masculinity predicated on generation and sexual power. In her argument, organizations like the Fatherhood Responsibility Movement or the National Fatherhood Initiative, all arriving in the early 1990s, demonstrate a direct masculine fight against the perceived usurping of the individual male's involvement in procreation. The identity of the father was being challenged by access to the one material that set a man apart from women and non-procreating men. Essentially, sperm donation and access to sperm rendered individual men largely superfluous outside of the initial donation, sending some more vocal men onto a crusade to reclaim if not their place in procreation than access to their "vital fluid" for the use of single women and same-sex couples.

The generation of such male initiatives to combat spaces that appear to be infiltrated by women evokes what many scholars note as earmarks of a "crisis of masculinity" as long and deeply held ideas of masculine performance are being challenged in ways that upset the narratives of personhood and self. US culture, at the moment, is in the midst of discussing another crisis in masculinity, with incredibly violent pockets of this particularly white male anxiety, and it would make sense that frustrations concerning gender and sexual performance would make their way into protected pockets. If we are able to listen more carefully to the pockets that defy cultural expectations or look at narrative that grapples with the negotiation of gender construction, I think that we can become more attuned to the reality of human existence. We can see the connection between the rise of sperm donation and the concomitant creation of men's movements to combat such spaces, for instance, and in that recognition, find the ways humans manufacture balms to confront deeply confusing paradoxes.

What I am gesturing toward here is what was captured in chapter 4. Wherever one looks for absolutes, there explodes a frustration when performances are not moving in the direction expected or shaped by the cultural discourse. We are surrounded by release valves, sometimes benevolent and sometimes unbelievably violent, but the constant undercurrent is that expectations and categorical frameworks fail every time. Just as the songs negotiate gender identities and failures through language and symbolic ordering, so too is it possible to see the same struggles in the contemporary world. Song narratives might be similar release valves for transgressive identities and should be planted in a similar fashion to buried identities, pockets of affinity spaces, external policing, and self-censoring. In song, we have the freedom to toy with the taboo and use metaphor as a disguise to protect the performance. We might also use those same spaces to try to generate a sense of power and control when we register sensations of subordination. I spoke of men's movements and violence, and I think that song narrative that captures linguistic violence, like in the use of terms such as "bitch" or "whore," serves the same symbolic purpose in assuaging masculine failure.[16] I believe that what scholarly conversations like this provide is a spotlight on the outlets that challenge accepted discourse and support the incredible power of narrative to capture these categorical disruptions. We are not meant to be corralled by categories—our vents make that clear. We are meant to move, encounter, evolve, and actively help shape a world that takes itself a little less seriously in some respects and offers far more opportunity for experimentation and unbound authenticity. In a word, we need less constraint.

These competing struggles are captured best in the idea of liminality, a concept that was suggested throughout each of the chapters and is at play in what I am arguing here in terms of release valves. Throughout Hugill's repertoire, liminality and categorical instability are registered in the depiction, particularly, of nonprocreative sex. The choice of anal sex or copulation through and against the backdrop of queer spaces necessitates a reading of characters evoking an identity category that explodes normative readings of assumed opposite-sex affiliation. Anal sex, especially for the era during which the chanteys were likely sung, was a sexual outlet that was subordinated to procreative sex and therefore relegated to the realm of deviance. When the narrator points to anal intercourse or erotic release through vague and queer "'oles" within several of the songs surveyed, it is possible to imagine the male characters as open to sexual outlets considered nonnormative and deviant.

Through those admissions, the sailing characters articulate an identity vulnerable to the dominant cultural ideal but also suggest a relative flexibility in their relationship with sex. Characters in the songs, then, become categorically liminal figures open to both normative and nonnormative sex for pleasure, protection, or to pointedly register sexual expectations and flout convention. The same-sex sexual implications of anal intercourse were discussed at length in chapter 5; however, the desire for anal sex with opposite-sex partners is also an affiliation with same-sex desires or at least an open admission to the pleasures of liminal space. The anus is an orifice that we all share regardless of gender or sexual preference, and through this identification, it is an orifice that is queered and evocative, and it is noteworthy that such sexual outlets are repeated across many of the songs from the manuscript.[17] The way that this connects to larger implications outlined here is that explosions like men's movements or molly house subcultures are places where actors have vented their misaligned identity performances. They have found places through which their lived realities can seep into protected spaces, and the repetition of nonprocreative pleasure outlets throughout almost all of the song narratives in the manuscript lends to a reading of these songs as being a place that the strain of carrying nonnormative desires infiltrates because it can no longer be held back. These narrative elements are the compulsion to speak identified by Foucault.

In Hugill's repertoire, liminality is often presented in terms of the repeated clash of land and sea, especially through the different characters and their own attachment to either land or water. The distinction between life on land and life on the water is symbolically represented through the various female figures throughout the songs surveyed, but it is also distinctly noted in terms of the narratives they are contained within. The "whores" who are encountered in the various ports seem to take on the role of representing the ebb and flow of water and land, desire and convention. The relationships with them are just as in flux as the sailor's travails on water, and female characters appear linguistically denoted as different and forever changing.

In "Saltpetre Shanty," the singer remarks, "Them young Chili whores, boys, we'll wish 'em in Hell," and in "The Gals o' Chile," the erotically charged women are "red-hot divils [sic] from the other side of hell." These women stand in marked contrast to "me charmin' Nancy Lee" and the daughter of Shenandoah, who is associated with love and familial affection. In the song "Shenandoah," this distinction between types of women and what one does with them is starkly apparent. In the comparison between Shenandoah's daughter and "the Old Man's daughter," it is clear that one daughter is slated for love, while the other is purely a vessel through which to secure sexual desires. "Shenandoah" captures a tension between desiring the mandates of landbound relationships for the sailor does vocalize a longing to copulate with the "Old Man's daughter"; however, it also presents the anger and frustration through the use of the term "fuck" and thereby captures a sliding scale of desire, conventional expectations, and juridical frustrations.

Indeed, Allan notes, regarding modern men's movements, that "the feeling of being 'just fucked,' [is] a not entirely uncommon sentiment among men and especially in the men's rights movements, [and] is enmeshed in castration and phallicism."[18] "Fuck" and also being "fucked" are each evocations of frustration, especially where women are concerned, and tied specifically to being divested of masculine power and authority and even tied to castration. It is a subordinating term, "the shameful and humiliating position"; "to be fucked, he has to submit, place himself beneath, and become bottom in the hierarchical structure of the language of fucking."[19]

The language of the songs helps to create a distinction between land and sea not unlike what I see of identities throughout. There are demarcations of us versus them, love versus sex, desire versus procreative expectation, and all appear predicated on the clash of land and water. These distinctions are even more apparent in comparisons involving race. Songs like "Shenandoah" and "The Hog-Eye Man" create a clear delineation between the bodies of white women and men and those that are nonwhite. At least in some songs, white women are a part of the love and commitment economy, and nonwhite bodies are aligned with quick and ready sex. Race plays out, throughout all the songs, as a line of separation and underscores the liminality and even the continuum more roundly. These examples betray the troubling nature of life, of being pulled between planes of existence and actors one encounters. Finding a place to moor is difficult and sometimes treacherous, and the answer is not always finite—just as in the case of navigating the high seas.

Historian Margaret S. Creighton indicates that "nineteenth century seaman may have been unique in their willingness to express their softer sides, for reasons having to do with their distance from home and from women."[20] In her discussion, Creighton captures the exact liminality extant in chanteys from Hugill, which appear to express this sometimes-painful reality of navigating the push and pull between land and water, the finite and the ever changing. Clearly, too, such navigation inspires a degree of frustration, fear, and rage. Though the man, especially the sailor, was expected to be in control and to evidence a manly fortitude in the emotional realm, the reality is captured best in these pockets within songs where the answer is not quite as simple. Both desire and convention pull with the same strength, and navigating those competing impulses was no less frustrating or confusing than navigating land and water. These images of land and water, the different types of women, and even the realities of life at sea versus life on land have a power to grasp at identity performance as it is: unstable, changing, and almost always situation dependent, not unlike the chanteys themselves, which are impromptu, situation specific, and ever changing.

The identity experiences I am suggesting do not speak to the realities of all men; certainly, I am by no means attempting to venture an argument concerning the intentions of Legman and Hugill, though they compiled the manuscript. Instead, what I am proposing is that we can think about all cultural spaces in a similar way and can have wider conversations concerning the kaleidoscope of identity performances that make the world such a rich and colorful place. The kaleidoscope metaphor, I think, connects well with what opened these concluding ideas. Just as I argued that rings reaching out from one beginning point capture the idea of identity being a constantly connected and unfolding thing, so too can we bring the kaleidoscope to bear on our understanding of identity formation. Not every man is going to have an experience of desiring the body of another man, as is discussed in chapter 5, and we cannot say that every person who encounters the songs from Legman and Hugill will find themselves reflected there in the ebb and flow between water and land either. In fact, the paucity of representation of some men and women, especially the racialized and therefore subordinated ways in which some characters are reproduced, creates a reading environment wherein the songs can only capture identity formation to a degree and one that is forever burdened by racism, misogyny, and xenophobia.

Just as several chapters suggested, however, these characters, flawed as they are, can remain as vessels through which to grapple with identity practices that are a part of every human. The clash of land and water, for instance, might be the most evocative of all for it gestures at the hard and steadfast and the undulating. Regardless of what is under discussion, when it comes to identity formation, we have to understand it as tidal. Water acts on land, eroding and changing it, in the same way that land constitutes the boundaries of water. Identity practices are not always performed to the same degree, nor do the songs always capture the full kaleidoscope of identity formation, but they present pockets of the more complex and frustrating aspects of navigating identity performance against the backdrop of juridical realities. They register the solid and the changing, and here, they do so for a group of men that requires far deeper exploration and analytical creativity.

Importantly, liminalities in these songs are delivered with a cavalier quality despite the pain and suffering that often come with exploring nonprocreative sex and unstable identities. This cavalier quality is likely in service of accessing male-bonding mechanisms and scripts. What the introduction to this inquiry posited was that all-male singing traditions access questions surrounding vulnerability as they are attached to questions of gender and sexuality and that the failures articulated permit space to bond through those failures. Indeed, these elements confirm that the Hugill songs are unique renderings of working-class identity and relay that popular depictions of working-class men neglect telling the whole story.

It appears that occupational song, more roundly, functions as a release valve likely because of, in part, the realities that attend the working-class man's life. He places his body and sometimes his life at the mercy of vocational dangers, which court him daily. He has expectations placed on him in terms of breadwinning, masculinity, and virility. The working-class man, at least the sailor, appears to grapple with comparing himself to others and to ideals and recognizes that he sometimes falls short. Many occupational songs, like Hugill's, underscore and celebrate the expected performances of masculinity, which privilege a strong and agentive male force in relationships with women, but these songs also clearly highlight the fragility of that masculine performance with a tonal shrug.

Each male character, though authoritative and self-centered in his approaches with women, meets with at least some element of masculine failure, whether it is being thrown out, poxed, or divested of money. It is apparent that songs like these, whether chanteys or other male homosocial song traditions, are imbued with complex narratives that access deeply felt social and emotional experiences that work to erode established masculine identity. In the space of the songs, the cavalier delivery of narrative elements is a way of articulating the idiosyncrasies of living within a particular identity—in this case, the working-class male—and the symbolic representations of failed or inadequate masculinity articulate the fear that lies at the base of any performance of masculinity. That fear is that, foundationally, they are socially constructed and therefore susceptible to failure. Admitting these vulnerabilities and sharing them with other men in a similar situation bond them together through those painful admissions.

By looking to other examples of male song tradition, with an eye trained on these vulnerabilities, scholars may begin to investigate the admissions hiding within them for what they hold about liminalities and admission. Of course, these observations of the instability of gender and sexual construction have long been a point of discourse across disciplines, but more conversation needs to occur around objects that present as firmly heteronormative on their surface. We need to engage in more penetrative readings to uncover what might be buried beneath the façade and certainly for a cultural group that has yet to be fully explored.

I want readers to think about the freedoms that this book provides and the avenues it opens for further inquiry. Its intention was to give "permission to think in different ways, to embrace the challenge of being less paranoid, less anxious, less worried . . . ambition that is ameliorative, aesthetic, and affective."[21] It is an invitation to begin thinking more about how something like humor or other folk ephemera function as obvious mechanisms by which fears, anxieties, vulnerabilities, liminalities, and complexities are vented, sometimes unattached to literal bodies.

I think it is possible for researchers and common readers alike to recognize collective human realities in a character like the hog-eye man or even in the beleaguered bumboy, disparate as they appear on the surface. If we are to think about these characters more as symbolic vessels that hold and represent the experiences of both men and women, then as now, we might begin to understand connections in time and space that did not appear as solid at first. I believe that modern and contemporary culture likes to imagine that our world is far removed from that of the nineteenth century and even farther removed from something like a nearly two-dimensional character in a folksong. Nothing, I think, is further from the truth. It is all connected; we are all connected. The differences are in degree and not kind and applying this framework of a continuum allows for these connections to come into greater focus. The sexually agentive hog-eye man and the subordinated bumboy, in this framework predicated on a continuum, have more in common than at first appears, and the connection really comes down to this negotiation of actions within arbitrary lines demarcating space and time. How much does the sea erode the land or is the land opening itself to its collision with the sea? Which, in the end, is the one holding control over the constitution of the other?

Paths Forward

For now, the intent is that this work will generate some ideas concerning how we might deal with the materials that we have at our disposal. Since it is possible to see these collected materials as registering enduring and imbedded qualities, similar inquiries into other collected examples of chanteys would prove evocative. At the moment, the critical investigation of collected texts for what they capture of the human condition has yet to materialize. This publication is the first time that the entire Hugill manuscript of unexpurgated chanteys has been shared with the scholarly and popular culture worlds. Though I have produced a few journal articles that analyze the texts provided by Hugill, this wider inquiry generates the need for more focused unpacking of individual songs.

Additionally, with the critiques of the work of both Legman and Hugill in terms of scholarly rigor and authenticity, the difficult work of connecting these songs to informants and origins is necessary. Since the focus of this text has been more on what the songs generally capture, a deeper historical investigation of the songs might render a different picture. There are a vast number of other untapped sources that would reveal a great deal about what is permitted within the confines of folk traditions. Within the unpublished manuscript alone, Legman presents multiple examples of unexpurgated folksong texts that are rich for what they relay about identity. Gordon's Inferno Collection, James Madison Carpenter's collection, and the vast Alan Lomax collection, among others, are primed for investigations similar to the one I have presented throughout this publication.[22] The work of Vance Randolph, too, comes to mind as an incredible collection of unexpurgated material that has yet to be unpacked, as does the online Jack Horntip Collection. The analytical approach to the chanteys provided by Hugill is an important first step in mining collected bawdy material. So much of the scholarship and investigation of folksong material have dealt with trying to collect, collate, and authenticate examples, and as important and fruitful as such vocations are, turning attention to studying these collections as cultural artifacts, akin to the work that is a part of spaces like literary criticism and even sociolinguistics, is just as necessary.

It is my estimation that much of this analytical work has not been ventured because so much of the chantey material collected is housed in spaces where access is limited, such as a manuscript repository and library holdings, and because the genre is plagued by questions of authenticity. Access to materials might be assuaged as more holdings are digitized and widely shared, as is the case with the James Madison Carpenter Collection digitized through the Vaughn Williams Memorial Library. Another issue has to do with the genre, and there are two potential plans for moving forward. The collected examples we do have obviously need some investigation in terms of authenticity. Ethnomusicologist Gibb Schreffler has begun this important and gargantuan process, at least in terms of examining collections for scholarly merit. When it comes to individual songs, the process of authentication would take more time and is a venture that may never yield strong and defensible conclusions. A final option, and one that can begin at any moment, is to take what we have at our disposal, admit the shortcomings of the genre and collected examples, and critically investigate the narratives as scholars do any other cultural object. Taking the approach of new criticism to analyze these texts would emancipate the examples from the crippling shadow of authenticity and attribution and would provide incredible material for literary study. All approaches outlined would be beneficial to the continued work in the field, but I am suggesting that the critical analysis of the texts is a more pressing and ultimately more rewarding venture to pursue.

We are experiencing a prime moment to investigate collections of chanteys for, in a world grappling with the reverberations of a global pandemic, we are positioned well to listen closely to the narratives of men who were also confined, lacked access to quality food, shelter, and compensation, lived with illness all around them, and wallowed in loneliness and isolation for sometimes months to years at a time. Between 2020 and 2024, a global culture struggled with and continues to battle tensions that the sailor would have understood—tensions of which are, quite literally, visited within the confines of collected chantey examples. The COVID-19 pandemic, which raged at its height from November 2019 to May 2023, is not unlike the many maladies that sailors confronted in the confined spaces of the sailing ship. Any sailing memoir will detail, at least to some degree, the physical suffering in shipboard confinement that was born of close quarters among many overworked and oftentimes-malnourished men. So, too, would the sailor understand being trapped in a floating world, cut off from family and friends. The confinement and isolation inherent in quarantine likely registered the same feelings of longing that found their way into collected examples of chantey tunes.

Recognition of tyranny and racial tensions were facets of the sailing life, which immediately connect to the struggles we have experienced as a global culture. Racial tensions, indeed, find themselves in both the historical tracing of chanteys and their lyrical materials. We are also in a moment of history when the fluidity of identity is at the forefront of conversation, something that creates tension as regards identity boundaries and policing. Lisa Gilman writes that "gender in lived life is fluid" and goes on to argue that "folkloric forms are just as much connected to the multiplicities of identities that exist within ideas about 'males or maleness' and 'females or femaleness,' a spectrum of identities across gender, and those who eschew gender categories altogether."[23] The chanteys, at least from Hugill, appear to support a relationship with gender and sexuality that is more contemporary and just as provocative. This renewed interest in a beloved folksong tradition demonstrates that we are in a cultural time and space where these narratives might have transformative power as well as illustrative potential. If we were to unpack the collected archival examples and turn the kaleidoscope in different ways, the connections to our world now and to the collective human experience would be stunning.

To close, this publication has been a labor close to my heart. I opened with sharing my own experience with working-class culture and my own early love of erotic narrative. Those parts are all still within the text. I think it is impossible to extricate personal identity from the object of study. On a deeper level, however, this book is an audible cry from the hidden parts within all of us: within our culture, ourselves, our friends, families, and lovers. I see literature and narrative as an outlet for the soul. Such literature and narrative can certainly be funny and entertaining, like the chanteys I have shared from Hugill, but in those moments when we are laughing, we are connecting with the intentions of the writer. We are recognizing the shared language that helps us understand what the writer is communicating. We like to joke, we like to share, we like to be in on a shared secret—Isn't that part of what writing and creation are all about? What I am suggesting in *Cabin Boys, Milkmaids, and Rough Seas* is that what we write down, what we sing, and what we share with the world are each a reflection of what we are experiencing, however buried and however individualized it may seem. Creating is a vulnerable practice. We are bearing our souls to anyone who is willing to listen, perhaps with the hope that those creations will reach individuals who recognize the same experiences we attempt to capture. In the case of some folk material, only certain people were supposed to hear it, yet here we are, looking at what does not necessarily belong to us and still finding connections to our own lives and struggles. In a way we—as researchers and curious onlookers—are taking a moment to look behind the curtain, and we have a chance to realize the collective reality that is always humming beneath the surface, barely perceptible because we are always in the process of surviving. We are the interlopers.

What I hope the reader might take from this analytical work is that identity is far too often prescribed for us and that there are release valves, all around, that we might interrogate further in order to understand the complexities of identity negotiation. The reality of performing who you are—the person you are when you think no one is looking, the person you are when you are among friends—does not always fit the social expectations that discipline selfhood when you are outside of those protected spaces. I hope that this investigation has related the provocative notion that what we create gives us entry into worlds that we often like to keep secret. Perhaps it may inspire more people, scholars and laity alike, to look at the opaque, to interrogate the things that appear to be status quo, and maybe even to challenge their own sense of self and other. Possibly, this could even open someone to a recognition of the continuum within all of us, a continuum that stretches out and touches others, reflecting back on us in the same circular and impactful patterns that Ahmed and Hurley both suggest. We are more connected to each other than we are disparate. So much of what we think of as absolute is unmoored. This is a moment in our collective culture to encourage more of these emancipatory conversations and to look back at past voices to see if there are echoes of these same inherent desires and curiosities. If we are open to listening in new ways, to situating ourselves so that we collide with possibilities that run counter to outworn narratives, there is a transcendence possible. If we take a page from folk song, we can also have fun while we are at it.

Appendix: Chantey Lyrics

Note: all underlining, spelling, punctuation (including ellipses and slashes), and idiosyncrasies that are not in square brackets are reproduced exactly as given in the original Legman manuscript with the exception that all caps have been changed to small caps for typographical reasons.

"The Shaver" or "The Bumboy"

When I was a tiny little boy,
I went to sea in Stormy's employ,
I shipped away as a little bumboy.
<u>When I was just a shaver, a shaver,</u>
<u>Oh, I wuz weary of the sea, when I was just a shaver.</u>
<u>When I wwas just a shaver.</u>

Oh, they whacked me up and they whacked me down,
The mate he cracked me on the crown,
He wanted me for his bit o' brown, <u>When, &c.</u>

When I went aloft by the lubber's hole
The mate he cried, Goddam yer soul!
An' he rammed his prick right up me 'ole, <u>When, &c.</u>

And when we lolloped around Cape Horn,
I wished to Christ I'd never been born,
The ice it froze the chief mate's horn, <u>When, &c.</u>

Oh, we left behind the ice an' rain,
An' once more to the tropics we came,
And the mate he was back on the job again.

When we made port, oh I skipped ship,
I'd had enough cock for one bleedin' trip,
With a boy-shaggin' mate, oh I'd never more ship.

<u>Sailing Ship Shanties</u>, 1925–1956.

"Blow the Man Down"

Oh, where are ye goin' to, my pretty maid?
    <u>Way-ay, blow the man down!</u>
Oh, I'm goin' a-milkin', kind sir, she said,
    <u>Gimme some time to blow the man down!</u>

Oh, have ye a sweetheart, my pretty maid?
I'm lookin' for one, kind sir, she said.

Then may I come with ye, my pretty maid?
Well yes, since ye axed me, sir, she said.

But I guess yer a bad un, kind sir, she said,
Yer out for to fuck me, but don't wanter wed.

Well, well, sez bold Jackshite, me thoughts ye have read,
Let's look for a haystack, 'twill make a fine bed.

Jack took her in tow, an' away they did go,
The bull with a hard-on, the cow sayin' No!

They came to a haystack, the maid she wuz shy,
They backed an' they filled, Jack's jibboom stove high.

The haystack capsizèd, Jack's jibboom got bent,
Straw hung from her arse-ole, her thing wuz all rent.

So he left her a-sittin' with her bloomers all torn,
He fucked her an' left her, that maid all forlorn.

Now all ye young sailors that round the Horn sail,
Don't take a young milkmaid away from her pail.

Don't ye try an' fuck her a-top of a stack,
Or ye might break yer jibboom, like did our poor Jack.

Look for a flash-packet what's got a nice bed,
Leave milkmaids to hayseeds, that's what poor Jack said.

<u>Sailing Ship Shanties</u>, 1927–1956.

"What Shall We Do? ~~With a Drunken Sailor?~~"

Alternate: "Drunken Sailor" written above "What Shall We Do?"

WHAT shall we do with a drunken sailor :3:
    <u>Earlye in the morning?</u>
    <u>Way, hay, an' UP she rises</u> :3:
    <u>Earlye in the morning.</u>

Scrape the hairs off his bollocks with a hoop-iron razor,
The hairs off his bollocks with a hoop-iron razor,
Scrape the hairs off his bollocks with a hoop-iron razor
    <u>Earlye in the morning, &c.</u>

What'll we do with the Queen o' Sheba :3:
Pull the hairs from her snatch with a pair o' tweezers./
What'll we do with the Queen o' Morrocker? :3:
Stick her in a cage, an' let a monkey fuck her.

<u>Sailing Ship Shanties</u>, 1930–1956.

"Ratcliffe Highway"

COME all ye young seaman an' listen ter me,
I'll sing ye a song all about the high seas.
Now it 'tain't very short nor it 'tain't very long,
'Tis of a Flying Fish sailor jist home from Hong Kong
    <u>Singing, too-relye-addie, too-relye-addie,</u>
    <u>Singin' too-relye-addiee, aye, too-relye-ay!</u>

Oh, as I wuz a-rollin' down Ratcliffe Highway,

A flash-lookin' packet I chanct for to see.
Of the port that she hailed from I cannot say much,
But by her appearance I took her for Dutch.

Her flag wuz three colours, her mast-head wuz low,
She wuz round at the counter and bluff at the bow :
From larboard to starboard an' so sailed she,
She wuz sailin' at large, she wuz runnin' free.

She wuz bowlin' along with the wind blowin' free,
She clew'd up her tawps'ls an' waited for me.
I fired me bow-chaser, the signal she knew,
She backed her main-tawps'l an' for me hove to.

I hailed her in English, she answered me clear,
I'm from the <u>Black Arrow</u>, bound to the <u>Shakespeare</u>.
So I wore ship wid a, What d'yer know!
I passed her me hawser an' took her in tow.

(In a snug little corner, oh soon we did moor,
I bought me some rum for this young Highway whore.
She told me her fancyman wuz at sea for a spell,
So I gave her me flipper an' we wuz both bound to Hell.)

I tipped her me flipper an' took her in tow,
An' yard-arm to yard-arm away we did go.
She then took me up to her lily-white room,
Into her paint-locker I stuck me jibboom.

She clew'd up her skirts, boys, we had much sea-room,
I raked her from forard wid a greasy jibboom.
Then I manned me gun an' I caught her at large,
Fired into her stern-port a filthy discharge.

We closed alongside, boys, I hauled in me slack,
I busted me bobstay—she busted her crack.
Now me shot-locker's empty, me powder's all spent,
Me gun needs repairin', it's choked at the vent.

She then dropped her courses, I lashed up and stowed,
I gave her some shillings 'fore I left her abode.
But it 'twarn't quite enough, boys, she wanted some more,
She cursed me an' called me a son-o'-a-whore.

She blazed like a frigate, at me she let fire,
Oh nothing could stem, boys, that Irish tart's ire.
She kicked me, she farted, she spat in me jaw,
An' I beat retreat through her open back-door.

I've fought with the Russians, the Prussians alsó,
I've fought with the Dutch and with Johnny Crapaud,
But of all the fine fights that I ever did see,
She beat all the sights o' the heathen Chinee.

Now all ye young sailors, take a warnin' I say,
Take it aisy, me boys, when yer down that Highway,
Steer clear o' them flash gals on the Highway do dwell,
Or they'll take up yer flipper an' yer soon bound to Hell!

<u>Sailing Ship Shanties</u>, 1925–1956.

"Do Let Me 'Lone, Susan"

Do let me 'lone, Susan, oh, do let me 'lone!
    <u>Hurrah! me looloo boys, <small>DO</small> let me 'lone!</u>
When I put me arm 'round Jinny's waist, Oh, Jinny jump away,
    <u>Hurrah! me looloo boys, <small>DO</small> let me 'lone!</u>

When I put me hand up Jinny's clouts, oh, Jinny jump about,
    <u>Hurrah! me looloo boys!</u>

Do let me 'lone, Flora, oh, do let me lone!
When I put me arm 'round Jinny's breasts, Oh, Jinny jump away,
When I put me hand on Jinny's snatch, Oh, Jinny jump about.

<u>Sailing Ship Shanties</u>, 1932–1956.

"The Hog-Eye Man"

Oh, the hog-eye man is the man for me,
With a prick from here to Tennessee!
<u>Oh, hog-eye O! Row the boat ashore for her hog-eye,
Row the boat ashore for her hog-eye O,
     She wants the hog-eye man!</u>

He came to the shack where Jinny she did dwell,
As soon as he saw her he tried to ring her bell./
O, Jinny's in the garden a-pickin' peas,
An' the hair of her snatch hangin' down to her knees.

She was too late to hide her snatch,
An' the hog-eye nigger jammed a bale down the hatch./
He caught-her all aback, an' he caulked her little crack,
She wriggled like the divil but she couldn't shift her tack.

Soon he had her like a schooner on the rock,
She was a little maid who had never seen a cock./
His bowsprit was hard, his bowsprit was long,
He tickled her innards while he sang this little song.

An' then he went away, 'cause he'd had his little fun,
He left her on her back, with her fanny in the sun./
Oh, her sweetheart (fancyman) came for to court his lass,
An' he saw his Jinny a-lyin' in the grass.

Oh, who's bin here since I've bin gone?
A big buck nigger wid a hard-on on./
If I cotch him here wid me Jinny anymore,
I'll tattoo his dusters, an' he won't fuck anymore.

Oh, the hog-eye man, he's lookin' for a ride,
When he's ashore, lock yer gals inside.

<u>Sailing Ship Shanties</u>, 1930–1956.

"Reefy Tayckle"

Every good ship has an anchor, every anchor has a stock,
Every boy that loves a flash gal has a bloody great—
<u>Slack away yer reefy tayckle, reefy tayckle, reefy tayckle,
Slack away yer reefy tayckle, me bollocks are jammed</u>!

Every good ship has a lifeboat, every lifeboat has some rollocks,
Every boy that loves a flash gal has a fine pair of—
Every good ship has a sidelight, every sidelight has a wick,
Every boy that loves a flash gal has a few fathom of—

Every good ship has a mainsail, every mainsail has a bunt,
Every gal that loves a sailor has a nice hairy—
Every good ship that goes alongside makes fast to the bitts,
Every gal that loves a sailor has a fine pair of—

<u>Sailing Ship Shanties</u>, 1932–1956.

"Miss Lucy Long"

Wuz ye never down on the Broomielaw,
When the Yankee boys wuz all the go?
<u>Timme way-ha-ay-hay, hay-hay, hay-hay,
Ah-ha, me bully boys, ah-ha</u>!
<u>Why don't ye try for to shag Miss Lucy Long</u>?

Oh, as I walked out one mornin' fair,
To view the view an' take the air./
Oh, 'twas there I met Miss Lucy fair,
'Twas there we met, I do declare.

I axed, 'Ow much? Will five bob do?
Is that enough for a quick blow-through?—
You dirty Limey, you stink o' tar,
Besides, I know what Limeys are!

With brassbounders of the Blackball Line,
I only spend me whorin' time./
They've got good cash, they treats ye well,

Their knobs are big for to ring the bell.

I showed her me knob, an' she changed her mind,
As one of her crew I was very soon signed./
The moral of this, when a-whorin' ye go,
If ye've got a big knob, ye will git a good tow.

Yer pockets, me son, can be empty as hell,
But with a big bowsprit, ye'll do yerself well./
For a whore is a woman, an' better than cash
She likes a big sailor, that's got a big lash!

Sailing Ship Shanties, 1931–1957.

"Cheerily Man"

Oh, Nancy Dawson, ai-o-eeyo—Cheerily man!
She's got no drawers on, ai-o-eeyo—Cheerily man!
An' likes it head-on, ai-o-eeyo—Cheerily man!
Oh, ally-high-ee-o-o—Cheerily man!

Oh, Sally Rackett, who'd like ter shaggitt, An' get a packet?
Oh, Flora Fernanah, She likes a banana, Stuck up her vagina.
Oh, widow Skinner, Likes cock for dinner, Long, thick or thi[n]
Oh, Missus Duckitt, Shits in a bucket, Who'd like to fuck it

Oh, Sally Riddle, I saw her piddle, Through a cinder-riddle.
Oh, Betty Baker, lives at Long Acre, I'd like to rake her.
Oh, Jinny Walker, Fucked by a hawker, Who had a corker.
Oh, Jennifer Bell, She fucks as well, An' never will tell.

Oh, Kitty Carson, She spliced a whoreson, Who likes it stern
Oh, Polly Hawkins, In her white stockings, Has had some fuck

Sailing Ship Shanties, 1927–19[illegible]

"The Liverpool Judies"

WHEN I was a youngster I sailed with the rest,
On a Liverpool packet bound out to the West.
We anchored way down in the harbour o' Cork,
Then we put out to sea for the port o' New York.
    <u>Singin' ho! ro! Ho, bullies, ho!</u>
    <u>Them Liverpool Judies have got us in tow!</u>

For forty-two days we was hungry an' sore,
Oh the winds was ag'in us, the gales they did roar.
Off Battery Point we did anchor at last,
With our jibboom hove in an' the canvas all fast.

The boarding-house masters was off in a trice,
A-shoutin' an' promisin' all that was nice.
An' one fat ol' crimp he got cottoned to me,
Says he, Yer a fool, lad, to follow the sea.

Says he, There's a job as is waitin' for you,
With lashin's o' liquor an' fuck-all to do.
Says he, What d'ye say, lad, will you jump her too?
Says I, Ye ol' barstard, I'm damned if I do!

But the best o' intentions they niver gits far,
After forty-two days at the door of a bar.
I tossed off me liquor, an' what d'ye think?
Why the lousy ol' barstard had drugs in me drink.

The next I remembers, I woke in the morn,
On a three-skysail yarder bound south round Cape Horn,
Wid an ol' suit of oil-skins an' two pair of socks,
An' a bloody big head an' a dose of the pox.

Now all ye young sailors, take a warnin' from me,
Keep a watch on your drinks when the liquor is free,
An' pay no attention to runner or whore,
Or your head'll be thick an' your prick'll be sore.

<u>Sailing Ship Shanties</u>, 1927–1956.

"Billy Boy"

Where have ye bin all the day, Billy Boy, Billy Boy?
    Where have ye bin all the day, me Billy Boy?
I've been walkin' on the quay with me charmin' Nancy Lee,
<u>An' sweet Nancy kittl'd me fancy, oh me charmin' Billy Boy</u>!

Is she fit to be your wife, Billy Boy, Billy Boy? <u>Is she, &c</u>.
Aye, she's fit to be me wife as the fork is to the knife./
Can she cook a bit o' steak, Billy Boy, Billy Boy?
She can cook a bit o' steak, aye an' make a griddle cake.

Can she make an Irish stew, Billy Boy, Billy Boy?
She can make an Irish stew, aye an' singin' hinnies too./
Does she sleep close unto thee, Billy Boy, Billy Boy?
Aye, she sleeps close unto me, like the bark is to the tree./

Can she make a feather bed, Billy Boy, Billy Boy?
She can make a feather bed, fit for any sailor's head./
Can she heave the dipsy lead, Billy Boy, Billy Boy?
Yes, she can heave the dipsy lead, but she's lost her maidenhea[d.]

Can she strop a block, Billy Boy, Billy Boy?
Aye, she can strop a block, an' she'll take a fathom o' cock./
Can she toss a bunt, Billy Boy, Billy Boy?
Aye, she can toss a bunt, an' she'll let you feel her cunt.

<u>Sailing Ship Shanties</u>, 1926–1956.

"John Brown's Daughter"

John Brown's daughter is a virgin, so I'm told,
Her arse-'ole's decked with diamonds and her cunt is
    decked with gold.
John Brown's daughter's got a wart upon her snatch,
John Brown's daughter's got a wart on her main-hatch.

<u>Sailing Ship Shanties</u>, 1928–1956.

"Can't Ye Dance the Polka?"

As I rolled down the Bowery one evening in July,
I met a maid who axed me trade : A Sailor John, sez I.

<u>Then away, you Santee, my fair maid (dear honey),
Oooh ye New York gals, cayn't ye dance the polka?
(Oooh ye New York gals, ye love us for our money!)</u>

To a fancy store I took her, I did not mind the expense,
I bought her two gold earrings, and they cost me fifteen cents./

Sez she, You Limejuice sailor, now see me home ye may,
But when we reached her own back door, she unto me did say :

My fancyman's a Yankee, wid his hair cut short behind,
He wears a pair o' long sea-boots, an' he's bosun in the
    Blackball Line./

He's homeward bound tomorrow, an' he will want his 'ole,
So if you want to dip yer wick, ye'll have to rock 'n' roll.

So I grabbed her right and proper, afore her flash man docked,
An' up the stairs we climbed right smart, an' soon her snatch
    wuz cooked./

I rode her long an' hard boys, she wriggled like an eel,
An' when I rammed it home two blocks, this maiden sure did
    squeal.

When I awoke next morning, me head wuz sore as hell,
She'd hit me with the piss-pot boys, and skint me pay as well./

I wrapped me glad rags around me, and to the docks did steer,
I'd never court another maid, I'd stick to rum and beer.

I joined a Yankee blood-boat, and sailed away next morn,
Don't ever fool around wid gals, yer safer off Cape Horn !

<u>Sailing Ship Shanties</u>, 1928–1956.

"Saltpetre Shanty"

To ol' Callyo we are bound away—<u>Arse-ole</u>! :2:
We're bound away at the break o' the day
To where them <u>putas</u> o' Chili will grab all our pay.
    <u>Arse-ole! Slap her arse (tits)</u>!
    <u>Ram it two-blocks up her arse-ole</u>!

Ol' Pedro the pimp, boys, he knows us of old :2:
He's a-primin' his <u>vino</u>, an' dopin' his beer,
To the Chinchas he'll ship us if we don't take care.

Ol' Madam the Judge stands her tarts in a row, :2:
She wants all her gals to put on a good show.
They're a-powderin' their fannies, they're scentin' their 'ole
Awaitin' us Jackshites to flush out their 'oles.

Them <u>putas</u> o' Chili they're hard to beat :2:
With a blow-through an' a <u>rumper</u> an' a skinful o' wine,
But them barstards is poxin' us all o' the time.

We'll wash down saltpetre with pisco an' wine :2:
When we're loaded an' ready for to sing a farewell,
Them young Chili whores, boys, we'll wish 'em in Hell.

<u>Sailing Ship Shanties</u>, 1926–1957.

"Serafina"

I<small>N</small> Callyo there lives a whore, her name is Serafina,
    <u>S<small>ER</small>-afina! S<small>ER</small>-afina</u>!
She sleeps all day an' works all night on the old Cally Marina,
    <u>S<small>ER</small>-afina! S<small>ER</small>-afina</u>!

She's the queen, me boys, of all the whores, that do a <u>rump the coolo</u>,
She used to fuck for monkey-nuts, but now she fucks for vino./
At robbin' silly sailor-boys, no whore was ever keener,
Y'could stow a barge inside her cunt, 'tis like a concertina.

She'll suck yer prick, yer balls an' all; that's how her mum did wean

She likes a prick like a chimney-stack, or the funnel of a White Star
    steamer./
Serafina's got no drawers, I've been ashore an' seen 'er,
She's got no time to put 'em on, that hard-fucked Serafina.

When I was young an' in my prime, I first fucked Serafina,
'Twas up the front in Callyo, an' up the back in Lima./
But the finest sight I'd ever seen was the cunt of Serafina,
Till I got a load, a right full-house, then I wisht I'd never bin ther[e.]

<u>Sailing Ship Shanties</u>, 1925–1957[.]

"The Fire Ship (II)"

. . . <u>We</u> went up to her bedroom, an' soon all sail was stowed,
Upon the brassbound bedstead, boys, to the bitter end we rode.
I caulked her seams with red-hot pitch, which made her jump for joy,
She cried that I had just the gun for a fire ship to employ.

Now all ye bully sailormen that sail the Western Sea,
An' all ye jolly 'prentice lads, a warnin' take from me:
Steer clear of lofty fire ships, for to me they brought bad luck,
For one burnt off me ol' Jibboom, an' now I cannot fuck.

<u>Sailing Ship Shanties</u>, 1930–1956.

"Sacramento"

As I wuz rollin' down the street,
    <u>Hoodah, to me hoodah!</u>
Two charmin' bitches I did meet,
    <u>Hoodah, hoodah, day</u>!

   <u>Blow boys, blow, for Californ-eye-o!</u>
   <u>There's plenty of grass, ter wipe yer arse,</u>
   <u>On the banks o' the Sacramento.</u>

I chose the one with the curly locks,
She wuz the one that gave me the pox./

Off to the doctor I did go,
Prick an' balls I had to show.

In came the nurse with a mustard poultice,
Chapped it on but I took no notice./
In came the doctor with a bloody big lance:
Now, young sailor, I'll make yer dance. . . .

I had to pay for me bed an' me room
By gettin' a knot on me ol' jibboom./
But a gal's a gal, an' sailors is men,
I'll still be a-cock when I see another hen.

An' when I'm well an' free from pain,
If I meet that whore, I'll fuck her again./
Sing, me boys, oh, heave an' sing,
Heave an' make her arse-ole spring.

<u>Sailing Ship Shanties,</u> 1923–1956.

"Sally Brown"

OH! Sally Brown's a big buck nigger,
    Way, hay, roll an' go!
Her arse-ole's big but her snatch is bigger,
    Spend my money on Sally Brown.

Sally Brown, I love yer daughter,
I love the place where she makes her water./
Sally Brown, I fucked your daughter,
Gave her twins an' stopped her water.

<u>Sailing Ship Shanties,</u> 1928–1956.

"The Gals o' Chile"

To Chile's coast we are bound away,
    <u>Timme arsy-ole, bungolero!</u>
To Chile's coast we are bound away,

<u>We'll shag an' all drink pisco (get pissed, boys)</u> !
To Chile's coast we are bound away,
Where them little Dago gals hawk their tripe all day,
    <u>Timme arsy bungolero</u>,
      <u>Sing olé! for a well-cut whore (a two-way whore)</u> .

An' when we gits to Vallipo :2:
They'll grab yer round the middle an' they won't let go,
To the whorehouse, bullies, with a roll 'n' go!
(To the <u>casa-de-puta</u> with a roll 'n' go!)

Them gals o' Chile they are hard to beat :2:
They shag like a hen when a cock it meets,
Oh, a <u>romper-la-cola</u> is a sailor's treat.

Them señoritas are smart an' gay :2:
They drink an' shag till the break o' day,
Then pitch ye out like a bale o' hay.

My trim little packet is a very smart craft :2:
You can have yer choice of a hole or a crack,
A peso up the front an' two fer up the back.

Rosita, Anna, an' Carmen too :2:
They'll greet ye with a hullabaloo,
An' they'll drop their drawers for a nice fuckeroo.

Them señoritas, as we know well :2:
They're red-hot divils from the other side of hell,
Keep yer hand on yer money when ye shag a Chile belle.

When the time comes for to say farewell :2:
Goodbye to the gals and our money as well,
With a dose of the pox from ol' Corynel.

<u>Sailing Ship Shanties</u>, 1925–1957.

"Maggie May"

Come all ye sailors bold, an' when me tale is told
I know ye all will sadly pity me.
For I was a goddam fool in the port of Liverpool,
On the voyage when I first paid off from sea.

Oh, Maggie, Maggie May, they have taken you away,
To slave upon Van Diemen's cruel shore.
Oh, you robbed many a whaler and you poxed many a sailor,
But ye'll never cruise 'round Paradise Street no more.

I paid off at the Home, after a voyage from Sierra Leone,
Two-pounds-ten a month had been me pay,
An' as I jingled in me tin, I was sadly taken in
By a lady of the name of Maggie May.

When I steered into her I hadn't got a care,
I wuz cruisin' up an' down ol' Canning Place,
She wuz dressed in a gown so fine, like a frigate of the line,
An' I, bein' a sailorman, gave chase.

She gave me a saucy nod, an' I like a farmer's clod,
Let her take me line abreast in tow,
An' under all plain sail we ran before the gale,
An' to the Crow's-Nest Tavern we did go.

When I got full o' beer, to her lodgings we did steer,
She charged me fifteen shillings for all night.
I wuz so ruddy drunk, as I got in her bunk,
Not knowing if I'd shagged or shove up shite.

Next mornin' when I woke,/me prick all bent an' broke,
I hadn't got a penny to me nyme.
So I had to pop me boots, me John L's an' me suit
Down in the Park Lane pawnshop Number Nine.

Oh you thievin' Maggie May, ye robbed me of me pay
When I slept wid you last night ashore.
Guilty the jury found her, for robbin' a homeward-bounder,

An' she'll never roll down Park Lane any more.

A week it passed away, an' in me bunk I lay,
Accursin' the day that I'd met Maggie May,
I'd got a dose o' clap, an' it ran just like a tap,
With a blueball and two chancres for me pay.

She wuz chained an' sent away from Liverpool that day,
The lads they cheered as she sailed down the Bay.
An' every sailor lad, he only wuz too glad
They'd sent the ol' whore out to Botany Bay.

<u>Sailing Ship Shanties</u>, 1926–1957.

"Johnny, Come Down to Hilo"

Now, who's bin here since I've bin gone?
Some big buck nigger wid a hard-on on.
    Johnny, come down to Hilo! oh, poor old man!
    Oooh! wake her! oh, shake her!
    Ooooh! wake that gal wid the blue dress on!
    When Johnny comes down to Hilo, oh, poor old man!

I won't wed a nigger, no I'm damned if I do,
He's got jiggers in his bollocks and his arse-ole too./
He travelled all around till he came to the shack
Where his Sally made a livin' oh, a-layin' on her back.

Went upstairs an' he looked through a crack,
Sally lyin' on the deck with her mains'l aback./
She'd just grabbed hold o' a piece o' plank,
Shoved it up her hatch (crack), an' gave herself a wank.

He opened the door—she gave a little cry,
An' then he stove his toggle up her ol' deadeye./
He was hard as a rock, an' he soon was two-blocks,
But in five days' time he had a dose of pox.

An' he swore he never would touch another bloomin' whore,

But was back on the job, next time he came ashore.

<u>Sailing Ship Shanties</u>, 1930–1956.

"Jinny Keep Yer Arse-'Ole Warm"

Now, m'lads, be of good cheer,
For the Irish land will soon draw near,
In a few days more we'll sight Cape Clear!
<u>   Ooooh! Jinny keep yer arse-'ole warm!</u>
<u>   Oh, jamboree, oh jamboree,</u>
<u>   Ai-i-i! ye big-pricked black man, sheet it home behind,</u>
<u>   Oh, jamboree, oh jamboree,</u>
<u>   Oooooh! Jinny keep yer arse-'ole warm!</u>

Now, m'boys, we're off to Holyhead,
An' there's no more casts of the dipsy lead,
'N' soon we'll lie in a fuckin' fevver-bed, <u>Ooooh! &c.</u>

Now the Bar Ship is in sight,
An' soon we'll be off the ol' Rock Light,
An' I'll be up yer flue tonight, <u>Ooooh! &c.</u>

Now we're haulin' through the dock,
All the pretty young gals on the pierhead do flock,
An' there's my Jinny, oh, she's hungry for the cock.

Now x we're tied up to the pier,
Oh, 'tis way down below an' pack yer bloody gear,
An' I'll soon be two blocks up you, me dear.

Now I'm safely on the shore,
An' I don' give a fuck how the windx do roar,
Oh, I'll drop me anchor an' I'll go to sea no more.

Now I've had two weeks ashore,
I'll pack me bag an' I'll go to sea once more,

An' I'll bid goodbye to me Liverpool whore, <u>Ooooh! &c.</u>

Sailing Ship Shanties, 1933–1956

"Shenandoah"

SHENANDOAH, I love yer daughter, <u>A-way! ye rolling river,</u>
Wish I wuz a-fucking of the Old Man's daughter,
    <u>An' away we're bound to go, 'crosst the wide Missoura.</u>

When I wux a young man in me prime, <u>A-way! &c.</u>
I'd shag them yeller gals two at a time./
Foretops'l halyards, the mate he will roar, <u>A-way! &c.</u>
Lay along smartly, ye son-o'-a whore!

Them little brown gals ain't got no drawers, <u>A-way! &c.</u>
They covers their things with bits o' straws./
Them Liverpool gals I do adore, <u>A-way, &c.</u>
But I'd sooner shag a little black whore.

Sailing Ship Shanties, 1933–1956

"Yaw, Yaw, Yaw!"

OH, mit mein niggerum, buggerum, stinkum,
    <u>Mit mein yaw, yaw, yaw!</u>
Mit mein niggerum, buggerum, stinkum,
    <u>Mit mein yaw, yaw, yaw!</u>
Vell, ve'll climb upon der steeples,
And ve'll shit (piss) down on de peoples,
    <u>Mit mein yaw, yaw, yaw.</u>

Sailing Ship Shanties, 1933–1956

Notes

Preface

1. For the first mention of Hugill sending unexpurgated texts to Legman, see EBarnacle, July 12, 2013, comment on Mudcat Café, "Stan Hugill Uncensored," https://mudcat.org/thread.cfm?threadid=145866.
2. Jonathan Lighter, email message to author, August 25, 2015.
3. Bob Walser, email message to author, October 9, 2014.
4. Judith Legman, email message to author, October 12, 2014.
5. Judith Legman, email message to author, October 30, 2014.

Chapter 1. Chanteys: The Sailor's Work Song among His Brothers

1. Mary K. Bercaw Edwards notes, "breath partakes of spirit (inspiration) that serves to unify, imparting a synergistic power to the group that adds up to more than the sum of its parts." Mary K. Bercaw Edwards, "Sailor Talk in Melville and Conrad," in *Secret Sharers: Melville, Conrad and Narratives of the Real*, ed. Pawel Jedrzejko, Milton M. Reigelman, and Zuzanna Szatanik (Szczecin: M-Studio, 2011), 249.
2. Eve Kosofsky Sedgwick, "Paranoid Reading and Reparative Reading; or, You're So Paranoid, You Probably Think This Introduction Is About You," in *Novel Gazing: Queer Readings in Fiction*, ed. Eve Kosofsky Sedgwick (Durham, NC: Duke University Press, 1997), 1–37.
3. Charles L. Briggs, "Disciplining Folkloristics," *Journal of Folklore Research* 45, no. 1 (2008): 99.
4. Briggs, "Disciplining Folkloristics," 103.
5. Sarah Lash, "Tilting the Ivory Tower: The Life, Works, and Legacy of Gershon Legman," *Folklore Historian: Journal of the Folklore and History Section of the American Folklore Society* 27 (2010): 25–41.
6. Briggs, "Disciplining Folkloristics," 94.
7. *Oxford English Dictionary*, s.v. "shanty," subentry "Etymology," accessed July 1, 2023, https://doi.org/10.1093/OED/3515706077.
8. Stan Hugill, *Shanties from the Seven Seas: Shipboard Work-Songs and Songs Used as Work-Songs from the Great Days of Sail* (Mystic, CT: Mystic Seaport Museum, 1996), 1–2.
9. Ethnomusicologist Gibb Schreffler argues, "Its [the spelling's] uniqueness sets it apart and makes it suitable for my [Schreffler's] project of distinguishing a distinctive genre rather than a generic and misunderstood catch-all term for sailors' songs as the spelling *shanty* might." Gibb Schreffler, email message to author, September 7, 2015.

10. For a thorough discussion of the song, its origins, and it use in popular culture, see Simon J. Bronner, *"Who's That Knocking On My Door?": Barnacle Bill the Sailor and His Mates in Song and Story*, Occasional Papers in Folklore 5 (Lansdale, PA: Loomis House Press, 2016).

11. Graeme Milne, "Collecting the Sea Shanty: British Maritime Identity and Atlantic Musical Cultures in the Early Twentieth Century," *International Journal of Maritime History* 29, no. 2 (2017): 375–81.

12. Schreffler is one of the only scholars to attempt a critical discussion of all published chantey collections. He indicates that many of the songs that scholars and chantey-revival bands alike use as primary source material have not been carefully critiqued or questioned and that a number of the chantey collections from the twentieth century are mixtures of primary source material, "cross-influence [from other sources], uncritical scholarship, or plagiarism." See Gibb Schreffler, "Twentieth-Century Editors and the Re-envisioning of Chanties: A Case Study of 'Lowlands,'" *The Nautilus* 5 (2014): 8. For a deepening of this investigation, see Gibb Schreffler, *Boxing the Compass: A Century and a Half Discourse about Sailor's Chanties*, Occasional Papers in Folklore 6 (Lansdale, PA: Loomis House Press, 2018).

13. Schreffler also captures the conflation of sea songs and chanteys, which he does best when he argues of chantey collector Stan Hugill's work:

> Hugill aimed to be as inclusive as possible. Any song that he heard which might have been sung "as a chanty" (a dubious criterion, implying that a song becomes a chanty if someone sings it during work on a sailing vessel) was included. In reading his text, one has no idea which of the items were known by more or less every chantyman (say, 40–50 out of the total 400+ items in the book?) and which were one-offs and provincial songs that are really outliers.

Gibb Schreffler, email message to author, September 6, 2015.

14. Stan Hugill, letter to Gershon Legman, September 2, [1962?], Judith Legman's personal collection. Emphasis original. For a discussion concerning the importance of genre and distinctions between genres, see Jacques Derrida and Avital Ronell, "The Law of Genre," *Critical Inquiry* 7, no. 1 (1980): 55–81. Schreffler argues that there was, at least by the 1890s, "increased recognition of chanties as a genre—a discrete topic of discussion." Schreffler, *Boxing the Compass*, 28.

15. Though there are several other chantey collectors who were sailors, none of their publications include such a succinct and pointed defense of their knowledge of chanteys. In fact, the material is presented in such a way that their pedigree as a sailor is expected to stand for itself. Frederick Pease Harlow is at least one of these sailor-collectors to reference. His collection *Chanteying aboard American Ships* is comprised of songs that he heard while he was employed as a sailor. The first chapter of his collection, "Chanteying on the Akbar," reads almost like a memoir, with songs interspersed between the narrative. See Frederick Pease Harlow, *Chanteying aboard American Ships* (Mystic, CT: Mystic Seaport Museum, 2004).

16. Richard Bauman, *A World of Others' Words: Cross-Cultural Perspectives on Intertextuality* (Malden, MA: Blackwell, 2004), 4.

17. James M. Carpenter, "Lusty Chanteys from Long-Dead Ships: Created as Working Songs of the Seaman, Especially on the Fast Clippers of the Last Century, They Are Now Collected through Research as Vital Reminders of the Age of Sail," *New York Times*, July 12, 1931, 12–13, 23.

18. Harlow, *Chanteying*, 7. The ties to work, in particular, may stem from the conjectured African American origin of chanteys, which Gibb Schreffler supports. See the seminal Schreffler, *Boxing the Compass*. It is also worth noting the work of Mary K. Bercaw Edwards and her specific focus on orality and the work of the sailor. See Mary K. Bercaw Edwards, *Sailor Talk: Labor, Utterance, and Meaning in the Works of Melville, Conrad, and London* (Liverpool: Liverpool University Press, 2021).

19. Though brief, for some commentary on bawdy songs in fraternity and US Navy culture, see Lois A. West, "Negotiating Masculinities in American Drinking Subcultures," *Journal of Men's Studies* 9, no. 3 (April 2001): 371. Specifically, West notes the fraternity song book K. White, *Tau Delta Phi Song Book* (College Park: University of Maryland, 1968). For discussion of rugby songs from both women and men, see Elizabeth Wheatley, "'Stylistic Ensembles' on a Different Pitch: A Comparative Analysis of Men's and Women's Rugby Songs," *Women and Language* 13, no. 1 (September 1990): 21. For a discussion of military cadences, see Mariana Grohowski, "Moving Words / Words that Move: Language Practices Plaguing U.S. Servicewomen," *Women and Language* 37, no. 1 (Spring 2014): 121.

20. Greg Dening, *Mr Bligh's Bad Language: Passion, Power and Theatre on the Bounty* (New York: Cambridge University Press, 1992), 57.

21. Erving Goffman, *Asylums: Essays on the Social Situation of Mental Patients and Other Inmates* (Harmondsworth: Penguin, 1961), 1–124.

22. Marcus Rediker, *Between the Devil and the Deep Blue Sea: Merchant Seamen, Pirates and the Anglo-American Maritime World, 1700–1750* (Cambridge: Cambridge University Press, 1987), 190.

23. Jane Ward, *Not Gay: Sex between Straight White Men* (New York: New York University Press, 2015), 107.

24. Ward, *Not Gay*; Scott Fabius Kiesling, "Men, Masculinities, and Language," *Language and Linguistics Compass* 1, no. 6 (2007); Scott Fabius Kiesling, "Homosocial Desire in Men's Talk: Balancing and Re-creating Cultural Discourses of Masculinity," *Language in Society* 34, no. 5 (2005); Scott Fabius Kiesling, "Playing the Straight Man: Displaying and Maintaining Male Heterosexuality in Discourse," in *Language and Sexuality: Contesting Meaning in Theory and Practice*, ed. Kathryn Campbell-Kibler et al. (Stanford, CA: CSLI Publications), 249–66; Michael Flood, "Men, Sex, and Homosociality: How Bonds between Men Shape Their Sexual Relations with Women," *Men and Masculinities* 10, no. 3 (2008).

25. Eve Kosofsky Sedgwick, *Between Men: English Literature and Male Homosocial Desire* (New York: Columbia University Press, 1985).

26. Barre Toelken, "Ballads and Folksongs," in *Folk Groups and Folklore Genres: An Introduction*, ed. Elliott Oring (Logan: Utah State University Press, 1986), 152.

27. Peter Narvaez, "'I Think I Wrote a Folksong': Popularity and Regional Vernacular Anthems," *Journal of American Folklore* 115, no. 456 (2002): 273.

28. Hugill, *Shanties*, 26. Other collectors identify these types differently; however, most create categories that evoke the general idea that there were shorter chanteys and longer chanteys depending on the type of work to be completed.

29. Percy Adams Hutchison, "Sailors' Chanties," *Journal of American Folklore* 19, no. 72 (1906): 26. Emphasis added.

30. Dorothy E. Smith, "Texts and the Ontology of Organizations and Institutions," *Studies in Culture, Organizations, and Society* 7, no. 2 (September 2001): 164.

31. According to the *Oxford English Dictionary*, a "capstan" is defined as follows:

> a piece of mechanism, working on the principle of the wheel and axle, on a vertical axis, the power being applied by movable bars or levers inserted in horizontal sockets made round the top, and pushed by men walking round, whereby the apparatus is made to revolve and wind up a cable round its cylinder or barrel; it is used especially on board ship for weighing the anchor, also for hoisting heavy sails, etc., and for raising weights out of quarries, mines, coal-pits (see gin n.1), and the like.

Oxford English Dictionary, s.v. "capstan," accessed September 1, 2023, https://doi.org/10.1093/OED/1788070678.

32. Jessica Floyd, "Engaging Imperfect Texts: The Ballad Tradition and the Investigation of Chanteys," *Restoration: Studies in English Literary Culture, 1660–1700* 44, no. 2 (2020): 111–38.

33. Lucy E. Broadwood and A. H. Fox-Strangways, "Early Chanty-Singing and Ship-Music," *Journal of the Folk-Song Society* 8, no. 32 (1928): 56.

34. Broadwood and Fox-Strangways, "Early Chanty-Singing," 58.

35. Broadwood and Fox-Strangways, "Early Chanty-Singing," 60.

36. Isaac Allen remarks,

I couldn't help but thinking that it [the sailor's song] had birth among the old buccaneers of the West Indies, the Vikings of the sixteenth and seventeenth centuries, who claimed and proved claim to the title of 'sons of the storm,' whether of the battle or the wave it mattered not to them; and it was easy to picture those firm old fellows, corseleted and helmeted, marching.... They have long ago passed away, but their spirit of daring still remains in the Anglo Saxon character, and their songs in the minds of our sailors.

Isaac Allen, "Songs of the Sailor," *Oberlin Students' Monthly* 1 (December 1858): 47. Speculative though it is, the comments attach to the likelihood of sailing songs tracing much further back than archival records suggest.

37. Floyd, "Engaging Imperfect Texts," 113.

38. Duncan Emrich, introduction to *American Sea Songs and Shanties*, by Richard Maitland, Noble B. Brown, Leighton Robinson, et al., Rounder Select / Recording Laboratory, Library of Congress, Archive of Folk Culture, SDC 13375, sound disc, 1980, liner notes, 3.

39. Gibb Schreffler, "'The Execrable Term': A Contentious History of *Chanty*," *American Speech* 92, no. 4 (November 2017): 453.

40. Carpenter, "Lusty Chanteys."

41. Floyd, "Engaging Imperfect Texts," 114.

42. Gershon Legman, *The Horn Book: Studies in Erotic Folklore and Bibliography* (London: Cape, 1964), 397.

43. Schreffler, *Boxing the Compass*, 6.

44. W. F. Arnold, "The Music of the Chanties," in *Songs of Sea Labour: Chanties*, by Frank Thomas Bullen (London: Orpheus Music, 1914), xi.

45. Kimberly J. Lau, "Serial Logic: Folklore and Difference in the Age of Feel-Good Multiculturalism," *Journal of American Folklore* 113, no. 447 (2000): 74.

46. Concerning changes that arrived during the Industrial Revolution, see Valerie Burton, "The Myth of Bachelor Jack: Masculinity, Patriarchy and Seafaring Labour," in *Jack Tar in History: Essays in the History of Maritime Life and Labour*, ed. Colin Howell and Richard J. Twomey (Fredericton, NB: Acadiensis Press, 1991), 179–98.

47. Kelby Rose, "Nostalgia and Imagination in Nineteenth-Century Sea Shanties," *Mariner's Mirror* 98, no. 2 (May 2012): 147–60.

48. Joanna C. Colcord, *Songs of American Sailormen* (New York: W. W. Norton, 1938), 14.

49. Schreffler, *Boxing the Compass*, 2.

50. Charles Conrad, "Work Songs, Hegemony, and Illusions of Self," *Critical Studies in Mass Communication* 5, no. 3 (1988): 196.

51. Hutchison, "Sailors' Chanties," 25.

52. Rediker, *Between the Devil*, 189n103.

53. Charles L. Briggs, *Rethinking Poetics, Pandemics, and the Politics of Knowledge* (Denver: University Press of Colorado, 2021), 61.

54. Robert Darby, "'An Oblique and Slovenly Initiation': The Circumcision Episode in Tristram Shandy," *Eighteenth-Century Life* 27, no. 1 (Winter 2003): 72–84.

55. For specific discussion of detachable penises, see Kathleen Lubey, *What Pornography Knows: Sex and Social Protest since the Eighteenth Century* (Stanford, CA: Stanford University Press, 2022), esp. "Genital Parts: Detachable Properties in the Eighteenth Century," 63–73.

56. Elizabeth Freeman, *Beside You in Time: Sense Methods and Queer Sociabilities in the American 19th Century* (Durham, NC: Duke University Press, 2019).

57. Freeman, *Beside You in Time*, 95.

58. Freeman, *Beside You in Time*, 106.

59. Freeman, *Beside You in Time*, 7.

60. Freeman, *Beside You in Time*, 9.

61. Freeman, *Beside You in Time*, 15.

62. Jason T. Eastman, William F. Danaher, and Douglas Schrock, "Gendering Truck Driving Songs: The Cultural Masculinization of an Occupation," *Sociological Spectrum* 33, no. 5 (2013): 417.

63. Charles W. Joyner, "A Model for the Analysis of Folklore Performance in Historical Context," *Journal of American Folklore* 88, no. 349 (1975): 257.

64. Joyner, "Model for the Analysis," 264.

65. Lau, "Serial Logic," 73.

66. Joyner, "Model for the Analysis," 264.

67. Schreffler, "Twentieth-Century Editors," 14. Fo'c'sle songs are songs that are sung while sailors are relaxing together in the fo'c'sle of the ship. Stan Hugill calls them "forebitters" or "main-hatch songs," which are "songs sailors sang when off-watch." See Hugill, *Shanties*, 27. Later in his discussion, Hugill claims that these forebitters are sometimes utilized as chanteys. He claims, "if they had a good chorus [forebitters] were often utilized for capstan and pump [songs]," which further demonstrates that sailors might utilize any song that they enjoy to lighten the heavy work of the ship. Ibid., 27.

68. Brad Beavan, "'One of the Toughest Streets in the World': Exploring Male Violence, Class and Ethnicity in London's Sailortown, c. 1850–1880," *Social History* 46, no. 1 (2021): 13.

69. Floyd, "Engaging Imperfect Texts."

70. Gerry Smyth, "Shanty Singing and the Irish Atlantic: Identity and Hybridity in the Musical Imagination of Stan Hugill," *International Journal of Maritime History* 29, no. 2 (May 2017): 400.

71. G. Smyth, "Shanty Singing," 404.

72. Rediker demonstrates that "work was a public activity, so public in fact that any seaman, even when off duty, knew what work was being done, and by whom, by the distinctive yell each tar gave during his various exertions. Crews were extremely sophisticated in judging the quality of each man's contribution to the sailing of the ship." Rediker, *Between the Devil*, 95.

73. Allen, "Songs of the Sailor," 49.

74. Allen, "Songs of the Sailor," 48.

75. Emphasis original, though originally underlined, which is the case for all the emphases in the Hugill songs throughout the chapters of this book. Legman also inconsistently used some slashes to indicate a line break between the lyrics, which have been omitted as well. However, the lyrics as originally presented in the Legman manuscript are reproduced in the appendix. And all other idiosyncrasies are original.

76. Gale P. Jackson, "Rosy, Possum, Morning Star: African American Women's Work and Play Songs," *Journal of Black Studies* 46, no. 8 (November 2015): 775.

77. R. W. Gordon, "Folk Songs of America: A Hunt on Hidden Trails," *New York Times*, January 2, 1927.

78. Schreffler, *Boxing the Compass*, 36.

79. Schreffler, *Boxing the Compass*, 64.

80. Roger D. Abrahams, *Deep the Water, Shallow the Shore: Three Essays on Shantying in the West Indies* (Mystic, CT: Mystic Seaport Museum, 2002), 1.

81. Schreffler, *Boxing the Compass*, 77.

82. David S. Cecelski, *The Waterman's Song in Maritime North Carolina* (Chapel Hill: University of North Carolina Press, 2001), xii.

83. Cecelski, *Waterman's Song*, xx.

84. Stan Hugill, letter to Gershon Legman, June 18, 1956, Judith Legman's personal collection.

85. Hugill, *Shanties*, 17.

86. Gordon, "Folk Songs of America," 22. "Chantey" and "chanties" are both used in this same quote. It is unclear why these two spellings are used within the framework of this sentence; however, the two spellings are interchangeable.

87. W. Jeffrey Bolster, *Black Jacks: African American Seamen in the Age of Sail* (Cambridge, MA: Harvard University Press, 1997), 9.

88. Michael J. Jarvis, *In the Eye of All Trade: Bermuda, Bermudians, and the Maritime Atlantic World, 1680–1783* (Chapel Hill: University of North Carolina Press, 2012), 246.

89. Abrahams, *Deep the Water*, 2.

90. Gershon Legman demonstrates that "hog-eye" should be understood to mean "a barge sailor, especially a Negro.... [Illegible] erotic significance is the female genitals, and not as implied by writers on sea-chanteys by confusion with *deadeye*, anus." Gershon Legman, "Sea Songs" (unpublished manuscript, last modified December 6, 2023), PDF of typescript. Judith Legman's personal collection. Emphasis original.

91. Roger D. Abrahams, "Afro-American Worksongs on Land and Sea," in *By Land and by Sea: Studies in the Folklore of Work and Leisure Honoring Horace P. Beck on His Sixty-Fifth Birthday*, ed. Roger D. Abrahams et al. (Hatboro: Legacy Books, 1985), 4.

92. Abrahams, "Afro-American Worksongs," 6. In the transcription of the song, Abrahams notes the chorus as both "Oh Jenny gone away" and as "Oh, Jenny gone away." It is not clear why the first two lines do not contain a comma while the other four lines contain the comma between "Oh" and "Jenny."

93. "Fancyman" was also understood, in the nineteenth century, to mean homosexual or same-sex affiliated. See M. Robinson, "Ornamental Gentlemen: Thomas F. Dibdin, Romantic Bibliomania, and Romantic Sexualities," *European Romantic Review* 22, no. 5 (2011): 685–706, https://doi.org/10.1080/10509585.2011.601684.

94. Schreffler, *Boxing the Compass*, 87.

95. Dorothy Noyes, *Humble Theory: Folklore's Grasp on Social Life* (Bloomington: Indiana University Press, 2016), 15.

96. Frank Thomas Bullen, *Songs of Sea Labour: Chanties* (London: Orpheus Music, 1914), vi.

97. Harlow, *Chanteying*, 92.

98. Carpenter, "Lusty Chanteys," 15.

99. Stan Hugill, letter to Gershon Legman, November 26, 1955, Judith Legman's personal collection.

100. Harold Whates, "The Background of Sea Shanties," *Music and Letters* 18, no. 3 (1937): 260.

101. W. B. Whall, *Ships, Sea Songs and Shanties* (Glasgow: James Brown and Son, 1913), xii. Emphasis original.

102. Ethan Blue, "Beating the System: Prison Music and the Politics of Penal Space," in *Isolation: Place and Practices of Exclusion*, ed. Alison Bashford and Carolyn Strange (London: Routledge, 2003), 54.

103. Blue, "Beating the System," 55.

104. Susanna Trnka, "Living a Life of Sex and Danger: Women, Warfare, and Sex in Military Folk Rhymes," *Western Folklore* 54, no. 3 (July 1995): 235.

105. David G. LoConto, Timothy W. Clark, and Patrice N. Ware, "The Diaspora of West Africa: The Influence of West African Cultures on 'Jody Calls' in the United States Military," *Sociological Spectrum* 30, no. 1 (2009): 96.

106. Kristen Bailey, "Brave Shanty Boys: The Songs of Timber Workers and Community in Pocahontas County, West Virginia," *Journal of Appalachian Studies* 27, no. 2 (2021): 159.

107. Toelken, "Ballads and Folksongs," 150.

108. Legman, *Horn Book*, 389.

109. Stuart M. Frank, "'Cheer'ly Man': Chanteying in *Omoo* and *Moby-Dick*," *New England Quarterly* 58, no. 1 (1985): 74.

110. Trnka, "Living a Life," 237.

111. Archie Green, "American Labor Lore: Its Meanings and Uses," *Industrial Relations: A Journal of Economy and Society* 4, no. 2 (1965): 55.

112. LoConto, Clark, and Ware, "Diaspora of West Africa," 97.

113. Hugill, letter to Legman, June 18, 1956.

114. Marcus Rediker, *The Slave Ship: A Human History* (New York: Penguin Books, 2008).

115. Blue, "Beating the System," 56.

116. Peter F. Murphy, *Studs, Tools, and the Family Jewels: Metaphors Men Live By* (Madison: University of Wisconsin Press, 2001), 38.

117. Elizabeth Freeman, *Time Binds: Queer Temporalities, Queer Histories* (Durham, NC: Duke University Press, 2010), 14.

118. Ronald L. Baker and Simon J. Bronner, "'Letting Out Jack': Sex and Aggression in Adolescent Male Recitations," in *Manly Traditions: The Folk Roots of American Masculinities*, ed. Simon J. Bronner (Bloomington: Indiana University Press, 2005), 316.

119. Lisa Gilman, "Folklore and Folklife of Women, Men, and Other Gendered Identities," in *The Oxford Handbook of American Folklore and Folklife Studies*, ed. Simon J. Bronner (Oxford: Oxford University Press, 2019), 921.

120. Mikhail Bakhtin, *Rabelais and His World*, trans. Helene Iswolsky (Bloomington: Indiana University Press, 1984), 319.

121. William Huddleston, "Kicking Off: Violence, Honour, Identity, and Masculinity in Argentinian Football Chants," *International Review for the Sociology of Sport* 57, no. 1 (2022): 37.

122. Huddleston, "Kicking Off," 48.

123. Huddleston, "Kicking Off," 48.

124. Murphy, *Studs, Tools*, esp. "Sex as War and Conquest," 76–97.

125. Trnka, "Living a Life," 232.

126. Eduardo Herrera, "Masculinity, Violence, and Deindividuation in Argentine Soccer Chants: The Sonic Potentials of Participatory Sounding-in-Synchrony," *Ethnomusicology* 62, no. 3 (2018): 470–99.

127. Anna Clark, *The Struggle for the Breeches: Gender and the Making of the British Working Class* (Berkeley: University of California Press, 1995), 33, 34.

128. Steven P. Schacht, "Misogyny on and off the 'Pitch': The Gendered World of Male Rugby Players," *Gender and Society* 10, no. 5 (1996): 560.

129. Eastman, Danaher, and Schrock, "Gendering Truck Driving Songs," 417. Emphasis original.

130. Trish Oberweis, Matthew Petrocelli, and Carly Hayden Foster, "Walking the Walk and Talking the Talk: Military Cadence as Normative Discourse," *Polymath: An Interdisciplinary Arts and Sciences Journal* 2, no. 4 (2012): 5. For how loggers in Appalachia similarly distance themselves, see also Bailey, "Brave Shanty Boys."

131. Murphy, *Studs, Tools*, 4.

132. Murphy, *Studs, Tools*, 7.

Chapter 2. Hugill's Repertoire and Training an Interdisciplinary Lens on Expressions of Gender and Sexuality

1. Hugill, letter to Legman, June 18, 1956.
2. Rose, "Nostalgia and Imagination," 147.
3. These are just a few of the authors who reference Stan Hugill and his work with chanteys: Andrew Bretz, "Sung Silence: Complicity, Dramaturgy, and Song in Heywood's Rape of Lucrece," *Early Theatre* 19, no. 2 (December 2016): 101; Paul Cowdell, "Cannibal Ballads: Not Just a Question of Taste," *Folk Music Journal* 9, no. 5 (2010): 723–47; Michael Pickering, Emma Robertson, and Marek Korczynski, "Rhythms of Labour: The British Work Song Revisited," *Folk Music Journal* 9, no. 2 (2007): 226–45; Stuart M. Frank, "Classic American Whaling Songs," *Maritime Life and Traditions*, no. 26 (Spring 2005): 16–33; Catherine Tackley, "Shanty Singing in Twenty-First-Century Britain," *International Journal of Maritime History* 29, no. 2 (2017): 407; G. Smyth, "Shanty Singing," 387; Rose, "Nostalgia and Imagination."
4. Gershon Legman, "Misconceptions in Erotic Folklore," *Journal of American Folklore*, 74, no. 297 (1962): 205.
5. Ed Cray, *The Erotic Muse: American Bawdy Songs* (Urbana: University of Illinois Press, 1992); Vance Randolph, *Roll Me in Your Arms: Folksongs and Music*, vol. 1 of *"Unprintable" Ozark Folksongs and Folklore*, ed. Gershon Legman (Fayetteville: University of Arkansas Press, 1992); Vance Randolph, *Blow the Candle Out: Folk Rhymes and Other Lore*, vol. 2 of *"Unprintable" Ozark Folksongs and Folklore*, ed. Gershon Legman (Fayetteville: University of Arkansas Press, 1992).
6. Murphy, *Studs, Tools*, 127.
7. The false-parts-motif version is uncannily similar to Jonathan Swift's "The Lady's Dressing Room" to the degree that one appears to have, potentially, influenced the other.
8. R. W. Gordon, "Blow the Man Down," 1917, 239, Robert Winslow Gordon Papers, Gordon Inferno Collection (1917–1933), American Folklife Center, Library of Congress, Washington, DC, accessed January 15, 2024, https://archive.org/details/1917gordoninfernocollection/page/n33/mode/2up?q=bullies. Available in Jack Horntip Collection, accessed January 12, 2024, https://www.horntip.com/html/books_&_MSS/1910s/1917-1933_gordon_inferno_collection_(MSS)/index.htm. All idiosyncrasies original.
9. Floyd, "Engaging Imperfect Texts."
10. Jessica Floyd, "Seamen, Semen, and Virility: Leaky Homophones on Land and at Sea," *English Studies* 102, no. 5 (2021): 533–51.
11. Lubey argues, "Vulnerable to having their genital property claimed by others, pornography makes eighteenth-century women an urgent case study for a question Lynn Festa asks about detachable attributes like wigs and hair." Lubey, *What Pornography Knows*, 19. Such an observation maps onto the detachable body parts of the woman in "Blow the Man Down" and presents a salient demand to attend to the ways in which certain body parts are aggrandized, detached, anthropomorphized, and more. Chapters 3 and 4 each delve more deeply into detachable genitals that sometimes take the place of the characters under discussion.
12. Schacht, "Misogyny," 560–61.
13. Hugill outlines, "I learnt [this chantey] from my old shipmate Paddy Griffiths. He told me that 'Bungyereye' was a slang term for a certain type of whiskey popular toward the end of the last century." Hugill, *Shanties*, 166. In terms of timing, it must be assumed that Hugill is referencing the end of the nineteenth century.
14. James Wright, "Blow the Man Down," n.d., 32, 03244, box 36, JMC/1/1/4/A, James Madison Carpenter Collection, Vaughan Williams Memorial Library, London, United Kingdom, accessed January 15, 2024, https://www.vwml.org/archives-catalogue/JMC. All idiosyncrasies original.

15. See Charles Tyng, *Before the Wind: The Memoir of an American Sea Captain 1808–1833*, ed. Susan Fels (New York: Penguin Books, 1999).

16. Hugill, *Shanties*, 157–58. Emphasis original.

17. Lubey opines that "by reading sex scenes across time, we can grasp their opposition to social hierarchies," which will be clear of the songs from Hugill. Lubey, *What Pornography Knows*, 3.

18. Walter Runciman Terry, "Foreword," in *The Way of the Ship: Sailors, Shanties and Shantymen*, by Richard Runciman Terry (Tucson: Fireship Press, 2008), n.p.

19. Roy Kerridge, "Ballad of the Sea Blue Yodeller," *Country Music World* 13 (September 1981). Chris Roche, personal collection, email message to author, April 28, 2017.

20. Kerridge, "Ballad."

21. Joyner, "Model for the Analysis," 262. Emphasis original.

22. Schacht, "Misogyny," 552.

23. Susan G. Davis, *Dirty Jokes and Bawdy Songs: The Uncensored Life of Gershon Legman* (Urbana: Illinois University Press, 2019), 45.

24. Gershon Legman, letter to Stan Hugill, June 8, 1956, Judith Legman's personal collection.

25. Hugill, letter to Legman, November 26, 1955.

26. Tom Brown, email message to author, February 22, 2017.

27. Joanne Begiato, *Manliness in Britain, 1760–1900: Bodies, Emotion, and Material Culture* (Manchester: Manchester University Press, 2020), 91.

28. Pauline Greenhill, "'Neither a Man nor a Maid': Sexualities and Gendered Meanings in Cross-Dressing Ballads," *Journal of American Folklore* 108, no. 428 (1995): 159.

29. Gershon Legman, *Rationale of the Dirty Joke: An Analysis of Sexual Humor* (New York: Grove Press, 1968), 22.

30. Begiato, *Manliness in Britain*, 127.

31. Legman, *Horn Book*, 426.

32. Begiato, *Manliness in Britain*, 69.

33. David A. McDonald, "Geographies of the Body: Music, Violence and Manhood in Palestine," *Ethnomusicology Forum* 19, no. 2 (2010): 202.

34. Legman, *Rationale*, 23.

35. Legman, *Horn Book*, 401.

36. Legman, *Horn Book*, 342.

37. Legman, *Horn Book*, 336.

38. Lash, "Tilting the Ivory Tower," 35.

39. Lash, "Tilting the Ivory Tower," 38.

40. Martha Cornog and Timothy Perper, "Make Love, Not War: The Legacy of Gershon Legman, 1917–1999," *Journal of Sex Research* 36, no. 3 (1999): 316.

41. Gibb Schreffler, email message to author, September 6, 2015.

42. Robert Lloyd Webb, review of *Shanties from the Seven Seas: Shipboard Work-Songs and Songs Used as Work-Songs from the Great Days of Sail*, by Stan Hugill, *Northern Mariner* 5, no. 3 (1995): 83–84.

43. Chris Roche, "Stan Hugill: 1906–1992," *Folk Music Journal* 6, no. 4 (1993): 558.

44. Sarah Lash shows that a great number of well-known and respected folklore scholars reference the work of Legman in their publications. She shows that "notable scholars as Christie Davies (2004), Brian Sutton-Smith (1978), Linda De'gh (1979, 1982), Simon Bronner (1978, 1984), Sandra Dolby (1977), Stanly Brandes (1977a, 1977b), Charles Doyle (1982), and more" reference the work of Legman. Lash, "Tilting the Ivory Tower," 37.

45. Stuart M. Frank, "Stan Hugill 1906–1992: A Remembrance," in *Shanties from the Seven Seas*, ed. Stan Hugill (Mystic, CT: Mystic Seaport Museum, 1994), xix.

46. Cornog and Perper, "Make Love, Not War," 316.
47. Briggs, "Disciplining Folkloristics," 92.
48. Cornog and Perper, "Make Love, Not War," 317.
49. Roche, "Stan Hugill," 558.
50. Robert Young Walser, email message to author, October 9, 2014.
51. Stan Hugill, letter to Gershon Legman, July 25, 1956, Judith Legman's personal collection.
52. Greenhill, "Neither a Man," 157.
53. Robert McCarl, "Occupational Folklore," in *Folk Groups and Folklore Genres: An Introduction*, ed. Elliott Oring (Logan: Utah State University Press, 1986), 76. Emphasis original.
54. McCarl, "Occupational Folklore," 76.
55. Sara Ahmed, *Queer Phenomenology: Orientations, Objects, Others* (Durham, NC: Duke University Press, 2006), 13.
56. Ahmed, *Queer Phenomenology*, 107.
57. For a framework to discuss sexualities in the early modern world, see David Halperin, *How to Do the History of Male Homosexuality* (Chicago: University of Chicago Press, 2002). Throughout, I use the terms "same sex" and "opposite sex" to describe relationships based on his research in historical realities of language.
58. Jonathan Allan, "Queer Theory and Critical Masculinity Studies," in *Routledge International Book of Masculinity Studies*, ed. Lucas Gottzen, Ulf Mellstrom, and Tamara Shefer (Abingdon: Routledge, 2019), 73.
59. Allan, "Queer Theory," 74.
60. Allan, "Queer Theory," 80–81.
61. Allan, "Queer Theory," 81.
62. Natasha Hurley, *Circulating Queerness: Before the Gay and Lesbian Novel* (Minneapolis: University of Minnesota Press, 2018). For a discussion concerning the narrative treatment of the sea as a vast and terrifying place, see John Peck, *Maritime Fiction: Sailors and the Sea in British and American Novels, 1719-1917* (Houndmills: Palgrave, 2001). Specifically, in his discussion of *Moby-Dick*, Peck outlines, "If the sea is conventionally vast, dangerous, and mysterious in the sea story, in *Moby-Dick* it is even more vast, dangerous and mysterious." Ibid., 115.
63. Valentina Bold and Pauline Greenhill, "*Frenchman's Creek* and the Female Sailor: Transgendering Daphne du Maurier," *Western Folklore* 71, no. 1 (2012): 54.
64. Peck, *Maritime Fiction*, 116.
65. Ahmed, *Queer Phenomenology*, 124.
66. Hurley, *Circulating Queerness*.
67. Ahmed, *Queer Phenomenology*.
68. For a deeper discussion of *pornocorridos* and the interesting interplay between male and female singers of these bawdy songs, see Yessica Garcia Hernandez, "A Vulgar Folklore: The Pornographic Fantasies of *Pornocorridos*," *Porn Studies* 10, no. 1 (2023): 50–65.
69. Michel Foucault, *Discipline and Punish: The Birth of the Prison*, trans. Alan Sheridan (New York: Random House, 1977).
70. Victor Tadros, "Between Governance and Discipline: The Law and Michel Foucault," *Oxford Journal of Legal Studies* 18, no.1 (1998): 78.
71. Simon J. Bronner, *Crossing the Line: Violence, Play, and Drama in Naval Equator Traditions* (Amsterdam: Amsterdam University Press, 2006), 25.
72. Bailey, "Brave Shanty Boys," 162.
73. Bailey, "Brave Shanty Boys," 160; William Main Doerflinger, *Songs of the Sailor and Lumberman*, rev. ed. (Glenwood: Meyerbooks, 1990).
74. Blue, "Beating the System," 60.
75. Bailey, "Brave Shanty Boys," 165. Emphasis original.

76. Legman, *Rationale*, 17.
77. Greenhill, "Neither a Man," 166.
78. Greenhill, "Neither a Man," 170.
79. Roger D. Abrahams, "Toward a Sociological Theory of Folklore: Performing Services," *Western Folklore* 37, no. 3 (1978): 176.
80. Abrahams, "Sociological Theory of Folklore," 169. Kristen Bailey notes this "outsider status" in terms of loggers and logging men, who not only were very similar to sailors but often traded places with sailors (i.e., men who were sailors and loggers often worked in both vocations at some point in their lives). Bailey, "Brave Shanty Boys," 159.
81. Gilman, "Folklore and Folklife," 931.
82. David A. Carter, "The Industrial Workers of the World and the Rhetoric of Song," *Quarterly Journal of Speech* 66, no. 4 (1980): 365.
83. Michel Foucault, *The History of Sexuality*, vol. 1, trans. Robert Hurley (New York: Random House, 1988), 32.
84. A. Green, "American Labor Lore," 55.
85. Greenhill, "Neither a Man," 165.
86. Gilman, "Folklore and Folklife," 927.
87. Lau, "Serial Logic," 80.
88. Conrad, "Work Songs," 189.
89. Carter, "Industrial Workers," 366.
90. Laura Gowing, *Common Bodies: Women, Touch and Power in Seventeenth-Century England* (New Haven, CT: Yale University Press, 2003), 106.

Chapter 3. Words of Warning and the Ebb and Flow of Identity

1. For confirmation of this identity performance of sailors, especially as it aligns and collides with images of the sailing man, see Peck, *Maritime Fiction*. Of note is the idea that this identity framework not only was represented in novels circulated at the time but also was an identity structure that some sailors assumed because of such representations.
2. Paul Gilje, *To Swear like a Sailor: Maritime Culture in America, 1750–1850* (Cambridge: Cambridge University Press, 2016), 238.
3. Steven Dashiell, "'You Feel That?' Examining Gay Porn Discourse as Hegemonic Discursive Soundtrack," *Porn Studies* 10, no. 1 (2022): 23.
4. Dashiell, "You Feel That?," 22.
5. Marcus Rediker, *Outlaws of the Atlantic: Sailors, Pirates, and Motley Crews in the Age of Sail* (Boston: Beacon Press, 2014), 177.
6. Burton, "Myth of Bachelor Jack," 181.
7. Legman, *Rationale*, 10.
8. Valerie Burton, "'Whoring, Drinking Sailors': Reflections on Masculinity from the Labour History of Nineteenth-Century British Shipping," in *Working Out Gender*, ed. Margaret Walsh (Aldershot: Ashgate, 1999), 88.
9. Begiato, *Manliness in Britain*, 178.
10. John Michael McCluskey, "'Rough! Tough! Real Stuff!': Music, Militarism, and Masculinity in American College Football," *American Music* 37, no. 1 (2019): 30.
11. Ben Wadham, "Brotherhood: Homosociality, Totality and Military Subjectivity," *Australian Feminist Studies* 28, no. 76 (2013): 225. For the use of sport and combat metaphors in male discourse, see also Murphy, *Studs, Tools*, esp. "Sex as Sport," 59–75, and "Sex as War and Conquest," 76–97.
12. Trnka, "Living a Life," 235.

13. Emphasis original. *Culo*, translated from Spanish, is "ass."
14. Herrera, "Masculinity, Violence, and Deindividuation."
15. Valerie Burton, "'As I Wuz A-rolling Down the Highway One Morn': Fictions of the 19th Century English Sailortown," in *Fictions of the Sea: Critical Perspectives on the Ocean in British Literature and Culture*, ed. Bernhard Klein (London: Routledge, 2002), 144.
16. John Cleland, *Memoirs of Fanny Hill* (London, 1749; Project Gutenberg, 2008), https://www.gutenberg.org/files/25305/25305-h/25305-h.htm.
17. Ahmed, *Queer Phenomenology*, 107.
18. Burton, "Whoring, Drinking Sailors," 96.
19. Burton, "Myth of Bachelor Jack," 182.
20. Edwards points to "intentional euphemistic opacity of the nautical terms" in describing an exchange in "John Davis's *The Post-Captain; or, the Wooden Walls Well Manned* (1806)," in her chapter "Sailors." See Edwards, *Sailor Talk*, 34. Edwards specifically discusses the use of nautical euphemism in "the racy meaning[s]" of terms like "*scud, lie-to, cat-heads, clean run, top-lights*, and *head-rails*." Ibid., 35. Emphasis original.
21. According to the *Merriam Webster Dictionary*, a "jibboom" is "a spar that forms an extension of the bowsprit." The "bowsprit" is "a large spar projecting forward from the stem of a ship." A "deadeye" is "a rounded wood block encircled by a rope or an iron band and having holes to receive the lanyard that is used especially to set up shrouds and stays." *Merriam Webster Dictionary*, s.v. "jibboom," accessed April 5, 2021, https://www.merriam-webster.com/dictionary/jibboom; *Merriam Webster Dictionary*, s.v. "bowsprit," accessed April 5, 2021, https://www.merriam-webster.com/dictionary/bowsprit; *Merriam Webster Dictionary*, s.v. "deadeye," accessed April 5, 2021, https://www.merriam-webster.com/dictionary/deadeye.
22. Burton, "Whoring, Drinking Sailors," 95.
23. Begiato, *Manliness in Britain*, 195.
24. Foucault, *Discipline and Punish*, 94.
25. Begiato, *Manliness in Britain*; Burton, "Myth of Bachelor Jack."
26. Jonathan Allan, "Circumcision Debates in *Sexology* Magazine (1934–1975)," *Journal of Men's Studies* 29, no. 3 (2021): 354–72. Here, Allan highlights the argument ventured that circumcision aided in preventing things like chancres caused by syphilis. It is tempting to connect the surgeon's lance to the tools of circumcision, and in wielding the lance, the surgeon is potentially circumcising the sailor to rid him of his chancres.
27. Margaret S. Creighton, "American Mariners and the Rites of Manhood, 1830–1870," in *Jack Tar in History: Essays in the History of Maritime Life and Labour*, ed. Colin Howell and Richard J. Twomey (New Brunswick: Acadiensis Press, 1991), 160.
28. Murphy, *Studs, Tools*; David M. Friedman, *A Mind of Its Own: A Cultural History of the Penis* (New York: Simon and Schuster, 2001).
29. Burton, "As I Wuz A-rolling," 149–50.
30. Begiato, *Manliness in Britain*, 68.
31. Begiato, *Manliness in Britain*, 83.
32. Judith Butler, *Bodies that Matter: On the Discursive Limits of "Sex"* (New York: Routledge, 1993), 65. Emphasis original.
33. Raymond Stephanson, *The Yard of Wit: Male Creativity and Sexuality, 1650–1750* (Philadelphia: University of Pennsylvania Press, 2004), 47.
34. The *Oxford English Dictionary* gives the definition of a "fire ship" as "a ship loaded with burning material and explosives, which is set adrift near enemy ships or installations to ignite and destroy them. Also *fig*. Now *hist*." *Oxford English Dictionary*, s.v. "fireship," accessed January 12, 2024, https://doi.org/10.1093/OED/1042058012. However, there is a further definition that is "*slang*. A person, esp. a woman, infected with a venereal disease. Also: a prostitute. Cf. firedrake n. 3d. Obs." Ibid. Emphases original.

35. Creighton, "American Mariners," 162.

36. See Foucault, *History of Sexuality*, 3–4. Here, Foucault discusses this specific turn to the procreative bedroom and the silencing and pathologizing of sexualities that were not procreative in their aim.

37. R. W. Connell, *Masculinities*, 2nd ed. (Berkley: University of California Press, 1995), 55.

38. David Brandon Dennis, "Seduction on the Waterfront: German Merchant Sailors, Masculinity and the 'Brucke zu Heimat' in New York and Buenos Aires, 1884–1914," *German History* 29, no. 2 (2011): 190.

39. Other nationalities are also lampooned later in this song. Russians, Prussians, the Dutch, Chinese, and also "Johnny Crapaud" are compared to "this Irish tart's ire," but none are as notorious as her.

40. The false-parts-motif version of "Blow the Man Down," located in R. W. Gordon's Inferno Collection, reproduces the collision of façade and reality. The female character is presented, at first, as a beautiful woman, and the sailing character happily follows her toward what he thinks will be incredible pleasure. Once in her room, the woman transforms as she removes parts of her body in front of the horror-struck sailor. A similar pull is presented here, where there is a sliding connection between exterior and interior, reality and façade. Gordon, "Blow the Man Down," 239.

41. See Burton, "Myth of Bachelor Jack," 179–98. Burton specifically points to how "the existing system of allotments involved the shipping company in making payments to seafarers' wives and dependents," which, in turn, "threatened the precariously structured system of dominance and subordination." Ibid., 194.

42. Lubey, *What Pornography Knows*, 32.

43. Lubey, *What Pornography Knows*, 32.

44. Ahmed, *Queer Phenomenology*, 68.

Chapter 4. Heteronormative Economies and Shadow Admissions

1. Rediker, *Between the Devil*, 190.

2. Jeana Jorgensen, "Masculinity and Men's Bodies in Fairy Tales: Youth, Violence, And Transformation," *Marvels and Tales* 32, no. 2 (2018): 353.

3. Jorgensen, "Masculinity and Men's Bodies," 352.

4. For some discussion concerning Gershon Legman's own attempt at approaching questions concerning the representation of men and women as characters in jokes and what those characters portray about the inner thoughts of the joke teller and audience, see S. Davis, *Dirty Jokes*, 209. Her comments summarize Legman, *Rationale*; and Gershon Legman, *No Laughing Matter: An Analysis of Sexual Humor*, vol. 1. (Bloomington: Indiana University Press, 1982).

5. This saying finds its way into at least one collected chantey. In the James Madison Carpenter Collection, a version of "Leave Her, Johnny, Leave Her" (1928) from the repertoire of Stanton King has a line that reads, "Its [sic] growl you may, but go on you must." Stanton King, "Leave Her, Johnny, Leave Her," 1928, no. 03326, Songs and Chanties, folder 37, JMC/1/1/4/B, James Madison Carpenter Collection, Vaughan Williams Memorial Library.

6. Connell, *Masculinities*, 77.

7. The term "bastard" is spelled with the additional *r* in the example of "Saltpetre Shanty" from Legman and Hugill. Legman, "Sea Songs."

8. Kiesling, "Playing the Straight Man," 264.

9. The notion of "failed males" is taken from Pol Dominic McCann, David Plummer, and Victor Minichiello, "Being the Butt of the Joke: Homophobic Humour, Male Identity, and Its

Connection to Emotional and Physical Violence for Men," *Health Sociology Review* 19, no. 4 (December 2010), 506.

10. Connell, *Masculinities*, 55.

11. Legman glosses "two-blocks" as meaning "tight together, like the sheaves of a pulley-block." Legman, "Sea Songs."

12. Herrera, "Masculinity, Violence, and Deindividuation," 484.

13. Connell, *Masculinities*, 55.

14. Tyng, *Before the Wind*, 88.

15. The racism inherent throughout many of the songs in Legman and Hugill is noteworthy considering that many of the songs were likely influenced by the African American song tradition. See Schreffler, *Boxing the Compass*.

16. Julia Kristeva, *Powers of Horror: An Essay on Abjection*, trans. Leon S. Roudiez (New York: Columbia University Press, 1982), 1.

17. Kristeva, *Powers of Horror*, 3.

18. Bakhtin, *Rabelais and His World*, 335.

19. Bakhtin, *Rabelais and His World*, 334.

20. Kristeva, *Powers of Horror*, esp. "Approaching Abjection," 10.

21. Katrina Dyonne Thompson, "'Some Were Wild, Some Were Soft, Some Were Tame, and Some Were Fiery': Female Dancers, Male Explorers, and the Sexualization of Blackness, 1600–1900," *Black Women, Gender + Families* 6, no. 2 (2012): 1–28.

22. Kristeva, *Powers of Horror*, esp. "Approaching Abjection," 10.

23. Legman contends that "rumper-la-cola" means "(arsebreaker), referring to anal intercourse." Legman, "Sea Songs."

24. Isabel Molina Guzman and Angharad N. Valdivia, "Brain, Brow, and Booty: Latina Iconicity in U.S. Popular Culture," *Communication Review* 7, no. 2 (2004): 211.

25. Siobhan Brooks, "Hypersexualization and the Dark Body: Race and Inequality among Black and Latina Women in the Exotic Dance Industry," *Sexuality Research and Social Policy* 7, no. 2 (2010): 79.

26. Karen V. Waters, *Perfect Gentleman: Masculine Control in Victorian Men's Fiction, 1870–1901* (New York: Peter Lang Publishing, 1999), 74.

27. Rosanne Currarino, "'Meat vs. Rice': The Ideal of Manly Labor and Anti-Chinese Hysteria in Nineteenth-Century America," *Men And Masculinities* 9, no. 4 (April 2007): 477. Michael S. Kimmel also discusses the notion of the "heroic artisan" and shows that he was "stiffly formal in his manners with women, stalwart and loyal to his male comrades. On the family farm or in his urban crafts shop, he was an honest toiler, unafraid of hard work, proud of his craftsmanship and self-reliance. With a leather apron covering his open shirt and his sleeves rolled up, Boston silversmith Paul Revere, standing proudly at his forge, well illustrates this type." Michael S. Kimmel, *American Manhood: Transformations in Masculinity from the Revolution to the Modern Era* (New York: Basic Books, 1993), 16.

28. Margaret S. Creighton, "Davy Jones' Locker Room," in *Iron Men, Wooden Women: Gender and Seafaring in the Atlantic World, 1700–1920*, ed. Margaret S. Creighton and Lisa Norling (Baltimore: Johns Hopkins University Press, 1996), 160.

29. Laura Mulvey, "Visual Pleasure and Narrative Cinema," in *Film Theory and Criticism: Introductory Readings*, ed. Leo Braudy and Marshall Cohen (New York: Oxford University Press, 1999), 841.

30. Mulvey, "Visual Pleasure," 839.

31. Anthropologist Elijah Adiv Edelman and sociolinguist Lal Zimman argue that the "reduction of the body to genitals, to one particular site of imagined difference or variation, is a model of what Grabham (2007) refers to as hyperembodiment, where only one portion

of the body becomes the focal point of personhood." Elijah Adiv Edelman and Lal Zimman, "Boycunts and Bonus Holes: Trans Men's Bodies, Neoliberalism, and the Sexual Productivity of Genitals," *Journal of Homosexuality* 61, no. 5 (2014): 675.

32. Lubey, *What Pornography Knows*, 52.

33. Cathy Lynn Preston, "'The Tying of the Garter': Representations of the Female Rural Laborer in 17th-, 18th-, and 19th-Century English Bawdy Songs," *Journal of American Folklore* 105, no. 417 (Summer 1992): 327.

34. Kate Manne, *Entitled: How Male Privilege Hurts Women* (New York: Penguin Random House, 2020), 70.

35. Manne, *Entitled*, 73.

36. At least in the eighteenth century, semen was considered a life-giving force that required care and protection. The needless spilling of semen was anxiety producing to the point that treatments were deployed for those who spilled semen in nonprocreative situations, and tracts of warning were circulated for the damaging impacts of masturbation (termed "onanism" in the period). In fact, in the 1724 treatise *Onania*, masturbation and the spilling of semen were argued to lead to the unseating of one's masculinity. *Onania; or, The Heinous Sin of Self-Pollution, and All Its Frightful Consequences, in Both Sexes, Considered* (London: H. Cooke, 1756; Wellcome Collection, 2014), accessed January 16, 2024, https://wellcomecollection.org/works/yxrtxsdy/items?query=fainting.

37. Toni Morrison's *The Bluest Eye* captures the racialized quality of the term "yellow" in the character of Maureen Peal. The term "high-yellow" is meant to be understood as a pejorative demarcation of biracial identity. The term denotes the lighter color of one's skin. For more discussion of Maureen Peal and race seen through that character, see Paul Douglas Mahaffey, "The Adolescent Complexities of Race, Gender, and Class in Toni Morrison's *The Bluest Eye*," *Race, Gender and Class* 11, no. 4 (October 2004): 155.

38. XYZ [W. Elmes, F.], *Jack in a White Squall, amongst Breakers—On the Lee Shore of St. Catherine's*, engraving, 1811, call no. PC 1 - 11826 (A size) [P&P], British Cartoon Print Collection, Library of Congress, accessed January 15, 2024, https://www.loc.gov/pictures/item/2006686609/.

39. Inger Lövkrona, "Erotic Narrative and the Construction of Gender in Premodern Sweden," *Journal of Folklore Research* 35, no. 2 (May 1998): 150.

40. Lövkrona, "Erotic Narrative," 147.

41. Greg Dening shows that, on the British naval ship the *Bounty*, "being found with the 'venereals' was not an offence for which a sailor might be flogged. For 'venereals,' there was a fine of fifteen shillings (more than half a month's pay) to be paid to the ship's surgeon." Dening, *Mr Bligh's Bad Language*, 63. Of note is the fact that African American sailing men especially identified the sailing vocation and the pay they received as marks of their masculinity. See Bolster, *Black Jacks*, 166.

42. See Breanne Fahs, Eric Swank, and Lindsay Clevenger, "Troubling Anal Sex: Gender, Power, and Sexual Compliance in Heterosexual Experiences of Anal Intercourse," *Gender Issues* 32, no. 1 (2015): 19–38.

43. Katherine Crawford, *European Sexualities, 1400–1800* (Cambridge: Cambridge University Press, 2007), 48. Leah Leneman underscores the idea that women in the early modern era were mindful of having children out of wedlock. She contends, "Implicit, and often explicit, in cases of damages for seduction, was the idea that a woman who bore a bastard child was ruined and had no hope of every [sic] marrying." Leah Leneman, "Seduction in Eighteenth and Early Nineteenth-Century Scotland," *Scottish Historical Review* 78, no. 205 (1999): 57.

44. Stephanson, *Yard of Wit*, 62.

45. Lövkrona, "Erotic Narrative," 153.

46. Mark Bracher, "Writing and Imaging the Body in Pornography: The Desire of the Other and Its Implications for Feminism," *American Journal of Semiotics* 8, no. 4 (1991): 108.

47. Creighton, "Davy Jones' Locker Room," 120.

48. For a discussion concerning the fact that sailors often shipped to sea because of their proximity to ports, see Daniel Vickers and Vince Walsh, *Young Men and the Sea: Yankee Seafarers in the Age of Sail* (New Haven, CT: Yale University Press, 2007). The sailing vocation was a last option for many young boys who were unable to find work elsewhere.

49. Bronner, *"Who's That Knocking?,"* 52. "Barnacle Bill the Sailor" is a sea song and not a chantey.

50. The vulnerability of the sailing body is a key component to the arguments ventured in Peck, *Maritime Fiction*.

51. Within the ballad notes for "Johnny, Come Down to Hilo," Legman glosses that "anal intercourse, [was] believed by sailors to involve less danger of venereal disease." Legman, "Sea Songs." Arnold David Harvey does reference, however—as regards the late 1700s to early 1800s in England—the fact that "there seems to have been a belief current among certain classes that, if one was suffering from venereal disease, the most effective way to get rid of it was to have sex with an uninfected person, to whom it would be automatically passed on, though this could hardly have been the only reason for sexual assaults on very young children." Arnold David Harvey, *Sex in Georgian England: Attitudes and Prejudices from the 1720s to the 1820s* (London: Phoenix Press, 2001), 79.

52. Jonathan Branfman, Susan Stiritz, and Eric Anderson, "Relaxing the Straight Male Anus: Decreasing Homohysteria around Anal Eroticism," *Sexualities* 21, no. 1–2 (2018): 110.

53. Stephen Maddison, "Is the Rectum *Still* a Grave? Anal Sex, Pornography, and Transgression," in *Transgression 2.0: Media, Culture, and the Politics of a Digital Age*, ed. Ted Gournelos and David J. Grunkel (New York: Bloomsbury Publishing, 2011), 92.

54. I explore semen, seamen, and liquid metaphors in Jessica Floyd, "Seamen, Semen, and Virility: Leaky Homophones on Land and at Sea," *English Studies* 102, no. 5 (2021): 533–51, https://doi.org/10.1080/0013838X.2021.1943895. Cultural anxieties around loss of semen arrived in treatises like the anonymous *Onania; or, the Heinous Sin of Self-Pollution* (1724) and Samuel Auguste David Tissot's later *A Treatise on the Diseases Produced by Onanism* (1832). One section of *Onania* cautions that masturbation will "cause fainting Fits and Epilepsies; in others of Consumption; and many young Men, who were strong and lusty before they gave themselves over to this Vice, have been worn out by it, and by its robbing the Body of its balmy and vital Moisture, without Cough or Spitting, dry and emaciated, sent to their graves." *Onania*, 13.

55. Kimberly R. McBride and J. Dennis Fortenberry, "Heterosexual Anal Sexuality and Anal Sex Behaviors: A Review," *Journal of Sex Research* 47, no. 2–3 (2010): 123.

56. Stephen Maddison, "Is the Rectum," 88.

57. Liam Wignall et al., "A Qualitative Study of Heterosexual Men's Attitudes toward and Practices of Receiving Anal Stimulation," *Culture, Health and Sexuality* 22, no. 6 (2020): 677.

58. For a depiction of female submission through the anus, see the contemporary erotic memoir Toni Bentley, *The Surrender: An Erotic Memoir* (New York: Harper Collins, 2004).

59. Jade Aguilar, "Pegging and the Heterosexualization of Anal Sex: An Analysis of Savage Love Advice," *Queer Studies in Media and Popular Culture* 2, no. 3 (2017): 279.

60. Aguilar, "Pegging," 287.

61. Branfman, Stiritz, and Anderson, "Relaxing," 114.

62. Fahs, Swank, and Clevenger, "Troubling Anal Sex."

63. Jonathan Allan, *Reading from Behind: A Cultural Analysis of the Anus* (Regina, SK: University of Regina Press, 2016), 174.

64. Allan, *Reading from Behind*, 187.

65. Richard Henry Dana Jr., *Two Years before the Mast* (Cleveland, OH: World Publishing Company, 1946), 46.

66. The line is rendered almost identical to the one in "The Gals o' Chile," in which women's sexual voracity and their penchant for anal sex are highlighted. In fact, the line from "Gal's O' Chile" begins, "Them gals o' Chile they are hard to beat," which boasts few choice differences as compared to a similar line in "Saltpetre Shanty." These similarities could be because one informant (Hugill) supplied the lines and rendered lines similarly across several chanteys or it could highlight the elastic quality of chanteys as whole lines and narrative frameworks were shared, remembered, and mix/matched among different songs. This cross-pollination is something that has been identified within many oral traditions, such as that which is found in the ballad.

67. Brian J. Rouleau, "Dead Men Do Tell Tales.: Folklore, Fraternity, and the Forecastle," *Early American Studies and Interdisciplinary Journal* 5, no. 1 (2007): 54.

68. See also S. Frank, "Cheer'ly Man," 74, where he discusses the fictitious juxtaposition of levity with danger in chanteys "sung" within several works by Herman Melville.

Chapter 5. Looking Queerly and the Pleasures That Defy Category

1. Herman Melville, *Billy Budd* (New York: Tom Doherty Associates, 1988), 10.

2. This fragmentation exemplifies the process of the scopophilic gaze that theorist Laura Mulvey identifies; she outlines that the sexual object is often fractured so that certain body parts are framed and come into focus more than others. Specifically, she is discussing how a woman's body is "fragmented by close-ups, is the content of the film, and the direct recipient of the spectator's look." Mulvey, "Visual Pleasure," 841. However, the theory is salient here.

3. Kristina Straub makes the argument that a specific focus on excrement might be tied to same-sex urges between men as early as the eighteenth century. She argues, concerning the feud between Alexander Pope and Colley Cibber, "Like the 'sodomite' Nokes, who dives 'in Excrements' rather than in the 'proper' place, Pope focuses more on the work of the ass than the work of the penis, and the former defines him sexually and literarily." Kristina Straub, *Sexual Suspects: Eighteenth-Century Players and Sexual Ideology* (Princeton, NJ: Princeton University Press, 1992), 75.

4. Cameron McFarlane, *The Sodomite in Fiction and Satire, 1660–1750* (New York: Columbia University Press, 1997), 166.

5. Begiato, *Manliness in Britain*, 175.

6. Begiato, *Manliness in Britain*, 169.

7. Hurley, *Circulating Queerness*, 45.

8. For a reading on sailors and tattooing, see Ira Dye, "The Tattoos of Early American Seafarers, 1796–1818," *Proceedings of the American Philosophical Society* 133, no. 4 (1989): 520–54.

9. This line and analysis expose the racist undertone to the song narrative. See Alan Rice, "'Who's Eating Whom': The Discourse of Cannibalism in the Literature of the Black Atlantic from Equiano's Travels to Toni Morrison's *Beloved*," *Research in African Literatures* 29, no. 4 (Winter 1998): 107. Rice's discussion exposes the idea of the bestial quality of the other, as is hinted here, and importantly cites Henry Louis Gates Jr., *The Signifying Monkey* (London: Oxford University Press, 1988).

10. For an extended analysis of "The Bumboy," see Jessica Floyd, "The Erotic Clash of 'A Boy-Shaggin' Mate' and a 'Little Bumboy': Ships Stations and Genital Imagery in 'The Shaver,'" *The Nautilus* 10 (2019): 7–42.

11. "Bum boy" is categorized under "Various Anal Terms" in *The Big Book of Filth* and is argued to have arrived in the lexicon in the nineteenth century. Jonathon Green, ed., *The Big Book of Filth: 6500 Sex and Slang Words and Phrases* (London: Cassel, 1999), 248.

12. The narrative of "The Bumboy" falls in line with historical sketches of sailing relationships on shipboard. These relationships were hierarchical, in which the more powerful man would often take advantage of the younger, more impressionable sailing boy. For a detailed discussion of hierarchical same-sex relationships on naval sailing vessels, see Barry R. Burg, *Boys at Sea: Sodomy, Indecency, and Courts Martial in Nelson's Navy* (New York: Palgrave Macmillan, 2007).

13. For example, some of "Lady Lil" focuses on an agentive penis. Ronald L. Baker, "Lady Lil and Pisspot Pete," *Journal of American Folklore* 100, no. 396 (1987): 192, https://doi.org/10.2307/540921. See also Baker and Bronner, "Letting Out Jack," 315–50. Research into military cadences demonstrates that narratives often center agentive penises and hypermasculine imagery. See Trnka, "Living a Life," 232–41. For a vast number of bawdy songs that often center male genitalia, see Cray, *Erotic Muse*.

14. Thomas P. Oates, "The Erotic Gaze in the NFL Draft," *Communication and Critical/Cultural Studies* 4, no. 1 (2007): 76, 81.

15. Oates, "Erotic Gaze," 83–84.

16. Julia Epstein, "Fanny's Fanny: Epistolary, Eroticism, and the Transsexual Text," in *Writing the Female Voice: Essays on Epistolary Literature*, ed. Elizabeth C. Goldsmith (Boston, MA: Northeastern University Press, 1989), 139.

17. Legman references, in the ballad notes for "Yaw, Yaw, Yaw," a description from William Main Doerflinger's collection that describes the song as "a pseudo-Dutch or imitative Squarehead." Doerflinger, regarding his version titled "Ja, Ja, Ja," argues that it "was a ditty at the expense of the 'Dutch,'" which Legman quotes in the body of his own annotations for "Yaw, Yaw, Yaw!" Legman, "Sea Songs"; Doerflinger, *Songs of the Sailor*, 86.

18. W. H. Smyth, *The Sailor's Word-Book: An Alphabetical Digest of Nautical Terms, Including Some More Especially Military and Scientific, but Useful to Seamen; as well as Archaisms of Early Voyagers, Etc.* (Glasgow: Blackie and Son, 1867; Project Gutenberg, 2021), https://www.gutenberg.org/cache/epub/26000/pg26000-images.html, 741.

19. Interestingly, there is a conflation of Dutch and German here. *Mein* is German for "my," whereas much of the narrative is predicated on a xenophobic rendering of Dutch-tinged English.

20. Historian Alan Bray shows, "It was not until the 1890s that the term homosexual first began to be used in English, and none of its predecessors now survive in common speech: Ganymede, pathetic, cinaedus, catamite, bugger, ingle, sodomite—such words survive if at all in legal forms or deliberate obscenity, or in classical and theological contexts from which they are drawn." Alan Bray, *Homosexuality in Renaissance England* (New York: Columbia University Press, 1996), 39.

21. Bray, *Homosexuality in Renaissance England*, 39. See also Foucault, *History of Sexuality*; Jonathan Goldberg, *Sodometries: Renaissance Texts, Modern Sexualities* (New York: Fordham University Press, 2010).

22. Ahmed, *Queer Phenomenology*, 13.

23. Eve Sedgwick argues, "My point is of course again not that we are here in the presence of homosexuality (which would be anachronistic) but rather (risking anachronism) that we are in the presence of male heterosexual desire, in the form of a desire to consolidate partnership with authoritative males in and through the bodies of females." Sedgwick, *Between Men*, 38.

24. According to *The Big Book of Filth*, "bit o' brown" arrives in our lexicon to describe same-sex engagements within the nineteenth century. J. Green, *Big Book of Filth*, 236.

25. Epstein, "Fanny's Fanny," 136.

26. A. A. Markley, "E. M. Forster's Reconfigured Gaze and the Creation of a Homoerotic Subjectivity," *Twentieth Century Literature* 47, no. 2 (Summer 2001): 278.

27. Philip C. Van Buskirk, diaries, 1851–1902, collection no. 3621, 18 microfilm reels, 37 vols., accession no. 3621-001, Philip C. Van Buskirk Papers, 1851–1902, Special Collections, University of Washington Libraries, University of Washington, Seattle, Washington. For a digital

version, see "The Journals of Philip C. Van Buskirk," Philip C. Van Buskirk Archive, CUNY Academic Commons, accessed January 17, 2024, https://vanbuskirk.commons.gc.cuny.edu/the-diary-of-philip-c-van-buskirk/.

28. See Mikhail Bakhtin's discussion of not only dismemberment but also specifically extraordinarily large penises and testicles that "grow to monstrous dimensions." Bakhtin, *Rabelais and His World*, 327.

29. Murphy, *Studs, Tools*, 3, 8.

30. For a close reading of sexual ordering, see Straub, *Sexual Suspects*. Specifically, see her analysis of the positioning of a young schoolboy and his more powerful and lecherous teacher. Ibid., 72. The same degree of sexually loaded hierarchy is apparent in crossing-the-line ceremonies, especially as observed by Jane Ward. See Ward, *Not Gay*.

31. For a small selection of the many articles dealing with the intersection of sexuality and male grooming, see Victoria Clarke and Virginia Braun, "How Can a Heterosexual Man Remove His Body Hair and Retain His Masculinity? Mapping Stories of Male Body Hair Depilation," *Qualitative Research in Psychology* 16, no. 1 (2019): 96–114; Janice Miller, "Manscaping and After: Power, Parody and the Hairy Chest," *Fashion Theory: The Journal of Dress, Body and Culture* 22, no. 6 (2018): 641–55; Elena Frank, "Groomers and Consumers: The Meaning of Male Body Depilation to a Modern Masculinity Body Project," *Men and Masculinities* 17, no. 3 (2014): 278–98.

32. EBarnacle1, "RE: Help: Meaning of a Few Drunken Sailor Verses," May 7, 2002, comment on Mudcat Café, accessed April 9, 2021, mudcatcafe.org.

33. Matthew Hall, "'When There's No Underbrush the Tree Looks Taller': A Discourse Analysis of Men's Online Groin Shaving Talk," *Sexualities* 18, no. 8 (2015): 999.

34. Hall, "When There's No Underbrush."

35. Semen is a particularly important facet of narrative and also history. Historically, semen was understood as a life-giving force to the extent that it was a protected entity. Philip C. Van Buskirk, in his *Journal of a Cruize*, cataloged his emissions and compared them against ailments he attributed to his spent sperm. Philip C. Van Buskirk, diaries. Raymond Stephanson argues that "semen was (along with animal spirits) one of the most spirituous and vital fluids, and therefore exceedingly important to the well-being of the male body; and the production of seed and its discharge were linked directly to the brain." Stephanson, *Yard of Wit*, 34.

36. Lisa Jean Moore, *Sperm Counts: Overcome by Man's Most Precious Fluid* (New York: New York University Press, 2008), 80. See also ibid., 71–91.

37. Thomas Waugh, "Men's Pornography: Gay vs. Straight," *Jump to Cut: A Review of Contemporary Media*, no. 30 (1985): 30–35, https://www.ejumpcut.org/archive/onlinessays/JC30folder/PornWaugh.html.

38. Waugh, "Men's Pornography," 33.

39. Waugh, "Men's Pornography," 34.

40. Waugh, "Men's Pornography," 35.

41. Geoffrey Lokke, "Cuckolds, Cucks, and Their Transgressions," *Porn Studies* 6, no. 2 (2019): 214.

42. Thomas P. Oates also recognizes the fetishizing of Black male bodies as commentators often capture the bodies of Black men in hyperbolic ways. Oates, "Erotic Gaze," 80.

43. Maryna Romanets, "Erotic Assemblages: Field Research, Palimpsests, and What Lies Beneath," *Journal of Ukrainian Studies* 27, no. 1 (Summer 2002): 282.

44. Romanets, "Erotic Assemblages," 282.

45. The final rhyming couplet of this version of "The Hog-Eye Man" evokes similar narrative ideas to that of contemporary cuckold pornography, even down to the racial dynamics

of characters portrayed. The consistent denoting of "the hog-eye man" as African American, using the pejorative terminology for Black men and women, runs roughly along similar narrative structures of cuckold pornography, in which the white male character encounters his wife copulating with a Black man. The scenes usually attach a homoerotic undercurrent, which is also readily apparent within this version of the song.

46. Lokke, "Cuckolds," 218.

47. Sedgwick, *Between Men*, 160.

48. Drew Ayers, "Bodies, Bullets, and Bad Guys: Elements of the Hardbody Film," *Film Criticism* 32, no. 3 (2008): 43.

49. Dennis, "Seduction on the Waterfront," 196.

50. Derek Massarella, "'And Thus Ended the Buisinisse': A Buggery Trial on the East India Company Ship *Mary* in 1636," *Mariner's Mirror* 103, no. 4 (2017): 427.

51. Barry R. Burg, *Sodomy and the Pirate Tradition: English Sea Rovers in the Seventeenth-Century Caribbean*, 2nd ed. (New York: New York University Press, 1995).

52. Bray, *Homosexuality in Renaissance England*; Crawford, *European Sexualities*.

53. Burg, *Boys at Sea*.

54. For an extended discussion of the connection among sodomy at sea, sailors, and their semen, see Floyd, "Seamen, Semen, and Virility." The work of Seth LeJacq is also important concerning the reality that sailors were well aware of emerging same-sex identities and affiliations in the early modern period. See Seth LeJacq, "Buggery's Travels: Royal Navy Sodomy on Ship and Shore in the Long Eighteenth Century," *Journal for Maritime Research* 17, no. 2 (2015): 103–16.

55. Van Buskirk, *Journal of a Cruize*, 161.

56. Ward, *Not Gay*, 158.

57. Ward, *Not Gay*, 30.

58. Floyd, "Erotic Clash."

59. Ward, *Not Gay*, 107.

60. For more information on fraternity initiation rites and mores, see Flood, "Men, Sex, and Homosociality"; Kiesling, "Homosocial Desire"; Kiesling, "Men, Masculinities, and Language."

61. Ward also points to the homoerotic rituals involved with crossing-the-line ceremonies in sailing folkways. Though much of the research on early modern examples of the crossing-the-line ceremony demonstrates only a registration of rigid hierarchy, there is room to imagine erotically charging the hierarchical metaphors that were a part of such rituals.

62. Aguilar, "Pegging," 285.

63. Ahmed, *Queer Phenomenology*, 13.

64. Judith Butler, *Gender Trouble: Feminism and the Subversion of Identity* (New York: Routledge, 1990); Butler, *Bodies that Matter*.

65. Legman, *Rationale*, 16. Emphasis original.

66. Ahmed, *Queer Phenomenology*, 13.

Conclusion. "What Shall We Do with a Drunken Sailor" and His Comrades?

1. Ahmed, *Queer Phenomenology*, 107.

2. *Online Etymology Dictionary*, s.v. "queer," accessed April 12, 2021, https://www.etymonline.com/word/queer.

3. The notion of circularity is borrowed from Hurley, *Circulating Queerness*.

4. Jessica Floyd, "TikTok's Sea Chanteys—How Life under the Pandemic Has Mirrored Months at Sea," The Conversation, January 26, 2021, https://theconversation.com/tiktoks-sea-chanteys-how-life-under-the-pandemic-has-mirrored-months-at-sea-153421.

5. Ballad scholar Mary Ellen Brown notes this same enduring quality concerning other oral traditional material. Brown makes the argument that "many things are called ballads. In fact, 'ballad making' is probably a continuing practice, an accessible artistic vehicle—at once local, regional, national, and transnational; popular ballad, broadside, and literary." Mary Ellen Brown, "Placed, Replaced, or Misplaced? The Ballads' Progress," *Eighteenth Century* 47, no. 2–3 (2006): 120. The same is evident in contemporary presentations of chantey material. For an example of contemporary singers creating songs like chanteys, similar to what Brown outlines here, see Zeynep Sasmazel, "Gay Pirates Were Very Real, and We've Even Got the Sea Shanty to Prove It," The Hornet, May 13, 2021, https://hornet.com/stories/gay-pirates-real/.

6. See the entirety of section 5 within the introduction to Legman, *Rationale*. There, Legman not only uses the term "fake-lore" but also indicts the mass production of folklore for popular consumption. Legman would likely lob a similar derision toward popular renditions of chanteys (taken out of context from shipboard work) as well as commercially produced material like Salty Dick's *Uncensored Sailor Songs* released in 2004.

7. Brown, "Placed, Replaced, or Misplaced?," 120.

8. Historian Seth LeJacq makes the argument, though, that eighteenth-century sailors did have a conception of same-sex affiliated identity. LeJacq, "Buggery's Travels." In researching courts-martial cases, he maintains, "The language, context and witnesses' interpretations of what had happened made it clear that 'Buggerer' referred to an identity and that these men fully understood their culture's thought and language about its urban sexual underworld." Ibid., 106.

9. Foucault, *History of Sexuality*, 32.

10. Tim Hitchcock and Michelle Cohen, "Introduction," in *English Masculinities: 1660–1800*, ed. Tim Hitchcock and Michelle Cohen (London: Routledge, 2014), 8.

11. Faramerz Dabhoiwala, "Sex and Societies for Moral Reform, 1688–1800," *Journal of British Studies* 46, no. 2 (April 2007): 290–319.

12. For further discussion of men grappling with gender and sexuality, especially in the modern era, see Jonathan Allan, "Phallic Affect, or Why Men's Rights Activists Have Feelings," *Men and Masculinities* 19, no. 1 (2016): 22–41; Sarah Maddison, "Private Men, Public Anger: The Men's Rights Movement in Australia," *Journal of Interdisciplinary Gender Studies* 4, no. 2 (1999): 39–51; Annie Potts, "'The Essence of the Hard On': Hegemonic Masculinity and the Cultural Construction of 'Erectile Dysfunction,'" *Men and Masculinities* 3, no. 1 (2000): 85–103.

13. Kiesling, "Men, Masculinities, and Language," 659.

14. Jonathan Allan, "Masculinity as Cruel Optimism," *NORMA* 13, no. 3–4 (2018): 182.

15. Allan, "Masculinity as Cruel Optimism," 181–82.

16. For further representation of how men use language as distancing and ordering mechanisms, especially in establishing othered identities and roles, see C. J. Pascoe, "'Dude, You're a Fag': Adolescent Masculinity and the Fag Discourse," *Sexualities* 8, no. 3 (2005): 329–46.

17. For an extended discussion of the anus, both literally and figuratively, see Allan, *Reading from Behind*.

18. Allan, "Phallic Affect," 29.

19. Allan, "Phallic Affect," 29.

20. Creighton, "Davy Jones' Locker," 125.

21. Jonathan Allan, "Falling in Love with Eve Kosofsky Sedgwick," *Mosaic: A Journal for the Interdisciplinary Study of Literature* 48, no. 1 (2015): 5.

22. For a thorough list of available collections of chanteys, along with critical commentary concerning each collection, see Schreffler, *Boxing the Compass*. Schreffler ventures the important argument that not all chantey collections are the same in the form or intent and any scholar undertaking an investigation of the genre should know the collector, the purpose of the publication, and the attempt, on the part of the collector, to connect the songs back to the

work of the sea. Schreffler critiques the collection and conclusions of Cecil J. Sharp in particular (ibid., 52–54) and other collectors who arrived during the height of folklore collection and study, citing that many of these researchers collected examples of chanteys but also relied on desk sources, like Frederick J. Davis and Ferris Tozer's collection, which was primarily circulated for popular performances.

23. Gilman, "Folklore and Folklife," 917–18.

Bibliography

Abrahams, Roger D. "Afro-American Worksongs on Land and Sea." In *By Land and by Sea: Studies in the Folklore of Work and Leisure Honoring Horace P. Beck on His Sixty-Fifth Birthday*, edited by Roger D. Abrahams, Kenneth S. Goldstein, Wayland Debs Hand, and Maggie Craig, 1–9. Hatboro: Legacy Books, 1985.
Abrahams, Roger D. *Deep the Water, Shallow Shore: Three Essays on Shantying in the West Indies*. Mystic, CT: Mystic Seaport Museum, 2002.
Abrahams, Roger D. "Toward a Sociological Theory of Folklore: Performing Services." *Western Folklore* 37, no. 3 (1978): 161–84.
Aguilar, Jade. "Pegging and the Heterosexualization of Anal Sex: An Analysis of Savage Love Advice." *Queer Studies in Media and Popular Culture* 2, no. 3 (2017): 275–92.
Ahmed, Sara. *Queer Phenomenology: Orientations, Objects, Others*. Durham, NC: Duke University Press, 2006.
Allan, Jonathan. "Circumcision Debates in *Sexology* Magazine (1934–1975)." *Journal of Men's Studies* 29, no. 3 (2021): 354–72.
Allan, Jonathan. "Falling in Love with Eve Kosofsky Sedgwick." *Mosaic: A Journal for the Interdisciplinary Study of Literature* 48, no. 1 (2015): 1–16.
Allan, Jonathan. "Masculinity as Cruel Optimism." *NORMA* 13, no. 3–4 (2018): 175–90.
Allan, Jonathan. "Phallic Affect, or Why Men's Rights Activists Have Feelings." *Men and Masculinities* 19, no. 1 (2016): 22–41.
Allan, Jonathan. "Queer Theory and Critical Masculinity Studies." In *Routledge International Book of Masculinity Studies*, edited by Lucas Gottzen, Ulf Mellstrom, and Tamara Shefer, 72–81. Abingdon: Routledge, 2019.
Allan, Jonathan. *Reading from Behind: A Cultural Analysis of the Anus*. Regina, SK: University of Regina Press, 2016.
Allen, Isaac. "Songs of the Sailor." *Oberlin Students' Monthly* 1 (December 1858): 46–49.
Arnold, W. F. "The Music of the Chanties." In *Songs of Sea Labour: Chanties*, by Frank Thomas Bullen. London: Orpheus Music, 1914.
Ayers, Drew. "Bodies, Bullets, and Bad Guys: Elements of the Hardbody Film." *Film Criticism*, 32, no. 3 (2008): 41–67.
Bailey, Kristen. "Brave Shanty Boys: The Songs of Timber Workers and Community in Pocahontas County, West Virginia." *Journal of Appalachian Studies* 27, no. 2 (2021): 158–76.
Baker, Ronald L. "Lady Lil and Pisspot Pete." *Journal of American Folklore* 100, no. 396 (1987): 191–99.
Baker, Ronald L., and Simon J. Bronner. "'Letting Out Jack': Sex and Aggression in Manly Recitations." In *Manly Traditions: The Folk Roots of American Masculinities*, edited by Simon J. Bronner, 315–50. Bloomington: Indiana University Press, 2005.

Bakhtin, Mikhail. *Rabelais and His World*. Translated by Helene Iswolsky. Bloomington: Indiana University Press, 1984.

Bauman, Richard. *A World of Others' Words: Cross-Cultural Perspectives on Intertextuality*. Malden, MA: Blackwell, 2004.

Beavan, Brad. "'One of the Toughest Streets in the World': Exploring Male Violence, Class and Ethnicity in London's Sailortown, c. 1850–1880." *Social History* 46, no. 1 (2021): 1–21.

Begiato, Joanne. *Manliness in Britain, 1760–1900: Bodies, Emotion, and Material Culture*. Manchester: Manchester University Press, 2020.

Bentley, Toni. *The Surrender: An Erotic Memoir*. New York: Harper Collins, 2004.

Blue, Ethan. "Beating the System: Prison Music and the Politics of Penal Space." In *Isolation: Place and Practices of Exclusion*, edited by Alison Bashford and Carolyn Strange, 53–66. London: Routledge, 2003.

Bold, Valentina, and Pauline Greenhill. "*Frenchman's Creek* and the Female Sailor: Transgendering Daphne du Maurier." *Western Folklore* 71, no. 1 (2012): 47–67.

Bolster, W. Jeffrey. *Black Jacks: African American Seamen in the Age of Sail*. Cambridge, MA: Harvard University Press, 1997.

Bracher, Mark. "Writing and Imaging the Body in Pornography: The Desire of the Other and Its Implications for Feminism." *American Journal of Semiotics* 8, no. 4 (1991): 105–30.

Branfman, Jonathan, Susan Stiritz, and Eric Anderson. "Relaxing the Straight Male Anus: Decreasing Homohysteria around Anal Eroticism." *Sexualities* 21, no. 1–2 (2018): 109–27.

Bray, Alan. *Homosexuality in Renaissance England*. New ed. New York: Columbia University Press, 1996.

Bretz, Andrew. "Sung Silence: Complicity, Dramaturgy, and Song in Heywood's Rape of Lucrece." *Early Theatre* 19, no. 2 (December 2016): 101–18.

Briggs, Charles L. "Disciplining Folkloristics." *Journal of American Folklore Research* 45, no. 1 (2008): 91–105.

Briggs, Charles L. *Rethinking Poetics, Pandemics, and the Politics of Knowledge*. Denver: University Press of Colorado, 2021.

Broadwood, Lucy E., and A. H. Fox-Strangways. "Early Chanty-Singing and Ship-Music." *Journal of the Folk-Song Society* 8, no. 32 (1928): 55–60.

Bronner, Simon J. *Crossing the Line: Violence, Play, and Drama in Naval Equator Traditions*. Amsterdam: Amsterdam University Press, 2006.

Bronner, Simon J. *"Who's That Knocking On My Door?": Barnacle Bill the Sailor and His Mates in Song and Story*. Occasional Papers in Folklore 5. Lansdale, PA: Loomis House Press, 2016.

Brooks, Siobhan. "Hypersexualization and the Dark Body: Race and Inequality among Black and Latina Women in the Exotic Dance Industry." *Sexual Research and Social Policy* 7, no. 2 (2010): 70–80.

Brown, Mary Ellen. "Placed, Replaced, or Misplaced? The Ballads' Progress." *Eighteenth Century* 47, no. 2–3 (2006): 115–29.

Bullen, Frank Thomas. *Songs of Sea Labour: Chanties*. London: Orpheus Music, 1914.

Burg, Barry R. *Boys at Sea: Sodomy, Indecency, and Courts Martial in Nelson's Navy*. New York: Palgrave Macmillan, 2007.

Burg, Barry R. *Sodomy and the Pirate Tradition: English Sea Rovers in the Seventeenth-Century Caribbean*. 2nd ed. New York: New York University Press, 1995.

Burton, Valerie. "'As I Wuz A-rolling Down the Highway One Morn': Fictions of the 19th Century English Sailortown." In *Fictions of the Sea: Critical Perspectives on the Ocean in British Literature and Culture*, edited by Bernhard Klein, 141–56. London: Routledge, 2002.

Burton, Valerie. "The Myth of Bachelor Jack: Masculinity, Patriarchy and Seafaring Labour." In *Jack Tar in History: Essays in the History of Maritime Life and Labour*, edited by Colin Howell and Richard Twomey, 179–98. Fredericton, NB: Acadiensis Press, 1991.

Burton, Valerie. "'Whoring, Drinking Sailors': Reflections on Masculinity from the Labour History of Nineteenth-Century British Shipping." In *Working Out Gender*, edited by Margaret Walsh, 84–101. Aldershot: Ashgate, 1999.

Butler, Judith. *Bodies That Matter: On the Discursive Limits of "Sex."* New York: Routledge, 1993.

Butler, Judith. *Gender Trouble: Feminism and the Subversion of Identity*. New York: Routledge, 1990.

Carpenter, James M. "Lusty Chanteys from Long-Dead Ships: Created as Working Songs of the Seaman, Especially on the Fast Clippers of the Last Century, They Are Now Collected through Research as Vital Reminders of the Age of Sail." *New York Times*, July 12, 1931, 12–13, 23.

Carter, David A. "The Industrial Workers of the World and the Rhetoric of Song." *Quarterly Journal of Speech* 66, no. 4 (1980): 365–74.

Cecelski, David S. *The Waterman's Song in Maritime North Carolina*. Chapel Hill: University of North Carolina Press, 2001.

Clark, Anna. *The Struggle for the Breeches: Gender and the Making of the British Working Class*. Berkeley: University of California Press, 1995.

Clarke, Victoria, and Virginia Braun. "How Can a Heterosexual Man Remove His Body Hair and Retain His Masculinity? Mapping Stories of Male Body Hair Depilation." *Qualitative Research in Psychology* 16, no. 1 (2019): 96–114.

Cleland, John. *Memoirs of Fanny Hill*. London, 1749; Project Gutenberg, 2008. https://www.gutenberg.org/files/25305/25305-h/25305-h.htm.

Colcord, Joanna C. *Songs of American Sailormen*. New York: W. W. Norton, 1938.

Connell, R. W. *Masculinities*. 2nd ed. Berkeley: University of California Press, 1995.

Conrad, Charles. "Work Songs, Hegemony, and Illusions of Self." *Critical Studies in Mass Communication* 5, no. 3 (1988): 179–201.

Cornog, Martha, and Timothy Perper. "Make Love, Not War: The Legacy of Gershon Legman, 1917–1999." *Journal of Sex Research* 36, no. 3 (1999): 316–17.

Cowdell, Paul. "Cannibal Ballads: Not Just a Question of Taste." *Folk Music Journal* 9, no. 5 (2010): 723–47.

Crawford, Katherine. *European Sexualities, 1400–1800*. Cambridge: Cambridge University Press, 2007.

Cray, Ed. *The Erotic Muse: American Bawdy Songs*. Urbana: University of Illinois Press, 1992.

Creighton, Margaret S. "American Mariners and the Rites of Manhood, 1830–1870." In *Jack Tar in History: Essays in the History of Maritime Life and Labour*, edited by Colin Howell and Richard J. Twomey, 143–63. New Brunswick: Acadiensis Press, 1991.

Creighton, Margaret S. "Davy Jones' Locker Room." In *Iron Men, Wooden Women: Gender and Seafaring in the Atlantic World, 1700–1920*, edited by Margaret S. Creighton and Lisa Norling, 118–37. Baltimore: Johns Hopkins University Press, 1996.

CUNY Academic Commons. "The Journals of Philip C. Van Buskirk." Philip C. Van Buskirk Archive. Accessed January 17, 2024. https://vanbuskirk.commons.gc.cuny.edu/the-diary-of-philip-c-van-buskirk/.

Currarino, Rosanne. "'Meat vs. Rice': The Ideal of Manly Labor and Anti-Chinese Hysteria in Nineteenth-Century America." *Men And Masculinities* 9, no. 4 (April 2007): 476–90.

Dabhoiwala, Faramerz. "Sex and Societies for Moral Reform, 1688–1800." *Journal of British Studies* 46, no. 2 (April 2007): 290–319.

Dana, Richard Henry, Jr. *The Seaman's Friend: Containing a Treatise on Practical Seamanship, with Plates; A Dictionary of Sea Terms; Customs and Usages of the Merchant Service; Laws Relating to the Practical Duties of Master and Mariners*. Mystic, CT: Mystic Seaport Museum, 1856.

Dana, Richard Henry, Jr. *Two Years before the Mast*. Cleveland, OH: World Publishing Company, 1946.

Darby, Robert. "'An Oblique and Slovenly Initiation': The Circumcision Episode in *Tristram Shandy*." *Eighteenth-Century Life* 27, no. 1 (Winter 2003): 72–84.

Dashiell, Steven. "'You Feel That?' Examining Gay Porn Discourse as Hegemonic Discursive Soundtrack." *Porn Studies* 10, no. 1 (2022): 20–32.

Davis, Susan G. *Dirty Jokes and Bawdy Songs: The Uncensored Life of Gershon Legman*. Urbana: University of Illinois Press, 2019.

Dening, Greg. *Mr Bligh's Bad Language: Passion, Power and Theatre on the Bounty*. New York: Cambridge University Press, 1992.

Dennis, David Brandon. "Seduction on the Waterfront: German Merchant Sailors, Masculinity and the 'Brucke zu Heimat' in New York and Buenos Aires, 1884–1914." *German History* 29, no. 2 (2011): 175–201.

Derrida, Jacques, and Avital Ronell. "The Law of Genre." *Critical Inquiry* 7, no. 1 (1980): 55–81.

Doerflinger, William Main. *Songs of the Sailor and Lumberman*. Rev. ed. Glenwood: Meyerbooks, 1990.

Dye, Ira. "The Tattoos of Early American Seafarers, 1796–1818." *Proceedings of the American Philosophical Society* 133, no. 4 (1989): 520–54.

Eastman, Jason T., William F. Danaher, and Douglas Schrock. "Gendering Truck Driving Songs: The Cultural Masculinization of an Occupation." *Sociological Spectrum* 33, no. 5 (2013): 416–32.

EBarnacle. Comment on Mudcat Café, "Stan Hugill Uncensored," July 12, 2013. https://mudcat.org/thread.cfm?threadid=145866.

EBarnacle1. Comment on Mudcat Café, "RE: Help: Meaning of a Few Drunken Sailor Verses," May 7, 2002. https://mudcat.org/thread.cfm?threadid=46594.

Edelman, Elijah Adiv, and Lal Zimman. "Boycunts and Bonus Holes: Trans Men's Bodies, Neoliberalism, and the Sexual Productivity of Genitals." *Journal of Homosexuality* 61, no. 5 (2014): 673–90.

Edwards, Mary K. Bercaw. "Sailor Talk in Melville and Conrad." In *Secret Sharers: Melville, Conrad and Narratives of the Real*, edited by Pawel Jedrzejko, Milton M. Reigelman, and Zuzanna Szatanik, 247–58. Szczecin: M-Studio, 2011.

Edwards, Mary K. Bercaw. *Sailor Talk: Labor, Utterance, and Meaning in the Works of Melville, Conrad, and London*. Liverpool: Liverpool University Press, 2021.

Emrich, Duncan. "American Sea Songs and Shanties." Library of Congress.

Epstein, Julia. "Fanny's Fanny: Epistolary, Eroticism, and the Transsexual Text." In *Writing the Female Voice: Essays on Epistolary Literature*, edited by Elizabeth C. Goldsmith, 135–53. Boston: Northeastern University Press, 1989.

Fahs, Breanne, Eric Swank, and Lindsay Clevenger. "Troubling Anal Sex: Gender, Power, and Sexual Compliance in Heterosexual Experiences of Anal Intercourse." *Gender Issues* 32, no. 1 (2015): 19–38.

Flood, Michael. "Men, Sex, and Homosociality: How Bonds between Men Shape Their Sexual Relations with Women." *Men and Masculinities* 10, no. 3 (2008): 339–59.

Floyd, Jessica. "Engaging Imperfect Texts: The Ballad Tradition and the Investigation of Chanteys." *Restoration: Studies in English Literary Culture, 1660–1700* 44, no. 2 (2020): 111–38.

Floyd, Jessica. "The Erotic Clash of 'A Boy-Shaggin' Mate' and a 'Little Bumboy': Ships Stations and Genital Imagery in 'The Shaver.'" *The Nautilus* 10 (2019): 7–42.

Floyd, Jessica. "Seamen, Semen, and Virility: Leaky Homophones on Land and at Sea." *English Studies* 102, no. 5 (2021): 533–51.

Floyd, Jessica. "'Serafina's Got No Drawers' and nor Does Anyone Else: The Absence of Undergarments in the Legman/Hugill Chanteys." *Critical Studies in Men's Fashion* 9, no. 2 (2022): 223–40.

Floyd, Jessica. "TikTok's Sea Chanteys—How Life under the Pandemic Has Mirrored Months at Sea." The Conversation, 26 January 2021. https://theconversation.com/tiktoks-sea-chanteys-how-life-under-the-pandemic-has-mirrored-months-at-sea-153421

Foucault, Michel. *Discipline and Punish: The Birth of the Prison*. Translated by Alan Sheridan. New York: Random House, 1977.
Foucault, Michel. *The History of Sexuality*. Vol. 1, translated by Robert Hurley. New York: Random House, 1988.
Frank, Elena. "Groomers and Consumers: The Meaning of Male Body Depilation to a Modern Masculinity Body Project." *Men and Masculinities* 17, no. 3 (2014): 278–98.
Frank, Stuart M. "'Cheer'ly Man': Chanteying in *Omoo* and *Moby-Dick*." *New England Quarterly* 58, no. 1 (1985): 68–82.
Frank, Stuart M. "Classic American Whaling Songs." *Maritime Life and Traditions*, no. 26 (Spring 2005): 16–33.
Frank, Stuart M. "Stan Hugill 1906–1992: A Remembrance." In *Shanties from the Seven Seas*, edited by Stan Hugill, xix–xxiii. Mystic, CT: Mystic Seaport Museum, 1994.
Freeman, Elizabeth. *Beside You in Time: Sense Methods and Queer Sociabilities in the American 19th Century*. Durham, NC: Duke University Press, 2019.
Freeman, Elizabeth. *Time Binds: Queer Temporalities, Queer Histories*. Durham, NC: Duke University Press, 2010.
Friedman, David. *A Mind of Its Own: A Cultural History of the Penis*. New York: Simon and Schuster Press, 2001.
Gates, Henry Louis, Jr. *The Signifying Monkey*. London: Oxford University Press, 1988.
Gershon Legman Collection. 1917–1999. Kinsey Institute, Indiana University, Bloomington, Indiana.
Gilje, Paul. *To Swear like a Sailor: Maritime Culture in America, 1750–1850*. Cambridge: Cambridge University Press, 2016.
Gilman, Lisa. "Folklore and Folklife of Women, Men, and Other Gendered Identities." In *The Oxford Handbook of American Folklore and Folklife Studies*, edited by Simon J. Bronner, 917–36. Oxford: Oxford University Press, 2019.
Goffman, Ervine. *Asylums: Essays on the Social Situation of Mental Patients and Other Inmates*. Harmondsworth: Penguin, 1961.
Goldberg, Jonathan. *Sodometries: Renaissance Texts, Modern Sexualities*. New York: Fordham University Press, 2010.
Gordon, R. W. "Folk Songs of America: A Hunt on Hidden Trails." *New York Times*, January 2, 1927, 3, 22.
Gowing, Laura. *Common Bodies: Women, Touch and Power in Seventeenth-Century England*. New Haven, CT: Yale University Press, 2003.
Green, Archie. "American Labor Lore: Its Meanings and Uses." *Industrial Relations: A Journal of Economy and Society* 4, no. 2 (1965): 51–68.
Green, Jonathon, ed. *The Big Book of Filth: 6500 Sex and Slang Words and Phrases*. London: Cassel, 1999.
Greenhill, Pauline. "'Neither a Man nor a Maid': Sexualities and Gendered Meanings in Cross-Dressing Ballads." *Journal of American Folklore* 108, no. 428 (1995): 156–77.
Grohowski, Mariana. "Moving Words / Words that Move: Language Practices Plaguing U.S. Servicewomen." *Women and Language* 37, no. 1 (Spring 2014): 121–30.
Guzman, Isabel Molina, and Angharad N. Valdivia. "Brain, Brow, and Booty: Latina Iconicity in U.S. Popular Culture." *Communication Review* 7, no. 2 (2004): 205–21.
Hall, Matthew. "'When There's No Underbrush the Tree Looks Taller': A Discourse Analysis of Men's Online Groin Shaving Talk." *Sexualities* 18, no. 8 (2015): 997–1017.
Halperin, David. *How to Do the History of Male Homosexuality*. Chicago: University of Chicago Press, 2002.
Harlow, Frederick Pease. *Chanteying aboard American Ships*. Mystic, CT: Mystic Seaport Museum, 1962.

Harvey, Arnold David. *Sex in Georgian England: Attitudes and Prejudices from the 1720s to the 1820s*. London: Phoenix Press, 2001.
Hernandez, Yessica Garcia. "A Vulgar Folklore: The Pornographic Fantasies of *Pornocorridos*." *Porn Studies* 10, no. 1 (2023): 50–65.
Herrera, Eduardo. "Masculinity, Violence, and Deindividuation in Argentine Soccer Chants: The Sonic Potentials of Participatory Sounding-in-Synchrony." *Ethnomusicology* 62, no. 3 (2018): 470–99.
Hitchcock, Tim, and Michelle Cohen. "Introduction." In *English Masculinities: 1660–1800*, edited by Tim Hitchcock and Michelle Cohen, 1–22. London: Routledge, 2014.
Huddleston, William. "Kicking Off: Violence, Honour, Identity, and Masculinity in Argentinian Football Chants." *International Review for the Sociology of Sport* 57, no. 1 (2022): 34–53.
Hugill, Stan. *Shanties from the Seven Seas: Shipboard Work-Songs and Songs Used as Work-Songs from the Great Days of Sail*. Mystic, CT: Mystic Seaport Museum, 1966.
Hurley, Natasha. *Circulating Queerness: Before the Gay and Lesbian Novel*. Minneapolis: University of Minnesota Press, 2018.
Hutchison, Percy Adams. "Sailors' Chanties." *Journal of American Folklore* 19, no. 72 (1906): 16–28.
Jack Horntip Collection. Accessed January 12, 2024. https://www.horntip.com/html/books_&_MSS/1910s/1917-1933_gordon_inferno_collection_(MSS)/index.htm.
Jackson, Gale P. "Rosy, Possum, Morning Star: African American Women's Work and Play Songs." *Journal of Black Studies* 46, no. 8 (November 2015): 773–96.
James Madison Carpenter Collection. Vaughan Williams Memorial Library.
Jarvis, Michael J. *In the Eye of All Trade: Bermuda, Bermudians, and the Maritime Atlantic World, 1680–1783*. Chapel Hill: University of North Carolina, 2010.
Jorgensen, Jeana. "Masculinity and Men's Bodies in Fairy Tales: Youth, Violence, and Transformation." *Marvels and Tales* 32, no. 2 (2018): 338–61.
Joyner, Charles W. "A Model for the Analysis of Folklore Performance in Historical Context." *Journal of American Folklore* 88, no. 349 (1975): 254–65.
Kerridge, Roy. "Ballad of the Sea Blue Yodeller." *Country Music World* 13 (September 1981): n.p. Chris Roche, personal collection, email message to author, April 28, 2017.
Kiesling, Scott Fabius. "Homosocial Desire in Men's Talk: Balancing and Re-creating Cultural Discourses of Masculinity." *Language in Society* 34, no. 5 (2005): 695–726.
Kiesling, Scott Fabius. "Men, Masculinities, and Language." *Language and Linguistics Compass* 1, no. 6 (2007): 653–73.
Kiesling, Scott Fabius. "Playing the Straight Man: Displaying and Maintaining Male Heterosexuality in Discourse." In *Language and Sexuality: Contesting Meaning in Theory and Practice*, edited by Kathryn Campbell-Kibler, Robert J. Podesva, Sarah J. Roberts, and Andrew Wong, 249–66. Stanford, CA: CSLI Publications, 2002.
Kimmel, Michael S. *American Manhood: Transformations in Masculinity from the Revolution to the Modern Era*. New York: Basic Books, 1993.
Kristeva, Julia. *Powers of Horror: An Essay on Abjection*. Translated by Leon S. Roudiez. New York: Columbia University Press, 1982.
Lash, Sarah. "Tilting the Ivory Tower: The Life, Works, and Legacy of Gershon Legman." *Folklore Historian: Journal of the Folklore and History Section of the American Folklore Society* 27 (2010): 25–41.
Lau, Kimberly J. "Serial Logic: Folklore and Difference in the Age of Feel-Good Multiculturalism." *Journal of American Folklore* 113, no. 447 (2000): 70–82.
Legman, Gershon. "Sea Songs." Unpublished manuscript, last modified December 6, 2023. PDF of Typescript. Judith Legman's personal collection.

Legman, Gershon. *The Horn Book: Studies in Erotic Folklore and Bibliography*. London: Cape, 1964.

Legman, Gershon. "Misconceptions in Erotic Folklore." *Journal of American Folklore* 74, no. 297 (1962): 200–208.

Legman, Gershon. *No Laughing Matter: An Analysis of Sexual Humor*. Vol. 1. Bloomington: Indiana University Press, 1982.

Legman, Gershon. *Rationale of the Dirty Joke: An Analysis of Sexual Humor*. New York: Grove Press, 1968.

LeJacq, Seth. "Buggery's Travels: Royal Navy Sodomy on Ship and Shore in the Long Eighteenth Century." *Journal for Maritime Research* 17, no. 2 (2015): 103–16.

Leneman, Leah. "Seduction in Eighteenth and Early Nineteenth-Century Scotland." *Scottish Historical Review* 78, no. 205 (1999): 39–59.

LoConto, David G., Timothy W. Clark, and Patrice N. Ware. "The Diaspora of West Africa: The Influence of West African Cultures on 'Jody Calls' in the United States Military." *Sociological Spectrum* 30, no. 1(2009): 90–109.

Lokke, Geoffrey. "Cuckolds, Cucks, and Their Transgressions." *Porn Studies* 6, no. 2 (2019): 212–27.

Lövkrona, Inger. "Erotic Narrative and the Construction of Gender in Premodern Sweden." *Journal of Folklore Research* 35, no. 2 (May 1998): 145–56, 183.

Lubey, Kathleen. *What Pornography Knows: Sex and Social Protest since the Eighteenth Century*. Stanford, CA: Stanford University Press, 2022.

Maddison, Sarah. "Private Men, Public Anger: The Men's Rights Movement in Australia." *Journal of Interdisciplinary Gender Studies* 4, no. 2 (1999): 39–51.

Maddison, Stephen. "Is the Rectum *Still* a Grave? Anal Sex, Pornography, and Transgression." In *Transgression 2.0: Media, Culture, and the Politics of a Digital Age*, edited by Ted Gournelos and David J. Grunkel, 86–100. New York: Bloomsbury Publishing, 2011.

Mahaffey, Paul Douglas. "The Adolescent Complexities of Race, Gender, and Class in Toni Morrison's *The Bluest Eye*." *Race, Gender and Class* 11, no. 4 (October 2004): 155–65.

Manne, Kate. *Entitled: How Male Privilege Hurts Women*. New York: Penguin Random House, 2020.

Markley, A. A. "E. M. Forster's Reconfigured Gaze and the Creation of a Homoerotic Subjectivity." *Twentieth Century Literature* 47, no. 2 (Summer 2001): 268–92.

Massarella, Derek. "'And Thus Ended the Buisinisse': A Buggery Trial on the East India Company Ship *Mary* in 1636." *Mariner's Mirror* 103, no. 4 (2017): 417–30.

McBride, Kimberly R., and J. Dennis Fortenberry. "Heterosexual Anal Sexuality and Anal Sex Behaviors: A Review." *Journal of Sex Research* 47, no. 2–3 (2010): 123–36.

McCann, Pol Dominic, David Plummer, and Victor Minichiello. "Being the Butt of the Joke: Homophobic Humour, Male Identity, and Its Connection to Emotional and Physical Violence for Men." *Health and Sociology Review* 19, no. 4 (December 2010): 505–21.

McCarl, Robert. "Occupational Folklore." In *Folk Groups and Folklore Genres: An Introduction*, edited by Elliott Oring, 71–90. Logan: Utah State University Press, 1986.

McCluskey, John Michael. "'Rough! Tough! Real Stuff!': Music, Militarism, and Masculinity in American College Football." *American Music* 37, no. 1 (2019): 29–57.

McDonald, David A. "Geographies of the Body: Music, Violence and Manhood in Palestine." *Ethnomusicology Forum* 19, no. 2 (2010): 191–214.

McFarlane, Cameron. *The Sodomite in Fiction and Satire, 1660–1750*. New York: Columbia University Press, 1997.

Melville, Herman. *Billy Budd*. New York: Tom Doherty Associates, 1988.

Miller, Janice. "Manscaping and After: Power, Parody and the Hairy Chest." *Fashion Theory: The Journal of Dress, Body and Culture* 22, no. 6 (2018): 641–55.

Milne, Graeme. "Collecting the Sea Shanty: British Maritime Identity and Atlantic Musical Cultures in the Early Twentieth Century." *International Journal of Maritime History* 29, no. 2 (2017): 370–86.

Moore, Lisa Jean. *Sperm Counts: Overcome by Man's Most Precious Fluid*. New York: New York University Press, 2008.

Mudcat Café. http://mudcat.org/.

Mulvey, Laura. "Visual Pleasure and Narrative Cinema." In *Film Theory and Criticism: Introductory Readings*, edited by Leo Braudy and Marshall Cohen, 833–44. New York: Oxford University Press, 1999.

Murphy, Peter F. *Studs, Tools, and the Family Jewels: Metaphors Men Live By*. Madison: University of Wisconsin Press, 2001.

Narvaez, Peter. "'I Think I Wrote a Folksong': Popularity and Regional Vernacular Anthems." *Journal of American Folklore* 115, no. 456 (2002): 269–82.

Noyes, Dorothy. *Humble Theory: Folklore's Grasp on Social Life*. Bloomington: Indiana University Press, 2016.

Oates, Thomas P. "The Erotic Gaze in the NFL Draft." *Communication and Critical/ Cultural Studies* 4, no. 1 (2007): 74–90.

Oberweis, Trish, Matthew Petrocelli, and Carly Hayden Foster. "Walking the Walk and Talking the Talk: Military Cadence as Normative Discourse." *Polymath: An Interdisciplinary Arts and Sciences Journal* 2, no. 4 (2012): 1–13.

Onania; or, The Heinous Sin of Self-Pollution, and All Its Frightful Consequences, in Both Sexes, Considered [...]. London: H. Cooke, 1756; Wellcome Collection, 2014. https://wellcomecollection.org/works/yxrtxsdy/items?query=fainting.

Pascoe, C. J. "'Dude, You're a Fag': Adolescent Masculinity and the Fag Discourse." *Sexualities* 8, no. 3 (2005): 329–46.

Peck, John. *Maritime Fiction: Sailors and the Sea in British and American Novels, 1719–1917*. Houndmills: Palgrave, 2001.

Philip C. Van Buskirk Papers. Special Collections. University of Washington Libraries.

Pickering, Michael, Robertson Emma, and Marek Korczynski. "Rhythms of Labour: The British Work Song Revisited." *Folk Music Journal* 9, no. 2 (2007): 226–45.

Potts, Annie. "'The Essence of the Hard On': Hegemonic Masculinity and the Cultural Construction of 'Erectile Dysfunction.'" *Men and Masculinities* 3, no. 1 (2000): 85–103.

Preston, Cathy Lynn. "'The Tying of the Garter': Representations of the Female Rural Laborer in 17th-, 18th-, and 19th-Century English Bawdy Songs." *Journal of American Folklore* 105, no. 417 (Summer 1992): 315–41.

Randolph, Vance. *Blow the Candle Out: Folk Rhymes and Other Lore*. Vol. 2 of *"Unprintable" Ozark Folksongs and Folklore*, edited by Gershon Legman. Fayetteville: University of Arkansas Press, 1992.

Randolph, Vance. *Roll Me in Your Arms: Folksongs and Music*. Vol. 1 of *"Unprintable" Ozark Folksongs and Folklore*, edited by Gershon Legman. Fayetteville: University of Arkansas Press, 1992.

Rediker, Marcus. *Between the Devil and the Deep Blue Sea: Merchant Seamen, Pirates and the Anglo-American Maritime World, 1700–1750*. Cambridge: Cambridge University Press, 1987.

Rediker, Marcus. *Outlaws of the Atlantic: Sailors, Pirates, and Motley Crews in the Age of Sail*. Boston: Beacon Press, 2014.

Rediker, Marcus. *The Slave Ship: A Human History*. New York: Penguin Books, 2007.

Rice, Alan. "'Who's Eating Whom': The Discourse of Cannibalism in the Literature of the Black Atlantic from Equiano's Travels to Toni Morrison's *Beloved*." *Research in African Literatures* 29, no. 4 (Winter 1998): 106–21.

Robert Winslow Gordon Papers. R. W. Gordon Inferno Collection (1917–1933). Library of Congress.

Roche, Chris. "Stan Hugill: 1906–1992." *Folk Music Journal* 6, no. 4 (1993): 558–59.

Romanets, Maryna. "Erotic Assemblages: Field Research, Palimpsests, and What Lies Beneath." *Journal of Ukrainian Studies* 27, no. 1 (Summer 2002): 273–85.

Rose, Kelby. "Nostalgia and Imagination in Nineteenth-Century Sea Shanties." *Mariner's Mirror* 98, no. 2 (May 2012): 147–60.

Rouleau, Brian J. "Dead Men Do Tell Tales: Folklore, Fraternity, and the Forecastle." *Early American Studies and Interdisciplinary Journal* 5, no. 1 (2007): 30–62.

Sasmazel, Zeynep. "Gay Pirates Were Very Real, and We've Even Got the Sea Shanty to Prove It." *The Hornet*, May 13, 2021. https://hornet.com/stories/gay-pirates-real/.

Schacht, Steven P. "Misogyny on and off the 'Pitch': The Gendered World of Male Rugby Players." *Gender and Society* 10, no. 5 (1996): 550–65.

Schreffler, Gibb. *Boxing the Compass: A Century and a Half of Discourse about Sailor's Chanties*. Occasional Papers in Folklore 6. Lansdale, PA: Loomis House Press, 2018.

Schreffler, Gibb. "'The Execrable Term': A Contentious History of *Chanty*." *American Speech* 92, no. 4 (November 2017): 429–58.

Schreffler, Gibb. "Twentieth-Century Editors and the Re-envisioning of Chanties: A Case Study of 'Lowlands.'" *The Nautilus* 5 (2014): 7–51.

Sedgwick, Eve Kosofsky. *Between Men: English Literature and Male Homosocial Desire*. New York: Columbia University Press, 1985.

Sedgwick, Eve Kosofsky. "Paranoid Reading and Reparative Reading; or, You're So Paranoid, You Probably Think This Introduction Is About You." In *Novel Gazing: Queer Readings in Fiction*, edited by Eve Kosofsky Sedgwick, 1–37. Durham, NC: Duke University Press, 1997.

Smith, Dorothy E. "Texts and the Ontology of Organizations and Institutions." *Studies in Cultures, Organizations and Societies* 7, no. 2 (September 2001): 159–98.

Smyth, Gerry. "Shanty Singing and the Irish Atlantic: Identity and Hybridity in the Musical Imagination of Stan Hugill." *International Journal of Maritime History* 29, no. 2 (May 2017): 387–406.

Smyth, W. H. *The Sailor's Word-Book: An Alphabetical Digest of Nautical Terms, Including Some More Especially Military and Scientific, but Useful to Seamen; as well as Archaisms of Early Voyagers, Etc*. Glasgow: Blackie and Son, 1867; Project Gutenberg, 2021. https://www.gutenberg.org/cache/epub/26000/pg26000-images.html.

Stephanson, Raymond. *The Yard of Wit: Male Creativity and Sexuality, 1650–1750*. Philadelphia: University of Pennsylvania Press, 2004.

Straub, Kristina. *Sexual Suspects: Eighteenth-Century Players and Sexual Ideology*. Princeton, NJ: Princeton University Press, 1992.

Tackley, Catherine. "Shanty Singing in Twenty-First-Century Britain." *International Journal of Maritime History* 29, no. 2 (2017): 407–21.

Tadros, Victor. "Between Governance and Discipline: The Law and Michel Foucault." *Oxford Journal of Legal Studies* 18, no. 1 (1998): 75–103.

Terry, Richard Runciman. *The Way of the Ship: Sailors, Shanties and Shantymen*. Tucson: Fireship Press, 2008.

Terry, Walter Runciman. "Foreword." In *The Way of the Ship: Sailors, Shanties and Shantymen*, by Richard Runciman Terry, n.p. Tucson: Fireship Press, 2008.

Thompson, Katrina Dyonne. "'Some Were Wild, Some Were Soft, Some Were Tame, and Some Were Fiery': Female Dancers, Male Explorers, and the Sexualization of Blackness, 1600–1900." *Black Women, Gender + Families* 6, no. 2 (2012): 1–28.

Toelken, Barre. "Ballads and Folksongs." In *Folk Groups and Folklore Genres: An Introduction*, edited by Elliott Oring, 147–74. Logan: Utah State University Press, 1986.

Trnka, Susanna. "Living a Life of Sex and Danger: Women, Warfare, and Sex in Military Folk Rhymes." *Western Folklore* 54, no. 3 (July 1995): 232–41.

Tyng, Charles. *Before the Wind: The Memoir of an American Sea Captain, 1808–1833*, edited by Susan Fels. New York: Penguin Books, 1999.

Van Buskirk, Philip C. *Journal of a Cruize*. Philip Clayton Van Buskirk Papers. 1851–1902. University of Washington Special Collections, University of Washington, Seattle, Washington.

Vickers, Daniel, and Vince Walsh. *Young Men and the Sea: Yankee Seafarers in the Age of Sail*. New Haven, CT: Yale University Press, 2007.

Wadham, Ben. "Brotherhood: Homosociality, Totality and Military Subjectivity." *Australian Feminist Studies* 28, no. 76 (2013): 212–35.

Ward, Jane. *Not Gay: Sex between Straight White Men*. New York: New York University Press, 2015.

Waters, Karen V. *Perfect Gentleman: Masculine Control in Victorian Men's Fiction, 1870–1901*. New York: Peter Lang Publishing, 1999.

Waugh, Thomas. "Men's Pornography: Gay vs. Straight." *Jump to Cut: A Review of Contemporary Media*, no. 30 (1985): 30–35. https://www.ejumpcut.org/archive/onlinessays/JC30folder/PornWaugh.html.

Webb, Robert Lloyd. Review of *Shanties from the Seven Seas: Shipboard Work-Songs and Songs Used as Work-Songs from the Great Days of Sail*, by Stan Hugill. *Northern Mariner* 5, no. 3 (1995): 83–84.

West, Lois A. "Negotiating Masculinities in American Drinking Subcultures." *Journal of Men's Studies* 9, no. 3 (April 2001): 371–92.

Whall, W. B. *Ships, Sea Songs and Shanties*. Glasgow: James Brown and Son, 1913.

Whates, Harold. "The Background of Sea Shanties." *Music and Letters* 18, no. 3 (1937): 259–64.

Wheatley, Elizabeth. "'Stylistic Ensembles' on a Different Pitch: A Comparative Analysis of Men's and Women's Rugby Songs." *Women and Language* 13, no. 1 (September 1990): 21–33.

Wignall, Liam, Ryan Scoats, Eric Anderson, and Luis Morales. "A Qualitative Study of Heterosexual Men's Attitudes toward and Practices of Receiving Anal Stimulation." *Culture, Health and Sexuality* 22, no. 6 (2020): 675–89.

XYZ [W. Elmes, f.]. *Jack in a White Squall, amongst Breakers—On the Lee Shore of St. Catherine's*. Engraving, 1811, call no. PC 1 - 11826 (A size) [P&P], British Cartoon Print Collection, Library of Congress. Accessed January 15, 2024. https://www.loc.gov/pictures/item/2006686609/.

Index

Page locators in *italics* indicate figures.

abjection, 139–41, 175
Abrahams, Roger D., 31, 32, 33, 81, 245n92
admissions: of compulsion to return to sites of pain, 123, 168; confession/disclosure, 82, 202–4, 208; of desire to remain on land, 160–61; of same-sex curiosity, 84, 166, 183, 186, 196, 198–201, 203, 212; of struggle to reproduce scripts of masculinity, 153, 161, 216; of unstable gender hierarchies, 117, 120; of vulnerability, 49–50, 153, 161, 166, 196, 198–99, 206, 212, 216
affinity groups, 39–40, 43
African/African American traditions, 29–35, 39, 241n18; women's, 30, 44
African dancers, 141
"Afro-American Worksongs on Land and Sea" (Abrahams), 33
agency, female, 109, 120–21, 124, 133–34, 163; avoidance of pregnancy, 155–56, 166; in heteronormative economies, 152–58, 159; and lived realities, 168–70; and nonprocreative sex, 154–56; and theft from men, 156–57; used to combat subordination, 134, 152; weaponization of venereal disease, 148, 153–54
agentive masculinity, 45–46, 95, 97–101, 123; and anal sex, 160–61; continuum of, 215–16; homosocial and homoerotic, 84, 173; in narration of song, 92–93, 132–33, 134–35, 144–46, 149–50; penis as agentive, 137, 197, 257n13; scopophilic, 173–74, 180, 197–99; subordination of, 93, 107, 114–19, 123, 134. *See also* hypermasculinity; masculinity

aguante, 46
Ahmed, Sara, 75, 86, 127, 220; on lines that divide space, 74, 86, 186, 201, 203; on seeing the world "slantwise," 74, 78, 100, 128, 186, 205
Allan, Jonathan, 73–74, 167, 210, 213, 251n26
Allen, Isaac, 29, 243n36
all-female singing spaces, 43–44
all-male song traditions, 4; connecting factors between song traditions, 42, 50, 133, 172, 181; connections between chanteys and work songs, 38–50; fraternity songs, 40; homophobia within, 47; hypermasculinity in, 45–46, 66, 75, 83–84; sexuality as key facet in, 84; "us-versus-them" mentality, 48–49, 82. *See also* football/rugby; military cadences
all-male spaces, 11–12, 45, 61, 67; emotion and desire in, 84, 200; fraternities, 12, 136, 201, 259n60; "fratriarchies," 97; sailing ship as doubly exclusive, 11. *See also* football/rugby; military cadences; sailing ship, early modern (tall ship)
"Alouette," 57
"American Sea Songs and Shanties" (Emrich), 18
anal sex: and agentive masculinity, 164–67; and female agency, 154–56, 166; gay and bisexual men associated with, 163–64, 166–67; hierarchical consequences of, 155–56, 163; pegging discourses, 166, 201; as protective, 156, 162–63, 166; "sodomy," historical understandings of, 184–85, 208–9, 211–12; violence of, 98, 140, 155, 165–67; vulnerable admission of desire for, 166. *See also* excrement; sexual acts; sexuality

Anderson, Eric, 163–64, 165
anus, 104; and abjection, 140, 143; fetishization of, 141–43; as focus of violence, 137; male, circular desiring for and disavowal of, 165–67; opposite-sex affiliated male desiring for, 164–66, 212; as shared and queered space, 100, 162, 212
anxieties: about cuckolding, 24–25, 197–98; about gender and sexuality, 46, 50, 100, 132; about identity performance, 82–84, 96; about masculinity, 24–25, 67, 128; about semen, 57, 165, 210–11, 254n36, 255n54, 258n35; around aging and decaying, 65; around anal penetration, 166–67; around male grooming, 194; and marriage expectations, 96; release valves for around masculine identities, 85, 90–91, 93, 161–63, 210; sex and work as for men, 111–12; of white men, 197, 210. *See also* castration anxiety
Argentinian football chants, 47, 98, 137
Army Slang Dictionaries, 42
Arnold, W. F., 21
"A-Roving," 19
artifacts, cultural: bonding objects and rituals, 12; as data set, 49–50, 65–66; hybridity of, 26; nuances and complexities of, 95; used to differentiate group members from outsiders, 12
audience: chanteys sung out of context for, 10; disciplined by warning songs, 109, 115, 116; inhibitory effect on performer, 62; involvement in scopophilic consumption, 177; sailing character's imagination consumed by, 150; songs created for, 8. *See also* queer gaze; scopophilic consumption
Ayers, Drew, 198

Bachelor Jack figure, 95, 96
"Background of Sea Shanties, The" (Whates), 37
Bailey, Kristen, 40, 79, 250n80
Baker, Ronald L., 45
Bakhtin, Mikhail, 24, 46, 140, 258n28
ballads, 9, 260n5; continuous tradition of, 207; cross influence with chantey, 19–20, 28; landbound, 20; as narrative, 13; *pornocorridos*, 77
Barbados, singers from, 31–32

"Barnacle Bill the Sailor," 8, 161, 255n49
Bauman, Richard, 9
Beavan, Brad, 28
Begiato, Joanne, 65, 66–67, 96–97, 107, 108, 111–12; on gaze in early modern culture, 175–76
belonging, need for, 81, 84, 89, 200
Beside You in Time (Freeman), 26
"Between Governance and Discipline" (Tadros), 78
Between Men (Sedgwick), 12, 197
Billingsgate fishwives' calls, 28, 43, 44
"Billy Boy," 131, 132, 134, 149, 213; desire for shore and domesticity in, 159–60; lyrics, 162, 230
Billy Budd (Melville), 174–75
blood, images of, 140–41
"Blow the Man Down," 24, 36, 247n11; comparison across collections, 56–61; false-parts-motif version, 247n7, 252n40; final line of, 128; gender order subverted in, 118, 209; hierarchical equality rendered in, 118; Hugill's version, 59–61; injury to penis in, 110–12, *111*, 128, 209; in James Madison Carpenter Collection, 58–59; lyrics, 56–57, 110, *111*, 222–23; milkmaid version in Inferno Collection, 56–57
Blue, Ethan, 38, 39, 44
Bluest Eye, The (Morrison), 254n36
Bodies That Matter (Butler), 113–14
body: abjection, 139–40; *ars erotica* of historical inquiry, 25–26; and historical inquiry, 25–26; hyperembodiment, 253n41; nexus with breath, 14; nonwhite, racialized abjection of, 139–41; regulated by work songs, 14–15, 39; voice linked with, 8, 14–15
Bold, Valentina, 75
Bolster, W. Jeffrey, 32
"Bosun's Wife," 42
"bowsprit," 251n21
Boxing the Compass (Schreffler), 20–21
Boys at Sea (Burg), 199
Bracher, Mark, 157
Branfman, Jonathan, 163–64
Bray, Alan, 184–85, 199, 257n20
breath, 13–15, 38, 41, 51, 77, 90, 240n1
Briggs, Charles L., 6, 24, 71–72
Broadwood, Lucy E., 15–18

Bronner, Simon J., 45, 79, 161
Brooks, Siobhan, 143–44
brotherhoods, 11, 51, 97
Brown, Mary Ellen, 207, 260n5
Brown, Tom, 64
Bryant, William Cullen, 33
"bugger," as term, 184
Bullen, Frank Thomas, 21, 35–36
"Bumboy, The," 166, 172, 203, 256n11, 257n12; lyrics, *182*, 221–22; male bodies on display in, 189, 192–93; same-sex erotic fixation in, 173, 180–83, 200
Burg, Barry R., 199
Burton, Valerie, 96, 98, 104, 108, 110, 159, 252n41
Butler, Judith, 83, 113–14, 202

call-and-response form, 16, 30, 39
"Can't Ye Dance the Polka?," 102, 120; lyrics, *122*, 231
Cape Breton milling ceremonies, 44
capstan/windlass chanteys, 13, 242n31; privileged in collections, 20; "Sacramento," 14–15, 93–95, *94*
Carpenter, James Madison, 10, 20, 27, 36–37, 72, 217. *See also* James Madison Carpenter Collection
Carter, David A., 82, 85
castration anxiety, 24–25, 80, 113–15; and men's rights movements, 213; theft from men as symbolic of, 156–57. *See also* anxieties; penis
categorical structures: combatted by warning songs, 87–88, 116–17, 121–23, 126–29, 130, 206; finite expectations, 85–86, 104, 124, 127, 131, 170, 171, 203; gender expectations not met, 48, 81, 89, 120–24, 128, 158, 171, 206, 209; instability of, 73–75, 130; land and sea as symbolic of, 126; liminality of, 116, 121, 130; pushing back against, 85, 121–23. *See also* heteronormative economies
Cecelski, David S., 31
censorship, 31, 37–38, 61–64
Chanteying aboard American Ships (Harlow), 10
chanteyman, 35–36; Black, 32; as composer, 11; first line sung by, 39; prized for ability to extemporize, 36

chanteys: and African/African American traditions, 29–35, 241n18; as American tradition, 27–31; approximations sung today, 10; attached to waterways, 23; authentication of tradition, 8–9, 217–18; beginning of interest in, 20–21; as British tradition, 27–31; call-and-response form, 16, 30, 39; capstan/windlass, 13, 242n31; collective human realities in, 216, 217; connection to work songs and all-male singing traditions, 38–50; continuous tradition of, 207; as cosmopolitan genre, 30, 35; as counter-cultural, 28; cross influence with ballads, 19–20; dating of, 15–27, 243n36; definitions, 10–15, 70, 240n9; embodied quality of, 8; evolution of over time, 18, 22–23, 28, 37; gendered imagery at center of, 26–27; hauling/halyard, 13, 20; historical periods and situations, 24; as homosocial bonding mechanism, 11–12; and homosocial/homoerotic slippage, 12–13, 88, 197–98; impromptu nature of content, 35–38; insulating function of, 11–12; interdisciplinary reading of, 4–5; interpretational issues, 9–10; lines of as ejaculation, 200; longevity of genre, 31; lyrics, 35–38, 39, 244n75; male bodies as entire inspiration for lyrics, 191; male control expressed through narrator, 144–47; military imagery in, 96–98; penis as vulnerable in, 80–81; possible places of origin, 27–35; racist language of, 33–34, 214; recycling function of, 13, 67, 83, 96, 129, 130, 141, 146, 158; renaissance during 2020s, 206–7, 219; retrofitted sea and shore songs, 9; rhythm matched to work process, 13; secondary function of, 54; self-analysis in, 67–68; sex and eroticism as main themes of, 47; sung by working men, 9–10, 27–35; as term, 7–8, 20, 22; "text" of, 14; tied to bonding rituals, 12; types of coordinated with types of work, 11, 13; vulnerability expressed through, 77. *See also* warning songs
chantez (imperative of *chanter* to sing), 8
chantie-impulse, 14
chanting, 8, 29, 43, 46
characters: abjection of nonwhite, 139–40, 177; collective human realities in, 156,

170, 216, 217; liminality of, 172, 196, 198, 212; named, 132; penis as, 191; vessel-like quality of male and female characters, 130–34

characters, female: as belonging to male narrator, 145–46; duality of women in warning songs, 121–22; as empty vessels, 133–34; fear of feminization displaced onto female or feminized characters, 47–48; as focus of sexual rage, debasement, and disregard for well-being, 134, 137; as foils to masculine identity formation, 131; language used to describe, 133–34; as out of control, 185–86; as punchlines, 138–39, 147; venereal disease weaponized by, 148, 153–54. *See also* women

characters, male: as collective "we," 131, 132–33, 178–79; control displayed by, 144–46, 180; elements of masculine failure met by, 215; liminality and bodies of, 172, 196, 198; subordination of sailing character in warning songs, 108–9, 114–15; yearning for shore and domesticity, 159–60

"Cheerily Man," 131, 149; lyrics, *150*, 228

Cibber, Colley, 172, 256n3

Circulating Queerness (Hurley), 77–78, 177

Clark, Anna, 47

Clark, Timothy W., 39, 42

Cleland, John, *Fanny Hill*, 25, 85, 99–100, 172, 175

Cohen, Michelle, 208–9, 211–12

Colcord, Joanna, 21–22

collections, 260n23; ballad-like songs privileged, 19–20; Black chanteys left out, 30–31; collector's aesthetic reflected in, 65; collectors and collection processes, 8–9, 27; differences elided in, 85; digitized, 217–18; essentialist, 27; limits of, 36–37, 241n12, 256n66; micro and macro considerations, 35; by sailor-collectors, 241n13, 241n15; self-censored by collectors, 30–31, 37, 62; sentimentality connected to, 21–22. *See also* folksong and folklore research

collective songs: collective "we" in, 131, 132–33, 178–79; during COVID-19 pandemic, 206–7, 218; emotional safety afforded by, 42, 90; gender anxiety in, 45–46; homophobia within, 47; masculine identity leveraged through, 42–43, 48; physical safety afforded by, 38–39; power garnered through lyrics, 43; woman's body as site for male agency, 147

collisions, concept of, 75, 77–78, 205, 252n40; between domesticity and hypermasculinity, 119–20; between ideas of land and water, 126, 128, 216

Common Bodies (Gowing), 86–87

composers, sailors as, 11, 87

confession, 82, 202–3, 208, 212

Connell, R. W., 117, 135, 137, 161–62

Conrad, Charles, 22–23, 85

consent, 147–48

contact zones, 23

Cornog, Martha, 69–72

cotton industry, 33

country music, 48–49, 85

courts-martial records, 199, 200

COVID-19 pandemic, 206–7, 218

Crawford, Katherine, 155, 199

Cray, Ed, 54–55

Creighton, Margaret S., 109, 116, 145, 158, 213–14

cross-dressing ballads, 80, 84

cross influence, 19–20, 28–30

crossing-the-line ceremony, 40, 57, 78–79, 258n30, 259n61; hoop-iron in, 194

"cruel optimism," 210

cuckolding, 102, 175, 178; in pornography, 24–25, 196–99, 258n45

"Cuckolds, Cucks, and Their Transgressions" (Lokke), 196–98

Currarino, Rosanne, 145

Curtis, Moses Ashley, 31

Dana, Richard Henry, Jr., 168

Danaher, William F., 26, 48–49

danger, 89; disregard for in working-class humor, 167–69; eroticism tied with, 57; insulated spaces of, 40–43; of land, 125–26; lyrics used to combat, 43, 79; of port towns, 57, 87–88, 104–8, 126; of working-class vocations, 81–82, 215

Daphnis and Chloe (Longus), 16

Darby, Robert, 24

Dashiell, Steven, 91, 93, 95

"daughters," in chanteys, 146–48, 160

Davis, Susan G., 68

"deadeye," 245n90, 251n21

Deep the Water, Shallow the Shore (Abrahams), 32
Dening, Greg, 254n41
Dennis, David Brandon, 112, 117, 119, 199
desire: in all-male spaces, 84, 200; anus as queer space for, 100; championed over societal expectations, 98; desire to be and the desire to be with, 13; instability of, 171; to look, 174–82; return to sites of pain, 122–24; unbound, 88, 122–24, 172, 185–86, 209
detachable body parts, 57, 79, 247n11; and castration anxiety, 113–14; and cinematic male gaze, 145; in description of bodily details, 174–75; "estrangement" of female genitals, 147, 252n40, 256n2, 258n28; hyperembodiment, 253n31; phallus, 113–14, 195
diasporic songs, 28, 30
Discipline and Punish (Foucault), 78
disclosure, 202–4
Doerflinger, William Main, 42
"Do Let Me 'Lone, Susan," 29–30, 33, 131; female agency in, 152–53; Legman's summary notes, 35; lyrics, 155, 225; sailor cast as vulnerable lover in, 160
domesticity: desire of sailors for, 159; nineteenth-century push toward, 96, 103–4, 108, 116–17, 119–20, 159
Dutch, ditties at expense of, 257n17, 257n19
Dutch shanties, 62

Eastman, Jason T., 26, 48–49
Edelman, Elijah Adiv, 253n31
Edwards, Mary K. Bercaw, 240n1, 251n20
Egyptian canopic jar, 132
either-or dichotomies, 202
Emrich, Duncan, 18
"Engaging Imperfect Texts" (Floyd), 15–16, 57
English Masculinities, 1660–1800 (Hitchcock and Cohen), 208–9, 211–12
Epstein, Julia, 183, 189
"Erotic Assemblages" (Romanets), 197
erotohistoriography, 25
European Sexualities, 1400–1800 (Crawford), 155
excrement, 149; and abjection, 139–40, 177; gay and bisexual men associated with, 163–64; urine linked with sea, 140
"Execrable Term, The" (Schreffler), 20

Fabri, Felix, 16
fairy tales, 133
familial connection, importance of, 160
"fancyman," 245n93
Fanny Hill (Cleland), 25, 85, 172, 175, 176; audience assumed to be male, 183; female narrator as cover for queer gaze, 182; focus on male bodies in, 189–90; sailing character in, 99–100, 200
female impersonation, 173, 176, 181–84, 187
feminization: damage to penis as, 114, 115, 119; male fear of, 44, 47–48, 161–62
firehouse culture, 73
fire ships, 112–13, 251n34
"Fire Ship (II), The," 112–14, 120; lyrics, 113, 233
fishwife, figure of, 28, 43
Flood, Michael, 12
fo'c'sle (forecastle) songs, 8, 28, 35, 244n67
folklore: arrival of gendered bodies in spaces of, 151; continuous tradition of, 87, 207–8, 216, 218–19; in digital space, 206–7; materials as registers of identity, 85–86; restrictive social norms contested by, 81
Folklore Society, 20–21
folksong and folklore research, 20–22, 260n23; categorization in, 8, 22; collaboration with nonacademics, 71–72; as history of expurgation, 68–69; informants, reticence of, 37–38, 62–63, 72. *See also* collections
"Folk Songs of America" (Gordon), 32
football/rugby: *aguante*, 46; American college, militaristic images in, 96, 97; "masculine rituals," 48; NFL draft, 181–83; *rough* and *tough* images, 98; secretiveness about informal activities, 62–63
football/rugby ditties, 4, 34, 45, 46; "Alouette" version, 57; Argentinian football chants, 47, 98, 137
Forster, E. M., 187, 188, 189
Fortenberry, J. Dennis, 165
Foster, Carly Hayden, 49
Foucault, Michel, 78, 107–8, 252n36; confession, concept of, 82, 202, 203, 208, 212
Fox-Strangways, A. H., 15–18
Frank, Stuart M., 41, 71
fraternities, 12, 40, 136, 201, 259n60
"fratriarchies," 97

Freeman, Elizabeth, 25–26, 45
frustrations: anger, fear, and rage, 213–145; around gender identity and masculinity, 67, 84, 92–93, 127–28, 130–31, 134, 137, 152–53, 169, 210–11; around sailing work, 15, 76–77, 89; around sexuality, 76–77, 89, 152–53, 208; channeled through two-dimensional characters, 134; of early modern sailors, 89; "fuck" and being "fucked" as evocations of, 213; of hierarchical sailing environment, 87–88; throughout song traditions, 92–93, 206, 208; of working-class life, 81–82, 134, 215

"Gals o' Chile, The," 138, 141–43, 145–46, 212, 256n66; female agency in, 152; lyrics, *142–43*, 234–35; oral sex in, 155–56; venereal disease in, 153–54; voyeuristic gaze in, 149; women as desiring in, 157
gay/queer individuals: anal sex and denigration of, 163–64; linguistic violence against, 47
gender, 5; anxieties about, 46, 50, 100, 132; and categorical expectations, 48, 81, 85–86, 89, 120–24, 128, 158, 171, 206, 209; as continuum, 23, 55, 67, 117, 171–72, 218–19; cracks in construction of, 83–84; in cross-dressing ballads, 84; frustrations around performance, 67, 84, 92–93, 127–28, 130–31, 134, 137, 152–53, 169, 210–11; as identity construct, 55, 206; instability of heteronormative, 87; juridical construction of, 83, 87–88, 93, 95; liminality of, 93, 116, 204; middle-class ideals, 158; performance of, 49, 84, 118, 160–61; subverted in warning songs, 116–21; theoretical framework for analysis, 73–89; in work song, 74–75
German merchant sailors, 117
Gilje, Paul, 91
Gilman, Lisa, 46, 81, 83–84, 218–19
Glyn, Edward, 97
Gordon, R. W., 27, 32, 72, 252n40; "Blow the Man Down" in collection of, 56–57; Inferno Collection, 54, 56, 217
Gowing, Laura, 86–87
Grabham, E., 253n31
Green, Archie, 42, 83
Greenhill, Pauline, 65, 73–75, 80
Guzman, Isabel Molina, 141

Hall, Matthew, 194
hardbody films, 172, 198–99
Harlow, Frederick Pease, 10, 36, 241n14
Harvey, Arnold David, 255n51
hauling/halyard chanteys, 13, 20
"Haul the Bowline," 18–19
hazing scenarios, 200
Henry VIII, 19
"heroic artisan," 253n27
heroic language, 97
Herrera, Eduardo, 47
heteronormative economies, 88; agentive masculinity in narration of song, 132–33, 134–35, 144–46, 149–50; anger and aggression linked with vulnerability, 158–70; clash of vessels, 134–51; clash of vessels and vulnerability, 158–70; destabilized by anal sex, 100; female agency in, 152–58, 159; and hierarchies of power at sea, 87–88; homosocial and homoerotic within, 84; instability of, 4, 130–31; men and women as vessels, 130–35; naturalized, 209; queer curiosity within, 84; queer readings of, 117, 121, 125–26; venereal disease in, 154; women's queer resistances in, 121
hierarchies: and anal sex, 155–56, 163; in crossing-the-line ceremonies, 194; instability of, 117, 120, 137; of power at sea, 14, 44, 76, 87–88; of sexuality, 61, 102, 117–18, 148, 163, 180–81, 199, 257n12, 258n30, 259n60
history: ahistorical lens, 25, 27; present connected to past, 10–11, 25–26; queering of, 25–26
History of Sexuality (Foucault), 82, 202, 208
Hitchcock, Tim, 208–9, 211–12
Hodge, George, 18
"Hog-Eye Man, The," 33, 34, 245n90, 258n45; as cuckold pornography, 24–25, 196; female narrator, 183; lyrics, *176*, 226; penis as character in, 192; scopophilic consumption of genitalia in, 172, 174, 190; "shifting tack," queered readings of, 185–86; tactile moments of watching and seeing in, 178; testicles in, 194; women's bodies in, 189
homoerotic, the, 12; awe as an entry point into, 173–74, 189, 190; "bugger," as term, 184; and cuckold pornography, 196–99;

eighteenth-century, 256n3; encounters between heterosexual men, 200–201; in hardbody films, 172, 198–99; "sodomy," historical understandings of, 184–85, 208–9, 211–12; in triangular relationships, 186–87

homosexuality: anal sex associated with, 163–64, 166–67; "homohysteria," 166–67; homosexual, as term, 80, 257n20, 257n23; homosocial, 12, 201; Legman's bias toward, 69–70; in male hazing rituals, 200; marriage as counter to, 96

Homosexuality in Renaissance England (Bray), 184–85

homosociality, 4; defined, 11; of early modern sailing identity, 96; homosocial/homoerotic slippage, 12–13, 88, 197–98; masculine vulnerability countered by, 78–79; as matter of life and death on sailing ship, 13. *See also* all-male song traditions

homosocial spaces, 133, 136, 197–202; comparison across enclaves, 12–13; human quandaries and experiences in, 3–4; as pressure cookers of emotion and desire, 84; songs deployed against backdrop of, 11; of women, 30, 43–44. *See also* sailing ship, early modern (tall ship)

hoop-iron, 194

Horn Book, The (Legman), 41, 68–69

Huddleston, William, 46, 47

Hugill, Stan, 4, 27; attempt to present true chantey relics, 9; *Bosun's Locker: Collected Articles 1962–1973*, 72; on Caribbean origin of songs, 39; on chanteys as chanting, 8; correspondence with Legman, 9, 63–64, 72, 241n14; on "forebitters," 242n67; hypermasculinity and vulnerability in performance, 65; as larger-than-life personage, 70–71; as "last chanteyman," 53, 70; linguistic power observed in, 144; narrative in repertoire of, 13; notes on "The Hog-Eye Man," 33; potential racial bias of, 34, 144; public and private productions, 10; reluctance to share bawdy lyrics, 37–38, 62; repertoire as closest to original form of chantey, 38; repertoire learned from Black/African American sailors, 31–32; *Sailortown*, 72; scholarly critique of, 69–70, 217; *Shanties from the Seven Seas*, 18, 20, 32; on soldiers of World War I, 42; songs learned from West Indian singers, 31–32; songs reproduced out of work context, 10. *See also Shanties from the Seven Seas*

Hugill's repertoire, 244n75; in archival form, 53–54, 61–62; authentic reality of chanteys represented in, 55–56; comparison with other collections, 54–55; content possibly created by, 64–65; as filthiest in chantey tradition, 55; as insider's view into the chantey, 63; limits of collection, 51, 64, 241n13; reasons for studying, 55–72; same-sex erotics in, 70; uncensored and fully unexpurgated versions, 59, 217

Hurley, Natasha, 75, 77–78, 86, 177, 220

Hutchison, Percy Adams, 14, 23

"hyper-" as prefix, 45

hypermasculinity, 75–76, 129, 144, 158, 173, 257n13; in all-male song traditions, 45–46, 66, 75, 83–84; bachelor culture of mid-nineteenth century, 98; Bachelor Jack figure, 95, 96; in chanteys, 83–84, 87–88; as cover for realities, 87; erosion of in song lyrics, 173; expectations of for working-class men, 133–35; foils to, 91–93; hyperbolic sexual power, 149–50; language, narrative, and imagery of, 45–46; male control from position of narrator, 144–47; misogynist culture of early twentieth century, 98; perceived threats to, 79, 82–83, 91, 108, 120; playing the role of, 93–106; societal views of, 66–67; and vulnerable male body, 65, 120. *See also* masculinity

"Hypersexualization and the Dark Body" (Brooks), 143–44

identity, 250n1; affinity groups, 39–40, 43; circulatory process of formation, 77, 206; dichotomy of power and lack, 48; either-or dichotomies, 202; folklore materials as registers of, 85–86; gender and sexuality as forms of, 55; group, 39–40, 51, 90; instability of, 79, 88, 90–91, 103–4, 119–20; queer negotiation of, 76–78, 90–91, 127–29; solidified by work song, 39–40, 49, 51; specific location of work song tied to, 39–40; struggle with unbound presentations of self, 186, 209; transgression of time and space by, 26; vessels, men and women as, 130–35; vessels of, 126–27, 130–31. *See also* masculinity; realities, lived

identity, sailing, 4, 13; competing drives from land and sea, 96, 121–28, 212–13; culturally manufactured, 12, 103; industrial age changes in expectations, 96; military imagery used to bolster, 96–98

identity formation: instability of, 90–95, 100, 118–19, 152; juridical, 78, 83, 87–88, 93, 95; kaleidoscope metaphor for, 4, 75, 85–86, 90–92, 152, 169, 214–15; liminality of, 92–93, 100, 107, 119; queering of, 80; as tidal, 214–15

identity performance: anxieties about, 82–84; in opposite-sex narratives, 88, 130–31; potential for failure, 158; release valves for, 82–83, 129–30, 219–20

Immortalia, 20

individuality, as discipline, 144–45

industrial age, 21, 96, 252n41

Inferno Collection (Gordon), 54, 56, 217

informants: research needed on, 217; reticence of, 37–38, 62–63, 72

initiation and bonding rituals, 11–12, 15, 40–42, 47, 82, 200; crossing-the-line ceremony, 40, 57, 78–79, 194, 258n30, 259n61. *See also* fraternities; military cadences

interdisciplinary scholarship, 6–7, 24

Irish music, 28

Jack Horntip Collection, 217

Jack in a White Squall, amongst Breakers—On the Lee Shore of St. Catherine's (cartoon), 150, *151*

Jackson, Gale P., 30

Jack Tar, myth of, 96, 100, 103, 107

James Madison Carpenter Collection, 54, 72, 217; "Blow the Man Down," 58–59. *See also* Carpenter, James Madison

Jarvis, Michael J., 32

"Jinny Keep Yer Arse-'Ole Warm": disregard for painful situations in, 168; lyrics, *164*, 238; queering reading of, 186; sailor cast as vulnerable lover in, 160–61; yearning for shore in, 159, 168

"John Brown's Daughter," 131, 146–48; lyrics, *147*, 230

"Johnny, Come Down to Hilo," 33, 102, 120, 123, 255n51; lyrics, *124*, 237–38

"Johnny Come Down de Hollow," 33

joie de vivre, 131, 167–70, 215

joking culture, male, 55, 65–66, 68, 87; and confession/disclosure, 202–4; disregard for pain, 167–69; female characters as punchlines, 138–39, 147; rationalization of, 80

Jorgensen, Jeana, 132, 133

Joyner, Charles W., 27, 62

juridical policing mechanisms, 206; combatting of, 121–24; countered by return to sites of pain, 122–24; and gender, 78, 83, 87–88, 93, 95, 202; and identity formation, 78, 83, 87–88, 93, 95; individuality as, 144–45; punishment as representation, 107–8; specters of loss, 114; for testing boundaries, 107–8, 209; venereal disease as an object of, 114–15

kaleidoscope metaphor, 203, 205–6; for identity formation, 4, 75, 85–86, 90–92, 152, 169, 214–15; rings and colors as multiplicity of identity and experience, 85–86, 214

Kiesling, Scott Fabius, 12, 136, 200, 209

Kort, Joe, 12, 201

Kristeva, Julia, 139–40, 175

"Lady's Dressing Room, The" (Swift), 247n7

land: continuum and tension between land and sea, 121–28, 158, 213–15; as more dangerous, 125–26; pleasure and pain equated with, 124–25; tension with water, 121–28, 158, 213–14. *See also* port towns; sea (water)

Lash, Sarah, 6, 69, 248n44

Latina bodies, 141

Lau, Kimberly J., 21, 27, 35, 84–85

"Leave Her, Johnny, Leave Her," 252n5

Legman, Gershon, 4, 27, 53, 244n75, 248n44; boundaries transgressed by, 6; "fakelore" term used by, 207, 260n6; focus of scholarship, 68; homosexuality, bias toward, 69–70; *The Horn Book*, 41, 68–69; Hugill's correspondence with, 9, 63–64, 72, 241n14; on job of folksong specialists, 54; on joking culture, 65–66; notes on "The Hog-Eye Man," 33, 245n90; *Rationale of the Dirty Joke*, 65, 68; on rationalization,

80; scholarly critique of, 69–70, 217; viewed as more open to salacious content, 63–64
LeJacq, Seth, 259n54, 260n8
Leneman, Leah, 254n43
liminality, 4, 211–16; and bodies of male characters, 172, 196, 198; and cavalier attitude, 131, 167, 215; of characters in songs, 212; of gender and sexuality, 93, 116, 130, 204; of identity formation, 82, 91–93, 100, 107, 119, 158, 204, 206; of lived realities, 77, 80, 82–83; negotiations of lax and fixed categories, 130; and opposite-sex erotic clashes, 130, 131, 158; and penis, 116; of sailing man, 11, 96, 100–101, 116, 128, 213–14; of sailor, 11, 100, 213–14; of sea, 75–76, 103–4, 128; of sexual expression, 96, 100–101, 104, 116, 204; and song, 77, 80, 82–83, 92–93; in warning songs, 121–28, 130
linguistic violence, 46–47, 135–39, 158, 211
literary theory, 5–6, 172
"Liverpool Judies, The," 93, 106–7; lyrics, 92, 229
LoConto, David G., 39, 42
loggers and logging songs, 38, 39–42, 44, 51, 78–79, 250n80
Lokke, Geoffrey, 196–98
Lomax, Alan, 31, 217
Longest Journey, The (Forster), 190
loss, specter of, 113–14
Lövkrona, Inger, 151, 157
Lubey, Kathleen, 120–21, 247n11, 248n17
lyrics, 35–38, 39, 244n75; as counter to dangers, 43, 79; sexuality and violence conflated in, 97–98; threats to masculinity combatted by, 44–45

Maddison, Stephen, 165
"Maggie May," 100, 113, 116, 118; lyrics, *101–2*, 236–37
Maitland, Richard, 18–19
Manliness in Britain (Begiato), 66–67
Manne, Kate, 147–48
"manscaping," 193–94
Markley, A. A., 188–89, 190
marriage, 96, 102–4, 110, 125
Masculinities (Connell), 117
masculinity: achieved by proxy, 47, 83, 139, 187, 197; across time, 26–27; admission of struggle to reproduce expectations, 153, 161, 216; *aguante*, 46; of Black men, 32; bonding as way to bolster masculine individuality, 91; as both finite and timeless, 24; consent as entitlement, 147–48; contemporary sense of failure at, 209–10; control expected for men, 99–102, 111–12, 144–45; core set of values and ideals, 51; cracks in façade of expected performance, 160; crises in, 210; cultural expectations for, 66–68; "cultural masculinization of an occupation," 48; deliberate transgression of expectations, 123; early American, 144–45; enduring qualities of, 23–25, 66; expected mode of working-class, 96, 112, 117, 133, 148–52; foils to, 92–93; hierarchies of, 87–88, 137, 145, 163, 199, 213, 257n12; idealistic views of, 91–93; imbedded in cultural reality, 66–67; instability of, 79, 90–91; male control expressed through narrator, 144–47; monogamic marriage as source of anxiety, 96; new expectations for in nineteenth century, 91, 96, 98–104, 107–8, 110–11; nineteenth-century English, 144–45; as oppositional to femininity, 93, 95–96; paradox of excesses of vice and desire, 67; and penetrability, 147, 153–54, 161, 164–67; "positive" and "negative," 151; queer negotiation of, 76, 91; sailing, expected mode of, 95–96; as social construct in need of confirmation, 79; "solitary man," 91; sperm donation as threat to, 210–11; subordination of women identified with, 48; as term, 74; threats to combatted by lyrics, 44–45; war/sports connected with, 46–47; working-class as insensitive, 117, 137. *See also* agentive masculinity; hypermasculinity; identity; penis; vulnerability, masculine; working-class men
masturbation, 57, 112, 190, 254n36, 255n54
McBride, Kimberly R., 165
McCarl, Robert, 73
McCluskey, John Michael, 97
McDonald, David A., 68
McFarlane, Cameron, 175
Melville, Herman, 41, 187, 188, 256n68; *Billy Budd*, 174–75; *Moby-Dick*, 75–76, 249n62; *Typee*, 177
men's movements, 210–11, 212, 213

"Merry New Dialogue, A," 57
middle-class gender ideals, 158
military cadences, 39, 41–42, 257n13; sexuality and violence conflated in lyrics, 97–98; sexuality as prevailing theme in, 47; "us-versus-them" mentality in, 49
military imagery, 96–98
military spaces, "feminine" duties in, 83–84
milkmaid, figure of, 56–57, 60–61
Milne, Graeme, 8
miners, 97
misogyny, as response to new cultural expectations, 98–99, 120
"Miss Lucy Long," 172, 175, 183, 187, 190; lyrics, *188*, 227–28
Moby-Dick (Melville), 75–76, 249n62
molly house subcultures, 209, 212
Moore, Lisa Jean, 195, 210
Morales, Luis, 165
Morrison, Toni, 254n36
Mulvey, Laura, 145–46, 148, 256n2
Murphy, Peter F., 44–45, 47, 49–50, 55, 191–92
Myra Breckinridge, 167

narrator: and agentive masculinity, 132–35, 144–46, 149–52, 164–67; cavalier attitude of, 167–68; as collective "we," 131, 132–33, 178–79; female, 183, 189; female impersonation as cover for queer gaze, 173, 176, 181–84, 187; feminized, 183; indeterminate gender of, 132, 175, 181, 183; as "just one of the guys," 144; male control from position of, 144–47
Narvaez, Peter, 13
nautical metaphors, 104–6, 127, 251n20; for penis, 174; queer readings of, 104, 118, 185–86; wind, 185–86
Neal, Steve, 198
"Neither a Man nor a Maid" (Greenhill), 73
nineteenth century: attitude toward old men's bodies, 65; bachelor culture, 98; domesticity, push toward, 96, 103–4, 108, 116–17, 119–20, 159; medical and cultural anxieties around sperm, 165; middle-class gender ideals, 158; new expectations of men, 96, 98–104, 107–8, 111–12; pornographic scripts, 157
nonprocreative sex: as counter to marriage expectations, 102–4, 110; and female agency, 154–56

nostalgia, 21–22, 54, 114
Not Gay (Ward), 200
Noyes, Dorothy, 35

Oates, Thomas P., 181–83
Oberweis, Trish, 49
obscenity laws, 20
occupational song, 38–43, 45, 50, 215. *See also* work song
"Oh, Jenny, Gone to New-Town," 33
"Oh Jenny gone away," 245n92
oral traditions, 23–24, 68
othering: belittling othered figures, 34; of isolated types of work, 39–40; through linguistic violence, 136–37; in war and sports, 46–47

pain and injury: cavalier attitude toward, 131, 167–70, 215; COVID-19 pandemic, 206–7, 218; desire to return to sites of, 122–24; land equated with, 124–25
patriarchy, 117, 135, 148
Peck, John, 75–76, 249n62
penis, 190–202; agentive, 137, 197, 257n13; of Black man, 196–97; castration fears, literal and figurative, 80; as cipher for realities of life, 80; comparisons between sizes, 190; diseases of as social and moral token, 114; as embattled, 99–100; equated with gun, 97–98, 104, *105–6*, 113; feminized by damage, 114, 115, 119; gaze of observer in position of, 146; injury to, 110–12, *111*, 114–15, 119, 128, 209; "jibboom," as term, 251n21; loss of control of, 99–102, 111–12; "manscaping" to enhance look of, 194; as metonymy for man, 192; as most paramount image of genitalia, 190–92; as nexus of reality and symbolism, 109–10, 115–16; other characters displaced by, 191; paradoxical power and vulnerability of, 115; as point of rationalization, 80; as social and moral token, 114, 115; as spectacle, 108–9, 112; as in state of conflict, 109–12; as target of humiliation, 109; vulnerability of, 80–81, 108–15; weaponized, 137, 154, 197. *See also* castration anxiety
Perper, Timothy, 69–72
persistence, lens of, 80
Petrocelli, Matthew, 49
phallus, 49, 84, 113–15, 166–67, 189, 195, 213

"Phequell, Roger," 75
piracy, golden age of (1500–1860), 199
"Placed, Replaced, or Misplaced?" (Brown), 207
Pope, Alexander, 172, 256n3
pornocorridos, 77
pornography: anal fixation in, 165; contemporary, 165, 195; cuckoldry in, 24–25, 196–99; eighteenth-century texts, 120–21, 247n11; gangbang, 197; as male bonding ritual, 195
port towns, 23; British, 28; dangers of, 57, 87–88, 156–57; dangers of in warning songs, 106–7, 126; Jolly Jack Tar image in, 91; Mobile Bay, 32; transient nature of, 28. *See also* land
Preston, Cathy Lynn, 147
prison work songs, 38–39, 44
prodigal son image, 117
published chanteys, 20–21
punishment, 107–8
putas (whores), 33–34

"queer": as destabilizing term, 73–75; meanings of, 177; *terkw* as root of, 205
queer gaze: desire to look, 174–82; female impersonation and narrators as covers for, 173, 176, 181–84, 187; male bodies on display, 187–90; narrative gaze trained on male bodies, 174–81; penis and testicles, focus on, 190–202; provided by queer narrative elements, 173–74; tactile moments of watching and seeing, 177–78, 193. *See also* scopophilic consumption
Queer Phenomenology (Ahmed), 76
queer readings, 171–204; of closing lines of warning songs, 126; destabilization of sex act, 100–103; of heteronormative economies, 117, 121, 125–26; of history, 25–26; lines that divide space, concept of, 74, 86, 186, 201, 203; narrative gaze trained on male bodies, 174–81; of nautical metaphors, 104, 118, 185–86; of NFL draft, 181–83; seeing "slantwise," 74, 78, 100, 128, 186, 205; "shifting tack," 185–86, 203; tension between care and violence, 177–79, 193; of time, 25–26; of warning songs, 91, 93, 100, 117, 121, 125–29; women's bodies, eliding of, 189–90, 193
queer spaces, 100–104, 121; anus as, 100; identity as unstable in, 128, 211; innards as,

174–75; sailing ship as, 76; sea as, 75–76, 125–26
queer theory, 73–75
"Queer Theory and Critical Masculinity Studies" (Allan), 75

Rabelais, Francois, 140
Rabelais and His World (Bakhtin), 46
Rabelaisian material, 43, 62, 140, 191–92
racialization, 33–34, 149–50; abjection of nonwhite characters, 139–40, 177; of Black penis, 196–97; blood, images of, 140–41; of disease and excrement, 34, 139, 177; linguistic subordination of nonwhite figures, 34, 139–44, *142–43*, 158, 213; violent dismissal of darker-skinned women, 143–44
racism, 33–34, 214, 253n15, 256n9
Randolph, Vance, 54–55, 217
Rape of Lucrece, The (Shakespeare), 19
"Ratcliffe Highway," 97, 104–6, 113, 150; gender order subverted in, 118; lyrics, *105–6*, 223–25
Rationale of the Dirty Joke (Legman), 65, 68, 203–4
realities, lived, 127, 173, 203, 205, 212; domesticity, turn to, 119–20; humor around, 167–69; instability of, 90–91, 167–68; liminality of, 77, 80, 82–83; symbolic fantasy of, 129; taboo as part of, 201. *See also* identity; release valves
Rediker, Marcus, 12, 24, 32, 43, 95, 132, 244n72
"Reefy Tayckle," 172, 181, 189, 194; dropped words in, 190–91, 192; lyrics, *227*
release valves, 210–11, 215; for anxieties around masculine identities, 85, 90–91, 93, 161–63, 210; confession/disclosure as, 82, 202–4; to counter female agency, 158; and exploration of taboo, 172–73, 181, 186–87; for instability of identity, 90–91; for intense emotions and desire, 83–84, 89, 206; literature and narrative as, 219; for performance of gender and identity, 82–83, 129–30, 158, 219–20; song as, 3, 83–85, 90–91, 93, 124–25, 186, 206–15 *See also* realities, lived
"reparative reading," 5–6
Restoration, 20
Revere, Paul, 253n27
rites of passage, 12, 40
Roche, Chris, 71

Romanets, Maryna, 197
Rose, Kelby, 21, 54
"Rosy, Possum, Morning Star" (Jackson), 30
Rouleau, Brian J., 168
Russell, W. Clarke, 27–28

"Sacramento," 14–15, 93–95, 251n26; anal sex suggested in, 98; lyrics, *94*, 233–34; phallic imagery of lance in, 114–15; sailing character as spectacle in, 108–9, 114; violent agentive masculinity in, 98–99
safety: as facet of shore life, 159; songs as tools for, 38–39, 42, 90
sail, great age of (1500–1860), 199
sailing, early twentieth century, 98
sailing ship, early modern (tall ship): Bermudian vessels, 32; cargo-carrying, 38; chantey as last surviving link with, 21; coordination of song, voice, and work, importance of, 10; death penalty for same-sex erotic encounters, 199; entrapment on, 76, 218; "feminine" duties on, 84; hierarchies on, 44, 76, 87–88, 145, 199, 257n12; homosociality as matter of life and death, 13, 76; images of, *16*, *18*; looking back at land from, 125; mixed-race crews, 30, 32–35; near "total-institution" framework of, 11; passenger and troop ships, 38; queer negotiation on, 76; rape of boys on, 189, 199–200; rhythmic nature of work, 13–14; rootedness given to by ceremonies, 79; as safer than port, 57–58; sails, *19*; slaving vessels, 141; social community of, 14; spars and rigging of, *17*; as symbol of queer realities, 104
sailing vocation: assumed to be white, Anglo-Saxon, 30; as cosmopolitan, 35; intimate and sexually charged quality of, 11; as last option for boys, 255n48
sailor: as akin to composer, 11, 87; as archetype of manhood, 91; cultural expectations for, 67–68; cultural falsehood of desire for life at sea, 159; disregard for danger and pain, 167–69; fear of danger as constant, 89; Jolly Jack Tar image, 91; liminality of, 11, 100, 213–14; military metaphors for, 96–97; not limited by strict hetero/homosexual dichotomy, 199–201; as oppositional to other men, 95; as symbol of nation, 67; as unbound to expectations, 102–3
"Sally Brown," 31, 34, 131, 140, 146–47; lyrics, *136*, 234
"Saltpetre Shanty," 33–34, 131, 135, 149, 153–54, 255n66; anal sex in, 155; disregard of painful situations in, 168; lyrics, *169*, 232; sailor cast as vulnerable lover in, 161; women as desiring in, 157
Sarsfield, Heather, 44
Schacht, Steven P., 47, 57, 62–63
Schreffler, Gibb, 19–21, 27–28, 69, 70, 218, 240n9, 241nn12–13, 260n23; on Black origins of songs, 30, 34, 39, 241n18
Schrock, Douglas, 26, 48–49
Scoats, Ryan, 165
scopophilic consumption, 84, 120, 194, 256n2; and agentive masculinity, 173–74, 180, 197–99; audience involvement in, 177; awe as an entry point into, 173–74, 189, 190; cinematic male gaze, 145, 146, 148; expectations for reader/viewer, 175–76; keyhole in the door, 100, 172; linguistic, 181; male gaze and voyeurism, 135; permission provided through songs, 87; protected spaces for, 172–73, 175, 186–87, 200–203. *See also* audience; queer gaze
scrotum and testicles, 177–78, 193–94
sea (water): as backdrop to chanteys, 75; continuum and tension between land and water, 121–28, 158, 213–15; freedom provided by, 25–126; indeterminacy of, 35, 75–76, 104, 122, 172; liminality of, 75–76, 103–4, 128; queer nature of, 75–76, 125–26; waterways, chantey attached to, 23
sea-related genres, 8–9
sea songs, 7–9, 241n13; "Barnacle Bill the Sailor," 255n49; mentioned in *Daphnis and Chloe*, 16
Sea Songs and Shanties (Whall), 38
Sedgwick, Eve Kosofsky, 5, 12, 188, 197, 257n23
semen: anxieties about, 57, 165, 210–11, 254n36, 255n54, 258n35; and milkmaid figure, 57; nineteenth-century medical and cultural anxieties around, 165
"Semen, Seamen, and Virility" (Floyd), 57
sense-methods, 26

"Serafina," 120; anal sex suggested in, 98; lyrics, *99*, 232–33
sexual acts: "any port in a storm," 96, 99–100; with humanoid animal, 178–80; masturbation, 57, 112, 190, 254n36, 255n54; nautical metaphors for, 59; nonprocreative, as counter to marriage expectations, 102–4, 110; queer reading as destabilization of, 100–102; quick and ready, 95–96, 99–100, 102–4, 110–11, 213; simulated through work actions, 15. *See also* anal sex
sexuality: anxieties about, 46, 50, 100, 132; discourse required of, 82, 208; frustrations around, 76–77, 89, 152–53, 208; hierarchical, 61, 102, 117–18, 148, 163, 180–81, 199, 257n12, 258n30, 259n60; liminal nature of, 103–4; performative character of, 80; and queer realities, 104; "same sex" and "opposite sex" as terms, 249n57; self-conscious presentation of, 49–50; terminology for in early modern world, 249n57; violence conflated with in lyrics, 97–98; vulnerable admissions, 49–50, 166, 196, 212; work conflated with, 44–45. *See also* anal sex
Shakespeare, William, 19
Shanties from the Seven Seas (Hugill), 18, 20, 32; censored, 37; expurgated chanteys in, 64; suggested list of motifs in, 58
shanty, as catch-all term, 8
"Shanty Singing and the Irish Atlantic" (Smyth), 28
"Shenandoah," 34, 131, 134, 137, 149–50, 213; lyrics, *138*, 239; male hierarchy subverted in, 137
"shifting tack," 185–86, 203
shore songs, 8
"shot locker," 150
sing-outs, 8
slavery, 29–32, 39, 42, 43; and blood imagery, 140–41
Slave Ship, The (Rediker), 43
Smith, C. Fox, 30–31
Smith, Dorothy E., 14
Smyth, Gerry, 28, 54
Sodomy and the Pirate Tradition (Burg), 199
"sodomy," historical understandings of, 184–85, 208–9, 211–12

song: liminality of, 77, 80, 82–83; as release valve, 3, 83–85, 90–91, 93, 124–25, 186, 206–15; as structuring mechanism that connects body, breath, and voice to work, 28–39, 41; uniting elements of, 41–42, 51, 77, 82, 85
Songs of Sea Labor (Bullen), 21
Songs of the Sailor and Lumberman (Doerflinger), 42
spaces: alternative, 100; defined by texts, 14; finite places for singing work songs, 14, 39–40; and narrative of song, 13; ship as safer than port, 57–58. *See also* all-male spaces; homosocial spaces; queer spaces
Sparling, Heather, 44
spectacle, 108–9, 112, 114, 120
Sperm Counts (Moore), 210
sperm donation, as threat to masculinity, 210–11
steam-powered ships, 8, 18
Stephanson, Raymond, 114, 115
stevedores or hoosiers, 33
Stiritz, Susan, 163–64
Straub, Kristina, 256n3, 258n30
strip clubs, darker-skinned women in, 143–44
subordination: of agentive masculinity, 93, 107, 114–19, 123, 134; and collective male gaze, 146–47; "docile bodies," 109; female agency used to combat, 134; homoerotic implications of anal sex, 164–66; linguistic, 34, 120, 135–39; linguistic, of nonwhite figures, 34, 139–44, *142–43*, 158, 213; of sailing character in warning songs, 108–9, 116–21; of women, masculinity shown by, 34, 48
Swedish folklore, premodern, 151, 157
Swift, Jonathan, 247n7

taboo: as part of shared reality, 201; release valves and exploration of, 172–73, 181, 186–87
Tadros, Victor, 78
tattooing, as form of ownership, 178
Terry, Richard Runciman, 62
"Texts and the Ontology of Organizations and Institutions" (Smith), 14
Thompson, Katrina Dyonne, 141
time, queering of, 25–26

Toelken, Barre, 13, 41
transgressive identity, performances of, 209
triangular relationships, 186–87
Tristram Shandy (Sterne), 24, 25
Trnka, Susanna, 41–42, 47, 97–98
trucking songs, 48–49
Tyng, Charles, 138–39
Typee (Melville), 177

union songs, 82
"us-versus-them" mentality, 48–49, 82, 93, 95, 129, 144

Valdivia, Angharad N., 141
Van Buskirk, Philip C., 190, 199, 258n35
venereal disease, 254n41, 255n55; economic implications of, 154; and female agency, 148, 153–54, 163, 168; and heteronormative economies, 130, 148, 153–54; in warning songs, 107–9, 113–15, 118–20, 126, 129; weaponized by female characters, 148, 153–54
vessels: clash of, 134–51; clash of, and vulnerability, 158–70; Egyptian canopic jar, 132; empty, female characters as, 133–34; identity categories as, 126–27; land and water as symbolic, 125; men and women as, 130–35; ships as, 131–32
violence: of anal sex, 98, 140, 155, 165–67; anus as focus of, 137; female characters as punchlines, 138–39, 147; linguistic, 46–47, 135–39, 158, 211; narrative, 135, 137–39, 141, 144, 155; as posturing or performance mechanism, 139; sexuality and war conflated in lyrics, 97–98
vulnerability: admissions of, 49–50, 153, 161, 166, 196, 198–99, 206, 212, 216; countering sense of, 83, 91, 96–99; of creating, 219; expressed through chanteys, 77; of female body, 154; liminalities, 80, 100, 107; shared through collective song, 42, 90
vulnerability, masculine: anger and aggression linked with, 158–70; in crossing-the-line ceremonies, 78–79; damaged body as register of, 79–80; desire for safety of shore, 159; feminization, fear of, 44, 47–48, 161–62; homosociality as means to combat, 78–79; male body as vulnerable, 106–16; penis as a focus of, 80–81; sex and work as anxieties, 111–12; specters of loss, 113–14; subordination of sailing character in warning songs, 108–9, 114–15

Wadham, Ben, 97
Walser, Robert Young, 72
war, sports conflated with, 46–47
Ward, Jane, 12, 200–201, 259n61
Ware, Patrice N., 39, 42
war metaphors for sailing work, 96–97, 158
war metaphors for sexuality, 96–98; fire ship, 112–13; penis equated with gun, 97–98, 104, *105–6*, 113
warning manuals, German, 117
warning songs, 57–58, 60–61, 90–129; absence of warnings about dangers on ship, 125; categorical structures combatted by, 87–88, 116–17, 121–23, 126–29, 130, 206; clash of land and sea in, 96, 121–28, 212–13; closing lines, 126; dangers of port, 106–7; expected mode of sailing masculinity in, 95–96; gender order subverted in, 116–21; idiosyncrasies of identity construction in, 87–88; juridical structures in, 107–10; liminality of, 121–28, 130; misogyny in, 98; penis in conflict in, 109–10; queer negotiation of identity in, 90–91, 128–29; queer readings of, 91, 93, 100, 117, 121, 125–29; return to sites of pain as counter to, 122–24; sexual acts with women as warning of dangers in port, 87–88, 104–8; surface and deeper readings of, 95; use of any orifice in, 97–100; venereal disease in, 107–9, 113–15, 118–20, 126, 129; vulnerability of male body in, 106–16. *See also* "Blow the Man Down"; "Liverpool Judies, The"; "Maggie May"; "Ratcliffe Highway"; "Sacramento"
Waters, Karen V., 144
waterways, chantey attached to, 23
Waugh, Thomas, 195–96
waulking songs, Scottish, 43–44
Way of the Ship, The (Terry), 62
Webb, Robert Lloyd, 70–71
West, Lois A., 242n19
West Indian singers, 31–32
Whall, W. B., 30, 38
Whates, Harold, 37
"What Shall We Do? (Drunken Sailor)," 172, 173, 178–80; collective "we" in, 178–79;

lyrics, *180*, 223; tension between care and violence in, 177–79, 193; women's bodies in, 189
Wignall, Liam, 165
Wittgenstein, Ludwig, 6
women: all-female singing spaces, 43–44; Billingsgate fishwives' calls, 28, 43, 44; bodies of as sites for men's relationship with their genitals, 197; bodies of elided in lyrics, 189–90, 193–94; "caging women up," 109, 178–80; children out of wedlock, 254n43; conflated with ships, 118, 120; disease attributed to nonwhite, 34; duality of characters in warning songs, 121–22; female agency, 109, 120–21, 124, 134, 152–59, 163, 168–70; female truckers, 49; as foils to masculine identity formation, 131; frustrations of sailing visited on, 15; homosocial spaces of, 43; power of increased in nineteenth century, 109, 117; power of in warning songs, 116–21; racialized in chanteys, 33–34; sexual dishonor, 155; subordination of identified with masculinity, 34, 48; types of in chanteys, 134, 213–14; as vessels through which to imagine desire, 131. *See also* characters, female
work: attachment between working-class life and song, 22–23, 215; connection of body, breath, and voice to, 38–39, 41; informal activities, 62–63, 81; isolated types of, 39–40, 81; as public activity, 244n72; sex simulated by, 15; sexuality conflated with, 44–45
working-class life, 6–7; dangers of vocations, 81–82, 215; frustrations of, 81–82, 134, 215; sailing as part of, 21; similar ideas across time, 26–27; song in spaces of, 22–23. *See also* sailing ship, early modern (tall ship)
working-class men: danger embraced by, 167–68, 215; early American, 144–45; eroticized in early modern culture, 175–76; expected mode of masculinity for, 96, 112, 117, 133, 148–52, 215; failure of bodies due to work conditions, 107; focus on tempering desires of, 111–12; "heroic artisan," 253n27; requirements of manual work, 117; vulnerability of, 41, 47, 65. *See also* masculinity; sailor

work song, 10; African American, 29–35; authority challenged by, 38; Billingsgate fishwives' calls, 28, 43; bodies regulated by, 14–15, 38–39; bonding / songs of comradery distinguished from, 40; as "call to action," 51; chanteys mapped onto, 39; connection of chanteys to, 38–50; embodied reality of workspaces as connecting factor, 42; finite places for singing, 11, 19, 39–40, 50; gender and sexuality in, 74–75; prison work songs, 38–39, 44; rhythm matched to work process, 13–14, 29; for rowing, 31; Scottish waulking songs, 43–44; vulnerability in male, 44, 47–48. *See also* chanteys; occupational song
World War I, 42, 108
Wright, James (sailor), 58–59

"Yaw, Yaw, Yaw!," 172, 175, 190, 257n17; lyrics, *179*, 239; same-sex curiosity in, 184; "yaw," meaning of, 184

Zimman, Lal, 253n31

About the Author

Photo courtesy of the author

Jessica M. Floyd is an interdisciplinary scholar who critically analyzes the expression of gender and sexuality in erotic cultural artifacts. Dr. Floyd is a professor of English at the Community College of Baltimore County, where she teaches undergraduate writing and literature, and is also an adjunct instructor in the Departments of History and Gender, Women's, + Sexuality Studies at the University of Maryland, Baltimore County, where she teaches undergraduate courses on gender and sexuality.

Printed in the USA
CPSIA information can be obtained
at www.ICGtesting.com
CBHW020117050824
12636CB00015B/53